Asymmetric Politics

Asymmetric Politics
Ideological Republicans and Group Interest Democrats

Matt Grossmann

Director, Institute for Public Policy and Social Research
Associate Professor of Political Science
Michigan State University

David A. Hopkins

Assistant Professor of Political Science
Boston College

OXFORD
UNIVERSITY PRESS

OXFORD
UNIVERSITY PRESS

Oxford University Press is a department of the University of Oxford. It furthers
the University's objective of excellence in research, scholarship, and education
by publishing worldwide. Oxford is a registered trade mark of Oxford University
Press in the UK and certain other countries.

Published in the United States of America by Oxford University Press
198 Madison Avenue, New York, NY 10016, United States of America.

© Oxford University Press 2016

Library of Congress Cataloging- in- Publication Data
Names: Grossmann, Matthew, author. | Hopkins, David A., author.
Title: Asymmetric politics : ideological Republicans and group interest
Democrats / Matt Grossmann, Director, Institute for Public Policy and
Social Research, Associate Professor of Political Science, Michigan State
University ; David A. Hopkins, Assistant Professor of Political Science,
Boston College.
Description: New York, NY : Oxford University Press, 2016. | Includes
bibliographical references. | Description based on print version record
and CIP data provided by publisher; resource not viewed.
Identifiers: LCCN 2016020568 (print) | LCCN 2016009497 (ebook) | ISBN
9780190626617 (E-book) | ISBN 9780190626624 (E-book) | ISBN 9780190630560
(Online Component) | ISBN 9780190626594 (hardcover : alk. paper) | ISBN
9780190626600 (pbk. : alk. paper)
Subjects: LCSH: Party affiliation—United States. | Republican Party (U.S. :
1854-) | Democratic Party (U.S.) | Political culture—United States.
Classification: LCC JK2271 (print) | LCC JK2271 .G76 2016 (ebook) | DDC
324.273—dc23
LC record available at https://lccn.loc.gov/2016020568

3 5 7 9 8 6 4 2
Paperback printed by Webcom, Inc., Canada
Hardback printed by Bridgeport National Bindery, Inc., United States of America

In Memory of Nelson W. Polsby

CONTENTS

ACKNOWLEDGMENTS

The roots of this collaboration date back to our experience as doctoral students at the University of California, Berkeley, where we both spent a number of rewarding years in the company of gifted colleagues and faculty. We are especially indebted to the Institute of Governmental Studies, which fostered a welcoming community of scholars devoted to the study of American politics. Both of us benefited immensely from our time as students of the late Nelson W. Polsby, whose intelligence, perceptiveness, and dedication to keeping political science connected to the political world continue to inspire us today.

Over the course of writing this book, we have received invaluable feedback and assistance from a legion of colleagues and experts whose responses and insights have enriched our work immeasurably. For kindly offering their thoughtful analysis, advice, and encouragement, we thank Chris Ansell, Julia Azari, Valentina Bali, Frank Baumgartner, Jonathan Bernstein, David Broockman, Jonathan Chait, Casey Dominguez, Lee Drutman, Patrick Egan, Jennifer Erickson, Daniel Galvin, Michael Heaney, John Henderson, Bryan Jones, David Karol, Ken Kersch, Herbert Kitschelt, Ezra Klein, Phil Klinkner, Tim LaPira, Yphtach Lelkes, Yuval Levin, Seth Masket, David Mayhew, Shep Melnick, Hans Noel, Brendan Nyhan, Paul Pierson, Jack Pitney, Paul Rosenberg, Andrew Sabl, Reihan Salam, Eric Schickler, Steve Schier, Daniel Schlozman, Kay Schlozman, Adam Sheingate, Gregory Shufeldt, John Sides, Peter Skerry, Cory Smidt, Paul Sniderman, Michael Stamm, Daniel Stid, Laura Stoker, Steven Teles, Dan Thaler, Alex Theodoridis, Craig Volden, and two anonymous reviewers. For generously sharing data and comments, we thank Robert Boatright, Peter Francia, William Jacoby, Eric Gonzalez Juenke, Jonathan Ladd, David Lewis, Hans Noel, Jesse Rhodes, Mark Richardson, Jennifer Nicoll Victor, and Christina Wolbrecht.

Our research was supported by a grant from the William and Flora Hewlett Foundation, as well as by the Departments of Political Science at Michigan State University and Boston College. We thank Brendan Bucy, William Isaac, Marty Jordan, Helen Lee, Marissa Marandola,

Jessica Schoenherr, and Adam Thomas for providing excellent research assistance. For their help with coding and content analysis, we thank Katie Burke, Marina Carabellese, Michael Cnossen, Alec D'Annunzio, Mikaylah Heffernan, Megan Holtz, Malu Silva Martins Gadelha, Christine Steigelman, Alex Swindle, Vincent Szczerowski, Lauren Tamboer, and Elizabeth Wittenbach. We also note with particular gratitude the dedication and enthusiasm of David McBride at Oxford University Press for steering this book to publication.

Finally, we wish to express our appreciation to the people closest to us for their love and support. Matt thanks Sarah Reckhow as well as Norah, Ari, Jan, Larry, and Mindy Grossmann; Dave thanks Monica Soare, Allen and Joan Hopkins, and Finnegan Hopkins, Caitlin DeAngelis, Molly Hopkins, and Sam Hopkins. This book would not exist without their encouragement, patience, and affection.

Matt Grossmann
East Lansing, Michigan

David A. Hopkins
Chestnut Hill, Massachusetts

CHAPTER 1

༄

Introduction

Two Different Kinds of Parties

In April 2015, former First Lady and Secretary of State Hillary Rodham Clinton confirmed widespread expectations that she would seek the Democratic presidential nomination in 2016, announcing her candidacy by releasing a two-minute Internet video entitled "Getting Started." The slickly produced film presented a succession of Americans speaking with anticipation about approaching milestones in their lives, such as graduating from college, buying a house, starting a business, having a child, and entering retirement. Clinton herself did not appear on camera until well over halfway through the video, noting that she, too, was embarking on a new challenge by running for president (albeit for the second time). While Clinton's brief remarks did not offer any specific philosophical or substantive rationale for her campaign, her vow that "everyday Americans need a champion, and I want to be that champion" implied that she would advocate policies benefiting the kinds of people pictured in the video in ways that would help them pursue their various personal endeavors.[1]

The conspicuous variety of racial, sexual, and generational identities among the "everyday Americans" included in the Clinton video attracted substantial notice in the political press. John Dickerson of *Slate* described the production as containing "superbly shot images of attractive, striving Americans" of "all ages and ethnicities," concluding that "all the voters she hopes to stitch into her coalition [saw] a version of themselves."[2] Susan Page of *USA Today* similarly noted the video's "carefully diverse collection of Americans," summarizing its intended message to voters as "It's not about me; it's about you."[3] Democratic supporters in the media cheered the campaign's theme. The video "openly attempted to re-define everyday Americans as more diverse, and unremarkable in their diversity," argued Megan Carpentier of the *Guardian*. "Clinton, it says, stands for an optimistic, future-focused . . . [and] racially representative America in which women are happy to work, raise kids, grow tomatoes, retire and then reinvent themselves in their retirement years (much like Clinton herself has)."[4] Robert Kuttner of the *American Prospect* agreed, noting that "the social theme [of the video] was stunning" and praising its "heavy emphasis on the racial and ethnic mosaic that is America. . . . If all the people who recognize themselves in this video—the young, the poor, minorities, single women—actually get excited and turn out to vote . . . Clinton wins."[5]

In contrast, detractors criticized the video for what they saw as a lack of policy heft and a crudely transparent reliance on activating voters' social identities as a means of winning popular support. "Working mom, check. Hispanic entrepreneur, check. Retiring grandma, check. Gay couple, check. African-American family, check. Hardworking small-businessman, check. South Asian, inter-racial, lesbian, check, check, check," sighed Ruth Marcus of the *Washington Post*. "If your demographic was not featured, you should write the campaign and it will probably splice you in."[6] Maureen Dowd of the *New York Times*, a long-standing Clinton critic, mocked the video for being "gauzy" and "demographically pandering" while depicting the candidate as "a sweet docile granny" and her campaign as "a paean to the calibrated, artful and generic."[7]

The news media's tendency to portray electoral campaigns as extensions of the candidates' own personalities may explain why so much analysis focused on a video with a style and message that could have been shared by virtually any Democratic candidate for elective office. For generations, Democratic politicians have claimed to fight for the interests of "the people" against the forces of entrenched power. The party perennially draws its strongest electoral backing from members of discrete social groups who perceive themselves and their fellow group members as benefiting from specific government policies and programs intended to ameliorate various forms of social inequality. The Clinton campaign's overt attempts to assemble a demographically diverse population of supporters merely extended a long tradition of Democratic politics that reflects the essential nature of the party as a social group coalition.

Some commentators faulted the two-minute announcement video for failing to mention any substantive issue positions advocated by the candidate. But it was not difficult to infer from its general theme—accurately, as it turned out—that the Clinton campaign would soon publicly endorse an extensive series of detailed policies designed to appeal to the groups represented on camera, such as tuition assistance for college students, government-guaranteed health insurance for independent entrepreneurs, mandated family leave requirements for parents of newborns, universal pre-kindergarten programs for young children, generous Social Security and Medicare benefits for retirees, and antidiscrimination protections for gay couples. The coalitional composition of the Democratic Party has long encouraged party leaders to assemble a policy agenda from the aggregated preferences of the party's numerous constituencies, courting the mass electorate with a large assortment of concrete benefits favoring targeted populations. Although the particular groups inside the Democratic "big tent"—as well as their specific programmatic demands—have evolved over time, the party's foundational partisan character has remained constant across decades of electoral history.

While the Democratic Party is fundamentally a group coalition, the Republican Party can be most accurately characterized as the vehicle of an ideological movement. Most Republican voters—and nearly all of the party's activists, financial supporters, candidates, and officeholders— identify as conservatives and voice support for the abstract values of small government and American cultural traditionalism. In contrast to the variety of single-issue interest groups and social movements that collectively constitute the activist population of the Democratic Party, Republican politics is dominated by a broadly organized, cross-issue conservative movement that now maintains control of the party apparatus. Likewise, the Republican base of support in the mass electorate is less an aggregation of conscious social groups mobilized by the activation of identity-based interests than a less diverse set of voters who perceive themselves as mainstream Americans defending the values of individual liberty and traditional morality against the encroachment of left-wing ideas.

This fundamental and long-standing partisan asymmetry, though regularly acknowledged by previous generations of scholarship, is not recognized by most contemporary studies of American political parties. Yet sustained observation of the distinct behavior of Democratic and Republican leaders, activists, and candidates—whether on the campaign trail, in elective office, in the news media, or in the policymaking process—suggests that the two parties do not operate as simple mirror images. The unique importance of conservative self-identity as a defining characteristic of Republican Party politics has been visibly illustrated over the past decade by the rise of the Tea Party movement, an electorally potent mobilization of populist sentiment on the American right that not only has exhibited vehement opposition to President Barack Obama and his Democratic allies in Congress but also has taken aim at many incumbent Republican officeholders for demonstrating insufficient loyalty to their own professed ideological commitments. Intense electoral pressure from Republican activists and primary voters to maintain doctrinal purity exerts visible influence on the behavior of the party's elected officials, while no counterpart to this dynamic exists on the Democratic side—a particularly consequential contemporary example of the imbalance within the American party system.

Because politicians in a representative democracy face incentives to cater to the preferences of ordinary voters as well as organized interests and activists, such an essential difference in the foundational nature of the two parties is likely to be rooted in, or reinforced by, a corresponding asymmetry in the mass electorate. Indeed, the American public has for decades held collectively left-of-center positions on most specific policy issues even as it has consistently preferred right-of-center perspectives on broader ideological debates over the general size and role of government. The bifurcated nature of American public opinion simultaneously encourages Democratic candidates to court voters by publicly advocating a "laundry list" of numerous specific issue positions and spurs Republicans to attract support by emphasizing larger themes of limited government and American cultural traditions. It also accounts for the means by which each party can stoke a popular backlash to the policies pursued by the other: Democrats attack the privileged interests favored by Republican rule and appeal to the social groups that view themselves as disadvantaged, while Republicans characterize Democratic initiatives as threatening individual liberties and violating traditional American values.

The asymmetric configuration of the two parties extends from the voting public through activists and interest groups to candidates and elected officeholders, encompassing formal and informal party actors at both the mass and the elite level. In this book, we explore the historical roots of this foundational imbalance, demonstrate its enduring importance across a range of political phenomena, and explain its critical implications for American politics and policymaking in the past, present, and future. The mismatched nature of the two partisan camps is especially visible in the era of the ethnically diverse "Obama coalition" and the fierce, Tea Party–infused Republican opposition, but the distinct characters of the Democratic and Republican parties have a long pedigree. Indeed, previous generations of party scholars regularly noted important differences in the internal organizations, governing styles, ideological homogeneity, and electoral appeals of the two parties.

PARTY ASYMMETRY IN THE 20TH CENTURY: FROM POPULAR LORE TO ACADEMIC SCHOLARSHIP

We are hardly the first observers of American politics to suggest that the Democrats and Republicans are, in important respects, fundamentally different kinds of parties. The belief that the two partisan sides acted in a visibly distinct manner amounted to conventional wisdom for much of the 20th century, although the specific ways in which the parties appeared to differ evolved over time. In the past, observers frequently perceived Republicans as orderly in their behavior, loyal to their leadership, and unified around a common policy agenda—especially in comparison to the Democrats, who were portrayed as fractious, undisciplined, and ideologically incoherent. The popular view of the Republican Party as primarily composed of like-minded members from similar socioeconomic backgrounds who marched in ideological lockstep contrasted dramatically with the perception of a Democratic Party populated by multiple factions perennially competing with each other over control of the party organization and policy platform: machine politicians versus good-government reformers, northerners versus southerners, civil rights activists versus racial segregationists, hawks versus doves, liberals versus moderates versus conservatives. As Nelson W. Polsby and William G. Mayer observed in 1999, "the image of the Democrats as a divided, discordant party—and specifically as a party more internally divided than the Republicans—is firmly established in American political folklore."[8]

The Democratic reputation for disunity stretches back at least to the 1930s. The "New Deal coalition" that assembled behind Franklin D. Roosevelt's four presidential candidacies added the discrete social groups of labor union members, African Americans, the urban poor and working class, and liberal intellectuals to the existing Democratic base of southern whites, northern immigrants, and Catholics. While this amalgamation of mass constituencies proved electorally formidable, allowing Democratic leaders to achieve repeated national landslide victories in both presidential and congressional elections, the political heterogeneity of the groups that gathered under the Democratic banner after 1932 presented serious challenges to the capacity of national leaders to agree on a common substantive agenda. The many voters who belonged to the party for non-ideological reasons, such as southern whites whose Democratic affiliation was based on regional identity and northern machine loyalists whose relationship to the party was largely transactional, were amply represented during this period among Democratic activists and officeholders, many of whom regularly opposed policy initiatives advocated by the party's liberal bloc. Such well-known events as Roosevelt's failed 1938 attempt to "purge" anti–New Deal congressional Democrats by personally campaigning for their opponents in primary elections and the walkout of several southern state delegations at the 1948 Democratic National Convention over the party's position on civil rights (which resulted in the breakaway candidacy of Democratic governor Strom Thurmond of South Carolina on the States' Rights Party ballot line that November) served as particularly visible examples of deep Democratic divisions on major political issues.

For decades, the significant challenge faced by Democratic politicians in developing and enacting a coherent policy program amid such serious internal dissent was a frequent subject of popular commentary and scholarly analysis alike. In *A Democrat Looks at His Party*, published in 1955, former U.S. secretary of state Dean Acheson observed:

> From the very beginning, the Democratic party has been . . . the party of the many . . . and a party which represents [the many] will have their many interests, many points of view, and many purposes also. . . . Labor, organized and unorganized, skilled and unskilled; white-collar workers, farmers, professional people; persons dependent on savings or pensions; intellectuals; people in search of housing or some minimum medical care; as well as businessmen—all these criss-crossing groups have interests and points of view which insistently demand attention and which in themselves form a rudimentary system of checks and balances. . . . [T]he Democratic party performs through its own processes a preliminary accommodation and regulation of various and different interests before the legislative process begins, or as part of it, and by this develops policies and programs national in their scope and base.[9]

Such accommodation did not always succeed, leaving party leaders frequently unable to enact their own stated legislative priorities. As House majority leader (and future Speaker) Tip O'Neill remarked two decades later while lamenting his inability to keep the party unified, "We Democrats are all under one tent. In any other country, we'd be five splinter parties."[10]

Several landmark academic studies also addressed Democratic divisions. V. O. Key Jr.'s *Southern Politics in State and Nation* (1949) thoroughly analyzed the political difficulties that the then-solidly Democratic (but frequently antiliberal) South presented to national Democratic organizational and legislative leaders. James Q. Wilson's *The Amateur Democrat* (1962) chronicled the tensions that emerged in northern cities as old-line machine Democrats primarily motivated by electoral pragmatism and the spoils system increasingly faced a challenge for control of local party organizations from a new generation of issue-oriented activists. In his 1966 study of post–World War II congressional voting patterns, David

R. Mayhew noted that the Democratic legislative agenda "was arrived at by adding together the programs of different elements of the party," such as crop subsidies for farmers, workplace regulation for labor unions, and housing projects for city dwellers, all of which were enacted via party-facilitated logrolling by members representing diverse constituencies. Congressional Republicans, in contrast, perceived their proper legislative role as standing for the principles of "free enterprise and economy in government."[11] "Toward a More Responsible Two-Party System," the 1950 report of the American Political Science Association's Committee on Political Parties, called for a series of reform measures intended to bolster the internal cohesion (and, by extension, governing ability) of party organizations and officeholders. Though the report ostensibly applied to both parties, it was inspired by the substantial institutional difficulties faced at the time by programmatic liberals in enacting their favored policy agenda despite long periods of nominal Democratic control of the federal government.[12]

The relative disunity of the Democratic Party extended to the mass electorate as well. "The Democrats tend to be more split internally than the Republicans," observed Norman H. Nie, Sidney Verba, and John R. Petrocik in their 1976 study *The Changing American Voter.* "The Democrats represent a large and quite heterogeneous portion of the population; the Republicans a smaller and more homogeneous portion. . . . A large proportion of the Democratic identifiers is on the left; but a substantial (though not as large) group is on the right." In contrast, "Republican identifiers remain heavily tilted to the right," while "data on the Republican activists indicate that they have a conservative bent like the ordinary Republicans, only much more so."[13]

The 1968 Democratic National Convention, when internal divisions over the prosecution of the Vietnam War not only produced a struggle over the party platform and nomination of a presidential ticket but also provoked violent conflict between antiwar protestors and police on the streets of Chicago, merely reinforced the party's reputation as a loose confederation of discrete and often mutually antagonistic factions. The 1968 election marked the onset of a two-decade period of Republican dominance of the presidency, interrupted only by a single narrow Democratic triumph by Jimmy Carter in the post-Watergate election of 1976, prompting many political observers—both inside and outside the party—to conclude that the lack of a common ideological bond among Democrats had become a serious electoral liability by leaving large blocs of party identifiers open to poaching by the Republican opposition. The campaigns of Republican presidential candidates Richard Nixon, Ronald Reagan, and George H. W. Bush frequently emphasized conservative themes and national identity, attracting sufficient support from moderate and conservative "Nixon Democrats" and "Reagan Democrats" to compensate for their own party's relative numerical disadvantage in the American electorate.

Nelson W. Polsby argued that the Democrats' post-1968 reforms of the presidential nomination process, which were intended to reduce the power of party leaders to influence the selection of candidates, bore some responsibility for the party's difficulties in competing for the presidency after the 1960s despite its enduring majority status among the voting public. "Factionalism in the Democratic party, a failure to build a broad coalition, exposes Democratic candidates in the general election to the full force of the wide variation that Democrats of different stripes maintain in their policy concerns and commitments," Polsby wrote in 1983. "Failure to embrace a coalition-building strategy risks defection in such circumstances far more surely than in the Republican case, where the party maintains a high rather than a broad church of co-believers and where, consequently, serious contestants for the Republican nomination are much more likely to think more or less alike about public policy."[14] The historically poor electoral performance of Senator George McGovern of South Dakota, the archliberal 1972 Democratic presidential nominee, exemplified this distinct vulnerability.

To be sure, the Republican Party has historically exhibited its own version of factional politics at times, although its social and ideological heterogeneity has consistently failed to match that of the Democrats. From the 1930s through the 1960s, the primary line of internal division within Republican ranks separated East and West Coast moderates, who took a relatively accommodationist tack with respect to the New Deal in domestic policy and an internationalist approach in foreign affairs, from midwestern (and, increasingly, southern) conservatives, who continued to espouse limited government at home and isolationist or unilateralist policies abroad. The dual shocks of the Great Depression and World War II combined to temporarily strengthen the influence of the moderate bloc within the party by appearing to render traditional conservatism electorally unviable in most of the nation. But the nomination of Senator Barry Goldwater of Arizona for president in 1964 marked the emergence of an increasingly powerful new conservative movement seeking to push the party in a strongly rightward direction across the entire spectrum of public policy.

The remarkable success of the modern conservative movement in capturing effective control of the national Republican Party—a process that was hardly stalled by Goldwater's landslide defeat at the hands of Democratic incumbent Lyndon Johnson and that reached fruition with the presidential nomination and election of Ronald Reagan in 1980—was due to the particular receptiveness of Republican politicians, activists, and voters to an ideological appeal, which undermined efforts by moderate and liberal Republicans to resist a conservative takeover. As Nicol Rae explained in 1989:

> [T]he secret of the right's success in Republican party politics after 1960 was the forging of an enduring ideological constituency out of a variety of causes and issues. In a crude form, their ideology can be stated as follows: Something is rotten in the American body politic; that rottenness is due to liberalism; and only by returning to the economic, moral, and foreign policy precepts of America's past can the promise of America be redeemed. . . . The moderate strategy of "me-tooism" made strategic sense as long as American party politics were firmly set along New Deal lines . . . [but] as the New Deal consensus began to unravel . . . [moderates] offered no alternative vision or challenge to the prevailing political establishment the way the purist style and uncompromising conservatism of the right did. [Moderate] Republicans were not short of ideas and policies, of course. What they lacked was a distinctive ideology.[15]

Whereas the organization of activists within the Democratic Party has tended to be divided into multiple social groups and issue areas—the labor movement, the civil rights movement, the antiwar movement, the feminist movement, the gay rights movement, the environmental movement, and so forth—the conservative ascendancy in the Republican Party occurred via a broad mobilization of ideologically motivated activists who promoted an alternative philosophy that applied across a broad spectrum of policy domains. The relationship between ideological identity and partisan affiliation strengthened further after Reagan's victory, to the point that claiming adherence to the conservative movement became a virtual requirement for national party officials to retain their credentials as Republicans in good standing. Rather than create internal disunity, the absorption of white southerners into the party's electoral and activist coalition during this era merely strengthened its identification with a conservative ideology that now encompassed economic, foreign policy, and cultural doctrines.

Jo Freeman perceptively identified the definitional importance of ideology for Republicans and group membership for Democrats in her 1986 study of party elites, arguing that each side exhibited a unique "party culture" encompassing its attitudes, organization, and style. The Democratic Party, she observed, was structured as an alliance of component constituencies, with caucuses representing subgroups that served as "primary reference groups" for their membership and often defined the fault lines of intra-party debate. The Republican Party, in contrast, was bound together by a common conservative identity, with internal conflicts representing disagreement over whether or not particular party members were true conservatives and, therefore, "real" Republicans. "The Republican party is not a poor imitation of a normal coalition-building party," she concluded, "but a different type of political organization that does things in different ways."[16]

PARTY ASYMMETRY IN CONTEMPORARY POLITICS

Over the past quarter of a century, the American political environment has changed in ways that have rendered obsolete some of the most prominent former manifestations of party asymmetry. The severe ideological divisions evident in the national Democratic Party after the 1930s, which at times shifted effective control of Congress to a cross-partisan "conservative coalition" of Republicans and southern Democrats at the expense of the Democratic leadership, began to decline significantly in the 1970s as party realignment in the South gradually replaced maverick "Dixiecrats" with conservative Republicans, resulting in a centralization of institutional power in Democratic leaders responsible to the liberal majority in the party's congressional caucus.[17] The improved electoral fortunes of Democratic presidential nominees since the 1980s has likewise refuted the previously widespread assumption that the relative heterogeneity of Democrats represented a serious obstacle to the task of uniting its voters behind the party's candidates for national office. In fact, conventional wisdom in the Obama era holds that the Democratic Party's social diversity has become an enduring advantage, at least in presidential elections, as a result of the steady population growth of racial and religious minority groups within the American electorate—a trend that is projected to continue for decades in the future.[18]

According to a consensus shared by academic scholars and popular pundits alike, the contemporary party system is distinguished by strong and growing ideological polarization among Democratic and Republican elected officials, candidates, and activists.[19] Whether this trend also extends to party identifiers in the electorate is still a matter of some debate among political scientists,[20] but experts agree that voters are now more likely to be "sorted" into the party that best matches their existing political beliefs, contributing to a sizable increase in the aggregate level of party loyalty in national elections.[21] The process of partisan sorting has particularly reduced the defection rate of Democratic voters to Republican presidential nominees over time, as the proportion of right-leaning Democratic identifiers in the mass public (who were traditionally open to persuasion by Republican candidates) has declined since the 1980s.

But the emergence of a more politically unified Democratic Party at both the mass and the elite level over the past several decades does not imply that the distinct characters of the parties have faded. The polarization of the parties has itself exhibited an asymmetric pattern: while congressional Democrats have collectively moved modestly to the ideological left since the 1970s (mostly as a result of the declining electoral fortunes of the party's ideologically atypical southern wing), Republicans in both chambers have shifted much further to the right over the same period, as measured by the NOMINATE scores developed by Keith Poole and Howard Rosenthal.[22] Among officeholders, activists, and voters alike, the proportion of nonliberals in the Democratic Party has remained significantly larger than the share of nonconservatives in the Republican Party.

Other manifestations of party asymmetry have remained intact, even in the current age of rampant polarization. As we will show, Democratic voters still tend to report that their attachment to the party is based on group identity or sympathy, while Republicans more frequently perceive party allegiance to be a product of ideology. Likewise, the previously noted tendency of American citizens to hold left-of-center views on most specific policy issues while simultaneously preferring conservative positions on broad ideological principles has continued to give Democratic candidates an incentive to base their campaigns around advocacy of specific domestic policy programs while encouraging Republican candidates to stress more general rhetorical themes of small government, nationalism, and traditional morality.

Moreover, new consequences of party asymmetry have emerged in recent years, with three of these developments becoming central attributes of contemporary American politics. The first is the formation of the modern conservative media universe, which holds considerable and increasing power within the Republican Party and, by extension, the political world as a whole. Talk radio, right-leaning Internet outlets, and Fox News Channel have become highly influential forces in Republican politics over the past 25 years by promoting conservative views, mobilizing Republican voters, and enforcing ideological loyalty among the party's candidates and elected officials. Though some enterprising liberals have attempted to build a corresponding infrastructure on the left, it has never approached the visibility and popularity of conservative media and has not demonstrated the capacity to motivate mass participation or exert significant leftward pressure on Democratic leaders.

Second, the two parties' governing styles have become even more distinct. Since the 1980s, Republican officeholders have increasingly embraced a highly confrontational approach that eschews inside strategies premised on the pursuit of compromise in favor of maximizing partisan conflict, emphasizing symbolic acts of ideological differentiation, and engaging in near-automatic obstruction of initiatives proposed by the opposition. While Democrats have also become more procedurally aggressive, several veteran observers of Washington workways have noted the Republican Party's disproportionate contribution to the trend of increasing political hardball.[23] The series of governing crises over the past two decades that have been precipitated by Republican demands, including multiple government shutdowns, a near-default on the federal debt, and the second impeachment of a sitting president in American history, serve as illustrative examples of the growing divergence between a Republican Party increasingly devoted to expressions of ideological commitment and a Democratic Party that remains responsive to a set of social constituencies prizing incremental policy goals.

Third, the traditional reputation of Republicans as highly disciplined and deferential to authority has been eroded by the rise of an increasingly unruly contingent of "Tea Party" officeholders and activists who frequently rebel against the leaders of their party. Contemporary Republican factionalism does not reflect significant ideological disunity; virtually all Republican politicians espouse a conservative political philosophy, relegating the party's once-sizable moderate bloc to a scattered handful of officials. Instead, the fault lines of internal debate and conflict tend to separate conservative purists who reject compromise and value constant symbolic confrontation from more pragmatic colleagues who prefer to pick their battles and demonstrate achievements in governing.[24]

The foundational difference between the two major parties thus endures even in an era marked by growing polarization among political elites and heavily party-line voting in the mass electorate, with significant implications for party politics in the present and future. As Geoffrey Kabaservice argues in his account of the Republican Party's post–World War II historical evolution, party polarization and asymmetry have combined to produce frequent paralysis within a constitutional structure that requires regular cooperation in order to function efficiently:

> While there are many possible reasons to explain the present American political dysfunction, the leading suspect is the transformation of the Republican Party over the past half-century into a monolithically conservative organization. Throughout American history, two principal political parties . . . had been coalitions of interest rather than ideological vehicles. . . . [T]he appearance of a Republican Party almost entirely composed of ideological conservatives is a new and highly unprecedented development.[25]

The assumption that the parties are more or less interchangeable in their composition, objectives, and behavior must be discarded in order to properly understand the most important attributes of contemporary politics, ranging from campaign strategy and governing style to the contours of public opinion and the role of the news media. Enduring party asymmetries challenge the development of unified theories of American parties intended to apply equally to Democrats and Republicans. Presuming that the parties act in a similar fashion in response to the same events makes for parsimonious theory, but the associated cost of inaccurate description and false equivalence is too high to bear. Understanding each party on its own terms is the first step toward building better theories of American politics and helping academic scholarship speak directly to the concerns of popular debate.

The persistence of party differences also contributes to the frequent inability of partisans on each side to comprehend the positions and actions of their counterparts in the opposite camp, further eroding the mutual understanding that is often a necessary condition for compromise and accomplishment within the American political system. Democrats and Republicans often demonstrate an elementary understanding of the basic distinction in the parties' operational approaches but habitually describe it in a manner that flatters their own party while disparaging the opposition. Republicans claim that they are the party of principles, whereas Democrats are the party of giveaways. Democrats view themselves as the party of productivity and problem solving, while criticizing Republicans as the party of extremism and obstruction.

But even these characterizations of party differences, replete as they are with inherent normative judgments, are more accurate than accounts that assume simple partisan equivalence. As political journalist and Vox founder Ezra Klein summarizes, "Democrats tend to project their preference for policymaking onto the Republican Party—and then respond with anger and confusion when Republicans don't seem interested in making a deal. Republicans tend to assume the Democratic Party is more ideological than it is, and so see various policy initiatives as part of an ideological effort to remake America along more socialistic lines."[26] These misapprehensions contribute to the current climate of incessant partisan vitriol. By offering a deeper exploration of the differences between the political parties, we hope to provide each side with a better understanding of the perspective and motivations of the other. The two parties face strong incentives to continue on their divergent paths, but they can also respect each other's objectives and learn from each other's strengths.

OUR ARGUMENT

The Democrats and Republicans are different kinds of parties, exhibiting distinct types of electoral supporters, activists, and institutional networks. Scholars and popular observers already recognize that the parties represent dissimilar constituencies and hold divergent substantive goals, but political science models often imply that the requirements for winning elections and achieving desired policy changes should produce symmetry in their strategic behavior and organizational structure.[27] These theories assume that the parties will adopt parallel approaches to electoral campaigns, policy debates, and governing activities when placed in similar circumstances, appearing as mirror images that represent different interests and perspectives but seek to achieve their desired ends through equivalent means. The (less theoretical) scholarly literature of past decades often described the parties as developing and maintaining distinct cultures. We aim to revive and reformulate this historical tradition, replacing its traditional focus on party organizations and national conventions with a broader approach that encompasses each party's associated activist networks and electoral supporters.

The Democratic Party, we argue, is a coalition of social groups that act as discrete voting blocs for candidates, constituencies for group leaders, and demanders of particular policy commitments.[28] Since the 1960s, changes in the relative size and influence of Democratic constituencies reduced the size of the party's conservative wing and expanded its policy agenda—but no organized liberal movement has emerged to dominate its internal organization or succeed in shifting its policies toward leftist positions. The Republican Party, in contrast, serves as the vehicle of a conservative ideological movement that succeeded after the 1950s in fusing its various intellectual strands, marketing its broad critiques of government, building a supportive organizational network, and moving party doctrine toward the policy commitments of its right wing. This underlying partisan asymmetry has produced distinct Democratic and Republican approaches to debating public issues, campaigning for votes, and pursuing policy change in government. The concurrent operational liberalism and symbolic conservatism of the American public has allowed each party to maintain its unique character while effectively competing for broader popular support.

Ideology, as we use the term here, is a broad system of ideas about the role of government. It serves a key role in unifying the Republican Party's popular and activist base and constraining its politicians. Group interests, in our definition, are the product of discrete constituencies with separable and specific policy concerns. The Democratic Party—in the electorate, as an organizational network, and in government—is organized around group interests. One could, of course, redefine conservatives as a dominant "group" in the Republican Party, rather than recognizing conservatism as a unifying ideology, but that conceptual shift would reduce clarity without changing the implications of our argument. Even if treated as a group interest, conservatives are not analogous to Democratic groups; they view the GOP as properly the vehicle of their views alone, rejecting the legitimate standing of nonconservatives within the party.

Alternatively, one might argue that the Republican Party is also coalitional in nature but merely contains a comparatively small number of more populous social groups. The parties indeed differ in the size of their electoral constituencies. Compared to Democratic-aligned groups, however, most Republican-leaning sectors of the electorate (such as whites, Christians, or married voters) are not as uniform in their collective partisan affiliation, are less likely to relate to the party according to a well-defined set of distinctive issue priorities, rarely view themselves as constituting a discrete component of a larger coalition, and are less identified with separate interest organizations and elected representatives that claim to speak for their particular concerns.

The fundamental distinction that we draw between ideological Republicans and group-interest Democrats is meant to unify our description and analysis of numerous specific ways and circumstances in which the parties exhibit consistent differences. Yet our findings and their implications do not necessarily require the adoption of these particular conceptual definitions or labels. We use the terms *ideology* and *group interest* descriptively rather than pejoratively, and we do not harbor normative judgments about the relative superiority of either party's foundational character.

Our argument also reconceptualizes important trends in American politics. Rather than assuming symmetric ideological polarization in public opinion or legislative behavior, we identify distinct trajectories: while the Republican Party has collectively moved broadly rightward on the ideological spectrum over time, the Democratic Party has shed its conservative coalition partners and is increasingly dedicated to the new issue concerns of its rising group constituencies. Although racial politics played a key role in enabling both shifts, we argue that the solidification of ideological conservatism among Republicans and constituency politics among Democrats extended well beyond the specific importance of civil rights in driving partisan change.

We also reinterpret trends in the role of partisanship, media and research use, and public mobilization that are widely blamed for contemporary dysfunction in governmental institutions. The heyday of extensive and expert-driven policymaking in the 1960s and early 1970s—a status quo to which many liberal commentators and scholars now wish to return—was, in our view, more the product of an elite-level political consensus than an outgrowth of durable popular support. Capitalizing upon public concern and resentment, conservatives responded by developing an alternative set of media, activist, and research institutions that succeeded in transforming the Republican Party into an obstructionist force that slowed the growth in the scope of government but failed to reverse specific prior expansions of federal power and responsibility. Democrats continued to rely on policy expertise, identifying new social problems and proposing specific solutions, but divided into disparate issue area networks tied to separate constituencies. Sensitive to the preferences of the American electorate, Democratic leaders increasingly came to justify support for individual policy reforms on empirical or group-interest grounds rather than mounting a broader philosophical defense of an expansive national government.

Despite these changes, we perceive considerable continuity in the role of party politics within the larger framework of governance. The exceptional conservatism of American political culture and public policy in comparison to other nations reflects the long-standing role of the Republican Party in fusing traditional American values with anti-government sentiment. Most contemporary governing difficulties in the United States reflect the existence of evenly matched parties with increasingly dissimilar goals operating within a decentralized institutional structure.

In the near future, there is little reason to expect either party to transform its fundamental character. Both Democratic and Republican politicians maintain sizable bases of fervent public support that correspond to the distinctive approaches preferred by their respective activist populations, even if clashes between the irreconcilable views of the two parties frequently produce gridlock and even crisis. We hope that our analysis can provide Democrats and Republicans alike with a greater perspective on how the behavior and strategy of the opposing party is consistent with a set of sincerely held beliefs and objectives, but it is overly optimistic to expect such understanding to spur a bipartisan movement for reform and cooperation. Party asymmetry, regularly reinforced by the leaders, activists, and voters on each side, instead appears likely to remain an enduring feature of American politics.

OUR EVIDENCE

This book seeks to demonstrate the long-standing existence of asymmetric partisanship across the American political system and assess its numerous manifestations and implications. We rely on varied data and analyses, drawing upon interviews and surveys of citizens, activists, and officials; government records and activity disclosures; experiments; historical archives and reviews; and text and audiovisual documentation. We build on the valuable work of other scholars who have already conducted relevant data collection and interpretation, though assessing our claims has often required substantial data updating, re-coding, and re-analysis. We review, synthesize, and apply prior findings from political science (in both the American and comparative subfields), history, sociology, psychology, communications, and law.

We also gather and analyze original data on candidate speeches and debates, party platforms, media coverage and opinion columns, and congressional speeches, letters, and committee hearings. To enable assessments of change over time, many of these new datasets provide continuous coverage of the period from 1948 to the present and extend widely across policy areas. Our analysis provides direct assessments of how often and in what contexts the parties refer to social groups, ideological concepts, public policies, symbolic imagery, and evidentiary sources. To improve readability, we provide full information in tables, figures, and footnotes but avoid detailed justifications for methodological choices within the main text. We also provide all data online for easy public access.

The party asymmetries that we identify and document are manifested widely and regularly in contemporary American politics. But our analysis has clear boundaries. We do not imply that partisan, ideological, or policy orientations necessarily arise from individual differences in genetics or personality. We uncover links between the parties' distinct policy agendas and their unique organizational and strategic characteristics, but we do not claim that the same differences have characterized the two parties throughout American history or that they apply equally well to all conservative or liberal factions worldwide. We specify the historical roots and potential contingencies associated with each of the salient differences that we identify between Democrats and Republicans at both the mass and the elite level and place both parties in international context.

This study pursues a holistic approach that connects mass political behavior to institutions and elites; situates contemporary events in historical and comparative perspective; and integrates the insights of practitioners, public commentators, and scholars from other disciplines. As a result, we sometimes restrict the detailed examination of any particular subject in favor of a wider scope of analysis. The array of approaches, analyses, and examples that we present are designed to document, explain, and contextualize partisan asymmetry across the broad landscape of American politics.

PLAN OF THE BOOK

Our analysis begins with American voters, proceeds to the organizations and networks maintained by the parties and their associated media and research enterprises, and concludes with an analysis of the role of party asymmetry in political campaigns and the policymaking process. Chapter 2 examines the parties' distinct sources of support in the mass electorate. We demonstrate that Republican voters commonly identify as conservatives, conceptualize political choices in ideological terms, view the parties as divided by broad principles, voice support for politicians who reject compromise in order to remain true to their beliefs, and demand a broad shift in the ideological direction of public policy. In contrast, Democrats are more likely to perceive political choices as invoking group interests, to view party conflict as arising from clashing group coalitions, and to support politicians who make compromises in order to achieve practical accomplishments. The parties can sustain these asymmetries in the electoral arena because a majority of the public holds left-leaning views on specific policy issues yet agrees more generally with conservative principles. Each party can thus claim to represent a popular majority and can readily mobilize public opinion in opposition to the actions of the other.

Chapter 3 turns to the party organizations and their affiliated networks, presenting a framework that distinguishes our account from prior theories of political parties. We review the historical development of the social group coalition that constitutes the Democratic Party and the ideological movement that came to control the Republican Party. We find that the Democratic electoral and interest group base is dominated by an array of discrete social minorities who provide loyal partisan support even if they decline to consider themselves ideological liberals, and that Republicans attract votes from social pluralities that identify with the party on ideological terms. Only Democratic interest groups link the party's voting blocs to specific legislative goals. We review the history of party organizational reforms and analyze each party's convention speeches and platforms, demonstrating that the Democratic Party has repeatedly served as an arena for group conflict whereas the Republican Party has long provided a vehicle for conservative ideological expression. We also situate the American parties in international context, demonstrating that the Republican Party stands alone among comparable democracies in its broad ideological commitment to conservatism.

Chapter 4 extends our analysis to debates over public policy issues, including the unique influence of conservative media and the different uses of scientific research by each party. Responding to the disproportionately liberal cast of journalism and academia, the conservative movement built its own network of alternative media outlets and think tanks. As a result, partisan identifiers and activists came to rely on distinct sources of political information, with Republicans more likely to consume media that are openly aligned with their political orientation and to distrust alternative sources. Talk radio and Fox News Channel, in particular, have extended the reach of conservative messages and helped to mobilize the conservative activist base. At the elite level, Democratic politicians disproportionately rely on research produced within universities, whereas Republicans are more closely tied to conservative think tanks. Democrats employ research to analyze the extent of social problems and the relative effectiveness of policy tools, while Republicans and conservative think tanks rely on policy experts to justify their broader vision of the proper role of government in society.

Chapter 5 illustrates the implications of party asymmetry for American political campaigns. We find that Republican candidates are more likely than Democrats to engage in ideological appeals to both the primary and the general electorate in campaign rhetoric, advertising, and media. Democrats, in contrast, are more likely to cite group identity and interests and to use targeted policies to court specific social groups. Challenges to incumbent officeholders in Republican primary elections are more likely to be based on ideology, whereas Democratic primary competition is more likely to involve group divisions. Minority candidates share demographic characteristics with their electoral constituencies more frequently in the Democratic Party. In primary elections, Republican candidates position themselves as conservatives in good standing, while Democrats emphasize group loyalties and the electoral viability of their candidacy. In general elections, Democratic candidates develop targeted proposals and defend existing government programs, whereas Republicans sound more abstract themes and warn of threats to American values.

Chapter 6 explores the implications of asymmetry for the parties in government. We find that Democratic officials treat the policymaking process as an attempt to address a catalog of social problems, each requiring a form of government action, whereas Republicans view policy disputes as manifestations of a broader conflict over the proper scope of federal responsibilities. Because realistic new policy alternatives are more likely to expand than to contract the role of government, Republicans focus on position taking and retrenchment, whereas Democrats prioritize substantive policy changes. Congressional rules evolved in the 1970s at the behest of Democrats frustrated by conservative influence over the committee system, but institutional reform ultimately coincided with a decline in liberal policymaking. A conservative and confrontational faction of Republicans then remade the congressional party in the image of movement activism in the 1980s—only to face regular rebellions by later generations of purist conservatives over insufficient ideological fidelity. In the policymaking arena, Democrats have responded to conservative critiques by advancing proposals that incorporate markets, build incrementally on existing institutions, minimize the role of bureaucracies, and decentralize responsibility. Republicans have thus succeeded in limiting visible expansions of government's size, but not in reducing the breadth of national policy goals.

Party asymmetry is at the root of much that is distinctive about American politics and government. We synthesize a wide variety of research in order to document the most consequential differences between Democrats and Republicans and emphasize their widespread implications. Our approach offers more accurate predictions for how political debates will evolve and how government will operate under the leadership of each party. Stagnation in theories of political parties, campaigns, and policymaking is often attributable to scholars' inability to equate the actions of one side with those of the other. Recognizing the distinct styles of each party can produce better explanations for political events and trends, including contemporary polarization and dysfunction. Each party's methods of campaigning, organizing, and governing exhibit strengths and weaknesses, collectively resulting in a persistently competitive national battle for electoral success and policy influence.

We hope that our approach can help partisans on each side better understand one another. Many contemporary critiques of American institutions are disguised conservative or liberal complaints about the other side's typical style of political organization and governance. Recognizing the mentality and strategies of the other party's membership can bolster the ability of political actors to advocate more effectively for their own views. A willingness to learn from both sides of the aisle will help improve our collective capacity to grasp the workings of American democracy and to sensibly guide its future.

CHAPTER 2

⌇

How Democrats and Republicans Think About Politics

The congressional midterm elections of 1994 resulted in a historic national landslide for the Republican Party. Benefiting from the mediocre job approval ratings of Democratic president Bill Clinton and a highly energized base of supporters, Republicans gained 8 seats in the Senate and 52 seats in the House of Representatives, winning majority control of both chambers and ending a 40-year span of uninterrupted Democratic rule of the House. No incumbent Republican member of Congress lost a reelection bid, while the plethora of Democratic electoral casualties included House Speaker Tom Foley of Washington, the first sitting Speaker since 1862 to be removed from office by his own constituents.

Victorious Republicans interpreted the results as a popular endorsement of their ideological agenda, promising a "Republican Revolution" once they took office the following January. "If this is not a mandate to move in a particular direction, I would like somebody to explain to me what a mandate would look like," crowed House Speaker-in-waiting Newt Gingrich of Georgia on the night of the election. According to Gingrich and his Republican colleagues, the American people had registered a decisive preference for their party's platform of small-government conservatism. "I believe that, starting today, the train is going to pull out of the station, and it is going to be a train that is bound for less government and more freedom," remarked Texas senator Phil Gramm the following morning.[1] Jon Christensen of Nebraska, one of many newly elected Republican "citizen legislators" who had never previously held political office, similarly argued, "The American people sent a clear message to us. . . . They elected a Republican majority to change the way Congress does business. After 40 years of liberal big government [and] big-spending politics, the American people said, 'Enough is enough.'"[2]

Evidence that voters preferred a conservative approach to governing extended beyond the election results. Public trust in government had sunk to a then-record low in the summer of 1994, with just 17 percent of Americans expressing confidence that the federal government would "do what is right" most or nearly all of the time.[3] A national Gallup poll conducted several months later during the week of the elections found that 55 percent of respondents agreed that "the government is trying to do too many things that should be left to individuals and businesses," compared to just 37 percent who believed that "government should do more to solve our country's problems."[4] In another Gallup survey conducted two months later, 67 percent of Americans named spending cuts a top legislative priority for the new Congress, while 55 percent of respondents in a *Washington Post* poll agreed with the statement that it was "absolutely critical" to reduce the federal budget deficit "as soon as possible." Republicans believed that they had little to fear from a confrontation with the politically weakened president: a January 1995 *Los Angeles Times* survey found that Americans believed, by a margin of 41 percent to 33 percent, that the new Republican congressional majority had "better ideas" than Clinton.[5]

As Republicans acted to advance their conservative policy agenda over the course of the 1995–1996 Congress, Democratic leaders—though initially stunned by the election results and derided as politically obsolete by the Washington pundit class—soon settled on a counter-strategy. Clinton decided to embrace rather than dispute the widespread interpretation of the Republican victory as an expression of symbolic antigovernment sentiment, seeking to demonstrate his responsiveness to the perceived will of the electorate. In his January 1995 State of the Union address, Clinton called for a "smaller, less costly, and smarter" government that would reject the "old way" of "large, top-down, inflexible bureaucracies . . . centralized . . . in Washington."[6] Instead, Democrats attacked the new Republican Congress by publicizing specific policy differences that separated the parties, especially those regarding funding levels for popular domestic spending programs that benefited key constituencies. When the Gingrich-led Congress passed budget legislation that included entitlement cuts and health care premium increases, Clinton responded with a veto, resulting in an impasse that led to a 27-day shutdown of the federal government over two separate periods between November 1995 and January 1996. Rather than characterize his position in broad ideological terms, Clinton emphasized the particular services and beneficiaries that he claimed would suffer under the Republican budget, arguing in a public statement that the

GOP was attempting to impose "deep" and "unwise" cuts to "Medicare, Medicaid, education, and the environment" while raising taxes on "the hardest-pressed working families in America."[7]

Despite their stated preference for small government in the abstract, most citizens surveyed by public opinion polls agreed with Clinton's call for more generous funding of these particular social programs, strengthening the president's position as he negotiated an agreement to resolve the crisis that ultimately excluded most of the Republicans' proposed spending reductions. A CBS News/*New York Times* poll found that respondents preferred preventing cuts to Medicare over balancing the federal budget by a margin of 67 percent to 27 percent.[8] Gingrich, widely blamed for shutting down the government in order to force his unpopular policies on the country, emerged from the budget battle as the most disliked politician in America. His attempts to repair the damage to his public reputation by adopting a more conciliatory approach in subsequent negotiations with Clinton alienated a number of conservative purists in his own party caucus, ultimately contributing to his departure from Congress after the disappointing results of the 1998 midterm elections.[9]

The events of the mid-1990s effectively illustrate the distinct nature of the two major parties, with a Republican Party that is primarily motivated by abstract ideology opposed by a Democratic Party that is dedicated to the defense of group interests. In this chapter, we present empirical evidence in support of the view that this partisan asymmetry is grounded in the political orientations of the American electorate. The distinct behavior of candidates, officeholders, and other elites on each side reflects corresponding differences in the bonds of identification linking citizen supporters to their chosen party and the nature of the demands that they make of their party's leadership. The Democratic Party's character as a social group coalition fosters a relatively pragmatic, results-oriented style of politics in which officeholders are rewarded for delivering concrete benefits to targeted groups in order to address specific social problems. Republicans, in contrast, are more likely to forge partisan ties based on common ideological beliefs, encouraging party officials to pursue broad rightward shifts in public policy. As a result, Republican voters and activists are more likely than their Democratic counterparts to prize symbolic demonstrations of ideological purity and to pressure their party leaders to reject moderation and compromise.

This partisan asymmetry is further reinforced by the distribution of political attitudes within the public at large. The American electorate consistently holds collectively left-of-center views on most policy issues even as it leans to the right on more general measures of ideology—as Lloyd A. Free and Hadley Cantril observed nearly five decades ago, the public is simultaneously operationally liberal and symbolically conservative.[10] This pattern has remained intact even as American politics has entered an era of rampant polarization among elites and partisan sorting within the mass electorate. Democratic politicians thus seek to direct voters' attention to the relatively popular positions taken by their party on specific issues, while Republican leaders benefit from framing political conflict as a clash between "big" and "small" government. As Gingrich discovered in his showdown with Clinton, the public's preference for limited federal power in the abstract often dissipates when voters are confronted with potential cuts to particular services. Democrats are surprised by the same pattern in reverse: Clinton's once-popular goal of implementing universal health insurance failed after Republicans in Congress successfully characterized it as a left-wing scheme to impose government control over the health care system and reduce the freedom of private citizens. Because the public collectively agrees with each party on its own preferred terms of debate, Democrats and Republicans can both claim to represent the views of an electoral majority—and each side maintains a powerful incentive to maintain its distinctive style of winning popular support.

THE CONCEPTUALIZATION AND MEASUREMENT OF MASS IDEOLOGY

In order to demonstrate that ideological thinking plays a more important role in shaping the political orientations of Republicans than those of Democrats, it is first necessary to address the complexity involved in defining and measuring ideology in the minds of voters. A pioneering 1964 study by Philip E. Converse identified multiple indicators of citizen ideology, including (1) self-identification with (and understanding of) ideological labels like "liberal" and "conservative," (2) conceptualization of political choices (such as favored parties or candidates) in terms of abstract principles and values, and (3) consistency of left- or right-leaning views over time and across an array of specific political issues (views that citizens sometimes calibrated by comparing their own position to those taken by liberal or conservative elites).[11] Converse's well-known conclusion that much of the American public remained "ideologically innocent" was based on the modest statistical associations that he found among these distinct indicators, as well as his discovery that most citizens did not hold uniformly liberal or conservative positions across disparate policy domains.

In recent years, the procession of ideological polarization among political elites has led scholars to investigate whether the mass electorate has reflected this trend, abandoning its prior philosophical incoherence. These analyses have tended to rely on measures of issue constraint—whether or not individuals maintain consistently liberal or conservative views on an array of specific policies—as the primary indicators of an ideological orientation toward politics.[12] Frequently, studies merge the reported positions of survey respondents on a battery of policy questions into a single numerical score representing a citizen's ideal point on a unidimensional left–right scale—a practice that may systematically underestimate the American public's degree of political extremity on most issues.[13] Furthermore, this approach omits the other manifestations of ideology identified by Converse. Ideological self-identification and devotion to abstract principles, though often imperfectly associated with the operational measures constructed by averaging together respondents' positions on multiple specific policy issues, can still retain significant independent influence over the opinions and behavior of voters. Even a citizen who fails to exhibit high levels of issue constraint may yet consider himself or herself a liberal or conservative and act accordingly in the political arena, with potentially significant consequences for partisan and electoral politics in the United States.

While Republicans are more likely to demonstrate an ideological conceptualization of politics than Democrats, this asymmetry does not reflect differential rates of policy consistency among the supporters of the two parties. Instead, Republican identifiers are more likely than Democrats to think about partisan politics in terms of ideology and to view their party as standing for a set of abstract values and principles. This form of ideological conceptualization does not necessarily produce issue constraint, nor does the presence of constraint necessarily reveal the existence of ideological reasoning (since citizens could also acquire consistent policy views from partisanship, social identity, or other sources). The analysis we present in this book draws upon indicators that measure the degree to which individuals perceive the political world, and their place in it, in abstract or value-laden terms.

We share the common assumption that ideology is a unidimensional attribute ranging from the liberal left to the conservative right. According to Christopher Ellis and James A. Stimson, the contemporary understandings of liberalism and conservatism can be summarized by an excerpt from a 1938 "fireside chat" radio broadcast by then-president Franklin D. Roosevelt:

> Roughly speaking, the liberal school of thought recognizes that the new conditions throughout the world call for new remedies . . . [that] can be adopted and successfully maintained in this country under our present form of government if we use

government as an instrument of cooperation to provide these remedies. . . . The opposing or conservative school of thought, as a general proposition, does not recognize the need for Government itself to step in and take action to meet these new
problems. It believes that individual initiative and private philanthropy will solve
them—that we ought to repeal many of the things we have done and go back [to
prior policies].[14]

Although the components of these ideologies have evolved over time, both
their general principles and the types of specific policies with which they
are associated have remained largely constant for 80 years. "The issues
that most define the dimension," report Ellis and Stimson, "are about government spending, about taxes, about the government reach, about benefits for the needy, and about income equality and inequality."[15] Similarly,
the relatively ideological nature of the Republicans and the group-based
organization of the Democrats are themselves stable and long-standing
attributes of the American two-party system, visible over decades of political history and remaining intact into the 21st century.

PARTY ASYMMETRY IN SYMBOLIC IDEOLOGY

Because American political culture has prized individualism and distrusted state authority since the nation's founding, conservative ideology has long held a strong popular appeal. Nevertheless, the more liberal
Democratic Party has maintained a persistent advantage in identifiers
within the national population since the 1930s. As Figure 2-1 demonstrates, the past six decades have produced an enduring gap between macropartisanship (the aggregate distribution of party identification in the
mass public, indicated here by the percentage of major-party identifiers
who identify as Democrats) and macro-ideology (indicated here by the
percentage of liberal identifiers among all liberal or conservative identifiers). Although the macropartisanship measure has generated controversy
regarding its (artificially) high level of instability, there is no dispute that
Democrats have usually held an advantage in partisanship despite the
consistent prevalence of conservative self-identification in the American
electorate. Since the 1950s, the gap between the two measures has averaged 20.5 points and has been relatively stable (with a standard deviation
of 5.2 points).

Both liberals and Democrats have represented a declining share of the
electorate since the 1950s, though the decline among liberals occurred
first. According to Ellis and Stimson, liberalism declined as the scope of
government expanded:

Figure 2-1   Macro-ideology and Macropartisanship

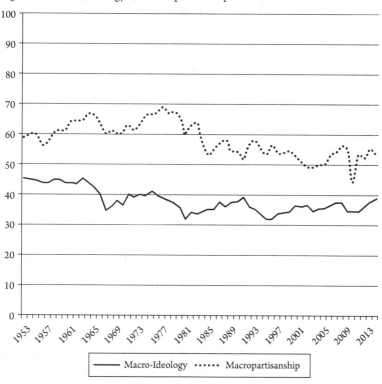

The dotted line shows the average percentage of respondents with Democratic identification out of all those identifying with one of the two major parties. The solid line shows the percentage of respondents with liberal identification out of all those identifying as liberal or conservative. For macropartisanship, James Stimson and Donald Green estimate percentages by using data from Gallup polls. Janet Box-Steffensmeier compiled data on macro-ideology. The authors updated the time series with (unadjusted) data from Gallup polls after 1997. Donald Green Replication Arhive is available at: https://sites.google.com/site/donaldpgreen/replication. Janet Box-Steffensmeier Dataverse is available at: https://dataverse.harvard.edu/dataverse/Steffensmeier

> Between 1963, when the Kennedy assassination made Lyndon Johnson president, and 1967, the third year of LBJ's Great Society, the ranks of self-identified liberals fell by 10.5 points—about one-fourth—and never recovered. . . . That movement would have been huge had it been temporary. As a permanent shift, it is a dominant story of American politics in the 20th century.[16]

The time series presented in Figure 2-1 confirms this decline in liberal self-identification during the 1960s but also finds thermostatic responsiveness to the direction of national policy: liberals made relative gains during the Republican presidencies of Richard Nixon and Ronald Reagan, while conservatives became more numerous during the Jimmy Carter and first Bill Clinton administrations; there has also been a more recent trend toward greater relative liberalism. The increase in relative identification with the Republican Party occurred later; it was particularly notable during the Reagan era and was driven especially by party realignment among conservative white southerners. Even though both liberals and conservatives have become better sorted into the "correct" parties over time, a sizable gap remains between the collective partisan and ideological self-identifications of American citizens.[17]

In a mass public containing more Democrats than Republicans but more conservatives than liberals, the Republican electorate will naturally include a greater proportion of party-consistent ideological identifiers than will the Democratic electorate. Figure 2-2 displays the distribution of ideological self-placement on the American National Election Studies (ANES) seven-point scale for Republicans (top) and Democrats (bottom) in 2012. The figure summarizes the distribution of ideology among all party members (black lines), among partisans who reported engaging in two or more activities in support of a candidate (gray lines), and among those who reported making political donations (marbled lines). Among both engaged citizens and the broader electorate, Republicans are strongly united by symbolic conservatism, while Democrats array themselves along a wider ideological spectrum. On the Republican side, self-identified conservatives constituted 74 percent of voters, 84 percent of activists, and 89 percent of donors, with virtually no party members located to the left of the ideological center. In contrast, among Democrats, only 47 percent of voters, 61 percent of activists, and 70 percent of donors identified as liberal; all three Democratic populations were more likely than their Republican counterparts to consider themselves ideological centrists, and 13 percent of Democratic voters and 12 percent of Democratic activists identified as a form of conservative. Clearly, shared ideology plays a central role in holding the Republican Party together: even Republicans with left-of-center attitudes on specific issues usually and disproportionately self-identify as conservatives.[18]

This finding does not merely reflect the particular ideological measure employed by the ANES, nor does it represent a unique preference of American citizens for the term "conservative." Figure 2-3 presents data from the 2011 wave of the World Values Survey (WVS) that similarly summarize the ideological placement of Democrats and Republicans. The WVS employs a 10-point ideological scale in which the endpoints are labeled "left" (1) and "right" (10), instead of "liberal" and "conservative," in order to facilitate international comparisons. The mean self-placement among Democrats was 4.8, with 45 percent of Democratic respondents choosing one of the two middle positions. The mean Republican position was 7.4, with two-thirds of Republican respondents placing themselves at

Figure 2-2 Ideological Self-Placement Among Partisans, Activists, and Donors

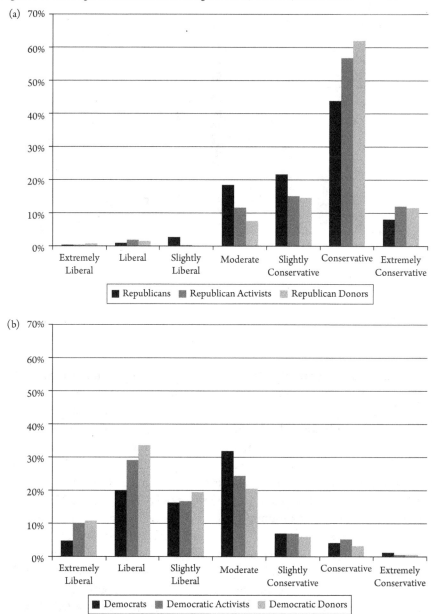

Percentages of Democratic and Republican activists, nonactivists, and donors who fit into each ideological category. Activists are those that reported participating in two or more campaign activities. Information drawn from the American National Election Studies 2012 Time-Series Study.

Figure 2-3 Distributions of Democrats and Republicans on a 10-Point Left–Right Scale

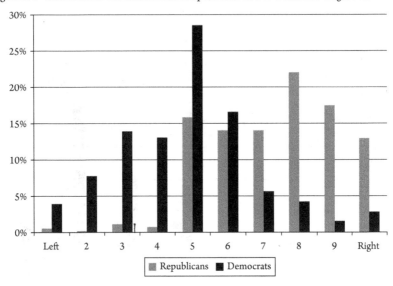

Percentage of Democrats and Republicans who classified themselves at each point on an ideological spectrum from "left" to "right." An additional 1 percent of Republicans and 2 percent of Democrats gave no answer. The mean answer for Democrats was 4.8; for Republicans, it was 7.4. Data are from the 2011 wave of the World Values Survey, available at www.worldvaluessurvey.org.

7 or above. For Democrats, the median and modal position was 5, while the median and modal Republican chose a self-placement of 8.

A similar asymmetry exists in the evaluations of ideological groups by partisans on both sides. The ANES asks respondents to rate political figures and groups on a "feeling thermometer" ranging from 0 (the most negative possible response) to 100 (the most positive possible response). Republican respondents to the 2012 national survey awarded "conservatives" a mean rating of 71.5 and "liberals" an average score of 37.9—a gap of 33.6 units, or one-third of the maximum possible difference. Democrats in 2012 gave liberals a mean score of 63.6 and conservatives a rating of 46.8, producing a difference of just 16.8 units, or only half the size of the Republican gap.

The ANES survey found comparable patterns in previous years, as illustrated by Figure 2-4. Over the past five decades, Republicans' average feeling thermometer rating of conservatives has always exceeded 60, and their average rating of liberals has always remained below 50, but the gap in Republicans' evaluations of the two ideological groups has grown significantly over time—fully doubling in size between 1968 and 2008. In contrast, Democratic identifiers did not collectively feel warmer toward liberals than toward conservatives until the 1980s; though Democrats have grown more favorable toward liberals, by 2012, the gap in their ratings of the two groups had only reached the magnitude of the corresponding

Figure 2-4 Differences in Feelings Toward Ideologues Over Time

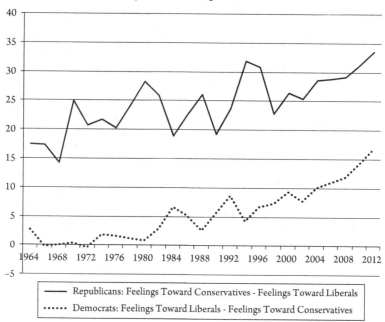

Differences between the average feeling thermometer ratings of conservatives and liberals by Republicans and of liberals and conservatives by Democrats. Data are from the American National Election Studies (only face-to-face interviews are included for 2012).

difference on the Republican side 40 years before. Although both parties have become more positive in their views of their own ideological group and more negative about the opposing ideological group, Republicans have consistently held both attitudes more strongly than Democrats.[19]

Both Republican favorability toward conservatives (over liberals) and Democratic favorability toward liberals (over conservatives) are increasing, reflecting a decades-long sorting of partisans: citizens on both the left and the right have become more likely over time to join the party that best matches their ideological orientation.[20] Yet Republicans had already demonstrated a clear preference for conservatives over liberals prior to the emergence of the sorting trend in the 1980s. Sorting has increased the proportion of Democrats who identify as liberal and view liberals more positively than conservatives, but because Republican identifiers have become even more uniformly conservative over the same period, the relative gap between the ideological homogeneity of the parties remains intact. Committed liberals represent a rising proportion of Democrats, but—unlike conservatives within the GOP—they do not dominate the party.

The ANES also reveals that Democrats and Republicans offer distinct evaluations of social groups and organizations, but none of these differences matches the size of the partisan gaps in favorability between the ideological groups. On average, Republicans rate business more positively than labor unions, while Democrats hold the reverse view, but the difference is small and mostly driven by unequal feelings toward unions rather than business. Reported feelings toward blacks and other demographic groups have grown more positive over time, with a slightly greater increase among Democrats (largely as a result of the larger share of minority respondents in the party). Polarization is mainly apparent in feelings toward ideological categories, rather than social groups.

Because self-identified conservatives consistently outnumber liberals in the American electorate, the phenomenon of ideological sorting can account for the declining magnitude of the Democratic advantage in macropartisanship after the 1970s (a trend evident in Figure 2-1). The Democratic Party's Roosevelt-era coalition contained a sizable proportion of conservatives attracted to the party on the basis of salient group identity—especially among southern whites and Catholics. Over time, the growing tendency of voters to choose a party aligned with their ideological preferences has coincided with a significant large-scale net shift of these voting blocs into the Republican Party. Although there has been a counter-movement among liberals toward the Democrats, the relative scarcity of liberals—especially liberal Republicans—in the mass public has limited the number of additional Democrats that could be supplied by this trend. An analysis by Alan Abramowitz and Kyle Saunders has attributed large declines in the Democratic identification advantage among Catholics, whites, and married voters over the past 30 years to ideological sorting, with conservatives within each group much more likely to identify as Republicans.[21] The collective ideological self-identification of white southerners and Catholics did not change between 1972 and 2004, but the partisanship of these groups slowly moved toward and eventually matched their prevailing conservative ideology.[22] Across all social categories except African Americans, conservatives have become more likely to identify as Republicans, though the continued importance of group identity in attracting social minorities to the Democratic Party guarantees that differences in partisan alignments (across all ideological categories) will persist among groups defined on the basis of ethnicity, income, gender, and religion.

IDEOLOGY VERSUS GROUP IDENTITY: HOW DEMOCRATS AND REPUBLICANS VIEW THE PARTIES

Republicans are not only the more ideologically homogenous party, but are also more likely to conceptualize politics as an ideological conflict over political principles between the left and the right. Democrats instead prefer to think of politics as a contest among social groups competing with each other for influence over the government. Each party therefore maintains distinct criteria for judging policy proposals and outcomes, with Republicans prizing compatibility with ideological doctrine and Democrats emphasizing the protection or advancement of group interests.

For more than six decades, the ANES has asked a sample of Americans what they like and dislike about each major party and presidential nominee, recording their open-ended responses to these questions. Philip Converse drew upon these items more than 50 years ago to create a "level of conceptualization" scale of categories that summarize citizens' responses in order to "provide some indication of the evaluative dimensions that tend to be spontaneously applied."[23] According to Converse's classifications, "ideologues" rely "in some active way on a relatively abstract and far-reaching conceptual dimension," while "group benefits" voters evaluate parties and candidates "in terms of their expected favorable or unfavorable treatment of different social groupings."[24] The other categories—"nature of the times" for those who hold one of the parties or candidates responsible for the overall direction of the nation and "no issue content" for those who mention personality traits or other nonsubstantive considerations— identify citizens whose preferences are not based on either the ideological alignments or the social group coalitions of the parties.[25]

While scholars have traditionally viewed these classifications as a hierarchical scale of political sophistication with ideologues at the top, we treat the "ideological" and "group benefits" categories as types rather than levels of conceptualization. (Following Converse, we use the term "ideologue" in a nonpejorative sense to refer to respondents who exhibit ideological reasoning.) The division shows that Republicans often view political conflict as fundamentally ideological in nature, while Democrats perceive it as a clash of competing group interests.

Although the most recent data from the ANES have not been fully coded, the following verbatim responses from Republican activists interviewed in 2012 would prompt their classification as "ideological":

- Democrats "want the government to run everything and they think the government can fix everything." Republicans "want people to be personally responsible for their own lives."
- The Democratic Party "promotes big government, secularism, elitism, and collectivism." The Republican Party "pushes for cutting the size of the federal government."
- Democrats are "quite socialistic, [giving] way too much power to the government." Republicans are for "fiscal responsibility and

conservatism . . . less government, more power to the states, encouraging jobs . . . with less dependency on the federal government."

The substantive words most commonly used by Republican activists interviewed by the 2012 ANES in describing their views of the parties included "conservative," "liberal," "spending," and "values." The 50 most frequently used words also included "moral," "responsibility," "smaller," "socialist," and "state." None of these words ranked among the top 50 mentioned by Democratic activists. The most common two-word phrases among Republican activists included "big government," "smaller government," and "less government," as well as "personal responsibility."

In contrast, the following open-ended responses from Democratic activists interviewed in 2012 would qualify them as "group benefits" voters under Converse's categorization:

- Democrats "support the poor and middle class." Republicans "look out for the rich and don't care about the poor and middle class."
- Democrats have "concern for the working class . . . [and have] always worked to help women." Republicans' "concern is for people who have money."
- Democrats are "the party of the common man." Republicans are "for rich, mainly white older folks who tend to be quite judgmental, narrow minded and unconcerned for their fellow Americans."

Across all Democratic activist responses on the 2012 ANES, the most commonly used substantive words included "class," "concern," "middle," "poor," "rich," and "women"; the words "gay," "interest," "programs," "policies," and "wealthy" also appeared among the top 50. None of these terms ranked among the top words mentioned by Republican activists. The most common two-word phrase among Democratic activists—by far— was "middle class."

In 2000, the most recent available data coded for level of conceptualization, the proportion of respondents categorized as ideologues was notably higher among Republicans—especially those who strongly identified with the party—than among Democrats or independents, as revealed by Figure 2-5. Respondents were classified as ideologues (or near-ideologues) if they cited ideological labels or referenced general principles in four open-ended responses, yet the vast majority of Democrats failed to qualify as ideologically oriented even under this generous definition.[26] Democrats used ideological reasoning in explaining their views of the parties even less frequently than they self-identified as liberals.[27] The percentage of respondents categorized as group-oriented voters was even more strongly

Figure 2-5 Ideological and Group-Based Conceptualization by Party Identification

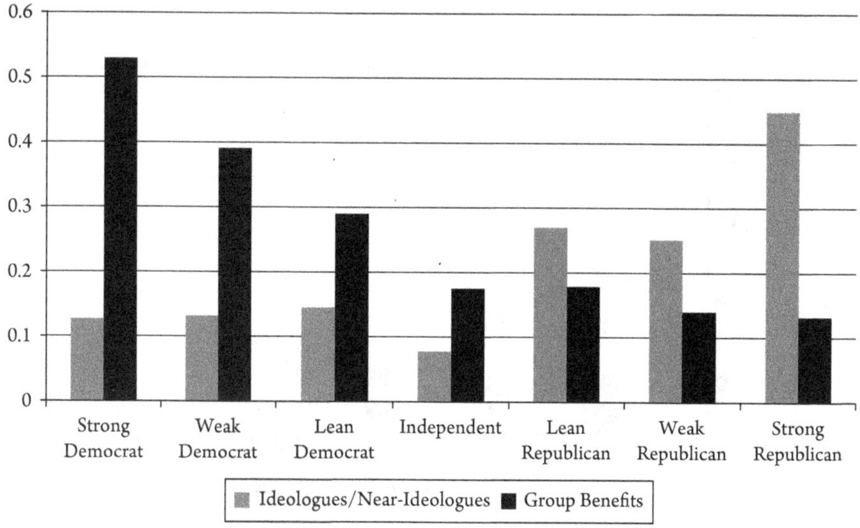

Proportion of respondents in each party identification category who were categorized as ideologues or near-ideologues and as group benefits voters on the levels of conceptualization scale. This scale is based on open-ended responses from the 2000 ANES survey regarding respondents' likes and dislikes of the two political parties and presidential candidates. The coding was conducted and reported by Lewis-Beck et al. (2008). These results were provided by Bill Jacoby.

associated in a linear fashion with the seven-point party identification scale. More than half of strong Democrats expressed their views of the parties and candidates in terms of group benefits, but only about 12 percent of strong Republicans did so.

Figure 2-6 confirms that this finding is not an artifact of the hierarchical scale of mutually exclusive categories, displaying the mean number of mentions of ideological concepts and social groups by respondents to the 2004 ANES within each of the seven categories of party identification. Once again, the Democratic propensity for viewing partisan conflict as defined by competing group interests contrasts sharply with the Republican tendency to characterize party differences in more abstract terms—a gap that holds after controlling for education, age, income, and other demographic factors.[28] In other words, the Republican propensity for ideological thinking does not depend on education or religion; it is instead a product of the conservative movement's successful communication of its version of the American political tradition to the party's electorate. One might expect that Democrats would frequently make connections between specific group identities and larger liberal themes, but Democratic respondents' citations of the social composition of the parties were only infrequently accompanied by appeals to abstract egalitarian, humanistic, compassionate, or democratic ideals.[29] The ideological

Figure 2-6 Number of Mentions of Ideology and Social Groups by Party Identification

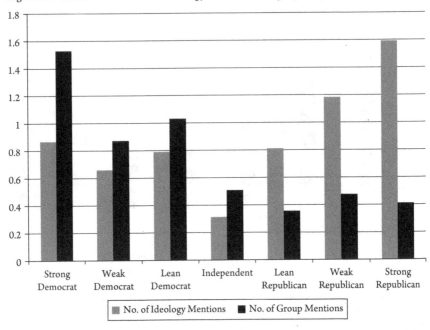

Average number of mentions of groups and ideological statements in open-ended responses from the 2004 ANES regarding likes and dislikes of the two political parties by respondents in each party identification category. The authors analyzed coding conducted by the ANES. The categories are described at http://www.electionstudies.org/studypages/2004prepost/nes04app.pdf.

language employed by Republicans did not consist of references to conservatives and liberals as social groups, though general citations of liberal or conservative viewpoints did constitute approximately 35 percent of respondents' ideological mentions.

This asymmetry extends beyond the particular context of recent elections. Figure 2-7 displays the difference between the proportion of strong Democrats and the proportion of strong Republicans who were categorized as ideologues and as group-benefits voters in available ANES surveys between 1964 and 2000. Republican identifiers have always been much more likely than Democrats to be ideologues, by margins ranging from 12 to 32 percentage points. Republicans use general concepts and principles to justify their partisan and candidate preferences more often than Democrats do, frequently emphasizing the need to limit the scope of government or preserve traditional American society. In contrast, Democrats have always been much more likely than Republicans to explain their political choices in terms of group benefits—often claiming that Republicans are the party of the rich and that their own party's candidates champion the disadvantaged—by margins varying from 25 to 48 percentage points.

Figure 2-7 Differences in Types of Conceptualization Among Democrats and Republicans

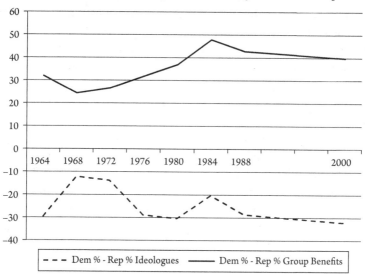

The solid line maps the difference between the percentage of strong Democrats and the percentage of strong Republicans who were categorized as thinking in terms of groups benefits; the dotted line maps the difference in the percentages who were categorized as ideologues on the levels of conceptualization scale in each election year. The categorization uses open-ended responses on the ANES Time-Series Study to questions about the likes and dislikes of the political parties and the candidates.

Strong Democratic identifiers consistently describe politics as a competition among social groups for favorable concrete policies and benefits, whereas strong Republicans explain the salient differences between the parties as concerning a more abstract conflict over the proper role of government. In every year for which data are available, strong Democratic respondents were much more likely to cite group benefits than ideological considerations by ratios ranging from 2:1 (in 1964) to more than 6:1 (in 1988), even as ideologues consistently outnumbered group-oriented voters by substantial margins among strong Republicans. While the political conceptualization of some partisans—and many more independents—fell within neither category, the relative Republican preference for ideological conceptualization and relative Democratic preference for the language of group interests remained constant across forty years of electoral history.[30] The differences are not a product of which party is in the majority or minority, in or out of government, or playing electoral offense or defense; they are instead largely stable.

Reflecting the prevailing Democratic advantage in national partisan identification, the average citizen has nearly always provided slightly more things they like and fewer things they dislike about Democrats compared to Republicans.[31] Political scientist Mark Brewer has categorized the most common specific comments made about each party across all respondents for every ANES survey between 1952 and 2004.[32] In every single survey, the most frequent response to the question of what citizens like about Democrats was that they are the "party of the working class" (or an analogous statement). Similarly, the most frequent response—in every single election year—to the question of what citizens dislike about Republicans was that they are the "party of big business and upper class" (or a similar statement). Brewer found some racial differences in the image of the Democratic Party; nonwhites were more likely to reference particular issues, whereas whites always predominantly perceived Democrats as representing the working class.[33]

Prior to 1964, respondents who were asked to describe the Republican Party cited a variety of positive attributes. But in 1964 and in every election since, the most commonly cited positive Republican quality has been the party's general "conservatism." Brewer found that the most frequently disliked characteristic of Democrats was not equally stable over time, yet in all but two years since 1960, the most popular response has been either "too much government spending," "too liberal," or "in favor of big government." The exceptions were 1972, when specific remarks about the party's unpopular presidential nominee George McGovern predominated, and 1980, when antipoverty policies topped the list of dislikes about Democrats. Among all voters, the images of the two parties revealed in these open-ended responses reflect consistent popular perceptions of a Democratic Party that represents relatively populous social groups and a Republican Party that stands for the more prevalent ideological view on the proper size and scope of government.

The liberal intellectual tradition in America often includes references to group membership in the service of broader egalitarian ideals, identifying the perceived status or privilege associated with various identities in order to justify public policies designed to advance the cause of social or economic equality. Yet most Democratic respondents explaining their partisan preferences to ANES interviewers in group-centered terms have emphasized one or more elements of the party's social coalition without a broader argument linking group identity to more abstract principles or values. Democratic identifiers and activists rarely cite concepts like equality, justice, or fairness in support of their political choices, employing these concepts even less frequently than their rare references to liberal or leftist identification or a general preference for government activism. In fact, many survey respondents who have been classified as "group benefits" voters have made no mention of policy or its effects, but instead have simply reported their perceptions of the kinds of people who belong to each party.

Characterizations of the Democratic Party as existing to advance the cause of liberalism are more commonly expressed by Republicans

explaining why they dislike the opposition. The view that political conflict occurs on a unidimensional spectrum between left and right poles
is shared much more by Republican identifiers and activists than by
Democrats, a pattern confirmed by a variety of measures of ideological
sophistication.[34] Republican ideological conceptualization extends far
beyond the word "conservative" and applies to other labels like "right"
and "left."

The relative Republican preference for eschewing group-centered
accounts of political conflict in favor of appeals to broader principles is
not merely the product of a rhetorical strategy to appease Republican-
oriented groups. Critics often view conservative ideology as merely a rationalization for advancing the material interests of a few privileged social
groups whom it is impolitic to champion explicitly. Not only have the
Democratic identifiers interviewed by the ANES frequently characterized the Republican Party as standing for the powerful, the wealthy, the
white, and the male, but liberal elites have also seized on any examples
of conservative inconsistency or hypocrisy as revealing an underlying in-
sincerity of belief. Yet the distinctive cast of modern Republican politics,
including the nature of internal partisan conflict as well as their style of
opposition to Democrats, reveals that party members take conservative
ideology quite seriously. Contemporary Republican ANES respondents
cite straightforward conservative principles such as limited government
and opposition to liberalism in explaining their views, rather than using
ideological language in the service of group-based appeals. In fact, it is
Democratic respondents who more commonly link their group references
to ideological language: even the minority of Democrats categorized as
ideologues often combine their stated principles with citations of group
interest.

The concentration of ideologically minded voters in the Republican
Party does not indicate that Republicans are more concerned with the
substance of policy than are Democrats. Members of both parties mention policies in their responses to the open-ended items on the ANES, but
they differ in the reasoning behind their stated positions. Democrats tend
to explain their views by citing the social groups that would be affected by
particular policies, while Republicans link specific issues to more general
beliefs about the proper role of government.

Since the New Deal era, the Democratic Party has served as the electoral vehicle by which discrete social minorities exert political pressure
to protect or advance their particular interests (often, the amelioration
of perceived disadvantage). In contrast, Republican candidates have traditionally drawn support from populous voting blocs that have tended
to view themselves less as self-conscious groups than as constituting the

default or mainstream American mass public of whom *other* groups make demands.[35] This attitude was memorably expressed by 2012 Republican presidential nominee Mitt Romney, whose controversial description of Democratic supporters as the "47 percent of the people ... who are dependent upon government, who believe that they are victims" was captured on video footage secretly recorded at a private fundraiser and leaked during the campaign.[36] Republican presidential candidates tend to attract support from social majorities or pluralities such as white voters, Protestants, suburbanites, and (heterosexual) married voters, while the Democratic Party resembles a "rainbow coalition" of racial, religious, economic, and sexual minorities who compensate for their smaller relative numbers by voting for Democratic candidates in lopsided proportions. The overwhelming margins by which many of these groups routinely support Democratic nominees contrast markedly with the comparatively modest rate at which their members express adherence to symbolic liberalism, thereby illustrating the central role of social identity in shaping the partisanship of Democratic identifiers. For many Democrats in the mass electorate, strong and durable party loyalty need not require ideological commitment to flourish in the presence of a highly salient social group membership.

The relative propensity of Democrats to exhibit group-based political orientations and Republicans to think in ideological terms is further demonstrated by several other items from the 2012 ANES, as summarized in Table 2-1. Respondents were asked which party is best for the interests of women, with "neither party" also offered as a response option. Democrats, especially those who had engaged in campaign activities, overwhelmingly agreed that their party better served women's interests, but Republicans were surprisingly reluctant to make similar assertions on behalf of the GOP. Fewer than half of Republican activists and only one-third of identifiers named the Republican Party as better for women, indicating an aversion to rhetoric that legitimizes group-specific interests even when it could simply serve as a symbolic act of partisan cheerleading.

The relative ideological orientation of Republican identifiers is also reflected in distinct partisan responses to ANES items asking interviewees to place themselves and both parties on a seven-point ideological spectrum. The vast majority of Republicans identified their own party as located to the right of the Democratic Party, while 13 percent of Democratic activists and one-third of other Democrats were unable to answer correctly.[37] Almost all Republican activists placed themselves closer to their own party than the opposition, but nearly 20 percent of Democratic activists and 30 percent of nonactivists placed themselves closer to the Republican Party or equidistant between the parties. These partisan

Table 2-1 VIEWS OF DEMOCRATIC AND REPUBLICAN PARTISANS
AND ACTIVISTS, 2012

	Democrats		Republicans	
	Non activists	Party Activists	Non activists	Party Activists
My Party Does Better for Interests of Women	76.4%	91.1%	33.3%	47.6%
Correctly Place Republicans as More Conservative	67.6%	77.3%	87.4%	94.4%
Place Self Closer to Own Party on Ideological Scale	69.6%	81.6%	83.9%	90.2%
Consistent View: Reason for Size of Government	64.7%	76%	80.2%	91.3%
Consistent View: General Government Services	40.9%	60.9%	64.5%	76%
Consistent View: Specific Social Programs	81.2%	84.5%	37.5%	55.9%

Percentage of Democratic and Republican activists and nonactivists who conform to their party's expected view on six questions: whether their party best represents the interests of women, whether they correctly place the Republican Party as more conservative than the Democratic Party, whether they place themselves as closer to their own political party, their view of the reason for the size of government ("involved in things people should handle themselves" for Republicans and "because problems have become bigger" for Democrats), their general view of government services ("provide more services" for Democrats and "provide fewer services" for Republicans), and their specific views of spending on government social programs (should increase in more categories than decrease for Democrats and should decrease in more categories than increase for Republicans). Activists are those who reported participating in two or more campaign activities. Data collected from the 2012 ANES.

differences in perceiving and conceptualizing politics in ideological terms have remained consistent for decades. The share of respondents who can place each party in the correct relative position on a liberal–conservative scale and also report their own position on the same scale rose from 48 percent in 1972 to 67 percent in 2004, but Republicans have always been better able to complete both tasks.[38]

Respondents were also asked two general questions about the size and scope of government: (1) whether government was large because it interferes with private decisions or because it addresses social problems, and (2) whether government should provide more or fewer services. Republicans, especially activists, chose the ideologically conservative response to both questions by wide margins. Democrats were less likely to give liberal answers, although the proportion of such responses rose substantially among activists. But Republican consistency on broad ideological predispositions did not extend to specific policy questions, reflecting the enduring gap between symbolic and operational conservatism. For 81 percent of nonactivist Democrats, the number of issue areas on which they supported an increase in spending exceeded the number of areas on which they supported spending cuts, but only 38 percent of nonactivist Republicans identified more programs to cut than items for which they favored spending growth. Democrats exhibit much stronger support for particular forms of government activity than for activist government as such, while Republicans are more united around broad principles of limited government than around the need for reductions in specific programs.

THE ROOTS OF PARTISANSHIP: IDEOLOGICAL PREFERENCE OR SOCIAL IDENTITY?

The different views of partisanship and partisan conflict held by Democrats and Republicans in the mass electorate can inform scholarly debates over the considerations linking citizens to their favored party. Drawing on sociological and social psychological theories that emphasize the centrality of group membership, Donald Green, Bradley Palmquist, and Eric Schickler describe party identification as primarily a product of social group identity, explaining that "people ask themselves two questions when deciding which party to support: What kinds of social groups come to mind as I think about Democrats, Republicans, and Independents? Which assemblage of groups (if any) best describes me?"[39] But Alan Abramowitz and Kyle Saunders have argued that Green, Palmquist, and Schickler did not test this claim or compare it with an approach based on ideology. Instead, contend Abramowitz and Saunders, "the questions most voters ask themselves in deciding which party to support are actually: 'What do Democrats and Republicans stand for?' and 'Which party's positions are closer to mine?'"[40]

Whether or not voters consciously ask themselves either set of questions, our findings of party asymmetry suggest that while both parties contain some members attracted by social identity and some by ideology, Democrats more closely match the social identity view offered by Green, Palmquist, and Schickler, whereas the ideological alternative proposed by Abramowitz and Saunders is more applicable to the Republican Party. Yphtach Lelkes and Paul Sniderman share this assessment, finding that Republicans are collectively much more ideologically sophisticated than Democrats, while Democrats are more motivated by group attraction.[41] Psychologists find that conservatives rely on a greater variety of moral foundations in their decision-making, whereas liberals focus on fairness and incorrectly assume that conservatives adopt dissenting positions because they instead value unfairness.[42] Political scientists sometimes resist acknowledgement of partisan and ideological asymmetry, but such views are less controversial within psychology.[43] Psychologists also recognize many differences in behavior that stem from thinking in practical versus abstract terms (often investigated as differences in "level of construal").[44] From this perspective, it is unsurprising that a party with more abstract conceptions of politics would act differently in many spheres.

Green, Palmquist, and Schickler employ the 1992–1996 ANES panel survey to assess whether voters' issue positions in a particular election prompted a change in their partisanship, finding that party identification remained consistent over time and predictive of a vote four years later, even with controls for issue attitudes.[45] Party identification is thus mostly a stable attribute rather than a "running tally" of issue positions and candidate evaluations that is updated for each election. Yet these panel models do not include ideological self-identification. Using the same panel, Abramowitz and Saunders show that ideology was also stable, and that prior ideology actually influenced current party identification (with prior party identification held constant).[46] Ideological self-identification is thus not simply adopted as a byproduct of party identification; though it is rare for citizens to switch parties after young adulthood, the changes that do occur tend to be in the direction of the voter's existing ideological affiliation.

Abramowitz and Saunders also find an increasing correlation over time between ideological self-identification and opinions on several issues, including national health insurance, spending and services, and abortion. However, they do not identify a clear trend in the association between ideology and opinions on job guarantees, aid to blacks, and defense spending.[47] The ideological categories are thus related to, but somewhat distinct from, specific issue positions and are not merely proxies for social group attitudes. When citizens are asked about groups and ideology simultaneously—that is, by questions that define the left as "the views of labor and other liberal groups"—their answers are actually more variable and less consistent than when asked about ideology alone.[48] Ideology and social group affiliation are distinct individual attributes, with each influencing citizens' choice of parties, but ideological identification cements more voter relationships with Republicans, and group ties provide more reasons to ally with Democrats.

RACIAL IDENTITY AND PARTY COMPOSITION

Racial and ethnic minority groups are an increasingly important component of the Democratic coalition. As African Americans have moved toward near-uniform support for Democrats, Hispanic Americans and Asian Americans (who also now prefer the Democratic Party over the

Republicans by ratios of 2:1 or even 3:1) have accounted for a growing share of the U.S. electorate. These trends have not resulted in overwhelming national Democratic majorities because whites have simultaneously become more likely to identify as Republicans and vote accordingly—though their collective partisan leaning is not as lopsided. This pattern of demographic sorting leads some Democratic-leaning political analysts to argue that both parties are racial group coalitions, with Republicans representing a white population that harbors racial resentment and anti-immigrant attitudes.

There is evidence that white opposition to policies designed to redress racial inequality is partially a product of remaining (but declining) traditional racism and (more widespread) symbolic racial attitudes, such as the denial that discrimination exists in contemporary American society and the belief that blacks are responsible for their own circumstances.[49] Likewise, anti-immigration policy views partially reflect negative attitudes about the ethnic groups that constitute the majority of recent immigrants. Yet the effects of these attitudes on the issue positions of white voters are at least as pronounced among Democrats as Republicans, largely because the conservative ideology of the latter group already encourages adoption of the same views. Scholars continue to disagree over the extent to which Republican opposition to affirmative action, for example, is a product of racial attitudes rather than conservative principles.[50] The most important aggregate impact of the persistence of symbolic racism is that the normal liberal majority for specific policy positions in the American public does not extend to race-targeted policies, which receive substantially less support among whites in both parties.[51]

Donald Kinder and Cindy Kam recently analyzed the role of ethnocentrism (encompassing both in-group pride and out-group hostility) in American politics, finding that "partisanship and ethnocentrism are virtually uncorrelated."[52] Measured by feeling thermometers toward racial groups, both whites and minorities rate their own group more warmly than others, but only whites use more negative stereotypes to describe out-groups. Both of these measures of ethnocentrism are related to multiple issue attitudes, including immigration and racial policies as well as subjects like homeland security and Medicare that are seemingly unrelated to race. But the political effects of ethnocentrism are largely independent of partisanship and ideological self-identification.[53] When the broader political environment activates ethnocentrism, however, it can have a partisan impact; for example, ethnocentric citizens were more likely to approve of George W. Bush following the terrorist attacks of September 11, 2001.

Barack Obama's status as the first African American major-party nominee and president also worked to activate racial considerations. Kinder and Kam find that ethnocentrism reduced voter support for Obama, but only among white Democrats and independents (Republicans were unlikely to cast their ballots for any Democratic candidate regardless of race).[54] African Americans were also more likely to turn out to vote and to support Democrats with Obama at the top of the ticket. A panel study reveals that a small number of racist whites moved toward Republican identification after Obama took office.[55] The tenor of the 2016 presidential campaign suggests that these partisan changes will likely endure beyond the Obama presidency. Even a small aggregate rise in Republican affiliation among whites or a permanent increase in African American participation rates could influence electoral outcomes in a closely divided electorate.

Racial identity plays an important role in minority citizens' attachment to the Democratic Party and its candidates. Although minority ethnocentrism is only weakly associated with Democratic partisanship, perceptions of common group fate among African Americans help cement their Democratic allegiance.[56] Latinos who view themselves as part of a pan-ethnic minority group may also be more likely to identify as Democratic.[57] Yet even minority voters who do not exhibit exceptional group identity now commonly support Democrats at high rates despite modest levels of liberal identification. According to media exit polls, 95 percent of African Americans supported Obama in the 2008 presidential election, even as only 28 percent of black voters identified as liberals. Similarly, just 25 percent of Latino voters in 2008 considered themselves to be liberal, while 67 percent voted for Obama. Racial minorities are also less likely than whites to apply the liberal label to their issue positions and more likely to mislabel liberal issue positions as conservative, suggesting a less ideological conceptualization of politics.[58]

In order to keep their multiracial coalition together, Democratic Party leaders face incentives to avoid activating their own white voters' antipathy to racial minorities—and to instead accuse Republicans of relying on white racial resentment. The absence of large minority constituencies within the Republican Party enables its leaders to reject group-based demands and to use racially coded language (such as "inner-city criminals") without risking criticism from their own supporters. Racial appeals, though they often provoke an elite backlash and attract negative media coverage, may help elites reach less sophisticated and unattached voters with ideologically inconsistent opinions that cohere more around racial views.[59] Through more explicit racial appeals than prior candidates, Donald Trump's 2016 presidential campaign reached many of these voters at the cost of reducing his popularity among swing voters and some traditional Republicans.

Race is also implicated, of course, in the larger debate over the long-term causes of southern realignment. Some scholars contend that white southern conservatives moved to the Republican Party as a result of inevitable ideological sorting, but there is evidence that symbolic racism is higher in the South and influenced southerners' increasingly Republican voting preferences.[60] Measures of symbolic racism remain controversial because it is not clear whether these attitudes are causes or consequences of policy positions and broader ideological views.[61] Regardless, symbolic racism is less associated with partisanship than is ideology; even among southern whites, the correlation between party and ideology after controlling for symbolic racism is .68, whereas the remaining correlation between party and symbolic racism is only .20.[62]

It is likely, however, that both traditional racism and symbolic attitudes regarding blacks' responsibility for their own condition have influenced the long-standing prevalence of conservative self-identification in the white South and the region's subsequent shift toward the Republican Party. Conservative ideology and opposition to race-based policies are now so strongly associated among citizens that it may be difficult to disentangle the relative importance of preexisting ideology and racially motivated views. Perhaps the move of southern whites toward Republicans was overdetermined by their antigovernment proclivities and their racial attitudes alike. Based on the open-ended responses of contemporary ANES respondents, we can report that few Republicans in any geographic region today express their conservative views in racially coded language; their ideological statements, for example, are not peppered with claims about criminals or welfare cheats.

While racial politics certainly play an important role in shaping the American party system as a whole, they cannot account for the asymmetries that we identify; all party differences remain large even when only whites in each party are considered. Chapter 3 reviews the specific histories that connected segregationist movements and white racial resentment with the ideological evolution of the parties. Racial attitudes continue to have significant effects on American public opinion, though the contemporary effects are concentrated in issue attitudes rather than in partisanship or ideology; these effects are often at least as—if not more—pronounced among white Democrats, who lack nonracial reasons to oppose remedies for discrimination. Racial resentment may also help explain both southern realignment and a small portion of nationwide Republican identification (particularly in the post-Obama era), but the party preference of most Republican voters reflects the durable popularity of conservative ideology in the American public.

AMERICAN PARTY IMAGES IN INTERNATIONAL CONTEXT

Asymmetries in group identity and ideology help citizens develop an image of each political party, but neither impression is uniformly positive or negative. The public collectively tends to ascribe distinct attributes to each side, as summarized in Figure 2-8. More citizens perceive the Democrats as caring about people like themselves, matching Democratic voters' characterization of their own party as representing the disadvantaged against the interests of the powerful. Citizens view the Republican Party as holding more extreme issue positions but the Democratic Party as wanting to "radically transform America," reflecting the public's distinctive combination of broad conservatism and left-leaning preferences on specific issues. These reputations can be quite long-standing: in the 1930s, 83 percent of Republicans (but only 15 percent of Democrats) believed that Franklin D. Roosevelt was "leading America toward dictatorship."[63]

The Republican Party is simultaneously perceived as more extreme on specific issues and less radical in its broader agenda. Voters are slightly more likely to report that the Republican Party shares their values than that the Democrats do, but the GOP is also seen as more influenced by

Figure 2-8 Party Reputations

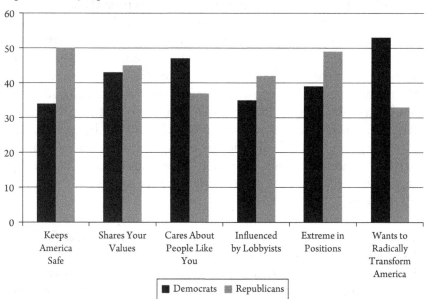

Percentage of Americans who report that each party fits each description. Results drawn from the 2014 Pre-Election American Values Survey conducted by the Public Religion Research Institute and made available at http://publicreligion.org/research/2014/09/survey-economic-insecurity-rising-inequality-and-doubts-about-the-future-findings-from-the-2014-american-values-survey/.

lobbyists. Democrats' group connections may not negatively affect their public image because Republican-aligned interests are less sympathetic. The Democratic Party's image as a group-based coalition largely has a positive valence; it is interpreted as a sign of caring about average Americans.

The Republican Party also maintains an advantage in citizen perceptions of its ability to keep America safe, reflecting the party's traditional "ownership" of the foreign policy and military domains.[64] Despite the stability of party images, however, judgments of party performance are more variable: the proportion of the public viewing the Democrats as better able to manage the economy has ranged between 38 percent and 77 percent, with several significant shifts across time, while the proportion that names Democrats as better able to "maintain the peace" has also varied widely, from less than 30 percent to over 70 percent.[65] Ideological self-identification better predicts views of partisan strengths when party positions are explicitly separated from assessments of leaders' performance.[66] The usual Republican advantage in popular responses to survey items asking which party keeps America safe is mostly a product of voters' perception that Republicans prioritize national security over other concerns.[67]

The American public's view of party strengths does not simply reflect the generic advantages held by all liberal and conservative parties worldwide. Figure 2-9 provides an international comparison of the American parties' relative performance on survey questions from the Comparative Study of Electoral Systems that measure which party better represents respondents' views and whether respondents feel closer to one party or the other. In other countries, these two questions produce pluralities for the same party; there is no general tendency for left- or right-of-center parties to perform better on one of these questions. Yet in the United States, more respondents report feeling closer to the Democratic Party than the Republicans, even as a plurality perceives the GOP as better representing their views. This apparent inconsistency matches the ideological and partisan disjuncture in public opinion: Americans regularly place themselves on the ideological right despite greater aggregate Democratic identification.

American public opinion is also internationally distinctive because of its combination of broad conservative attitudes and specific liberal issue positions. Table 2-2 illustrates differences in views on economic inequality across 25 nations, comparing the positions of Democrats, Republicans, and independents in the United States with opinions across the world by reporting the percentage of respondents agreeing with each statement. Large majorities of the public in most nations believe that the rich should pay a higher share of taxes (80 percent agree, on average), and

Figure 2-9   Center-Left Party Advantage on Feeling Close and Representing Views

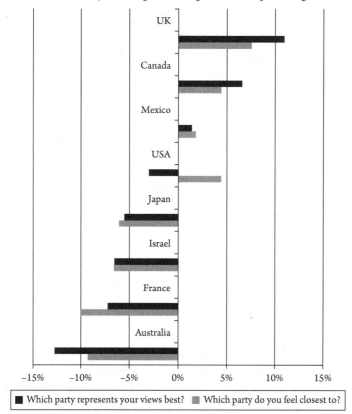

Difference in the percentage of each country's respondents who choose the center-left party versus the center-right party on two different survey questions: one asking which party best represents the respondent's views and one asking which party the respondent feels closest to. Positive numbers indicate a better performance for the center-left party (the Democrats in the United States), and negative numbers indicate a better performance for the center-right party (the Republicans in the United States). Data are from the second wave of the Comparative Study of Electoral Systems and are available at http://www.cses.org/.

that it is the government's responsibility to reduce differences in income (70 percent agree). In the United States, however, a majority of each partisan group agrees with the first statement, but only a minority agrees with the second. Americans are distinctive in supporting the specific policy of progressive taxation without sharing the principle behind it, standing out in international comparisons more for their opposition to liberalism in the abstract than for their level of support for particular liberal policies. In fact, even self-identified Democrats are slightly less likely to support the left-of-center position (progressive taxation) than are other citizens of the world.

The share of respondents agreeing that the government holds responsibility for reducing economic inequality is lower in the United States than

Table 2-2 OPINIONS OF PARTISANS ON INEQUALITY
IN INTERNATIONAL CONTEXT

	Government Responsible for Reducing Income Differences	Rich Should Pay Higher Share of Taxes	Income Differences Too Large	People Get Rewarded for Own Skills
Democrats	46%	76%	72%	74%
Republicans	23%	57%	57%	78%
Independents	33%	61%	67%	72%
World Average	70%	80%	84%	39%

Percentage of respondents who agree with each statement. Data are from the International Social Survey Programme Social Inequality III module from 1999.

in any other nation surveyed. Americans are also distinctive for their belief that social advancement is a product of individual skill. Americans' attitudes on the subject of economic redistribution are unique in both their negative views toward government and their positive views of individualism, but not in their policy positions. Republicans, in particular, exemplify these distinctive American tendencies.

The symbolic conservatism of the American public consistently stands out in comparative context. As Patrick Egan observes, Americans are "unusually skeptical about government's ability to solve problems," despite endorsing a long list of particular policies requiring government action.[68] According to the Pew Global Attitudes survey, Americans agree that the "freedom to pursue life's goals without interference" is more important than the government playing an active role to "guarantee that nobody is in need," a view shared with only a few developing nations; in the vast majority of countries, most people endorse the opposite view.[69] The anti-government stance of the Republican Party serves as the vehicle by which this attribute of the nation's unique political culture is expressed within American domestic politics, whereas the Democratic Party relies on a more internationally typical pattern of social group identification and shared policy agreement for the maintenance of its popular support.

THE DISTINCTIVE GOVERNING DEMANDS
OF THE TWO PARTY BASES

The substantial public appeal of symbolic conservatism in the United States has encouraged the Republican Party to define its own central purpose as the advancement of broad conservative principles. The wide

acceptance of this raison d'être within the ranks of Republican supporters has produced a constant and even intensifying popular demand
imposed on the party's officeholders to remain loyal to conservative
doctrine. The decisive collective rightward shift of the congressional
GOP in both chambers since the 1970s, a trend that accelerated after
1994 and rendered the party's moderate bloc essentially extinct,[70] has
not satisfied the preferences of most Republicans for an even more conservative national party. As Figure 2-10 illustrates, most Republican
identifiers consistently express a desire for their party to become more
conservative, while a majority of Democrats prefer that the Democratic
Party become more moderate rather than more liberal; this difference
predates the Obama presidency. The asymmetric polarization of party
leaders visible in Congress reflects the unequal pressure placed on officeholders by their respective popular bases.

Democratic and Republican identifiers also differ with respect to favored governing style, as revealed by Figure 2-11. Republicans in the electorate consistently express more admiration for politicians who "stick to
their positions," while Democrats favor those who "make compromises."
This discrepancy remained intact even during the final years of the George
W. Bush administration, when many liberal commentators openly urged
Democratic leaders toward more aggressive confrontation with Bush and
his partisan allies.[71] Though they voiced strong disapproval of the Bush

Figure 2-10 Share of Supporters Preferring Ideological Purity to Moderation by Party

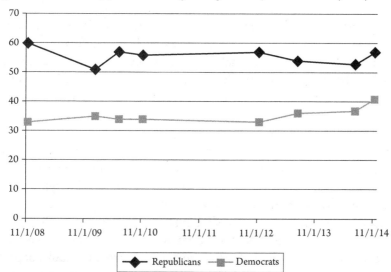

Share of each party's identifiers who say that they want their party's leaders to "move in a more liberal/conservative
direction" (as opposed to "a more moderate direction"). Data are from Pew Research Center surveys conducted in
2008, 2010, 2012, 2013, and 2014.

Figure 2-11   Percent Preferring Principles over Compromise by Party

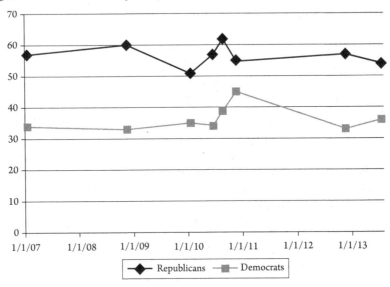

Share of each party's identifiers who say that they admire politicians "who stick to their positions" (as opposed to those "who make compromises"). Data are from Pew Research Center surveys conducted in 2007, 2008, 2010, 2012, and 2013.

presidency, rank-and-file Democrats still expressed a collective preference for compromise in government—a tendency that carried over to the Obama era. Likewise, Republicans have consistently valued doctrinal purity over pragmatic dealmaking, regardless of which party is in power.

Although data from comparable survey questions are not readily available for prior decades, evidence suggests that these differences are longstanding. The Pew Research Center previously asked citizens whether they liked politicians "who make compromises in order to get the job done" without specifying an alternative option of principled confrontation. As illustrated by Figure 2-12, Republicans have been less likely than Democrats since at least 1987 to voice support for politicians who compromise in the service of pragmatic accomplishment.

Criticism from media figures, interest group leaders, or financial donors that elected officials have betrayed the ideological commitments of their party via excessive compromise thus perennially finds a more sympathetic reception on the right than on the left. Although some prominent liberals accused Democratic politicians of failing to effectively oppose the actions of George W. Bush, especially on foreign policy, no coordinated effort arose to expel perceived moderates and apostates from the ranks of party officeholders, suggesting the limited appeal of this argument even within the Democratic base. In contrast, the 2008 election of Barack Obama immediately provoked a national mobilization of conservative activists under

Figure 2-12 Percent Liking Politicians Who Make Compromises to Get Job Done

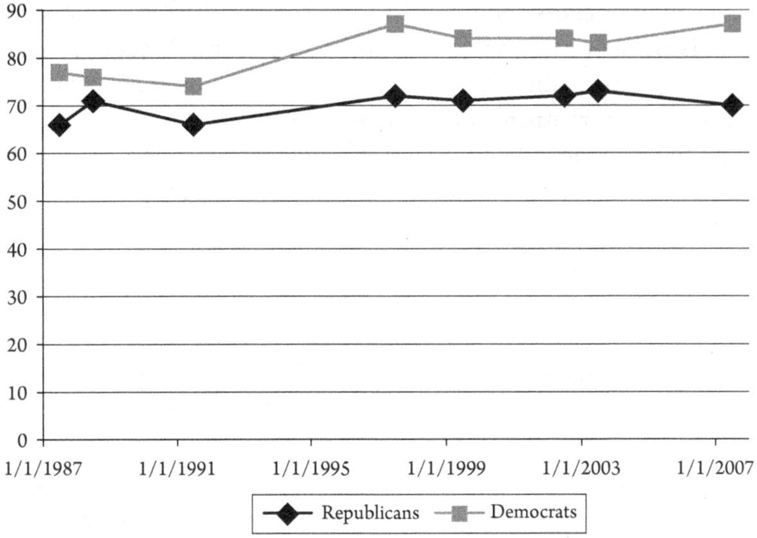

Share of each party's identifiers who say that they like politicians "who make compromises in order to get the job done." Data are from Pew Research Center surveys from 1987–2007 and are reported at http://www.people-press. org/2007/01/22/broad-support-for-political-compromise-in-washington/.

the banner of the Tea Party, motivated by the twin beliefs that Obama's policies endangered the very health of the nation and that the Republican Party had drifted unacceptably from its foundational principles. Similar waves of conservative backlash against perceived liberal advancement (and against the supposed co-optation of the Republican national leadership) have arisen regularly in American politics, previously occurring during the presidencies of Bill Clinton and Jimmy Carter; even the Republican administrations of Dwight Eisenhower, Richard Nixon, Gerald Ford, and George H. W. Bush produced large-scale and organized efforts to stimulate grassroots conservative opposition to "establishment" figures.[72]

Asymmetric ideological pressure from activists and voters may also help to explain why politicians tend to perceive their constituents as holding more conservative views than they actually do. Combining nationwide surveys of state legislative candidates and citizens, David Broockman and Christopher Skovron found that politicians dramatically overestimated the proportion of their constituents who agreed with conservative positions on abolishing welfare programs, implementing universal health coverage, and allowing same-sex marriage.[73] Though politicians in both parties exhibited this bias, Republicans overestimated conservative issue positions by a much larger margin than did Democrats—usually by more than 20 percent, implying that they viewed the average legislative district as more collectively conservative than the nation's most conservative districts are in actuality.[74] If the constituent pressure usually faced by Republican politicians consists of broad ideological critiques rather than specific issue advocacy, however, this degree of misperception is easily explained: political elites' estimates of public opinion reflect the degree of symbolic conservatism among their constituents and its concentration among the Republican Party's most motivated core supporters. In other words, Republican officials may perceive the presence of a conservative electorate because they regularly receive constituent pressure and a threat of voter backlash primarily from their ideological right.

THE SPECIFICALLY LIBERAL—AND GENERALLY CONSERVATIVE—AMERICAN PUBLIC

The asymmetry of the two parties is reinforced by the collective proclivity of the larger American electorate to endorse liberal positions on most individual political issues while simultaneously holding conservative views on the general size and role of the state—a durable tendency first noted nearly 50 years ago.[75] Republican politicians' appeal to voters, outside their party as well as within it, is primarily based on the broad themes of limited government and traditional American values. Democratic candidates, in contrast, draw popular support by advocating specific policies that provide tangible benefits to both their constituents and the wider citizenry.

Table 2-3 illustrates the divided political mind of the American public by summarizing the liberal or conservative direction of public opinion in both individual issue areas and broader ideological attitudes. It displays the average percent of liberal responses to public opinion questions (out of all noncentrist responses) asked by pollsters each year since 1981; figures below 50 percent represent a conservative majority, and those above 50 percent correspond to a liberal majority. Liberal positions have remained more popular than conservative positions, and sometimes substantially so, on nearly all domestic policy issues, even those—such as crime or welfare—sometimes thought to be "owned" by the Republican Party. Yet conservative responses predominate on items measuring ideological self-identification or attitudes regarding the general size and power of government. Depending on the scope of the questions asked, this summary of American public opinion reveals both a center-right and a center-left nation. This pattern of philosophical conservatism matched with operational liberalism persists across policy areas and types: the public prefers less spending and regulation overall, but more spending and regulation in each particular area of government responsibility.

Table 2-3 AVERAGE PERCENT OF LIBERAL
RESPONSES TO POLICY AND IDEOLOGY
SURVEY QUESTIONS

Specific Policy Opinions

	Liberal %
Macroeconomics	59.8
Civil Rights	51.9
Health	74.9
Labor	53.3
Education	69.3
Environment	74.6
Energy	54.1
Transportation	77.9
Crime	54.2
Welfare	56.8
Commerce	59.3

General Ideological Attitudes

	Liberal %
Self-Identification	35.1
Power of Government	28.9
Size of Government	34.4
Government Services	39.9

Percentage of liberal responses (out of total liberal and conservative
responses, not including moderate or unplaced responses) to
survey questions regarding policy opinions and general ideological
attitudes. Percentages are the average of all years since 1981. Data
drawn from a dataset compiled by James Stimson and available via
the Policy Agendas Project (www.policyagendas.org); see also Ellis
and Stimson (2012). Issue areas are categorized at policyagendas.
org. Power of government includes the variables FEDSTATE and
GOVPOW. Size of government includes the variables MTOOBIG
and THREATFX. Government services includes the variables
HEPLNOT, WATEALOT, NTYBIGGV, and SERVSPND.

These findings reflect a long-standing contradiction in collective public
opinion that allows each party to claim popular support for its policy
objectives. A majority of the American public has consistently agreed
with conservative preferences on general questions regarding the size of
government even as it has continued to favor the liberal position on most
specific policy issues. This gap between the operational and symbolic ideology of the American public has existed since at least 1958, as illustrated
by Figure 2-13.[76] The dashed line in the figure represents the average liberal share of all noncentrist responses to hundreds of specific public policy
survey questions (combined across all issue areas), revealing a modest but

Figure 2-13 Average Percent of Liberal Responses to Poll Questions on Policy and Ideology

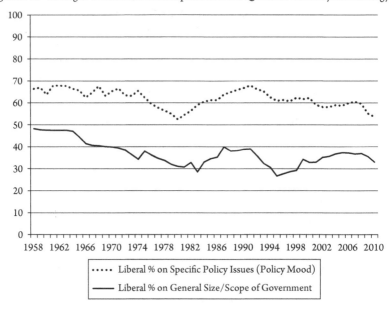

Average percent of respondents (out of all noncentrist responses) giving liberal answers to questions about specific policy issues and the general size and scope of government. Measures are drawn from data collected by James Stimson and available at policyagendas.org.

persistent liberal majority over time. The solid line represents a summary of responses to items measuring respondents' general preferences with respect to the power and scope of national government, demonstrating an equally consistent collective preference for the conservative position. Americans simultaneously believe that government should do less in general and that the reach of most individual government programs should be maintained or increased. This finding does not imply that public opinion never ebbs and flows; the public does often shift "thermostatically" against the direction of policy, becoming more conservative in response to liberal policy change and vice versa.[77] As government grew in the 1960s and 1970s, both opinions on specific policies and general attitudes moved rightward, followed by a reverse trend in the liberal direction during the presidency of Ronald Reagan (1981–1989).

Yet the gap between the general and specific directions of public opinion has been remarkably stable over more than 50 years, with an average difference of 25 points (on a 100-point scale) and a standard deviation of only 4 points. Americans' views on the general size and scope of government closely track macro-ideology (the black line from Figure 2-1, discussed above): the two measures are correlated at .87. Both macro-ideology (a measure of relative liberal self-identification) and the proportion of the public reporting liberal opinions on the general scope of government average 37 percent (in

Table 2-4 OPERATIONAL AND SYMBOLIC PREFERENCES
IN THE AMERICAN ELECTORATE

		Symbolic	
		Liberal	Conservative
Operational	Liberal	29%	29%
	Conservative	4%	15%

Percentage of Americans who report liberal or conservative self-identification (symbolic) and
liberal or conservative opinions on policy issues (operational). Approximately who self-identified
as moderates or did not answer the policy questions are not included in the table. Data drawn
from the General Social Survey from 1973–2006 and compiled by Ellis and Stimson (2012).

their overlapping years) and move in tandem; aggregate liberal identification thus usually matches the share of the population willing to express ge-
nerically positive views about a large central government.

Table 2-4 demonstrates how seemingly contradictory opinions within
the mass public reflect a gap between what is usually called "symbolic" and
"operational" ideology.[78] We use measures created by Ellis and Stimson,
who define operational liberals (or conservatives) as those respondents
who give mostly liberal (or conservative) responses to specific policy
questions and symbolic liberals and conservatives as those who explicitly
self-identify as such.[79] Operational liberals, though they substantially outnumber operational conservatives in the electorate, are no more likely to
identify as symbolic liberals than they are to identify as symbolic conservatives. Other research shows that even self-professed liberals are reluctant
to use the "liberal" label to describe their own (liberal) attitudes, whereas
conservatives apply the "conservative" label to many of their own views, regardless of whether such a classification is accurate.[80] Americans decidedly
prefer conservatism to liberalism in the abstract, even as many hold left-of-
center positions on a number of concrete issues. In addition, the American
public contains two ideologically cross-pressured subgroups that favor
either conservative positions on moral issues and liberal positions on economic issues or vice versa; both groups have collectively become more
Republican over time, even though they each only agree with the party
on mutually exclusive sets of issues.[81] Republican elites are thus on firmer
political ground, even among their own party's supporters, when they emphasize general ideological views over specific policy positions.

This collective inconsistency between general principles and particular
positions is not merely a product of confusion or misunderstanding in the
electorate. The operational liberalism of the mass public does not reflect a
refusal to consider costs or trade-offs; even survey respondents who are told
that spending in particular areas might require higher taxes or budget deficits

still prefer the liberal position at nearly the same rate.[82] Further, individuals with contradictory attitudes are not necessarily uninformed. "Citizens who mismatch operation and symbol are, in most cases, considerably more engaged and more committed to politics than nonideological moderates and as or nearly as engaged as consistent liberals," observe Ellis and Stimson.[83] The combination of conservative ideology and liberal issue positions "is found across all levels of political sophistication, all levels of attentiveness to politics, and all levels of extremity in either operational or symbolic beliefs."[84]

Why, then, do many Americans (and the nation in aggregate) jointly exhibit these seemingly contradictory views? Ellis and Stimson offer a two-part explanation. First, political conservatism draws from the long-established religious and cultural conservatism of the American people. Most citizens view the country as having a religious heritage and voice respect for tradition, social order, and family ties. Americans wish their widely shared personal value system to guide public life as well, but they do not necessarily associate this general proclivity for traditionalism, patriotism, and religiosity with specific policy positions:

> Candidates can occasionally gain electoral advantage by mobilizing morally and religiously conservative voters around some manufactured cultural issue of the time (gay marriage, for example). But individual issues of this sort have little staying power in American politics, and their impact on political choices is often overstated. In addition, the importance of any particular "cultural" issue to religiously conservative voters is likely to vary considerably, and the number that will care a great deal about any given issue will likely be small.[85]

Social and cultural conservatism, like economic conservatism, is a general orientation rather than a clear guide to applications in public policy. Religious tradition and devotion have played important and evolving roles in Republican politics and the conservative movement. Yet morally conservative citizens have a similar relationship to the party system as that seen in other Republicans: they identify with their favored party based on broad values rather than specific policy positions.

The second part of the explanation offered by Ellis and Stimson cites elite reinforcement. Each party recognizes and emphasizes its unique strengths, leading citizens to accept messages from both parties:

> Given that both the symbols of conservatism and the specific social benefits of liberalism are firmly entrenched as majority political preferences, it is of course not rational for any policymaker to try to clarify the relationship between operation and symbol: Both liberals and conservatives have found the frame that works best in explaining their own views. And the growing polarization of elite positions over the past 30 years has not solved the problem.[86]

Media reports repeat statements from politicians to the public that match the existing advantages of each party, and neither set of party leaders fights against the dominant frame presented on the other side.

Other research supports the claim that elite rhetoric reinforces the asymmetries in public support for the views expressed by each party. William Jacoby finds that voters respond to differences in Democratic and Republican politicians' rhetoric on government spending, with Republicans drawing on broad themes and Democrats emphasizing specific positions. The parties know that voters favor most individual categories of spending but disfavor spending in general, agreeing with each party on its own terms.[87] Republican politicians, as Ellis and Stimson put it, "attack popular social programs at the margins, saying that they are inefficient, poorly administered, or the like. But they rarely directly attack the worth of the program goals themselves."[88] Saundra Schneider and Jacoby find that these diverging frames matter even in welfare spending: the public moves against social welfare in response to conservative framing, not as a result of attitudes toward welfare recipients.[89]

These explanations are largely convincing, though we offer a few different emphases. First, the public preference for conservatism in the abstract stretches well beyond the "conservative" label. It also encompasses a broad preference for limited government and extends to other labels for the right and left poles of the ideological spectrum, representing agreement with the right in principle as well as symbol. Second, specific liberal issue positions are often associated with benefits for particular constituencies. Democratic elites may be responding optimally to the group-specific demands of their heterogeneous following rather than simply reframing their defenses of government activism in general. Citizens can reach agreement with liberal policy goals via shared identity or via sympathy with groups Democrats try to help.

Third, general conservative and specific liberal positions do not represent an inherent logical contradiction. A citizen could favor most current proposals for policy action in isolation, holding other policies constant, while still fearing that a collective implementation of the entire agenda would entail too broad a role for government. (Struggling dieters recognize an analogous dilemma: many people would like to ingest fewer calories overall, even if they are attracted to most particular opportunities to consume more.) Because the size and scope of federal responsibilities tend to grow over time, even elite skeptics of government activism must decide whether to accept (and make workable) new policies or to (unsuccessfully, in most cases) attempt to repeal them. Some conservative leaders reasonably reconcile these impulses by favoring a broad slowdown of spending and regulation even while working on behalf of particular expansions of government authority.

Although the discrepancy between the public's broad (conservative) and specific (liberal) views on public policy has been consistent for decades, there is some evidence that Republicans have been increasingly successful in instilling public fear of "big government." Figure 2-14 illustrates public responses to Gallup polls asking respondents to identify "the biggest threat to the country" over time, comparing "big government," "big business," and "big labor." The percent fearing "big government" has risen considerably, whereas the percent fearing "big business" (a common rhetorical enemy of Democrats) has remained flat. Interestingly, "big labor" has lost its perceived power to threaten the country (alongside declines in unionization). This may suggest that Republicans have succeeded in moving economic policy discussion away from a competition between two different interests (in the mind of the public) and toward an ideological battle over the size and scope of government.

The fundamental inconsistency in prevailing public opinion may tempt some analysts—especially those sympathetic to the Democratic Party—to treat voters' specific issue positions as reflecting their "real" political views, to dismiss symbolic ideology as a less important or legitimate attribute of individual opinion, and to consider Republican political victories to

Figure 2-14 Percent of the Public Most Fearful of Big Business, Big Labor, and Big Government

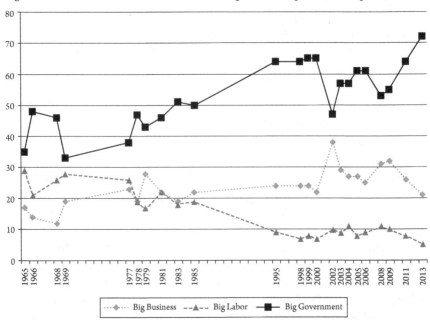

Percent of respondents answering "big government" (black line), "big labor" (dary grey dashed line), and "big business" (light grey dotted line) as the "biggest threat facing the country." Data drawn from Gallup polls available at: http://www.gallup.com/file/poll/166568/Greatest_Threat_131218.pdf

be a less representative expression of the public will. We strongly caution against such an interpretation. Internal contradictions between a voter's symbolic and operational ideology are not guaranteed to be resolved in favor of the latter; on average, 61 percent of citizens with liberal issue positions and conservative self-identification vote Republican for president, whereas only 34 percent of these conflicted voters support Democrats.[90] Individuals who side with liberals on specific policies but agree with conservative ideas about government in general are sometimes swing voters, but are more likely to prioritize their ideological self-identification over their issue positions when making electoral choices. As Democratic leaders have unhappily discovered, conservative symbolic ideology need not be accompanied by philosophically consistent policy views in order to exert a powerful influence on the political behavior of American citizens.

THE POLITICS OF THE AFFORDABLE CARE ACT: A CASE STUDY IN MASS PARTY ASYMMETRY

Barack Obama was elected president in 2008 with 53 percent of the national popular vote—the largest share of support received by any single presidential candidate in two decades, and the strongest electoral performance by a nonincumbent Democratic nominee since Franklin D. Roosevelt defeated Herbert Hoover in 1932. Like Roosevelt, Obama benefited from broad popular dissatisfaction with the state of the national economy under Republican rule, which had driven the job approval rating of his predecessor George W. Bush down to levels as low as 25 percent shortly before the election.[91] Obama was not the only member of his party to take advantage of this favorable political environment; the 2008 elections also produced Democratic majorities of 59–41 in the Senate (later augmented further by the defection of moderate Republican senator Arlen Specter to the Democratic Party, a move that temporarily gave Senate Democrats a filibuster-proof majority) and 257–178 in the House of Representatives, ensuring that the new president would have a friendly Congress with which to work as he advanced his legislative agenda.

Many of Obama's policy initiatives responded directly to the nation's dismal economic condition, including a sizable stimulus package and additional regulations of a financial services industry widely blamed for causing the crisis. But the Obama administration and Democratic congressional leaders were also committed to enacting ambitious health care reform legislation designed to implement a near-universal health insurance program—an objective that had remained at the top of the party's domestic policy agenda for decades. Like many previous Democratic presidential candidates, Obama had openly favored such a proposal during the 2008 campaign, lamenting the plight of the uninsured and promising to use the power of the federal government to guarantee comprehensive and affordable coverage.

Obama's health care plan had become a target of Republican criticism during the campaign—his opponent John McCain argued during a televised debate that Obama "wants to set up health care bureaucracies [to] take over the health care of America" and sarcastically characterized his opponent's proposal as "big government at its best"[92]—yet the new president had reason to believe that the public would support his efforts to implement an ambitious new federal program once he and his fellow Democrats took office. Not only had Obama won a decisive national victory running as an advocate of reform (his campaign had even produced a 30-minute infomercial largely devoted to the issue), but several preelection surveys had also found that voters trusted the Democratic Party to handle the issue of health care by a net advantage of 30 percentage points or more over the Republicans.[93] National exit polls on Election Day asked respondents which issue mattered most to them in determining their choice of candidate; 73 percent of those who chose health care reported voting for Obama.[94] Americans seemed enthusiastic about the possibility of major reform, with 40 percent of those surveyed by the Pew Research Center in early 2009 agreeing that the American health care system needed to be "completely rebuilt" and another 36 percent favoring "fundamental changes." The same poll revealed that 61 percent of the public expressed support for the proposition that health insurance should be provided to all Americans, "even if it means raising taxes."[95]

As Obama's plan for comprehensive reform began its journey through the legislative process on Capitol Hill in the spring of 2009, however, Republican leaders and conservative-aligned media figures responded with increasingly sharp-edged opposition. Some critics targeted specific provisions of the bill, both real (such as the mandate that Americans either acquire health insurance or pay a penalty to the government) and imagined (such as the claim, first voiced by former Republican vice presidential nominee Sarah Palin in a Facebook post, that Obama's reform bill would create a federal "death panel" empowered to decide whether citizens were "worthy of health care" based on their "level of productivity in society"). More commonly, however, Republican attacks sounded broader ideological themes designed to activate the symbolic conservatism of the American public. Employing a phrase that soon became a common element of Republican rhetoric, House Minority Leader John Boehner of Ohio characterized the Democratic proposal as a "complete government takeover of our health care system."[96] Senator Jon Kyl of Arizona described the bill as a "stunning assault on liberty," while fellow Republican Jim Bunning of Kentucky agreed that its provisions would "trample on the freedoms of Americans."[97] Asked whether the Democratic health care reform proposal amounted to "socialism," Republican National Committee chairman Michael Steele simply replied, "Yes. Next question."[98]

These arguments found a receptive audience among both Republican identifiers and the larger electorate. By mid-July 2009, only six months after Obama took office and at a point when reform legislation was still being developed by the relevant House and Senate committees, national surveys of public opinion began to reveal that the proportion of Americans who disapproved of the Democratic health care reform proposal had surpassed those in support of the measure.[99] Members of Congress who returned to their home states for the traditional August recess encountered substantial demonstrations of opposition to reform, often initiated by citizens identifying with the nascent Tea Party movement. Large, raucous crowds demanding that Congress abandon the reform effort became regular fixtures at public events; physical brawls even broke out at several town hall meetings, requiring police response to ensure the safety of the elected officials hosting them.[100] "I sense that people are scared for our country, and that's why we're having big turnouts," observed Republican senator Charles Grassley; one of Grassley's Iowa constituents further described the controversy over health care as "no less than liberty versus tyranny, good versus evil, and there's no middle ground."[101]

Democratic leaders did not appear to expect such an impassioned negative response, and many found such apocalyptic language utterly bewildering. To supporters, Obama's plan was hardly a "government takeover" or manifestation of leftist dogma, but rather a relatively pragmatic attempt to expand health care coverage and enact consumer protections without disrupting the existing private insurance already held by a majority of Americans; many proponents observed that the plan shared a number of key provisions with previous reform proposals advanced by Republican politicians. Democrats also noted that conservative activists attacked the Obama plan as liberty-denying socialism even as they vociferously defended existing entitlement programs that were even less consistent with small-government, free-market principles. Obama himself reported receiving letters from senior citizens saying, "I don't want government-run health care. I don't want socialized medicine. And don't touch my Medicare"—even though Medicare, a single-payer, federally administered insurance program for the elderly, was more of a "government-run" health care system than the regulated markets for private insurance plans that Obama's own reforms employed to expand coverage to the uninsured.[102] The best-known anecdote in this vein was furnished by Republican congressman Robert Inglis of South Carolina, who told the *Washington Post* that one town hall meeting attendee had warned him to "keep your government hands off my Medicare."[103]

These and other demonstrations of some Obama critics' imperfect command of the facts inspired Democratic smirks, but the ideologically framed negative characterizations popularized by conservative leaders succeeded in galvanizing ferocious opposition to the bill among Republican voters while simultaneously eroding support within the broader electorate. As Democrats discovered to their dismay, while the Republican electorate's professed aversion to handouts in principle does not necessarily indicate an unwillingness to take or defend existing benefits, its antigovernment sentiment still remains influential in directing the behavior of voters. The upset victory of an antireform Republican Senate candidate in a January 2010 special election in the normal Democratic stronghold of Massachusetts nearly derailed the passage of the reform legislation, dubbed the Affordable Care Act (ACA), and Obama's signing of the ACA into law that March did little to quell the growing popular backlash—despite Democratic hopes that the legislation might grow in popularity once it was enacted.

Public disapproval of "Obamacare," as the ACA was popularly known, played a significant part in producing massive Republican gains in the 2010 congressional midterm elections, handing the party control of the House of Representatives for what turned out to be the remainder of Obama's presidency. Democratic incumbents who favored health care reform lost a significant share of electoral support as a result of their vote, with most of the effect accounted for by constituents who perceived endorsement of the ACA as an indicator of the excessive liberalism of their representative.[104] Conservative voters linked health care to other Obama initiatives such as the economic stimulus package, perceiving a supposedly broader effort by Democratic leaders to expand the role of government and implement a liberal or socialist agenda. These voters mobilized to oppose Democratic politicians and to pressure Republicans to publicly commit themselves to reversing the tide of activist policymaking.

The partisan controversy over health care reform during the Obama presidency—a conflict that continues years after the passage of the ACA—serves as a valuable illustration of the larger foundational difference between the parties. Democratic leaders view their partisan constituencies as demanding practical solutions to expand and improve health insurance and as willing to tolerate considerable ideological flexibility and compromise in pursuit of these goals. For example, left-wing congressional

Democrats such as Barbara Lee and Dennis Kucinich put aside their preferences for a "public option" (a government-run insurance program that
would compete with private insurers), or even a Medicare-style single-
payer system, in order to support the ACA in 2010, concluding that the
ultimate objective of reducing the number of uninsured citizens was more
important than the precise means by which it was realized. Democratic
officials attempted to rally support among the party rank-and-file by emphasizing the specific benefits that certain classes of voters would receive
from the legislation: young people would gain the right to be covered by
their parents' insurance plans until age 26; women could not be charged
higher premiums than men and would receive mandated access to contra-
ception; the economically disadvantaged would gain expanded Medicaid
eligibility.

In contrast, Republican leaders demonstrated their own party's tendency to evaluate politics through the lens of abstract ideology, mobilizing supporters in the mass electorate by characterizing the health care
reform measure as violating the principles of individual liberty and limited government. They regularly described the ACA not merely as flawed
or misguided policy but as a more fundamental threat to cherished values;
the frequently lodged charge of "socialism" suggested that Obama and his
allies subscribed to an ideologically extreme and perhaps un-American
belief system. The viscerally negative popular response to the ACA among
conservative activists ensured that Republican officeholders would maintain a highly visible stance of opposition, lest they risk a challenge from
their ideological right in the next primary election. After Republicans
took control of the House of Representatives in 2011, party leaders held
dozens of votes on legislation repealing the ACA in part or in full; though
these measures stood no chance of enactment as long as Obama remained
president, Republican members found them useful as symbolic gestures
of opposition designed to appeal to their own party base and attract continued public attention to an unpopular law. More substantive resistance
came from Republican governors and state legislators who declined to
expand Medicaid eligibility, even though the federal government covered
the vast majority of the increased cost.

The contrast between the symbolic conservatism and operational liberalism of the American public was reflected in citizen attitudes toward the
ACA, as illustrated by Table 2-5, which summarizes the results of a typical 2013 survey.[105] From the summer of 2009 forward, most Americans
expressed disapproval of the law as a whole, with the vast majority of
public opponents agreeing that it represented "too much government involvement in health care." Yet nearly all of the ACA's specific provisions
continued to receive strong popular support.

Table 2-5 PUBLIC OPINION ON AFFORDABLE CARE ACT PROVISIONS

Provision	Total Approval %	Democratic Approval %	Republican Approval %	Approval Difference (D – R)
Small Business Tax Credits	88	96	83	13
Close Medicare "Donut Hole"	81	90	74	16
Health Insurance Exchanges	80	87	72	15
Stay on Parents' Plan Until Age 26	76	84	68	16
Subsidies for Insurance Purchase	76	91	61	30
Medicaid Eligibility Expansion	71	88	42	46
Ban on Denial Due to Preexisting Condition	66	75	56	19
Medical Loss Ratio	65	72	62	10
Medicare Tax Increase on High Incomes	60	80	37	43
Large Employer Mandate/ Penalty	57	79	36	43
Individual Mandate/Penalty	40	55	21	34
Affordable Care Act	**40**	**58**	**18**	**40**

Data from Kaiser Family Foundation, "Kaiser Health Tracking Poll: March 2013," http://kff.org/health-reform/poll-finding/march-2013-tracking-poll/.

These patterns in public opinion can inspire frustration in both parties. Democrats lament the political damage sustained by their party over the passage of the ACA, even though many of the voters who strongly opposed the law—and expressed their disapproval by voting against Democratic candidates—agreed with, and perhaps personally benefited from, one or more of its specific provisions. For Republicans, expressions of opposition were relatively costless before the law took effect, or when they were limited to a series of show votes in Congress. If a future Republican president attempts to repeal the ACA, however, the party will become vulnerable to Democratic attacks that draw upon the popularity of the law's specific provisions and accuse them of taking away health insurance from millions of Americans. As the case of the ACA demonstrates so strikingly, the distinct character of the parties and the bifurcated nature of American public opinion provide each party with grounds to lead a popular backlash against the policies of the other—thus contributing to a contemporary political environment characterized by ceaseless partisan conflict.

ASYMMETRIC PARTY SUPPORT
IN THE AMERICAN ELECTORATE

The unequal pressure that the leaders of both parties face from their respective electoral bases reflects an underlying difference in each party's type of public support. Democrats and Republicans each maintain the capacity to mobilize a potential public majority, though on markedly different terms. Democrats can attract voters who endorse part of their specific policy agenda, who identify with a social group within their coalition, or who sympathize with the party claiming to fight the powerful on behalf of the downtrodden. In contrast, the Republican Party's potential attractiveness rests on symbolic conservatism and a shared general perspective on the proper role of government in society. These distinctive forms of public support correspond to each party's electoral and activist constituencies. United by conservatism and a common adherence to abstract principles, the Republican faithful demand that party leaders stick to their convictions. The Democratic Party in the electorate contains diverse constituency groups that favor pragmatic action to achieve specific policy results. This foundational difference in the two party bases explains a great deal about the distinctive behavior of each party's elected officials and the diverging paths taken by their party organizations, as we explore in Chapter 3.

Our analysis of public opinion also offers some independent lessons for theories of mass political behavior, beginning with the conceptualization of ideology. Any definition of citizen ideology that conflates specific issue positions and broader views of government will provide inconsistent results, failing even to answer decisively whether the United States is collectively a center-left or center-right nation. The complexity of citizens' attitudes does not simply reflect the misunderstanding of ideological labels; instead, symbolic conservatism fuses an abstract ideological perspective with a popular self-definition. Put simply, the public mostly agrees with Republicans in philosophical terms but with Democrats in policy terms.

Theories of partisan identification should incorporate the possibility that citizens ally with each major political party for different reasons, or at least that they view their relationship to their favored party in unique ways. The Democratic Party includes many adherents who define themselves politically through their social group ties and describe their party as representing the group or groups with which they identify in an ongoing conflict with opposing groups. Republican Party supporters are much less likely to share this view; instead, they more commonly characterize the GOP as representing their vision of government and society in a battle with a Democratic Party that does not share their values.

The trends of ideological sorting and polarization have affected each party but have not necessarily made them more similar in kind. The departure of conservative Catholics and southerners from the Democratic Party has made it smaller and more ideologically homogenous, but committed liberals remain a numerical minority that competes with other party constituencies formed around single issues or identities. While liberal ideologues constitute a rising share of Democrats—albeit from a low starting point—conservatives have overwhelmed the Republican Party and become more aggressive in their ideological division of the political world. As we show in the next chapter, partisan electorates on both sides have evolved in tandem with the broader institutional development of each party's organizational and support networks. The distinct party bases are not epiphenomenal to this process: they constitute the unique environments within which each party developed its contemporary structure and style.

The dual prevalence of operational liberalism and symbolic conservatism in the American electorate also holds significant implications for elite strategies to marshal public opinion. Democratic politicians, emboldened by electoral successes and public opinion data demonstrating majority support for the specific issue positions in their party's platform, often act to fulfill their campaign promises once in office, only to encounter waning popular support because of the resonance of ideologically based attacks from the Republican opposition—as Obama and his congressional allies discovered in the first two years of his presidency. The demonstrated tendency of many Americans to maintain antigovernment ideological orientations even as they benefit from, and fiercely defend, specific government programs may be interpreted as mere confusion, ignorance, or hypocrisy. Yet symbolic conservatism need not be accompanied by operational conservatism to exert a substantial influence on the views and behavior of voters, as demonstrated by the multitude of citizens who attended town hall meetings and Tea Party rallies, wrote letters to the president, and turned out in the 2010 midterm elections to express their fervent opposition to the ACA; their imperfect logical consistency hardly prevented them from exerting considerable political influence.

Campaigning against big-government liberalism (or even socialism) and in favor of traditional values is often an effective strategy for Republicans to galvanize popular support within the party base and the public at large. Once they gain power, however, Republican leaders face a dilemma of their own, since the majority preference for smaller government in the abstract often decays when applied to the reduction or repeal of specific public programs—as Newt Gingrich discovered in his battles with Bill Clinton during the 1990s. What Republicans perceive as a mandate for their vision of limited government does not translate into support for the specific reforms (and associated reductions in government activity) necessary to put that vision into practice. Party asymmetry, as reinforced by the simultaneous operational liberalism and symbolic conservatism of the electorate at large, presents a significant challenge to the efforts of both Democrats and Republicans to achieve broad and lasting support for their policy initiatives, contributing to the frequent procedural stalemates and partisan rancor that have become familiar attributes of contemporary American politics.

CHAPTER 3

∽

An Ideological Movement Versus
a Social Group Coalition

The Conservative Political Action Conference (CPAC), a four-day annual event near Washington, D.C., has evolved over its 40-year history into a popular site for the congregation of the American conservative movement—and therefore a central, though ostensibly unofficial, venue for Republican politicking. Each year, a large troupe of politicians attends CPAC in order to impress an attentive audience of ideological activists, interest group leaders, and news media personalities who represent the base of the Republican Party. Candidates routinely use appearances at CPAC to emphasize their commitment to conservatism both as a personal identity and as a manual for governing, portraying their past and future political career as unerringly guided by ideological principles.

In the midst of his successful campaign for the Republican presidential nomination in 2012, Mitt Romney took a detour from personally courting voters in states with impending primary elections in order to deliver a well-publicized address at CPAC. Romney attempted in his speech to rally activist support by describing his candidacy in strongly ideological terms. "As conservatives, we are united by a set of core commitments," he argued, most notably the belief that "the principles embodied in the Constitution and the Declaration of Independence are uniquely powerful, foundational, and defining. . . . Conservatives all agree that departing from these founding principles is a departure from the greatness of America." Romney maintained that "history will record the Obama presidency as the last gasp of liberalism's great failure and a turning point for a new conservative era" and described the approaching presidential election as "a moment that demands we return to our basic values and first principles." In conclusion, he argued, "the task before us now is to re-affirm the convictions that unite us and go forward shoulder to shoulder to secure the victory America deserves."[1]

Romney used the word "conservatism" or "conservative" 25 separate times in his 25-minute address, including references to "conservative values," "conservative principles," "conservative constants," and "con-servative convictions." He attracted particular attention from the news media for claiming to have been a "severely conservative" governor of Massachusetts—a choice of words that struck some journalists as an awkward overcompensation for Romney's actual record in office, which was marked by several departures from right-wing doctrine (including the enactment of the nation's first state-level universal health insurance program). By the time that he became a presidential candidate, how-ever, Romney had adopted orthodox conservative positions on virtually every major issue, including support for the repeal of national health care reform; he had even spent most of the 2012 primary campaign at-tacking his Republican opponents from the ideological right, position-ing himself as the most conservative plausible nominee in the race.

Romney was far from the only Republican presidential contender to rely heavily upon openly ideological rhetoric; in a debate held in ad-vance of the 2012 Florida primary, the four participating candidates (Romney, former House Speaker Newt Gingrich, former senator Rick Santorum, and Representative Ron Paul) collectively uttered the term "conservative" a total of 25 times, making it the third most common substantive word in the debate transcript after "taxes" and "economy."[2] This was not an aberration. Republican candidates regularly appeal to officials, activists, and voters within their party by presenting them-selves as conservatives in good standing while attacking intra-party rivals for demonstrating insufficient devotion to ideological principles. Nearly every major Republican presidential candidate since Ronald Reagan has claimed the mantle of Reagan-style conservatism, with Reagan representing a frequently invoked embodiment of conservative purity.

It is difficult to imagine a major Democratic candidate for president delivering a prominent public address in which he or she repeatedly pledged an unswerving dedication to "liberal values," "liberal princi-ples," and "liberal convictions" or boasted of a "severely liberal" or "se-verely progressive" governing record. Moreover, no equivalent major event to CPAC compels Democratic politicians to extol the philo-sophical tenets of left-wing orthodoxy, nor does a comparable "liberal movement" serve as the conscious organizational foundation of the

Democratic Party. While both parties contain policy-oriented activists, donors, and organizations whose influential support is sought by ambitious politicians, the Democratic side is composed of a more diverse and complex coalition of actors whose affiliation with the party is mediated by a variety of specific interests and identities. Unlike their Republican counterparts, Democratic officeholders seldom attempt to satisfy the demands of their partisan base by proclaiming their devotion to timeless ideological truths; instead, they demonstrate their sensitivity to the particular present-day concerns of these discrete party constituents, such as labor unions, feminists, racial minorities, and environmentalists, by endorsing the more specific, and usually more concrete, agendas advanced by each of these groups.

In this chapter, we trace the evolution of the Democratic and Republican party organizations over nearly a century of American history, describing how each party developed a uniquely configured network of affiliated activists and interests. The fundamental character of the Democratic Party as a coalition of social groups whose various priorities are merged to create a collective policy platform has remained consistent over time, even as the particular constituencies and issue positions of the party have evolved in response to changes in the political environment. On the Republican side, a self-defined modern conservative movement founded in the 1950s by an alliance of public intellectuals, grassroots organizers, and entrepreneurial politicians almost immediately achieved substantial influence and managed to capture unchallenged control of the party apparatus by 1980, when Ronald Reagan was nominated and elected president. The power of conservative ideas and activism in Republican politics has only grown further in the succeeding decades; nearly all party leaders and elected officials now voice agreement with a common set of key ideological precepts and proudly identify themselves as members of the conservative movement.

We place this historical survey within the context of relevant theories explaining the purpose, development, and configuration of American party organizations, contending that they would be bolstered by the recognition of partisan asymmetry. We also compare the American parties to their counterparts in other nations, further confirming their distinctive nature—especially with respect to the relative conservatism of the Republican Party. Further supporting data are drawn from political endorsements, surveys of party activists, and content analyses of public speeches and platforms. In total, this evidence reveals how the distinctive characters of Democratic and Republican politics reflect the divergent agendas of their respective organizational bases.

PLACING ASYMMETRY IN PARTY THEORY

Most theories of American political parties are designed to apply equally to Democrats and Republicans. For example, in his landmark study *Why Parties?* John Aldrich identifies candidates and elected officials as the "central" and "most important" actors in both parties, arguing that partisan institutions have existed to serve the instrumental goals of ambitious office-seekers since the early years of the nation. According to Aldrich, politicians create and maintain parties to regulate ballot access, to solve collective action problems involved in mobilizing voters, and to ensure the stability of strategically beneficial legislative coalitions.[3]

Several recent analyses have challenged the politician-centered account of organizational development by arguing that each party is instead governed by an "extended party network" that includes activists and interest groups located outside as well as within the formal structures of government institutions and national, state, and local party committees.[4] One new theory contends that political parties represent aggregations of "intense policy demanders" who are engaged in politics to pursue specific programmatic goals; many of these actors exert influence on the party with which they are aligned from ostensibly nonpartisan positions in interest group organizations, the business sector, or the news media.[5] In this vein, David Karol describes parties as "coalitions of groups with intense preferences on particular policies" and identifies these groups as "self-aware collection[s] of individuals who share intense concerns [in the same issue area]."[6] According to this new theory, "ideology reflects a coalitional bargain among diverse policy demanders" rather than a shared set of values among citizens or politicians.[7] Because many voters are relatively uninformed about the parties' agendas and positions, party leaders are relatively free to satisfy the interests of these highly engaged, attentive constituencies without alienating the more indifferent broader public.

Activist-centered theories of political parties can account for the acquiescence of ambitious politicians to the preferences of informal networks, but they share with politician-centered theories the implication that the two major parties exhibit comparable internal configurations and approaches to courting voters.[8] As Jacob Hacker and Paul Pierson recently noted, Anthony Downs's model of electoral politics as the symmetric competition of two equivalent office-seeking parties for the support of voters arrayed along an underlying ideological dimension has served for decades as a "master theory" of political science.[9] By predicting that parties act on the basis of identical strategic incentives, Downsian views of political conflict assume mirror-image comparability between the Democrats and Republicans.

Yet previous generations of scholars often identified ways in which the organizational characteristics of the two parties failed to match. In his 1971 study of activists, David Nexon found that the parties "are different not only in name, program, and coalitional components but also in type."[10] Explaining the distinctiveness of the American political system, Nelson W. Polsby observed that "Democrats are primarily a mosaic of interests making claims on government; Republicans are bound together much more by ideological agreement."[11] And Jo Freeman's 1986 comparison of party convention delegates, organizations, and rules described distinct prevailing cultures on each side of the partisan divide.[12]

Studies in American political development substantiate the historical distinctiveness of each party's evolutionary path. As Daniel Galvin argues, Democrats and Republicans have followed unique organizational trajectories, developed distinctive internal norms, and aligned with dissimilar partner networks; these differences have been self-reinforcing, causing party leaders to maintain distinct practices over time.[13] Galvin notes that Republicans have consistently been a more homogenous party and "the Democratic Party has been home to a coalition of opposed types."[14] In *The Divided Democrats*, William Mayer argues that the lower levels of ideological agreement among Democratic elites and voters (reviewed by us in Chapter 2) explain the party's relatively deep internal divisions—illustrated by fractured presidential nomination processes and high levels of defection by Democratic voters to Republican presidential candidates between 1968 and 1988.[15]

Accounts of party differences that emphasized the unique fractiousness of the Democrats became scarcer after the 1990s, as rates of loyalty and cohesion within the party increased at both the mass and the elite level. By the presidency of Barack Obama, Republicans had become the more visibly divided party for the first time in living memory, as the rising Tea Party movement backed a series of primary challengers to incumbent officeholders and rebelled against the Republican leadership in Congress. Yet this internal conflict did not represent a transformation of the GOP's traditional ideological character. Tea Party activists and their "establishment" opponents within the Republican Party largely agreed on major principles, issues, and legislative priorities; areas of difference involved rhetorical style, governing strategy, and degree of devotion to acts of defiance directed at Democratic initiatives and leaders.

Although journalists often portray the rise of the ideologically purist Tea Party movement as a novel development in American politics, academic research suggests deeper historical roots. After interviewing Tea Party activists, Theda Skocpol and Vanessa Williamson observed:

> To say that Tea Partiers are part of a long-standing conservative tradition is to agree with many of our interviewees, who celebrate previous generations of conservatives as their political forebears. . . . An extraordinary number dated their first political experiences to the 1964 Goldwater campaign. . . . [T]he Tea Party is fundamentally the latest iteration of long-standing, hard-core conservatism in American politics.[16]

Christopher Parker and Matt Barreto also note this pedigree, arguing that the Tea Party "is simply the latest in a series of national right-wing social movements that have cropped up in America since the nineteenth century."[17] The two sets of scholars disagree about whether Tea Party members are primarily motivated by small-government doctrine or by anxiety over social and ethnic change,[18] likely because Skocpol and Williamson interviewed organizational leaders, whereas Parker and Barreto examined sympathizers identified in opinion polls of mass electorates. Yet both studies identify key antecedents to contemporary conservative populism, raising the question of why the Democratic Party lacks a comparable tradition of electorally powerful mobilization around a broad left-wing belief system.

"COALITION MERCHANTS" AND THE RISE OF PARTY POLARIZATION

Contemporary accounts of American politics commonly portray Democratic and Republican officeholders as steadily diverging over time from the political center toward the left and right poles, respectively, on an ideological spectrum. This perception is substantiated by quantitative analyses of roll-call voting that confirm a growing difference in the collective position-taking of the congressional parties.[19] The well-known progression of partisan polarization has forced an intellectual reevaluation of an American party system once thought internationally distinctive for the weakness of its internal discipline and its relative absence of policy coherence (especially among Democrats). Even previous periods of elevated polarization in Congress, such as the late 19th and early 20th centuries, are usually interpreted as reflecting stable electoral coalitions and the distribution of party patronage more than sharp ideological differences between Democratic and Republican elites.

In *Political Ideologies and Political Parties in America*, Hans Noel argues that contemporary party divisions neatly coincide with the emergence of affiliated coalitions of liberal and conservative activists for the first time in American history. Noel further contends that these divisions developed as a product of "coalition merchants," who assembled and marketed liberal and conservative ideologies (composed of a set of policy positions associated with support from corresponding public constituencies) to the leaders of the two respective parties.[20] In his account, previously distinct partisan and ideological coalitions converged over the second half of the 20th century because liberal and conservative activists, interest group leaders, and news media figures simultaneously succeeded in selling their respective bundles of policies and supporters to politicians and other elites in the Democratic and Republican parties.

Noel offers a convincing description of conservative ideology as having "married religiosity with anti-Communism and economic libertarianism."[21] He also recognizes the centrality of this ideology to Republican Party politics: "There are conservatives who accept only part of the package, but the package as a whole has a well-developed intellectual tradition, and the Republican Party as a whole advances all parts. The conservative ideology has become the core of the Republican Party."[22]

This account is consistent with historical studies that emphasize a "fusionist" movement in which elite actors strategically merged three strands of conservative ideology.[23] Conservatives have frequently described this movement as a "three-legged stool" that united free-market capitalism, a hawkish approach to national defense, and moral traditionalism, crediting the metaphor—perhaps apocryphally—to their patron saint Ronald Reagan. Yet the standard-bearers of the conservative movement did not merely market a collection of assorted political views to the existing leadership of the Republican Party; they embarked on a more ambitious project with both intellectual and electoral components. Conservative intellectuals succeeded in integrating their three traditions into a coherent, comprehensive political philosophy—an effort largely executed in the pages of the flagship opinion journal *National Review*, founded by William F. Buckley Jr. in 1955.[24] Meanwhile, a like-minded population of political professionals working in concert with sympathetic politicians mobilized conservative activists and voters to achieve a root-and-branch takeover of the Republican Party's organizational infrastructure and representation in government, thus marginalizing the moderate faction that had temporarily gained significant influence within the party in the wake of the New Deal and World War II.[25]

A sociological review noted that the intellectual movement's founders, such as Buckley, James Burnham, Frank S. Meyer, and Russell Kirk, "saw their contribution in promoting cohesion among the right's various factions" by leading "an effort to reconcile tensions among conservatism's competing strands."[26] Even resistant purists devoted to a single element of conservative thought later acknowledged the success of this fusion.[27] According to movement chronicler George Nash, the "three-legged stool" of modern conservatism was most effectively united by opposition to liberal policies:

> To the libertarians, modern liberalism was the ideology of the ever-aggrandizing bureaucratic, welfare state. If unchecked, it would become a totalitarian state, destroying individual liberty and private property—the wellsprings of a prosperous society. To the traditionalists, liberalism was a disintegrative philosophy which, like an acid, was eating away at the ethical and institutional foundations of Western civilization, creating a vast spiritual void into which totalitarian false gods would enter. To the Cold War anti-Communists, modern liberalism—rationalistic, relativistic, secular, anti-traditional, quasi-socialist—was by its very nature incapable of vigorously resisting an enemy on its left.[28]

Even after this conservative fusion was in place, movement leaders placed considerable emphasis on maintaining unity as a means of maximizing their political influence, an aim that was marked by "a succession of efforts to formulate a new synthesis of conservative aspirations." They endeavored to preserve an internally consistent ideology with foundational tenets that could be easily grasped by mass electorates as well as elite thinkers, and to remain active within the Republican Party as an avenue to implementing their ideas via government policy. As late as the 1990s, influential conservative leader Grover Norquist advocated the promotion of a "Leave Us Alone" coalition of conservative interest groups and movement leaders united by opposition to various forms of government regulation—an effort that fell within this venerable tradition.[29]

In an era of steadily widening ideological polarization between the parties, it is natural to assume that the Democratic Party has followed a similar trajectory over the past half-century, becoming the agent of a corresponding liberal or "progressive" movement that has mirrored the conservative ascendancy on the Republican side. Yet it is much more difficult to identify specific liberal "coalition merchants" or to trace the conscious development of modern liberalism as an abstract political philosophy within the boundaries of the Democratic extended network. Noel argues that "a liberal ideology" did "accomplish ... much of the same thing among the Democrats," identifying *New Republic* co-founder Herbert Croly as a left-of-center counterpart to Buckley, but Croly's Progressive Era formulation of an intellectual case for government intervention on behalf of redistributive economic goals predated Franklin D. Roosevelt's popular association of this reasoning with the Democratic Party via the New Deal—Croly died in 1930, two years before Roosevelt's election—and is even less applicable to other issue domains such as foreign policy or civil rights.

Although FDR's presidency ensured that the Democratic Party would serve as the natural political home for liberal intellectuals, other powerful groups within the Democratic coalition—including labor unions, southern conservatives, urban machines, and farmers—resisted efforts to redefine the party as consistently standing for a coherent liberal ideology, leading to perennial internal conflict that regularly threatened Democratic office-holders' ability to govern effectively. Committed liberals might have been content with a smaller but more cohesive party, but many elected officials and organizational leaders saw little reason to risk a proven national popular majority in pursuit of greater ideological unity. As Noel acknowledges, "Elements of the Democratic Party . . . continue to resist this [liberal] coalition. The party had a winner with the old New Deal coalition. It was not yet clear that the new, liberal ideological coalition would lead to similar electoral success. Liberalism would seem to alienate too many swing voters, or so many Democratic leaders fear."[30] Indeed, the widely perceived trade-off between ideological purity and popular appeal has remained central to the strategic calculations of Democratic officials up to the present day.

To be sure, the Democratic Party has moved collectively to the left over time—principally as a result of the defection of the white South to the Republicans—and party members have become more likely to adopt a common set of political views, especially at the elite level. Noel's analysis of newspaper columns demonstrates that the issue positions of liberal columnists were increasingly converging by the 1970s, matching a similar trend among conservative columnists. This similarity in levels of issue constraint leads Noel to suggest that the parties are ideological mirror images, using a definition premised on his notion that "a shared worldview or perspective . . . does not become an ideology . . . until it predicts a set of policies." His analysis of opinion journalism finds other manifestations of ideology but avoids assessing them: "Opinions can be considered in terms of policy prescriptions, groups (or individuals) that are affected, or abstract principles that are invoked." He focuses only on the first two, "especially policy."[31]

Our conception of ideology, as described in Chapter 2, instead emphasizes the role of abstract principles. Since Republicans more often invoke philosophical tenets or general threats to American values than do Democrats, conceptualizations of ideology that omit these manifestations will be less sensitive to partisan asymmetry. Issue constraint may not reflect the degree of devotion to a set of broader ideals; in some cases, citizens may learn "what position goes with what" by remaining attentive to the pronouncements of party leaders without developing an ideological self-identification, while others may be motivated politically by potent symbolic predispositions even as they struggle to correctly apply these principles to certain specific policy questions.

A significant subset of Democratic elites and opinion leaders self-identify as liberals and subscribe to common values such as egalitarianism that bring consistency to their views on a variety of particular issues. Yet the historical evolution of the Democratic Party contains no true analog to the rise and ultimate triumph of the modern conservative movement within Republican politics; similarly, the role of coalition merchants in developing a conscious ideology with which to identify is far less evident on the Democratic side. Even the popular view of the Democratic Party as moving steadily leftward since the 1960s (thus mirroring the Republicans' decided march to the right over the same period) is overly simplistic; such a shift is apparent on cultural matters such as abortion and gay rights, but the substantive positions of Democratic leaders on economic issues such as taxation and the welfare state in fact became *less* liberal after 1980.[32] Democratic officials have also consistently demonstrated much more reluctance than their Republican counterparts to openly pledge devotion to an ideological cause; it is notable that all four of the Democratic presidents that have served since the modern conservative movement achieved its first major breakthrough with Barry Goldwater's 1964 nomination—Lyndon Johnson, Jimmy Carter, Bill Clinton, and Barack Obama—declined to identify either themselves or the Democratic Party with symbolic liberalism as such, and all but Obama took measures to publicly distance themselves from more liberal members of their party.

We turn next to a more complete account of the evolution of each party's organization and extended network over nearly a century of American political history. The distinctive historical path followed by each set of party officials, activists, and politicians explains why the nature of the two parties remains distinct even in a polarized political era. On the Republican side, a highly disciplined, intellectually cohesive, and politically organized conservative movement managed, in a relatively short period of time, to achieve unquestioned primacy within the party, successfully defining the creed of "true" Republicanism as equivalent to its own ideological commitments. Democratic leaders, in contrast, have spent the past several generations managing an evolving coalition of social groups within the party organization and extended network as well as the broader electorate.

HOW THE CONSERVATIVE MOVEMENT CAPTURED THE REPUBLICAN PARTY

The rise of the modern American conservative movement, and its spectacular success in gaining control of the Republican Party, is an oft-told story that has inspired an extensive historiography.[33] Recent literature reviews in the fields of history and sociology reach similar conclusions: conservatism was a vibrant intellectual movement that built institutions to promote broad principles and cultivated a strong base of popular support, establishing itself over the past 50 years as the main intellectual and popular engine of Republican politics.[34]

The Republican Party has long been predominantly conservative. Progressive Republicans challenged the "Old Guard" right for party control in the early 20th century, temporarily gaining ascendancy during the presidency of Theodore Roosevelt (an event brought about by the assassination of his more conservative predecessor, William McKinley), but conservatives soon regained dominance. According to historian Heather Cox Richardson, "By 1920, Progressive Republicanism had lost all coherence and significance as a movement."[35] Political scientist John Gerring's analysis of party platforms found that Republicans had fully shifted from advocacy of central government to conservative economic policies by 1928.[36] But the onset of the Great Depression during the presidency of Herbert Hoover (1929–1933) discredited conservative Republicanism in the popular mind while bringing into power a renewed Democratic Party dedicated as never before to expanding federal power in order to ameliorate the effects of economic catastrophe.

Most conservatives opposed the New Deal and initial American intervention in World War II prior to the bombing of Pearl Harbor. But as Democratic policies led to the growth of government and a more internationalist role for the nation, Republicans divided over their party's proper response. One traditionalist faction, led by Senator Robert Taft of Ohio, "clung with a stranglehold to the idea that government activism was socialism . . . [that] would destroy the country," while a more moderate bloc associated with Governor Thomas E. Dewey of New York "gradually came to accept that the modern economy required government intervention."[37] Faced with the formidable strategic challenge of competing against a new national Democratic popular majority, Republicans nominated a series of presidential candidates who partially accommodated the New Deal and internationalist policies, including Wendell Willkie in 1940 and Dewey himself in 1944 and 1948, over the opposition of hard-line conservatives.[38]

Dwight D. Eisenhower, a World War II military hero whose landslide 1952 victory broke a 20-year Democratic hold on the White House, voiced conservative philosophical inclinations but aligned himself with Dewey's approach of largely accepting the existing New Deal. Regardless of his personal views, Eisenhower believed that Republicans needed to make peace with the modern welfare state for politically pragmatic reasons, as he explained in a 1954 letter to his brother Edgar:

I believe this country is following a dangerous trend when it permits too great a degree of centralization of governmental functions. . . . [But] the Federal government cannot avoid or escape responsibilities which the mass of the people firmly believe should be undertaken by it. . . . Should any political party attempt to abolish social security, unemployment insurance, and eliminate labor laws and farm programs, you would not hear of that party again in our political history. There is a tiny splinter group, of course, that believes you can do these things. . . . Their number is negligible and they are stupid.[39]

The "tiny splinter group" of staunch conservatives dismissed by Eisenhower softened its support for immediate repeal of New Deal programs in the face of what appeared to be impossible political odds but soon sought to reestablish its principles as the essence of proper Republicanism. As Eisenhower himself tacitly acknowledged, Republican acceptance of a larger and more active federal government after two decades of Democratic electoral dominance was more firmly based on considerations of political necessity than any fundamental rethinking of party doctrine. Small-government conservatism, though temporarily weakened even within its natural partisan home during the 1940s and 1950s, nevertheless drew upon a resilient strain of American political culture that emphasized the dangers that an expanded state posed to individual liberty.[40]

Dissatisfied conservatives devoted themselves to the task of building a new political movement that could simultaneously regain firm control of the Republican Party and discredit left-of-center politics in the eyes of the wider electorate. The intellectual component of this effort can be traced via a succession of prominent books that received substantial public notice: *The Road to Serfdom* by Friedrich von Hayek (1944), *Ideas Have Consequences* by Richard Weaver (1948), *God and Man at Yale* by Buckley (1951), *The Conservative Mind* by Russell Kirk (1953), *The Conscience of a Conservative* by Barry Goldwater (1960), and *Capitalism and Freedom* by Milton Friedman (1962). These works emphasized the development of conservative political ideas via reasoning from first principles. At the same time, a midcentury reimagining of the founding of America (illustrated by such trends as the resurgent popularity of the Federalist Papers) coincided with a revival of transatlantic conservative thought (such as the importation of the writings of Edmund Burke).[41] This intellectual tradition is still active today, regularly infused with new work like the integration of supply-side economics in the 1970s and the critique of the welfare state offered by Charles Murray in *Losing Ground* (1984). More than their liberal counterparts, American conservatives demonstrate a proclivity for venerating classic texts. When Newt Gingrich, a former professor of history, became Speaker of the House in

1995, he assigned a reading list to legislative staffers as relevant preparation for their new responsibilities.

In contrast to left-wing intellectual discourse, which often remains separate from—and even indifferent to—the rough-and-tumble world of practical politics, thinkers on the right aimed to advance their cause via the electoral process by popularizing conservative ideas among the American public and exhorting their followers to become politically active. After losing a 1958 state legislative race, L. Brent Bozell, the ghost-writer of Goldwater's *Conscience of a Conservative* (and a brother-in-law to William F. Buckley), argued that "a conservative electorate has to be created out of that vast uncommitted middle—the great majority of the American people who, though today they vote for Democratic or [moderate] Republican candidates, are not ideologically wedded to their programs or, for that matter, to any program. The problem is to reach them and to organize them."[42] Even the uber-intellectual Buckley entered the electoral arena himself by running for the mayoralty of New York City in 1965 to gain public attention for conservative positions; his older brother James L. Buckley served a term as a U.S. senator from New York after winning a multi-candidate race in 1970 as the nominee of the state's Conservative Party.

Each component of the conservative movement's "three-legged stool" drew upon arguments emphasizing fundamental values and appealing to overlapping sets of public supporters whom Nash describes as "loosely related groups" separated by "no rigid barriers."[43] First, cultural conservatism encompassed Judeo-Christian religiosity, the defense of Western traditions, and opposition to social change. Second, libertarianism and neoliberal versions of laissez-faire economics provided the intellectual architecture for business-sector conservatism, which increasingly evolved as the movement progressed from emphasizing balanced budgets to prioritizing tax cuts and regulatory relief. Third, staunch anticommunism and neoconservatism emphasized national security and patriotic conceptions of America's role as the world's leading power. All three traditions extensively employed symbolic rhetoric. As John Saloma, founding president of the Ripon Society (the most prominent moderate Republican organization of the era) later observed, conservatives "appropriated powerful words and symbols—freedom, family, work, religion—in a way that caught the liberals unaware."[44]

Though each tradition followed its own trajectory, all three developed in ways that enabled them to converge in a larger conservative movement based inside the Republican Party.[45] Cultural conservatism benefited from the 1950s-era social trends of increasing religious devotion and church attendance. Eisenhower played a key role in encouraging civic displays of religiosity. He actively promoted the idea of America as a Judeo-Christian nation via symbolic gestures such as adding "In God We Trust" to paper money and "one nation under God" to the Pledge of Allegiance, and introduced such initiatives as the Presidential (later National) Prayer Breakfast and opening invocations at public events.[46] Eisenhower and other Republicans of the era effectively merged notions of American exceptionalism with religious imagery, providing a foothold within political institutions.

Social conservatism always maintained a powerful base of support within the conservative grassroots—especially southern evangelical Christians spreading west. Organizations like Campus Crusade for Christ and the School of Anti-Communism helped spread socially conservative values as they integrated with the broader conservative mobilization of the 1950s. According to historian Darren Dochuk, evangelical Christians "joined other conservatives in aggressively promoting free enterprise. To be sure, this was only a small step to make. Already by the late 1940s southern transplants embroiled in the labor wars had chosen to support free market principles over industrial unionism. Even before that, southern plain folk had always seen themselves as defenders of pristine capitalism and Jeffersonian economics."[47] While most southern conservatives were still Democrats in the 1950s, the Republican Party had already begun to make regional inroads—Eisenhower carried five southern states in 1952 and eight in 1956—that presaged the more fundamental realignment to come.

Libertarians, along with their allies in business, also sought to advance their values in the public domain. Historian Elizabeth Fones-Wolf describes libertarian offerings of postwar economics education (and indoctrination) initiatives that aimed to "shape not only economic policies but also American values" by emphasizing freedom, individualism, and productivity.[48] These included specific outreach programs for church leaders and teachers to help inculcate capitalist values in youth. Libertarians also offered fellowships for young faculty on the philosophical foundations of free enterprise, testing the effects of these teachings with surveys.[49] Immediately following the 1948 election, won by Democratic president Harry Truman on a platform of economic populism, an ambitious new advertising campaign extolled the broad ideas of free enterprise. Spiritual Mobilization (a New Deal era attempt to engage ministers with business values) struggled until businesses and foundations backed it after World War II, sponsoring a radio program and newspaper columns. Business leaders responded to liberal proposals of the era with "hysterical warnings that the American way of life was under attack" in a battle for survival between socialism and capitalism.[50]

Intellectually, the Hayek-founded Mont Pelerin Society served as a formal association for self-identified libertarians; Milton Friedman cited its founding as the beginning of the conservative resurgence in economics. Libertarians also used the Foundation for Economic Education (FEE) and the Intercollegiate Studies Institute to promote their views. Ayn Rand, whose novels *The Fountainhead* (1943) and *Atlas Shrugged* (1957) remain widely read today, served as an influential popularizer of libertarian beliefs. Although Rand personally resisted the submergence of her Objectivist philosophy within the larger conservative movement, she supported Goldwater's 1964 presidential campaign and participated in mass political mobilization efforts. Rand is far from universally admired on the right (partly because of her outspoken atheism), but she played an important role in spreading antigovernment ideas; many conservative Republicans, including Alan Greenspan, Jack Kemp, and Paul Ryan, later credited her as an intellectual influence.[51] Eventually, some libertarians departed the conservative mainstream and the Republican Party to create the Society for Individual Liberty (1969) and the Libertarian Party (1971). But, as Nash observes, "for all the sound and fury and discussion of a 'burgeoning split,' one durable fact stood out: the conservative center was not disintegrating in practical terms. The dissenters remained dissenters."[52]

While the foreign policy strand of modern conservative thought departed from the limited-government doctrine advocated by the ideological right in the domestic realm by supporting an expanded national military capacity and interventionism abroad, intellectual leaders managed to integrate it successfully into the larger movement, mostly displacing the older isolationist streak of American conservatism. Their efforts benefited greatly from a postwar international order in which a Soviet Union founded on left-wing authoritarianism represented the primary threat to American hegemony, reinforcing the conservative perception of a worldwide ideological conflict between liberty and capitalism on the right and statist collectivism on the left. Indeed, anticommunism became a powerful unifying force within the modern conservative movement: foreign policy conservatives argued that American interests required preventing the expansion of Soviet spheres of influence, economic conservatives condemned the central planning and classless societal structure advocated by Marxist thought, and cultural traditionalists decried its hostility to religion.

Conservative Republicans recognized that anticommunism could also serve as a powerful symbolic cause around which to build popular support.[53] In 1948, Whittaker Chambers accused Alger Hiss, a former United Nations and State Department official who was president of the

Carnegie Endowment for International Peace, of serving as a Soviet spy; Chambers repeated his charges before the House Committee on Un-American Activities and appeared on *Meet the Press*. Chambers's allegations were later proven correct, and Hiss was convicted of perjury in a well-publicized trial. Republican senator Joseph McCarthy of Wisconsin took up the issue in the 1950s, claiming to know of 205 Communist Party members working for the U.S. government. McCarthy received substantial public attention and support for several years before the false nature of his accusations was exposed (most notably in a 1954 report by Edward R. Murrow of CBS News) and he was censured by the Senate; his attacks on the "communist-coddling" Truman administration had been widely credited in Washington with contributing to Republican victories in the 1950 and 1952 elections.

Anticommunism became a popular cause in conservative areas like Southern California, where citizens watched alarming documentaries and held regular public meetings in which liberal policies were presented as communist conspiracies.[54] Evangelical ministers, according to Dochuk, were "bridging gaps between religious and secular conservatives through the construction of a broad association of anticommunist activism."[55] Republicans, Cox Richardson noted, had long "interpreted virtually every attempt to use government to level the playing field between workers and employers as the creeping tentacles of communism," but this argument gained new currency in the Cold War era.[56] Goldwater and other conservative leaders blamed liberals who were "weak on communism" for putting America on a path to losing the Cold War.[57] As Nash observed, the conservative resurgence was "immensely assisted by the cement of anti-Communism throughout the years of self-definition ... nearly all conservatives were bound together by consciousness of a common mortal enemy. The threat of an external foe (which included liberalism, too) [was] invaluable."[58] Conservatives still occasionally employed old isolationist arguments against American reliance on international institutions, but their views developed into an "understanding of foreign affairs as a titanic conflict of ideologies, religions, and civilization"—a point of view that was particularly advanced by the growing ranks of neoconservatives, most of whom were former liberals and leftists who advocated aggressive policies of hard-power American intervention around the world.[59]

By the 1960s, conservative fusionists had succeeded in uniting these various schools of thought into a formidable intellectual and political movement—an effort that was made easier by a new burst of domestic policy activism led by Democratic presidents and congressional majorities.[60] After an interregnum in the late 1940s and 1950s, the size and scope of national government expanded dramatically from 1961 to

1976, mobilizing and shaping conservative opposition.[61] The conservative movement, assisted by a measurable antiliberal backlash in public opinion that emerged in the late 1960s, built lasting institutions designed to generate and publicize ideas for policymaking and public advocacy, including the expanded American Enterprise Institute and the new Heritage Foundation (1973), the Cato Institute (1977), and the Manhattan Institute (1978), as well as numerous state think tanks, which by the 1990s had sprung up in 75 percent of the states; we explore this development more fully in Chapter 4.[62]

The ascendant conservative movement took aim at moderate and liberal factions within the Republican Party while attempting to reframe inter-partisan conflict as a clash of competing ideologies. This approach not only satisfied conservatives' own conception of politics as an intellectual arena in which they battled liberal ideas but also attempted to shift the salient cleavage in the national electorate from a partisan conflict in which Republicans represented a perennial minority of voters to an ideological divide in which self-identified conservatives outnumbered liberals. National Republican electoral victories during this era required Democratic-leaning voters to cross party lines at nontrivial rates, and the most promising targets for defection were the significant share of Democrats who disapproved of liberalism. Republicans were therefore happy to characterize themselves as conservatives while labeling their electoral opponents, accurately or not, as "liberal Democrats."

Figure 3-1 illustrates these trends using the Google Ngram Viewer, which displays the historical usage of words and phrases in books. The lines represent the frequency of occurrence of four two-word phrases in each year (as a percentage of all two-word phrases used in American English books): "conservative Republican," "liberal Democrat," "liberal Republican," and "conservative Democrat." Conservative Republican

Figure 3-1 Google Books Mentions of Ideological and Partisan Labels

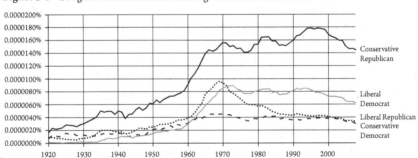

Proportion of all book phrases associated with the four terms in all books archived by Google. Available via the Google Ngram Viewer, http://bit.ly/1SAxn7V.

politicians have long been the most commonly identified group of the four, but the 1960s produced a conflict between two classes of Republicans (including a minority of liberals); by 1970, Republicans were nearly always referred to as "conservative" and liberal Republicans were moving toward extinction. The usage of "liberal Democrat" also rose and remained elevated, but most of the references involve Republicans calling their opponents liberals rather than Democrats adopting that definition for themselves.[63]

Conservative leaders and allied Republican politicians have often struggled to regulate and direct the grassroots forces that their movement has unleashed. Elites constantly attempted to benefit strategically from the mobilization of the populist right without associating themselves with its less politically advantageous elements or becoming a target of its activism themselves. Robert Welch, a candy executive on the board of FEE, founded the John Birch Society (JBS) in 1958 (named after a Christian missionary and Air Force officer killed by Chinese Communists in 1945) in order to pressure Eisenhower from the ideological right. The group grew as an outlet for far-right sentiment in the early 1960s, notably attacking liberal policies as communistic, but its penchant for conspiracy theories threatened larger movement-building goals. Buckley has often been credited with expelling the JBS from the conservative movement via a scathing 1962 editorial that also gained the endorsement of Barry Goldwater, although Buckley directed his criticism at Welch himself—calling him "a man whose views [are] . . . far removed from common sense"—while defending other members of the group as honest patriots.[64]

Much of the conflict between purist activists and movement regulars took place within affiliated party organizations like the College Republicans, the Young Republicans, and the National Federation of Republican Women. One leader of the rightist network called The Syndicate reflected: "We thought we knew exactly what it meant to be conservative until we saw these people. . . . We found ourselves—mostly pro-Goldwater—becoming 'middle-of-the-roaders' in comparison to the extremists."[65] Many key conservative figures, including Lee Atwater, Phyllis Schlafly, and Karl Rove, began their political careers by winning internal battles within these organizations.[66] In the process, conservatives won control of national, local, and state party groups.[67]

The movement to nominate Goldwater for president, first in an abortive effort in 1960 and then in a successful campaign in 1964, was the primary means by which conservatives merged their elite network with the broader popular constituency for right-wing ideology. Goldwater was assisted early on by most important conservative intellectuals and publications.[68] Before he entered the presidential race (or in some cases, even knew about the efforts), an alliance of grassroots activists had built a movement on his behalf, in the process gaining control of numerous affiliated Republican organizations.[69]

Goldwater's slogan "In Your Heart You Know He's Right" appealed to purist conservatives of all stripes. In his 1964 Republican nomination acceptance speech, Goldwater argued that "extremism in the defense of liberty is no vice, and moderation in the pursuit of justice is no virtue," a passage written by conservative professor Harry Jaffa. Goldwater also actively consulted conservative intellectuals and legal experts; most notably, he requested an opinion on the unconstitutionality of the 1964 Civil Rights Act from future Supreme Court nominees William Rehnquist and Robert Bork. His campaign also stimulated massive grassroots activism, with up to 500,000 campaign volunteers by Election Day.[70] Even his landslide defeat led to the creation of the American Conservative Union, the influential group that founded CPAC. Despite losing the White House, conservatives had "seized the party and legitimized the movement," leading to large increases in grassroots organization membership and conservative magazine circulation following the election.[71]

Another burst of grassroots mobilization by conservative activists occurred in the late 1970s and 1980s. This effort focused on motivating evangelical Christians—who had previously maintained some ambivalence toward organized participation in electoral politics—to support conservative Republicans in general and Ronald Reagan in particular. New "Religious Right" organizations like Focus on the Family (1977), Christian Voice (1978), and the Religious Roundtable (1979) helped televangelist Jerry Falwell launch the most well known of the groups, the Moral Majority (1979). Despite its visible emphasis on social and cultural issues, this effort sought integration into both the larger conservative movement and the Republican Party, and also promoted conservative views on economics and foreign policy.[72] A long history of evangelicalism in the South and Southwest preceded this political revival; many group members had long participated in existing conservative organizations by the time the media took note.[73] According to Julian Zelizer, new evangelical religious leaders combined "vast membership groups in churches" with the "infrastructure of television shows, publications, and radio shows that were crucial to the right."[74] Although these leaders often called for additional government intervention (for example, to outlaw abortion and pornography), they also framed their movement as a defense against state intrusion on private institutions.[75]

The popular mobilization of conservative Christians into Republican politics continued well into the 1990s but had no stable interest group leadership. A succession of groups claiming the banner of religious conservatism rose and then quickly lost momentum: the Moral Majority dissolved in 1989 and was replaced by the Christian Coalition, a legacy of televangelist Pat Robertson's 1988 campaign for the Republican presidential nomination, which itself declined in size and clout in the late 1990s. Yet even in its heyday, the Christian Coalition employed only three full-time lobbyists in a small office.[76] According to Jeffrey Berry's analysis of congressional hearings, the groups achieved little success in either bringing issues to Congress or winning legislative battles.[77]

The lack of stable, independent political organizations representing the Christian right reflected the rapid integration of social traditionalists into the broader conservative movement and Republican Party, reducing the need for a separate institutional infrastructure. By 1993, religious conservatives controlled 38 of 58 Republican central committees.[78] Christian Coalition executive director Ralph Reed, portrayed by the news media as one of the most influential political figures of the 1990s, was not a minister or theologian by training, but instead a professional Republican operative. Reed advocated conservative policies across a broad issue spectrum, explaining that his organization would "speak to the concerns of average voters in the areas of taxes, crime, government waste, health care, and financial security" in addition to culture and morality.[79] Religious conservative activists and organizations became involved in electoral campaigns on behalf of the Republican Party whether or not the candidates shared their religious background and convictions. According to Berry, conservative groups have historically focused less on lobbying and more on "becoming part of the leadership of the national party." He identifies Reed, Gary Bauer, Jerry Falwell, Grover Norquist, Howard Phillips, Phyllis Schlafly, and Paul Weyrich as conservative leaders that "have all regarded themselves more as Republican strategists than as legislative lobbyists."[80]

The Religious Right is sometimes identified as a separate wing within the Republican electorate that competes with economic conservatives for influence over the party. In our view, actual conflicts between these factions over policy are rare, with any tensions between them mostly stemming from disagreements over the relative emphasis or priority of economic and social concerns. Like other Republican supporters, evangelical Christians may have been initially drawn to the party by a particular facet of its appeal—in this case, shared cultural values—but Republican elites and religious leaders alike worked to integrate the group into the larger party organization and ideological movement by promoting conservative positions on a wide range of issues. While movement leaders accommodated the Religious Right over the course of the 1980s and 1990s by expanding the definition of orthodox conservative doctrine to include opposition to abortion and homosexuality, evangelical authorities likewise advocated a Christian worldview that encompassed conservative positions on economics and foreign policy as well as culture and morality, encouraging the adoption of a broad ideological orientation rather than a focus on a subset of issues.

Unlike religious conservatives, gun rights advocates continued to maintain a powerful network of single-issue interest organizations even as they similarly sought integration into the wider Republican Party. But the strategic behavior of the National Rifle Association (NRA), the most powerful of these groups, likewise demonstrates the tendency of political actors on the American right to sound general ideological themes and forge connections with the broader conservative movement. The contemporary NRA represents the interests of gun owners in the political arena not primarily by advocating conservation of hunting lands, or even by emphasizing the role that firearms might play in guaranteeing citizens' physical security and self-defense, but instead by portraying gun ownership as a constitutional right intentionally established by the nation's founders to prevent government overreach. The rhetoric of NRA leaders—who regularly warn their supporters that liberals are planning to confiscate the nation's gun supply in order to remove a popular check on the growth of federal power—thus blends naturally with the conservative movement's larger antigovernment message. Frequent reports of increased sales of firearms and ammunition upon the election of a Democratic president or the introduction of gun control legislation in Congress suggest that gun ownership has acquired a strong political dimension as a result of this ideological integration.

The presidency of Ronald Reagan sealed the conservative movement's ascendance within the extended network of the Republican Party and the unchallenged adoption of conservative positions on economics, culture, and foreign policy as official party doctrine. Reagan's formidable electoral success demonstrated that the party did not need to maintain a sizable moderate wing for the purposes of electability, and the realignment of the South provided the GOP with a large supply of new conservative voters, elected officials, and organizational leaders. More than 35 years after his presidency began and more than 10 years after his death, Reagan remains a figure with unequaled symbolic power, revered by Republican politicians and activists for representing, in their eyes, the personification of conservative principles. There is little room in the current party for challenging Reagan-identified conservative orthodoxy; instead, internal Republican disagreements more frequently involve accusations of insufficient allegiance to the Reagan legacy.

THE CONSERVATIVE MOVEMENT TAKES
ON THE "LIBERAL ESTABLISHMENT"

From its earliest days, the modern conservative movement declared political war on a perceived liberal elite that, in its view, had taken control of the American government, news media, and educational system.[81] As Kabaservice reports, William F. Buckley "gave the name 'liberal establishment' to the interlocking directorate of individuals, institutions, and ideas that he fought in his quest to revive conservatism in postwar America."[82] This alliance of power was hardly a figment of Buckley's imagination: Ivy Leaguers such as McGeorge Bundy moved between universities, media institutions like the *Washington Post*, philanthropies like the Ford Foundation, and the John F. Kennedy and Lyndon Johnson administrations. They acted as a bipartisan social clique of "the best and the brightest," advising political leaders on both foreign and domestic policy.

Buckley positioned himself in opposition to this establishment; as Nash observed, "*National Review* in its first years was dominated by the conviction that its preeminent intellectual enemy—and they insisted that it was an enemy—was liberalism. It was the liberals, said Buckley in the first issue, 'who run this country.'"[83] This argument provided Buckley and other well-born conservatives with a patina of populism that helped to build movement support outside of elite circles. Kabaservice notes that Goldwater supporters at the 1964 Republican National Convention "lacked Buckley's nuanced view of the establishment, but they responded on a gut level to his belief that he 'would rather live in a society governed by the first 2000 names in the Boston phone directory than in one governed by the 200 members of the Harvard faculty.'"[84] Later, Richard Nixon's vice president Spiro Agnew took up the cause, campaigning against an "effete corps of impudent snobs who characterize themselves as intellectuals" and blaming them for violence and campus unrest.[85]

Although members of the conservative movement readily referred to their political opponents as "liberals," many of their targets did not accept the label—and fewer still viewed themselves as leading a corresponding ideological movement of the left. The "establishment" of the 1950s and 1960s deemed fundamental disagreements over the size and purpose of government and America's proper role in the world to have been permanently resolved, leaving the competent management of the modern state as the primary remaining responsibility of the nation's political leadership. Sociologist Daniel Bell declared "the end of ideology" in his 1960 volume of the same name; Seymour Martin Lipset likewise ended *Political Man* (1960) with a chapter on "the end of ideology."[86] As Kabaservice puts it, "The members of the establishment had always thought of themselves as pragmatists, not ideologues."[87] Political scientist Ira Katznelson noted the existence of "a non-ideological (self-consciously technical, trans-ideological) orientation to reform grounded in a very high degree of self-satisfaction with the country's economy and society."[88] From this perspective, conservatism was a psychological impulse, rather than a fount of competing ideas.[89]

As a result, the increasing role of elites and expertise in government was viewed by establishment figures as a natural development that hardly required intellectual defense. A postwar scientific ascendance (led by the successful nuclear program and later invigorated further by the space race) was assumed to be a product of public consensus. Eisenhower had served as the president of Columbia University before entering the White House, promoting the conduct of research useful for informing public debate. The Great Society was a triumph of technocracy, further integrating the findings of social science into the development of public policy. As Johnson told the Brookings Institution, "There is hardly an aspect of the Great Society's program that has not been molded, or remolded, or in some way influenced by the community of scholars and thinkers. The flow of ideas continues—because the problems continue."[90] An educated class of experts advised policymakers in new advisory government research institutions, and thousands of professionals with advanced degrees joined the federal bureaucracy.[91] As Steven Teles argues, policy reforms drew from a "diminishing role of popular mobilization in setting the government's agenda and the increasing role of ideas generated in the academy, professions, and government itself."[92] Robert Weisbrot and Calvin Mackenzie agree that the "federal government was acting not as the agent of the American people responding to their demands, but as an independent force seeking to solve problems that its experts had identified and to which they had applied the tools of modern analysis."[93]

Wishing to challenge this perceived consensus, the conservative movement built alternative institutions to train its own set of elites. The American legal system offers an instructive example. Opposition to "activist" judges helped unite business and religious conservatives. Conservative foundations funded new public interest law firms (to counter a variety of firms organized around group rights) and made inroads into American law schools through law and economics programs.[94] The Federalist Society created a lasting network of conservative lawyers. Teles emphasizes a movement "increasingly directed by a conservative new class of ideologically motivated actors" who "invested significant resources in serious, first-order discussion of fundamental commitments with little if any short-term payoffs."[95] By the Reagan era, Federalist Society members were forming a network in the policy community, making it easier to hire and ally with like-minded conservatives.[96]

Although sectors of the American left have also viewed the "establishment" unfavorably at times, they did not succeed in building a parallel institutional infrastructure, mobilizing a sizable bloc of voters, or capturing the organizational network of a major political party. Only the conservative movement combined a substantial institutional capacity with an openly ideological perspective, coming to represent the most prominent opposition to an elite mainstream that collectively leaned left of center on many policy matters but was neither primarily motivated by the goal of furthering an ideological cause nor organized to do so. Conservatives' vilification of the "liberal establishment" was not simply partisan conflict in another guise; many establishment figures were Republicans, and the early years of the conservative movement were devoted as much to reestablishing conservative principles as Republican Party doctrine and gaining firm control of the Republican organizational apparatus as they were to providing energetic opposition to Democrats. While this effort found considerable success, no counterpart movement on the left ever emerged to remake the Democratic Party in its own image, ensuring that the foundational asymmetry of the parties endured into a new millennium.

THE PERSISTENCE AND EVOLUTION
OF THE DEMOCRATIC GROUP COALITION

The evolution of the Democratic Party, though not steered by a broad liberal ideological movement, nonetheless has exhibited significant historical change. In the early 20th century, the party was ruled by a coalition of white southerners—whose partisan affiliation was an expression of regional loyalty rather than policy agreement—and urban machines in the North largely supported by immigrants and their children. Neither organizational faction was particularly motivated to press for the adoption of a defining liberal ideology. As James Michael Curley, a colorful and corrupt four-term mayor of Boston who also served in Congress and as governor of Massachusetts, reportedly quipped, "Redistribution of the wealth would be all right, but in America the best we can achieve is redistribution of the graft."[97]

To be sure, Woodrow Wilson and other progressive Democrats pursued an ambitious program of economic intervention and internationalism. But the Democratic Party in the 1920s, according to historian David Burner, transformed from a rural party to an urban machine party based on the "self-interest of urban political pressure groups, both ethnic and economic."[98] Democrats were united behind Roosevelt's early New Deal legislative program, advanced as a response to the Great Depression, but tensions remained—especially between the northern and southern wings of the party—that deepened further as the 1930s wore on. Southern members of Congress played a key role in modifying many of Roosevelt's proposals; winning their often-pivotal support usually required the decentralization of enforcement mechanisms and the exclusion of farm and domestic labor from regulation (compromises seen in the Social Security Act of 1935).

Historian Alan Brinkley argues that the New Deal encompassed two different liberal visions and coalitions: one quasi-socialist effort advocated substantial federal regulation of markets, labor, and wealth, while another placed sole emphasis on a Keynesian role for government in managing economic cycles. In Brinkley's account, the Keynesian faction ultimately prevailed because big-government ideas and proposals provoked opposition from "anti-statist impulses deeply embedded in American political culture."[99] Calls for a "religion of government" thus gave way to more modest reform measures.[100] World War II and its prosperous aftermath reduced the demand for economic interventionism, undermining the rationale for further government expansion. The primary liberal organization of the postwar era, Americans for Democratic Action (founded in 1947), sought to counteract the influence of conservative southerners in the Democratic Party while simultaneously marginalizing leftists—and, eventually, the breakaway Progressive Party led by former vice president Henry Wallace (who had communist ties and favored reconciliation with the Soviet Union).

Brinkley, Katznelson, and labor historian Nelson Lichtenstein all argue that the opportunity for a true leftist party to emerge in the United States closed in the 1940s with "the transformation of the labor movement from a social democratic insurgency into a mere interest group."[101] An accord between labor and capital in the 1940s that was linked with a move toward firm-based collective bargaining and privatized welfare meant that "labor's ambitions were thereafter sharply curbed, and its economic program was reduced to a sort of militant interest group politics . . . [replacing] labor's earlier commitment to economic planning and social solidarity."[102] The potential for a legitimate American socialist movement was from that point on merely "a notation in the archives of history" in the 1950 words of Daniel Bell; more than sixty years later, Michael Kazin observed that Bell's "judgment [still] stands."[103]

The postwar American government became an arena for group competition. The 1940s, Katznelson argues, "changed the locus of political debate from questions of social organization and class relations to issues of technical economics and interest group politics. . . . [T]he collapse of the labor movement as a potentially social democratic force and the evaporation of the theoretical and academic bases for left-wing policy-making within American politics, demoralized the American left."[104] These developments enabled the rise of a diverse interest group coalition; as Brinkley describes, these postwar liberals

> still called themselves New Dealers, but they showed relatively little interest in . . . the New Deal's abortive experiments in economic planning . . . its vigorous if short-lived anti-monopoly and regulatory crusades, its open skepticism toward capitalism and its captains, its overt celebration of the state. . . . Thus reconciled to the structure of their economy, liberals of the postwar world could move forward into new crusades [such as civil rights and environmentalism].[105]

This new agenda "focused less on the broad needs of the nation and the modern economy than on increasing the rights and freedoms of individuals and social groups."[106] David Plotke concurs: "[Democrats] treated politics as group activity. . . . [Groups] were conceived as unavoidable components . . . and as legitimate starting points for political action. Democratic constituencies were addressed as groups by the state and party."[107]

But Democrats did create a policy agenda that united its urban constituencies, despite the lack of shared ideology, as John Mollenkopf describes:

> The disparate urban constituencies of the national Democratic Party—machines as well as reform groups, big business as well as labor, blue collar ethnics as well as minorities—could each find reasons to be united behind a program of growth and development. . . . [N]ational political leaders used federal programs not only to bring local constituencies together, but also to unite them organizationally. . . . Government programs could thus solidify national political power.[108]

Johnson's Great Society was also an attempt to respond to diverse party groups. As David Broder argues,

> Johnson had to shape his program to include incentives and rewards to each of the elements of his wide-ranging constituency. This . . . explains why Johnson offered such an incredible array of programs, rather than concentrating on a few fundamental reforms. . . . [E]ach had practical or symbolic value for some element of his constituency. . . . Johnson rarely dealt with The Public; he dealt with many little publics, and he dealt with them through their established leaders.[109]

Johnson was successful at pragmatic policymaking while disdaining broader ideological efforts, instead favoring group pluralism mediated by bargaining and compromise among politicians: "The biggest danger to American stability is the politics of principle, which brings out the masses in irrational fights for unlimited goals," he said, "for once the masses begin to move, then the whole thing begins to explode."[110] Johnson's 1964 reelection effort notably included 26 different citizens' committees representing an array of demographic constituencies.[111]

A "New Left" movement arose in the 1960s, founded by activists who viewed the Democratic Party as having been co-opted by existing centers of power. Like the "New Right" conservatives of the period, the New Left took aim at a political "establishment" that it viewed as insufficiently devoted to moral principles and excessively deferential to status and expertise. Yet the two strains of activism differed in their political objectives and favored strategies. "New Right" organizations such as the student group Young Americans for Freedom (YAF) sought and achieved integration into the broader conservative movement, the Goldwater presidential campaign, and the Republican Party, cementing relationships with other actors on the right and emphasizing the pursuit of partisan and electoral influence. In contrast, left-wing activists were far more likely to entangle themselves in doctrinal disputes and maintain ambivalence toward engagement with the Democratic Party or the electoral system—often favoring alternative forms of political activity such as direct protest.

These dissimilar approaches are immediately evident upon comparison of the YAF's founding Sharon Statement with the analogous Port Huron Statement drafted two years later by the Students for a Democratic Society, the leading left-wing student organization of the 1960s. As Daniel Akst observes, "the one-page [Sharon Statement] is a model of brevity and coherence, especially compared with the rambling 64-page Port Huron Statement."[112] He summarizes:

> The great economy of the Sharon Statement simply reflected its much clearer message: the less government, the better. The basic idea was to let people take care of themselves, a viewpoint not very difficult to elaborate then or now. The Port Huron Statement is so much longer because its many earnest drafters had a much heavier lift. They were determined not only to perfect relations among "men" but to safeguard against the undue power government and business tend to arrogate to themselves—even as they demanded that the same inept and militaristic state they reviled somehow manage housing, capital allocation, and other things by now demonstrably beyond its competence.[113]

Much of the New Left was demoralized by electoral politics in the 1960s, observe Maurice Isserman and Kazin, who note that "most New Leftists abandoned whatever hopes they still cherished of reforming the existing political system" after the bloody 1968 Democratic National Convention in Chicago. "Declaring themselves allies and disciples of third-world Communist revolutionaries like Mao Zedong and Che Guevara," they focused instead on opposing American intervention abroad.[114] According to Kazin, "Having dismissed patriotism as a smokescreen for imperialist war and the squelching of dissent . . . [the New Left's] general contempt for national symbols provided Richard Nixon, Ronald Reagan, and like-minded conservatives with an opportunity to brand all foes of military intervention as naïve at best and treasonous at worst."[115]

American liberals and leftists failed to construct a fusionist movement dedicated to working within existing partisan and electoral institutions to implement a shared ideology across a range of policy domains. Instead, political activism on the left was divided into a series of movements that focused on specific issue areas and advanced the views of discrete constituents, such as the civil rights movement, the women's rights movement, the gay rights movement, the environmental movement, and the antiwar movement. The leaders of each cause tended to sympathize with the others, but their organizational representation remained separate, and the constituencies for whom they claimed to speak did not necessarily perceive themselves to be members of an integrated "left wing" of American politics.

The absorption of these organizations, groups, and voters into the Democratic Party provoked considerable resistance from several of the party's existing key constituencies, producing persistent signs of strain within the Democratic coalition. White southerners and conservative Catholics, two loyally Democratic voting blocs who supplied much of the party's mass electoral support, became increasingly alienated by the party's leftward shift on racial, cultural, and foreign policy issues. Even the labor movement, which had provided the foundation of socialist and other comprehensive left-wing political mobilization in other Western nations, resisted alliance with these new causes. "In contrast to Western Europe," explains leftist Mike Davis, "where the insurgencies of 1968–1973 led to profound upheavals that set new agendas for the labor movement and recomposed its activist leadership, the American rank-and-file struggles did not succeed in re-orienting the unions. . . . [They] only left enduring legacies of frustration and demoralization."[116]

The tension among the various constituent groups under the Democratic "big tent" erupted into open conflict in 1972 when the party nominated South Dakota senator George McGovern for president.

McGovern successfully captured the nomination running on a socially liberal, antiwar platform ("acid, amnesty, and abortion," cracked
Republican Senate minority leader Hugh Scott), but it soon became apparent that his liberal image presented serious political liabilities in the
general election. McGovern failed even to unite his own party: the AFL-
CIO declined to endorse him, southern Democratic leaders kept their
distance, and over one-third of Democratic voters ultimately crossed
party lines to support Republican incumbent Richard Nixon.

To most Democratic officials, McGovern's landslide defeat demonstrated that outspoken liberalism retained a limited popular appeal even
within the Democratic Party and was thoroughly unacceptable to a majority of the American electorate. Whatever enthusiasm McGovern's
nomination evoked from students, hippies, feminists, gays and lesbians,
and culturally liberal professionals was outweighed many times over by
his alienation of the larger social groups that supplied the Democratic
Party with the votes it needed to win national elections. Even some of
McGovern's own supporters acknowledged this problem in retrospect.
Campaign strategist Frank Mankiewicz later complained that the campaign was "always subject to this pressure from the cause people. We
reacted to every threat from women, or militants, or college groups. If
I had to do it all over again, I'd learn when to tell them to go to hell."[117] As
George Miroff observes, McGovern's defeat "stigmatized the left wing of
the Democratic Party for the next generation and became a rationale for
the party's drift to the center. . . . Many Democratic leaders, among them
McGovern campaign alumni, were drawn after 1972 to the pragmatic
position that the party must shed its association with liberalism to survive
in the emerging conservative era."[118] Indeed, the McGovern campaign's
Texas state coordinator was a young law student named Bill Clinton who,
two decades later, became the most prominent and successful of the "New
Democrats" seeking to move the party in a more moderate ideological direction in order to expand its popularity.

The specter of McGovern's defeat, according to Miroff, has reinforced
the asymmetry between the parties: "[Liberals] erupt in frustration election after election that their party, unlike the Republicans, does not stand
for firm principles. Originating in the trauma of 1972, the Democrats'
identity crisis reflects a party afraid it will pay the kind of price that
George McGovern paid if, like him, it says what it believes."[119] Yet attempts by election-minded Democratic leaders to keep their traditional
coalition together faced challenges well beyond McGovern's campaign.
The Democratic big tent could only stretch so far; according to one historical survey, the absorption of the 1960s-era social movements into
the party "delivered the final blow to the New Deal order by opening a

gaping hole between two vital Democratic party constituencies," separating blacks and liberals from white Southerners and cultural conservatives. Consequently, "the Democratic party lost its majority status as well as its ability to define the nation's political agenda."[120]

The party also suffered from diminished public enthusiasm for economic redistribution after the 1960s. According to historian Jefferson Cowie, "the new occupational opportunities for women and minorities arrived just as the call for broad economic justice was in decline. The result was heightened competition for dwindling opportunity. The political calculation shifted in the sixties and seventies from changing the division of the pie to making sure everyone had an equal chance to compete for a slice."[121] Democrats still advanced New Deal–style economic policies until the early years of the Jimmy Carter presidential administration (1977–1981), including proposals for full employment through national planning that included giving the jobless the right to sue the government.[122] But Carter abandoned these efforts in the face of opposition from other Democratic constituencies.

In the absence of a broad internal movement with the power to enforce ideological discipline within the party, Democratic leaders attempted to keep this new group coalition satisfied by making specific policy concessions while resisting efforts to associate the party with either left-wing economics or unapologetic cultural progressivism, both judged ballot-box poison in the wake of the McGovern defeat. As Katznelson observed, "[In] the absence of either an engaged working-class social base . . . or realistic prospects for social democratic policies, the party embraced interest group pluralism as the only coherent strategy available. As a result, it found itself vulnerable to charges that it was nothing more than a holding company for special interests."[123] In the process, the poor and industrial unions lost influence within the party to newer movements constructed around social identity. For example, today's Democratic politicians celebrate United Farm Workers co-founder Cesar Chavez (1927–1993) as a hero of Latino political engagement rather than as a leader for unionization and economic equality.[124]

The Democratic Party focused on building single-issue groups, which became its dominant constituency representatives. The Ford Foundation initially funded 16 public interest law firms with different perspectives,[125] and this network connected with government officials, coming to play a large role in the rights revolution.[126] Ralph Nader founded a series of Washington lobbying organizations to battle business interests in every sector. By 1980, these groups and others that copied their approach were institutionalized participants, each in a different policy area.[127] Even originally generalist groups like Common

Cause developed a specific agenda focused on open government and campaign finance.

The various social movements of the 1960s became institutionalized in an array of interest organizations representing specific identities. In addition to more than 100 organizations representing racial and ethnic groups, this populous associational universe today includes the National Organization for Women and the National Abortion Rights Action League for women's rights; the Human Rights Campaign for gay rights; and the Sierra Club, World Wildlife Fund, and League of Conservation Voters for environmentalism. In contrast to the fusionist, comprehensively ideological conservative movement, the extended network of the Democratic Party contains a plethora of specialized groups that each make their own separate demands on candidates and elected officials. In order to be a "card-carrying" American liberal, it is necessary to have a particularly roomy wallet.

These groups and their affiliates achieved significant success in shaping Democratic policy. As Teles notes, "The new Democratic Party that emerged by the mid-1970s ... incorporated interest groups and social movements that had once defined themselves in opposition to the party. A loosely coordinated network that bridged state and society ... came into being as these activists moved into the professions, foundations, educational organizations, and the media."[128] Each issue network, including executive agencies, elite institutions, and advocacy groups, expanded its issue agenda and sought incremental progress toward its goals.[129] Yet Mayer found that the new movements "seemed just as structured around group appeals as [their] supposedly out-moded predecessor."[130]

Political scientist Theodore Lowi famously declared the results as "the end of liberalism" in a 1979 book of the same name, arguing that government had devolved into a system of satisfying client groups in each policy domain. Later scholars perceived a transformation rather than a decline of left-of-center activism. As Jeffrey Berry's book *The New Liberalism* (1999) begins, "One of the truisms of American politics is that liberalism is dead. Labor is weak; the welfare state has collapsed. . . . But liberalism is not dead. . . . [It has] changed its stripes. Today American liberalism stresses culture, status, life-style, morality, and rights. . . . Citizen lobbying groups are the moving force behind modern liberalism."[131] According to Berry,

The success of conservative Republicans in elections since 1980 may have been enough to cause the traditional liberals' decline. It seems plausible, however, that advocacy aimed at promoting economic equality has been adversely affected by the rise of environmentalism, consumerism, and other liberal, postmaterial causes. . . . [I]t may be that [white-collar] Ralph Nader liberalism helped to crowd out [blue-collar] Hubert Humphrey liberalism.[132]

Nader himself did not claim such a victory; in 2000, he broke with the Clinton-era Democratic Party over its business-friendly policies, running for president as the nominee of the Green Party.

The idealistic left remains politically fragmented. A sociological review found significant "institutional weaknesses on the [American] left," including limited organizations within the Democratic Party, in unions, among the working class, and in grassroots organizing.[133] According to Kazin, when the left has won, that victory has "never occurred under its own name."[134] Even protesters have been divided by identity in ways that fit the Democrats' interest group politics: activists include "adherents to an ever-expanding variety of causes—black freedom, Chicano rights, women's liberation, gay liberation, the rights of the disabled, and more."[135] Whereas the New Right activists of the 1960s became involved in Republican campaign politics and conservative groups, New Left activists mostly retreated to academia and journalism.[136] They made considerable inroads in universities but again divided into distinct demographic categories, helping to institutionalize the focus on identity across social science and humanities departments.[137] The activists who did remain politically involved, according to Isserman and Kazin, divided by issue area: "By the 1980s, left Democrats represented a variety of 'single-issue' movements—black, Chicano, feminist, environmentalist, peace, gay and lesbian, and elderly—as much as they did the party apparatus itself."[138] The Democrats gained policy success in many issue areas—especially in advancing the rights of identity groups—by effectively integrating a growing list of constituencies with separable concerns into a functional popular coalition.

The contemporary Democratic Party, though increasingly united around left-of-center positions on specific political issues, has continued to resist identification with liberalism as a symbolic partisan cause. Rather than developing political positions from first principles and philosophical creeds, Democrats continue to address the concrete agendas of discrete social groups, preferring a governing style of technocratic incrementalism over one guided by a comprehensive value system. The Democratic activist base uses its influence over candidates and elected officials to further the interests of the party coalition's constituent elements—such as the internal pressure that persuaded Barack Obama to reverse his public position on same-sex marriage during the 2012 presidential campaign (though Obama, a typical Democratic pragmatist, did so only after his political advisors concluded that he would not seriously damage his chances of winning a second term in office).

But Democratic politicians are notably less vulnerable than their Republican counterparts to accusations of ideological infidelity. Leftist activism in America not only commands a much smaller popular base than does analogous mobilization on the right, but is also weakly and intermittently engaged in the world of practical politics—as exemplified by the Occupy movement (founded in 2011), which attempted to rally public sentiment in opposition to economic inequality but soon disappeared into a haze of postmodern theorizing that rejected policy specificity, organizational structure, or constructive engagement with partisan and electoral institutions.[139] As journalist and activist Harold Meyerson lamented in 2016, the "tragic-comic history of the American left" amounts to "a largely marginal tendency in American politics that has often squandered its moments of opportunity with displays of purity and rigidity that have only left it more marginal."[140] More than half a century after its founding, there remains no true liberal counterpart to the American conservative movement, leaving the social group–dominated Democratic Party to evolve along its own unique path.

ASYMMETRY IN AMERICAN PARTY DEVELOPMENT

In addition to fitting narrative historical reviews, party asymmetry is also consistent with systematic studies of party development focused on party organizations and internal factions. To illustrate, Table 3-1 summarizes factions within each political party since the mid-20th century, as identified by Daniel DiSalvo (2012) and party responses to presidential election defeats, as identified by Philip Klinkner (1994). For reference, we include the margin of each presidential election victory in the popular and electoral vote and update these scholars' categorizations with the addition of the Tea Party faction and our assessments of losing party responses since 1996.

DiSalvo identifies internal factions that actively attempt to control the organizations and presidential nominations of each party. He recognizes three party factions that successfully influenced the Democratic Party: Populist Democrats in the early 20th century,[141] Liberal-Labor Democrats at midcentury, and New Politics Democrats in the 1960s and 1970s. He also finds two Democratic factions that did not succeed: the Southern Democrats (active through 1976) and the New Democrats (active from 1988 to 2004). DiSalvo classifies the Liberal-Labor Democrats and New Politics Democrats as both having a "target constituency," or interest group within the party. According to DiSalvo, the Liberal-Labor faction "tended to push controversies over ideological commitments to the background,"[142] while New Politics Democrats helped remake the party around identity politics. Later, New Democrats

Table 3-1 PRESIDENTIAL ELECTIONS, LOSING PARTY RESPONSES, AND PARTY FACTIONS

Election Year	Electoral Vote Margin	Popular Vote Margin	Losing Party Responses		Democratic Factions				Republican Factions		
			Democratic Response	Republican Response	South	Liberal-Labor	New Politics	New Democrats	New Right	Liberal	Tea Party
1956	72.3%	15.5%	Policy		▓	▓				▓	
1960	15.6%	0.2%		Organizational	▓	▓				▓	
1964	80.7%	22.6%		Organizational	▓	▓	▓		▓	▓	
1968	20.4%	0.7%	Procedural		▓	▓	▓		▓		
1972	93.5%	23.2%	Procedural		▓	▓	▓		▓		
1976	10.6%	2.1%		Organizational		▓	▓		▓		
1980	81.8%	9.7%	Procedural/Organizational			▓	▓		▓		
1984	95.2%	18.2%	Procedural/Organizational			▓	▓		▓		
1988	58.6%	7.8%	Procedural/Organizational			▓	▓		▓		
1992	37.5%	5.6%		Organizational				▓	▓		
1996	40.9%	8.5%		Organizational				▓	▓		
2000	0.9%	−0.5%	Organizational					▓	▓		
2004	6.5%	2.5%	Organizational					▓			
2008	35.7%	7.3%		Organizational				▓			▓
2012	23.4%	3.9%		Organizational				▓			▓

Characteristics of each presidential election campaign, the responses of the losing party (indicated by shading). Losing party responses are updated from Table 16 of Klinkner (1994). Intra-party cactions are updated from DiSalvo (2012). Electoral College data, popular vote margin and losing party response after 1996, and the Tea Party faction were added.

attempted to move the party toward the ideological center, characterizing it as "expert at satisfying various constituencies but inept at promoting an overall notion of the public interest"; they were, however, inhibited by the lack of a powerful sympathetic constituency within the party.[143]

According to DiSalvo, only one faction, the New Right, was successful in transforming the Republican Party, notably pushing it in a conservative direction beginning in 1964.[144] Although the New Right included libertarians, older conservatives, neoconservatives, and the Religious Right, he finds that the faction's "central thrust was antistatism."[145] Rather than representing a single interest group constituency, it drew from the broader conservative movement. DiSalvo identifies 1968 as marking the effective death of the liberal Nelson Rockefeller faction's influence over the party. Rockefeller had warned of conservatives' "determined and ruthless effort to take over the party, its platform, and its candidates on their own terms" and later acknowledged defeat in his attempt to prevent such an outcome.[146] More recently, the Tea Party faction has encouraged a confrontational style of politics and moved the party even further to the right.

Klinkner analyzes party change by closely observing the responses of the Republican and Democratic national committees (the RNC and DNC, respectively) in the wake of presidential election defeats. He finds that Democrats have sometimes responded by changing their policy positions (in 1956) and sometimes by revising their organizational and electoral strategies (in the 1980s). The most common Democratic response, however, has been the enactment of changes to internal nomination procedures.[147] Most importantly, the Democrats implemented a wave of fundamental party reform after 1968 at the urging of the McGovern-Fraser Commission that included requiring written delegate selection rules; establishing affirmative action for the representation of blacks, women, and youth in state delegations; and prohibiting the winner-take-all allocation of delegates to candidates.[148] These reforms introduced a caucus- and primary-driven nomination process with a "de facto quota system" for demographic representation and delegates "much less connected to traditional power structures."[149]

Convinced that they could succeed electorally by better balancing their constituencies, Democrats again modified their procedures after losses in 1972, 1980, 1984, and 1988. The Democratic National Committee long maintained an official list of constituency caucuses, reforming them in 1982 to allow anyone with 10 percent of member signatures to start a new caucus; this produced a cascade of groups—Asians, liberals, lesbians and gays, businesses, Native Americans, farmers, Israeli sympathizers, the disabled, and European ethnics—all "clamor[ing] for recognition and seats on the executive committee."[150] Later, the party further reformed this system in an effort to avoid balkanization, but demographic constituencies remain an important component of Democratic organizational structure. Even when Democratic leaders implemented internal reforms intended to improve their electoral fortunes, the new procedures maintained recognition of the party's diverse constituencies. After 1980, Democrats sought to raise more money by establishing a business council, labor council, small business council, and women's council, but this operation, "much more so than the RNC's, was fraught with the same questions of voice and representation that had permeated the controversies over procedural reform since 1968."[151]

Republican Party responses were far less varied: every single response to presidential defeat focused on organizational reform related to electoral strategy. Republicans always sought to rebuild their party infrastructure rather than change their policy positions, satisfy competing internal constituencies, or reach out to new groups with targeted appeals. However, according to Klinkner, "The quest for inclusiveness that spurred much of the Democrats' procedural efforts is not absent in the Republican party. Many, if not most, Republicans want to broaden their party, particularly regarding women and minorities, but they are willing to do so only as long as these new entrants act as individual Republicans, rather than as organized groups."[152]

Republicans often interpret electoral defeat as a consequence of insufficient, rather than excessive, ideological purity. After incumbent Gerald Ford lost the presidency in 1976, Senator Jesse Helms—a supporter of Reagan's challenge to Ford in the presidential primaries that year—argued that "now more than ever, the Republican Party must be transformed to a broad-based conservative party," championing an organizational takeover of the "machinery of the party" by staunch conservatives.[153] This approach gained even more favor after conservative hero Reagan won huge popular and electoral vote victories in 1980 and 1984—with conservatives facing little internal or popular backlash.

Yet it may be most instructive to compare each party's response to a disastrous electoral performance. Both Goldwater and McGovern lost the popular vote by 23 percent, but neither party reacted by avowedly moving to the center. After 1964, even the liberal Republican faction focused on organizational responses by working through RNC chair Ray Bliss; Klinkner reports that it was "seemingly oblivious to the fact that the party's focus on such tactics had helped to diminish their influence over the previous four years."[154] The Democratic response after 1972 also "seems to contradict theories of victory-oriented parties," Klinkner observes. "[T]he regulars and the professionals, who one would think would be concerned only with winning elections, were in fact quite open to appeals to procedural fairness—even in the fact of massive electoral defeat and sharp reduction of their influence within the party."[155]

Since the 1990s, the RNC and DNC have become less important in party nominations, rules, and conventions. They now act as fundraisers, media spokespersons, and service organizations to the presidential candidates, who are usually selected well before the convention. But in 2008 the Democrats again faced charges of procedural unfairness in response to the role of "superdelegates"—party officials who retained voting rights at the national convention. The questions of internal democracy raised by these delegates' potentially decisive influence over a closely contested nomination contest were especially sensitive because of the well-defined rival demographic constituencies (women and African Americans, respectively) of candidates Hillary Clinton and Barack Obama. On the other side, after losses in 2008 and 2012, Republican activists quickly rejected RNC attempts to soften the party image by endorsing policies to attract racial minorities.

Differences in party positioning also appear in the most important presentations at party conventions: the nomination acceptance speech by the party's presidential candidate. Table 3-2 reports differences in the content of these speeches from our original content analysis of a random sample of speech excerpts since 1948. We coded each nomination acceptance speech paragraph for any mention of ideology or philosophical principles, social groups or interest groups, public policy, or symbolic imagery. We found that Republicans are somewhat more likely to mention principles than

Table 3-2 CONTENT OF PRESIDENTIAL NOMINATION ACCEPTANCE
SPEECHES SINCE 1948

Number of Mentions Per Paragraph	Republicans	Democrats
Ideology or Principle	.48	.41
Conservative (Republican) and Liberal (Democratic) Ideological Principle	.33	.2
Public Policy	.41	.58
New Policy Proposal	.07	.13
Social or Interest Group	.16	.28
Demographic Group (Class, Race, Religion, Gender, Age)	.07	.13
Combined Social or Interest Group with Public Policy	.06	.1
American Imagery	.56	.48
Claim of American Exceptionalism or Threat to American Way of Life	.24	.17

Data drawn from an original content analysis of a random sample of 1,000 paragraphs from all convention nomination acceptance speeches since 1948. We assessed each paragraph for mentions of each type. Our data, content analysis codebook, and analyses of reliability are available online at mattg.org.

Democrats, especially principles consistent with their party's ideology—in fact, 27 percent of paragraphs reference a conservative ideological principle. Republicans are also quite likely to use symbolic imagery draped in the flag, with 22 percent of paragraphs referencing American exceptionalism or a threat to the American way of life. (Since the table reports the average number of mentions, both numbers are higher because of multiple mentions of each type in the same paragraph.) Democrats are more likely to mention public policies and social groups, especially specific policy proposals and demographic groups, and to combine references to target constituencies and associated policies. The speeches of presidential candidates bear the marks of their party's distinctive priorities.

CONTEMPORARY AMERICAN PARTIES IN COMPARATIVE CONTEXT

In addition to examining history to understand the divergent trajectories of the two American parties, we can also gain leverage from international comparisons. The deeply ideological nature of the Republican Party renders it a consistent outlier in comparative studies of political parties. To illustrate, Figure 3-2 provides a summary of party

Figure 3-2 Comparative Ideological Placement of American Political Parties

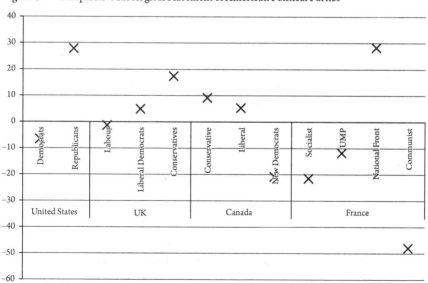

Conservative (high) or liberal (low) placement of the political parties based on the rhetoric in their party platforms. The data uses the most recent platforms and is based on a content analysis conducted by the Comparative Manifestos Project.

ideological placement based on a content analysis of platform language in the United States, United Kingdom, Canada, and France.[156] The Republican Party is significantly more conservative than center-right parties in these nations (and all others); in this group, the most similarly placed party to the Republican Party is the French National Front, a far-right nativist party. The Democratic Party is very slightly left-of-center in international terms.

This view of the Republican Party as an ideological outlier in international comparisons is confirmed by expert surveys that further differentiate among dimensions of policy conflict. Figure 3-3 illustrates the average placement of the two American parties on five different ideological scales in comparison to the international average across parties in 88 countries.[157] Across these dimensions, the Republican Party holds the most consistently conservative positions of any political party in the world.[158] Though parties like the French National Front score as more conservative than the Republican Party on the national identity dimension, even these other right-wing parties do not take equally conservative positions on economic redistribution, the role of the state, and public spending. The

Figure 3-3 Ideological Placement of American Political Parties on Several Dimensions

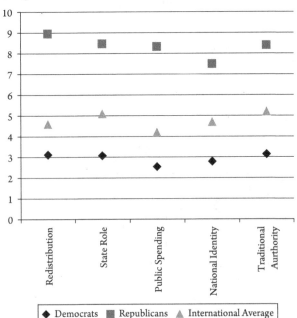

Conservative (high) or liberal (low) placement of the political parties based on expert coding. The Republican Party has the highest average conservatism of any party in the world. Data are based on a survey of experts in 88 countries conducted in 2008–2009 by Herbert Kitschelt and available via the Democratic Accountability and Linkages Project dataset.

Democratic Party rates as slightly left of the international average on all five ideological dimensions.

Because the American political system has only two competitive political parties (the fewest in the industrialized world), the Democratic Party also stands out in international comparisons—but not for its ideological consistency. Rather, compared to all other parties, the Democrats have assembled the broadest coalition of social groups and associated civil society linkages. Figure 3-4 compares each American party's group connections to the international average across parties (based on the same expert surveys). The Democrats are often rated as maintaining links to all six group categories tested: labor, business, religious, ethnic, geographic, and gender. The Republican Party is also more widely linked than the average party, but primarily because of its strong ties to business and religious groups. For both parties, these group links appear even though the expert survey questions were designed to assess the targets of clientelist exchanges. Neither the Republicans nor the Democrats are clientelist parties: they no longer offer government jobs or selective programs in exchange for party votes. But nonclientelist parties can still rely

Figure 3-4 Political Party Linkages with Social Groups

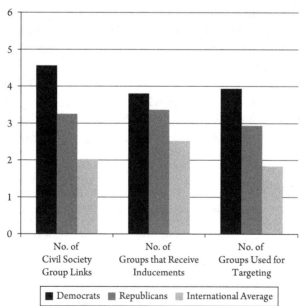

Number of civil society groups (out of six) to which political parties have links, to which parties provide target inducements, and through which political parties connect with target constituencies. The Democratic Party has the broadest social linkages of any developed political party in the world, with connections to unions, business, religious, ethnic, geographic and gender groups. Data are based on a survey of experts in 88 countries conducted in 2008–2009 by Herbert Kitschelt and available via the Democratic Accountability and Linkages Project dataset.

on group-based appeals because policy programs have disproportionate impacts on group interests.[159] If parties develop coherent agendas matching the perceived interests of their group coalition, they can sustain both types of linkage systems, although programmatic group-based appeals sometimes provoke a right-wing backlash and may be less consistent with conservative ideology.[160]

A comparative analysis of American parties is thus consistent with our historical account. The Republican Party's strongly ideological orientation, reflecting the role of the conservative movement in controlling its organizational network, is unique in the world. In contrast, the Democrats stand out in international comparison as a "big tent" party that incorporates a diverse array of groups, taking relatively moderate issue positions in comparison to center-left parties in other nations.

ASYMMETRY IN PARTY STRUCTURE

Partisan asymmetry is also visible in systematic analysis of the networks linking Democratic and Republican party organizations and officeholders to activists and interest groups. Quantitative indicators from a variety of studies demonstrate that the two parties' distinct historical orientations remain intact today, as exemplified by patterns of candidate endorsements. Theories of "extended parties" portray endorsements as the key mechanism by which party networks coordinate around favored candidates in an age when party committees and conventions no longer directly control the nominee selection process.[161] Yet Democratic primaries are more likely to produce wider competition over diverse group endorsements. Table 3-3 lists the number of national interest groups that issued endorsements in congressional campaigns prior to the 2002

Table 3-3 NATIONAL INTEREST GROUPS ENDORSING PRE-PRIMARY CONGRESSIONAL CANDIDATES

	Democratic Candidates		Republican Candidates	
	N	Percent of Total	*N*	Percent of Total
Economic	282	63.2	120	51.1
Identity	70	15.7	28	11.9
Single-Issue	69	15.5	62	26.4
Ideological	25	5.6	25	10.6

Number and proportion of national interest groups endorsing candidates of each political party in each category. Data drawn from an analysis by Casey Dominguez (2011) of the 2002 congressional elections.

primary elections.[162] More than twice as many interest groups were active in Democratic primaries than in Republican primaries. Unions dominated on the Democratic side, but there were also significantly more identity-based groups active in Democratic campaigns. The number of ideological groups was equal for both parties but constituted a larger proportion of the interests involved on the Republican side.

Table 3-4 provides a similar analysis of presidential primary endorsements since 1980, using data from Marty Cohen, David Karol, Hans Noel, and John Zaller.[163] Democrats have attracted more endorsements per contest, but these endorsements are more divided between the eventual nominee and other candidates (41 percent have gone to the winner versus 53 percent for Republicans). A greater proportion of Democratic endorsements come from groups—labeled "intense policy demanders" in the dataset—rather than individual party leaders. These group endorsements are more likely to favor the nomination winner in Democratic contests; only 5 percent of the total endorsements received by eventual Republican nominees came from such groups. Democratic candidates also draw support from demographic or interest group constituencies with which they share personal or policy identification, which the authors call "in-groups"; many of each candidate's endorsements in fact come from their own constituency.

The relative importance of groups within the Democratic Party is also confirmed by surveys of party convention delegates. Democratic delegates report many more organizational ties than Republicans, especially to organizations representing social group constituencies. Table 3-5 lists

Table 3-4 ENDORSEMENTS OF PRESIDENTIAL CANDIDATES

	Democrats	Republicans
Endorsements Per Contest	801	629
Endorsements Per Winner	325	333
Percent of Endorsements from "Intense Policy Demanders"	14.1%	8.2%
Winner's Percent of Endorsements from "Intense Policy Demanders"	12.0%	4.9%
In-Group Endorsement Types		
Race/Ethnicity	148	0
Religion	66	32
Gender	21	25
Interest Group	53	28

Number of endorsements received by all candidates and winning candidates from 1980–2004, along with the percent of endorsements that came from "intense policy demanders" and not party organization leaders. We also report the number of each type of in-group endorsements recorded. Data drawn from Cohen et al. (2008) and available at http://www.martycohen.net/5.html. The "intense policy demander" and "in-group" designations are available on the "extra variables" spreadsheet entitled "Endorsement+data.xls."

Table 3-5 ORGANIZATIONAL MEMBERSHIPS
OF CONVENTION DELEGATES

	Democrats	Republicans
2008 National Convention Delegates		
Political Memberships Per Delegate	1.22	0.9
Total No. Organizations Mentioned	238	184
Degree–Degree Correlation	0.353	0.101
Identity Organizations as Percent of Total	29%	20.1%
Ideological Organizations as Percent of Total	4.6%	8.7%
1980 State Convention Delegates		
Interest Group Memberships	1.57	1.06

Differences between the two political parties' 2008 convention delegates, as reported in a survey of convention delegates by Heaney et al. (2012). Degree–degree correlation measures the hierarchical concentration of organizational memberships (with numbers closer to 1 indicating that membership ties are less concentrated in a small number of organizations). The comparison from 1980 state convention delegates is based on information collected by Rapoport, Abramowitz, and McGlennon (1986). For more information, see http://bit.ly/M9vPUs.

characteristics of delegate organizational ties at each party's 2008 national convention. Individual Democrats average 35 percent more organizational memberships than Republicans, while Democratic delegates are collectively associated with 29 percent more organizations. Republican delegates disproportionately report membership in ideological organizations, whereas Democrats are more likely to cite an affiliation with identity-based organizations. Prior analysis of the structure of network ties in these data demonstrated that organizational ties are much more concentrated among a small number of groups in the Republican Party.[164] Democratic associational memberships, in contrast, are much more evenly dispersed among single-issue and identity-based organizations.

These findings are not specific to 2008 delegates. For comparison, Table 3-6 also presents data from a survey of 1980 state convention delegates across the United States.[165] Despite the different time period and level of government, Democrats exhibited much more organizational involvement than their Republican counterparts. This pattern is also evident in the 2000 national-level Convention Delegate Survey, which specifically asked respondents whether their activism within demographic or ideological groups was more personally important than their party activism.[166] A majority of Democrats identified their demographic group activities as more important; some Republicans also agreed (with the primary demographic group referenced by Republicans being geographic—usually their home state) but were more likely than Democrats to report that their activity on behalf of an ideological group was more important. In the 2012 wave of

Table 3-6 SHARED MAILING LISTS WITHIN EXTENDED PARTY NETWORKS

	Democrats	Republicans
Organizations in Extended Party Network	183	70
Mailing List Ties Between Organizations	318	96
Linked Interest Groups	44	7
Most Central Organizations	1. Americans for Democratic Action 2. *American Prospect* 3. Sierra Club 4. People for the American Way	1. *Human Events* 2. *National Review* 3. *Weekly Standard* 4. Republican National Committee

Differences between the two political parties' extended networks, as revealed by mailing list exchanges between organizations. Koger, Masket, and Noel (2009) collected these data by making donations to political organizations and candidates under different assumed names and tracking the other solicitations they received. Linked interest groups are those that were part of one of three party factions in each political party. See Koger, Masket, and Noel (2009, 2010).

the Convention Delegate Survey, Democrats were similarly more likely to report demographic and single-issue groups as their "most important" group, while Republicans were more likely to cite ideological groups.[167]

This divergent pattern of interest group involvement also appears in extended party networks. Gregory Koger, Seth Masket, and Hans Noel made donations to political organizations and candidates using different pseudonyms and recorded what other mail each "donor" received—a clever way to track shared mailing lists among Democrats and Republicans.[168] As Table 3-6 shows, donors to Democratic candidates and causes are rewarded with much more junk mail. There are more than three times as many shared mailing list ties on the Democratic side than among Republicans and 2.6 times as many organizations sharing contacts. Interest groups are a much more central part of the Democratic network, with six times as many interest groups in the major Democratic Party factions as there are among Republicans.[169] Interest groups, including those with single-issue concerns, top the list of most central organizations in the Democrats' extended party network. On the Republican side, ideological newsmagazines are the most central organizations sharing names. Republican party organizations exchanged their mailing lists with four media outlets and two candidates; Democratic party organizations exchanged their lists with nine interest groups, three media outlets, and three candidates.

A study of the employment histories of tax-exempt political (527) organization staff also found significant party differences.[170] The Republican Party network was relatively hierarchical, with more dominant roles played by party organizations and presidential administrations. The Democratic Party network included a broader role for unions and single-issue groups and was more internally divided by issue concern. Even when taking into account the frequent circulation of staff members through multiple affiliated organizations, it is clear that the parties maintain dissimilar informal infrastructures.

Republican organizational leaders are also much more likely than Democrats to weigh ideology heavily when evaluating potential candidates. A survey of 6,000 county-level party chairs asked respondents to describe their ideal candidate; nearly half of Republican Party leaders spontaneously mentioned ideology in their description compared to only 20 percent of Democrats.[171] When these leaders were asked to choose their preferred candidate among hypothetical alternatives that were randomized across many different candidate attributes, Republican leaders were 40 percent less likely to select candidates who were very liberal relative to their party, and ideology had a larger impact on candidate choice than any other attribute, including experience, background, and talents.[172]

These differences extend to the donor class. Table 3-7 summarizes attitudes expressed by campaign donors (defined as those who gave at least $200 during the 1990s) in each party. As measured by feeling thermometers, Republican donors expressed very positive evaluations of conservatives and very negative evaluations of liberals; Democrats maintained the reverse view but did not hold it as strongly in either case. Democratic

Table 3-7 FEELINGS OF DEMOCRATIC AND REPUBLICAN DONORS IN CONGRESSIONAL ELECTIONS

	Democratic Donors	Republican Donors
Average Feeling Toward Ideological Allies	70.7	78.9
Average Feeling Toward Ideological Opponents	23.8	13.7
Average Rating of Affiliated Interest Groups	57.6	47.3
Average Rating of Opposing Interest Groups	12.8	13.5
Candidate's Ideology Is Always Important	72.1%	80.4%
Endorsement from Group Is Always Important	16.1%	10.8%
Influencing Government Policy Is Very Important	69.7%	64.5%
Agree that Donors Are Motivated by Ideology	49.2%	67.3%

Average feeling thermometer ratings of Republican and Democratic donors toward their ideological allies and opponents (liberals and conservatives) and their average ratings across three interest groups on each side (Chamber of Commerce, National Rifle Association, and Christian Coalition on the Republican side; Sierra Club, National Organization for Women, and AFL-CIO on the Democratic side). We also report the percentage of Democratic and Republican donors that rated different factors as always or very important and the percentage that agree that donors are motivated by ideology. Results drawn from a survey of donors who contributed $200 or more to congressional candidates in 1996. Analysis by Francia et al. (2003), who provided us with additional data for this table.

donors felt more positively than did Republican donors about the interest groups affiliated with their party, though both expressed negative evaluations of the groups associated with the opposition. In choosing which candidates to support, Republican donors were more likely to say that (conservative) ideology is always important; they were also much more likely to agree that donors are motivated by ideological goals. In contrast, Democratic donors were more likely to view an interest group's endorsement as critical.

Recent research confirms that Democratic donors are more interested than Republican donors in demographic representation and less concerned with ideological fidelity.[173] Even among donors to organizations ostensibly designed to increase women's representation in public office, Republican supporters were focused on electing conservatives rather than increasing the share of female candidates. This matches a broader pattern among all party organization donors: Republicans aim to reduce the size and scope of government whereas Democrats wish to pursue a variety of single-issue causes. The Republican donor base is made up of ideological conservatives, whereas the Democratic donor base is a collection of policy issue activists, often motivated by social identity group concerns.

The difference in focus between the left and the right is also apparent in analyses of columnists in major newspapers and opinion journals. Based on Noel's content analysis of liberal and conservative opinion columns,[174] Table 3-8 reports the share of columns dedicated to general discussion of political ideology and specific domestic policy issues by writers on each ideological side (in the two most recent years of the dataset). Conservative columnists devoted more than three times as many columns to political ideology as left-leaning writers in 1970 and seven times as many in 1990. There was no consistent difference in the percentage of columns dedicated to domestic policy issues, but liberal writers supported about three times

Table 3-8 IDEOLOGY AND POLICY POSITIONS IN LIBERAL AND CONSERVATIVE OPINION COLUMNS

	No. of Domestic Policy Proposals Supported		Percent Covering Domestic Policy Issues		Percent of Opinion Columns on General Ideology	
	1970	1990	1970	1990	1970	1990
Liberal	23	28	31.5%	27.2%	4.4%	1.8%
Conservative	7	10	25.5%	33.9%	15%	12.6%

Number of policy positions favored by newspaper and journal opinion columnists and the percent of their columns that primarily cover domestic policy issues or the size and scope of government (ideology). Raw data drawn from Noel (2013) and recoded to create aggregate categories.

as many specific policy proposals.[175] In Chapter 4, we return to these data to document the differences in the columns' rhetoric and content.

The official platforms of the national parties also reflect their persistent asymmetry. Using data from the Comparative Manifestos Project, Figure 3-5 illustrates the differences in the share of each party's platform between 1936 and 2012 that was devoted to (1) general ideological rhetoric and (2) particular social group constituencies or public policies.[176] On average, 20 percent of the Republican platform was dedicated to discussing the size and scope of government, whereas Democrats allocated just 11 percent to the same subject. Policy positions and references to specific groups represented 43 percent of the language in the typical Democratic platform. Other analysis shows that Democratic platforms have long been more focused than their Republican counterparts on policies oriented toward minority social groups.[177]

We also conducted an original analysis of Democratic and Republican platforms since 1948. Table 3-9 summarizes the findings, reporting the average number of mentions of each type within a random sample of quasi-sentences. Republican platforms are more likely to discuss ideological principles, especially those that are consistent with their party's

Figure 3-5 Differences in Platform Discussion of Ideology and Specific Policies and Groups

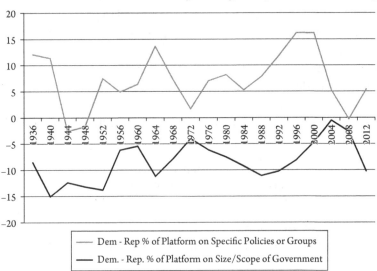

Three-year weighted mean (including .25 for both the prior year and the following year) of the percent of the Democratic and Republican party platforms that were dedicated to discussions of ideology (the size and scope of government) or specific social groups and public policies for all presidential elections since 1936. Some discussions fit into neither of these aggregate categories. Data were compiled from sentence-level hand-coding of party platforms by the Comparative Manifestos Project. The ideological indicator includes categories 203, 204, 301–305, 401, and 412–414. The social group and public policies indicator includes categories 402–404, 401, 504–507, 605, 606, 701, and 703–706. More information is available at https://manifesto-project.wzb.eu/.

Table 3-9 CONTENT OF PARTY PLATFORMS

No. of Mentions Per Sentence	Republicans	Democrats
Ideology or Principle	0.42	0.34
Conservative (Republican)/Liberal (Democratic) Ideological Principles	0.31	0.19
Explicitly Political Principles	0.37	0.27
Public Policy	0.65	0.73
Specific New Policy Proposals	0.18	0.26
Social Group or Interest Group	0.22	0.29
Combined Mentions of Social or Interest Group with Public Policy	0.12	0.15
Uses of American Imagery	0.16	0.14
Claims of American Exceptionalism or Threats to American Way of Life	0.06	0.04

Data from an original content analysis of a random sample of 2,000 quasi-sentences from all political party platforms since 1948. We assessed each quasi-sentence for the number of mentions of each type. Our data, content analysis codebook, and analyses of reliability are available online at mattg.org.

ideology and are explicitly political. Democratic platforms more often discuss public policy and social groups. The results generally match our content analysis of nomination acceptance speeches (from Table 3-2, discussed above), but both parties' platforms include more policy discussion and less usage of American imagery than the speeches. Nevertheless, each party difference is apparent in both written platforms and presidential candidates' speeches.

INTEREST GROUPS AND VOTING BLOCS IN PARTISAN SUPPORT COALITIONS

The enduring structural differences between the parties arise from and reinforce the electoral voting blocs and associated interest groups that constitute each party's base of support. In the 1930s, the Democrats produced a sizable national majority known as the New Deal coalition by cobbling together a group of disparate economic, demographic, and regional constituencies and satisfying the demands of their various political leaders.[178] Although political issues and identities have evolved since the 1930s, there is considerable continuity in the general character of the two parties' popular coalitions.

Table 3-10 summarizes the popular party coalitions in recent presidential elections. African Americans, fully integrated into the electorate by the Voting Rights Act, represent a significant and now even

Table 3-10 SOCIAL GROUP COALITIONS OF THE PARTIES
IN THE ELECTORATE

Republican Coalition

Percentage of Group Voting Republican

Groups	Percentage of 2012 Electorate	2012	2008	**2004**	**2000**	1996	1992
Whites	72	59	55	**58**	**54**	46	40
White Protestants	39	69	65	**67**	**63**	53	47
Married	60	56	52	**57**	**53**	46	41
Suburbanites	47	50	48	**52**	**49**	42	39

Democratic Coalition

Percentage of Group Voting Democratic

Groups	Percentage of 2012 Electorate	**2012**	**2008**	2004	2000	**1996**	**1992**
Blacks	13	**93**	**95**	88	90	**84**	**83**
Latinos	10	**71**	**67**	56	67	**72**	**61**
Asians	3	**73**	**62**	56	54	**43**	**31**
Jews	2	**69**	**78**	74	79	**78**	**80**
Nonreligious	12	**70**	**75**	67	60	**59**	**62**
Union Household	18	**58**	**59**	59	59	**59**	**55**
Big City Residents	11	**69**	**70**	60	71	**68**	**58**
Gays, Lesbians, Bisexuals	5	**76**	**70**	77	71	**71**	**72**

Percentage of each group voting for each party according to national exit polls, 1992–2012. Bold numbers indicate years in which the party won the electoral vote.

more loyal Democratic constituency despite their low levels of symbolic liberalism. Democrats' large share of the vote among the rising population of Latinos represents another significant bloc, and the party also receives significant support from religious minorities, especially those alienated by the religious right.[179] Jews, whose socioeconomic attributes and foreign policy opinions might suggest Republican leanings—and who do not necessarily ally with parties of the left in other nations—are reliable Democratic constituents.[180] Union households, though a dwindling share of the electorate, provide another Democratic voting bloc, as do urban residents and gays and lesbians. As feminists have developed a policy agenda and sought representation within the Democratic Party, single women have become another reliable party constituency.[181]

The Republican Party draws its mass support from constituencies that are more populous than pro-Democratic groups but usually tilt less decisively toward their favored party. Whites increasingly vote Republican, though less heavily than nonwhites vote Democratic. Restricting the analysis to white Protestants reveals a smaller group with more intense support, rivaling that of some Democratic constituencies. Evangelicals, in particular, have consistently voted decisively for Republicans—except during the 1976 presidential election, when significant numbers defected to Jimmy Carter, a born-again Southern Baptist. Republican nominees also usually prevail among married voters, but their advantage is not overwhelming. While suburbs were once reliable bastions of Republicanism, since the 1990s Republican candidates do not always carry a majority of suburbanites and often do better among rural voters.

Most citizens think of big business as the primary group active in Republican politics. Corporate America lacks a significant supply of popular votes, but executives and affiliated political action committees (PACs) do provide substantial financial support to the party. Yet business support has sometimes been divided. A business bloc was aligned with the New Deal and supported Democrats in favor of trade liberalization and union accommodation.[182] Eastern businesses supported Kennedy during his presidency, as he advanced their trade, tax, and antitrust agenda.[183] Johnson assembled a broad business base against Goldwater, including several Eisenhower-supporting executives frightened by the Republican challenger's extremism.[184] Even in 1980, some business leaders defected from Reagan.[185] In the 1990s, Bill Clinton led a concerted effort by the national Democratic Party to court business support.

The conservative movement was historically skeptical of close ties to business even while it relied on large financial contributions from businesspeople regarded as allied true believers. Hayek built the Mont Pelerin Society with business contributions but wanted to avoid co-option or "even the appearance of being dependent on any material interests."[186] After facing early troubles related to ties to businesses with short-term interests who had adapted to active government, the conservative legal movement tried to accept financial support but commit only to its own broader agenda.[187]

Business groups have become more politically mobilized since the 1970s: they numerically dominate Washington lobbying and maintain an extensive network of PACs that direct most of their financial support to Republican candidates. Yet their resources often shift to Democratic incumbents when they control Congress, and business-allied contributions have slowly supplanted donations from unions as a source of funding for Democratic campaigns.[188] With the K Street Project of the 1990s and early 2000s, Republican congressional leaders tried, with some success, to generate a firm commitment from business lobbyists to hire Republicans and support the party's candidates.[189] But although many Republican financial benefactors rely on business as the source of their wealth, they give to party candidates for ideological reasons rather than instrumental benefit. Following loosened legal restrictions on political money, a number of wealthy conservatives and libertarians—such as the well-known donors Sheldon Adelson, Foster Friess, and the brothers Charles and David Koch—have spent millions of dollars on electoral campaigns, super PACs, think tanks, and other political causes that favor their ideological commitments, far exceeding any direct financial return that they would likely receive. Hollywood liberals serve a similar role in the Democratic Party, representing an important financial constituency but not a populous voting bloc.

Republicans have been far less successful than Democrats in mobilizing interest groups that represent public constituencies. Figure 3-6 displays the number of advocacy groups mobilized in Washington, divided by ideological orientation and the kind of public groups they claim to represent.[190] Although (mostly Republican-leaning) business groups are much more plentiful, most issue groups are aligned with the Democrats. A much greater proportion of conservative groups take a broad ideological perspective, but liberals have mobilized both broad groups and an astounding array of single-issue groups. Figure 3-6 categorizes the

Figure 3-6   Percent of Advocacy Organizations and Political Staff by Ideology and Type

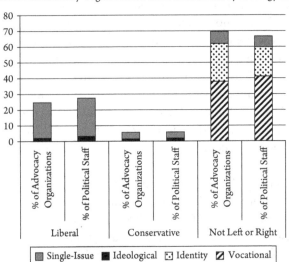

Percentage of Washington advocacy organizations and political staff in each category in 2005. Data collected by Matt Grossmann and reported in Grossmann (2012).

identity-based groups as nonideological, but most of these groups represent social minorities and operate like liberal single-issue groups.

Liberal groups also have more staying power: in an analysis of congressional hearings from three different years, Berry found only two conservative groups that were involved in hearings in 1979 and 1991, and only one (the National Rifle Association) active in 1963 as well; in contrast, there were 18 liberal groups involved in hearings in both 1979 and 1991, and 9 involved in all three years. Many liberal groups were able to survive the departure of their original founder, whereas conservative groups served more often as personal political vehicles.[191] The extensive liberal single-issue and identity group infrastructure in Washington often matches the voting constituencies of the Democratic Party, with hundreds of advocacy groups claiming to represent the interests of the Democratic blocs listed in Table 3-3 and few claiming to serve that role for the Republican constituencies.

Democrats' broad interest group infrastructure emerges in electoral and policymaking linkages. Figure 3-7 illustrates the ties between interest groups that endorse the same candidates (gray lines) and those that support the same legislation (black lines) within each party, based on an analysis of pre-primary candidate endorsements in the 2002 congressional elections and of coalitions favoring or opposing specific legislation in the prior Congress.[192] Lines connect actors endorsing more than one of the same candidate or bill.

The Democratic network features a greater number of groups than the Republican network, while these groups reflect the party's ties to discrete mass constituencies—including those with specific issue positions, general economic interests, and social identities. The Republican network includes few central players, mostly businesses. The Democratic network contains dense ties across the issue spectrum for both candidate and legislative endorsements, and the Democratic Party also maintains strong links between its electoral and legislative coalitions, with the two types of network ties being strongly correlated. The diverse groups that unite to support the same candidates also collaborate in order to pass bills in Congress. The Republican Party lacks similar ties between its electoral and legislative interest group coalitions, relying instead on a broad conservative movement.

RACIAL POLITICS AND PARTY COALITIONS

Racial minorities constitute a significant and growing share of the Democratic electorate and are represented by a series of prominent interest

Figure 3-7 Interest Group Support Networks for Party Candidates and Legislation

(a) Democratic Network

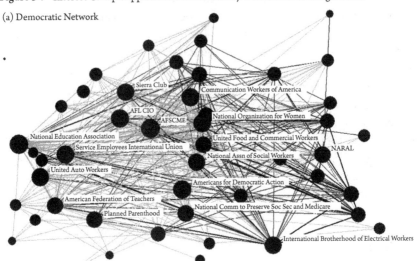

(b) Republican Network

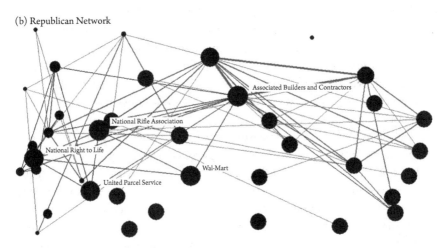

Ties between interest groups that support the same candidates (grey lines) and legislation (black lines) within each political party. The top network is composed of Democratic groups; the bottom network is composed of Republican groups. Lines connect actors that share one or more candidate or bill, with line width proportional to the number of ties. Size of nodes is determined by the number of coalition partners (degree centrality); nodes with more than 30 ties are labeled. Data from Dominguez (2011). See also Grossmann and Dominguez (2009).

groups affiliated with the party. Even though white voters are not as consistently Republican-leaning as nonwhites are pro-Democratic, and few organizations officially claim to speak for whites as a group, some Democrats perceive the Republican opposition as a party that is similarly defined by the salient racial identity of prejudiced whites. Before concluding this chapter, we wish to consider the changing historical role of race within the organizational structure of both parties, both within and outside the South.

From the 1930s to the 1950s, racial issues were largely engaged within the divided Democratic coalition, since the party then contained both the primary proponents (African Americans and northern liberals) and opponents (white southerners) of racial equality. Noel finds that the subject was discussed mostly in liberal media, with conservative interest in racial issues not peaking until a backlash against affirmative action and busing for school desegregation in the 1970s. The pattern was similar, but more strategic, among legislators: "Race [was long] an internal struggle among progressives, and one that was probably of low priority. In Congress . . . Republicans used race strategically to embarrass Democrats. Neither party raises the issue often."[193] Even when pro-segregation arguments encompassed conservative themes such as antistatism, opposition to judicial activism, and support for states' rights, the conflict remained largely an internal battle among Democrats prior to the partisan realignment of the South.

Over the same period, however, leaders of the conservative movement were quite aware that their own advocacy of a small-government, socially traditionalist philosophy would naturally appeal to southerners and racists, and some of them—most notably William F. Buckley—publicly defended the Jim Crow system. Although attacks by conservative Republicans on centralized government power long preceded the Republican Party's viability in the South, party leaders began to actively promote the congruence between conservative ideology and the interests of southern whites.[194] The national Republican Party's outreach to the South from the 1950s forward emphasized ideological conservatism and opposition to liberal northern Democrats.[195]

Yet Republican politicians adopted a message that could appeal to racial resentment without explicitly invoking racist appeals. By the 1960s, conservative Republicans like Barry Goldwater and Ronald Reagan were widely using the language of "color blind" policy, opposing Jim Crow racism as well as efforts to eradicate it via regulations on employment, housing, and education. Despite his national landslide defeat, Goldwater carried five states in the Deep South after opposing the Civil Rights Act of 1964 on federalist grounds. Nixon and Reagan accepted civil rights laws permitting formal equality but used similar rhetoric to attract southerners and white backlash voters. Southern evangelical Billy Graham, who led massive "crusades" aligned with Republican presidential candidates from the 1950s onward, endorsed the same language and agenda.[196]

By the 1970s, liberal legislative victories had moved the national debate over racial policy beyond the removal of legal segregation and the extension of voting rights in the South to a new set of initiatives designed to combat less formal barriers to equality nationwide. These new policy proposals, such as affirmative action and busing, were less popular with northern whites and inconsistent with traditional conservative ideology, producing increasingly united Republican opposition. Racial attitudes were also easily integrated into support for "law and order" responses to crime and unrest as well as opposition to urban corruption, welfare, and elite planning. Because most white southerners and many northern white ethnic constituencies already considered themselves conservatives, Republicans could attract their votes without voicing explicitly racist messages.

Historians have extensively studied these trends in racial politics. As Ronald Formisano found in Boston, white ethnic groups initially "practiced politics [not] as a way of maximizing the public good, but rather, in nonideological fashion, as a means to upward mobility by gaining status and patronage, and distributing jobs, favors, and contracts."[197] Conservatism fit somewhat naturally alongside their growing skepticism of elite planning; some anti-busing activists had previously opposed "highway construction, urban renewal, and airport expansion promoted by social engineers, bureaucrats, and above all, outsiders."[198] Busing plans to mix poor white ethnic enclaves and black areas were developed by elites and enforced by judges but were immediately unpopular and lost support over time, even among blacks.[199] Jonathan Rieder's analysis of racial backlash in Brooklyn concluded that northern desegregation produced a broader aversion to liberalism, which locals came to associate with "profligacy, spinelessness, malevolence, masochism, elitism, fantasy, anarchy, idealism, softness, irresponsibility, and sanctimoniousness," and support for conservatism, which they associated with "pragmatism, character, reciprocity, truthfulness, stoicism, manliness, realism, hardness, vengeance, strictness, and responsibility."[200] Of course, government policies had also subsidized and helped build white ethnic enclaves and the suburbs to which whites often fled, but voters were not moved by this fact.

The building of a Republican organizational and electoral infrastructure across most of the South did not occur until after the fight over legal segregation had been resolved and overtly racist sentiments had become less frequent in political rhetoric. This provided deniability for politicians who attempted to exploit racial resentment in more subtle ways but also allowed new constituents (including members of younger generations, northern migrants, and rural residents moving to the suburbs) to accept the small-government conservative message without consciously adopting its racial connotations. Southern segregationists had long voiced conservative themes of free enterprise and opposition to federal intervention, naming many of their groups taxpayers' or property owners' associations.[201] They attacked the Civil Rights Act as a threat to capitalism, a cause backed by foreign communists, and an infringement on individual rights. Lester Maddox, the last holdout of segregationist restaurant owners in Atlanta who later served as a Democratic governor of Georgia from 1967 to 1971, claimed that civil rights was a threat to "states' rights, constitutional government, individual freedom, and the American free enterprise system, racial pride, racial integrity, independence, the right to employ or be employed, freedom of speech, the right to buy, own, or rent property, and, yes, the right to live in a free country."[202]

The southern Republican Party inherited the region's racially troubled legacy but was also bolstered by the steady postwar migration of transplants from the North. These newcomers were often ideologically conservative but uninterested in preserving traditional southern heritage and actively repelled by overtly racist appeals. From the 1970s to the 1990s, half of all southern Republican identifiers and many of its new politicians were born in the North.[203] Newt Gingrich provides a useful example. As a native northerner who attended college in Atlanta in the early 1960s, he honed Republican messages for use in the exurban district he later represented. In an interview with Nelson W. Polsby, Gingrich presented a clear view of Georgia politics since he had moved to the state:

> You have a decisive shift of poor southern whites starting with Goldwater, which was essentially a racist reaction, combined with the emergence of. . . entrepreneurial, wealth, business oriented [people] . . . who see the Democratic Party as the party of labor, weak foreign policy, and confusion domestically . . . [but] not [in] a racist way, combined with the racist reaction against Lyndon Johnson and the Civil Rights Bill. The duality of these two could lead to . . . the emergence of a genuine network of Goldwaterites who permanently changed then to the Republican Party. . . . You've got a floating racist coalition, which was Republican on the national ticket but very Democrat locally. . . . You have the rising suburbanites who are Republicans unless the Republican gets too racist. . . . You have a wave of college-educated southerners merging with the influx of Yankees.[204]

Just as national political change forced southern segregationists to revise their rhetoric, Republicans produced a message that appealed to sincere conservatism as well as residual segregationist sympathies. As historian Kevin Kruse put it, "White southern conservatives were forced to abandon their traditional, populist, and often starkly racist demagoguery and instead craft a new conservatism predicated on a language of rights, freedoms, and individualism."[205] "Removed from their obviously racial origins," Kruse explained, "segregationist phrases, such as 'freedom of choice' or 'neighborhood schools,' as well as segregationist identities, such as the angry taxpayer or concerned parent, could be easily shared by middle-class whites who had no connection to the segregationist past but who gladly took part in crafting the suburban future."[206]

Southerners increasingly voted on the basis of their general ideological views and opinions on social welfare policy (rather than their racial attitudes), first in presidential elections and later in House and Senate contests.[207] As the South developed economically, newly rich areas contributed more support to the ascendant Republican Party than did the poor white areas with proximate large black populations that had served as the voting base for segregationist candidates Strom Thurmond in 1948 and George Wallace in 1968.[208] By the 1970s, the richest southern whites had moved away from the Democratic Party, whereas poor whites remained, matching the class division long present in the North; middle-income whites followed their richer counterparts into the GOP by the 1990s, making Republicans the dominant regional party in congressional as well as presidential elections.[209]

Today, whites who hold symbolically racist beliefs are more likely to find a home in the Republican Party, though racially influenced issue attitudes are equally common among white Democrats.[210] But the evidence does not suggest that conservatism is an inherently racist ideology or that Republicans are primarily attracted to their party on the basis of white solidarity.[211] Political scientists, though they disagree about whether white southerners subsumed their racial attitudes within a broader conservative ideology or simply abandoned their racial ties to the Democrats in favor of an ideological alignment with the Republicans, agree that these voters' contemporary partisanship is based on adherence to conservatism more generally, not their views on racial issues alone.[212] At the same time, Republican candidates are more likely than Democrats to use racially coded language and to express anti-immigrant views, which hampers their party's ability to attract popular support from nonwhite citizens.

The building of the modern conservative movement in the 1950s was not primarily motivated by racial animus, and its battles with moderates over control of the Republican Party did not principally involve racial disagreements.[213] However, many conservative movement leaders, including Buckley and Goldwater, opposed federal intervention in the South on behalf of civil rights, whether because of racist sympathies (as in Buckley's case) or because of opposition to the revocation of state and local authority (as in Goldwater's). Goldwater's 1964 presidential nomination permanently decimated what was left of the black Republican vote, which removed a constituency within the party in favor of continued support for, and prioritization of, civil rights programs. As the debate over racial policy moved toward more nationally controversial issues that provoked increasing white opposition across regional lines, Republicans were well-positioned to attract support from voters motivated by racial resentment, even though the party's positions could also be justified in ideological terms.

The decreasing prevalence of racial bias in the American public in the late 20th century did not produce a corresponding decline in popular adherence to conservatism more generally, further suggesting that the relationship between the two orientations is not a matter of simple equivalence. Yet the visible influence of white racism in partially motivating citizen opposition to the Obama presidency, as well as the role of anti-immigrant and anti-Muslim attitudes in fueling Donald Trump's unexpectedly popular campaign for the Republican presidential nomination in 2016, demonstrate that partisan and ideological conflict remains entangled with the continued presence of racial, ethnic, and religious prejudice in the United States. The stark and growing gap in racial diversity between the two partisan constituencies indicates that members of minority groups continue to overwhelmingly perceive their political interests as best served by the politicians and policies of the Democratic Party.

ASYMMETRY IN PARTY DEVELOPMENT AND NETWORKS

The two party organizations and their associated extended networks have distinct foundations, with the Republican Party serving as the political vehicle of a powerful conservative movement and the Democratic Party maintaining a big tent populated by a collection of social groups with particular interests. Both the conservative conquest of the Republican Party and the post-1960s evolution of the Democratic group coalition are well-documented historical developments. These essential differences and distinct trajectories are revealed in studies of party factions, rules changes, and nomination battles. The parties' different structures are also evident in their internal endorsements, extended networks, interest group affiliations, and platforms, as well as in the opinions of their activists and donors.

This evidence supports the view that the American parties are asymmetric, rather than the mirror images often assumed by previous theories. Although both parties contain extended networks, the Democratic Party matches the ideal type of a coalition of discrete groups that are "intense policy demanders" much better than the Republicans. The history of the GOP's adoption of conservative doctrine, in contrast, is much more consistent with accounts of ideological "coalition merchants" who consciously reshaped party constituencies; no comparable coalition-builders have been able to unite Democratic supporters around a liberal ideology and move the party broadly to the left.

On this point, the qualitative narratives of historians and the quantitative evidence supplied by political scientists are largely consistent with each other. They collectively represent a challenge to the simple account of symmetrical partisan polarization that is often assumed by contemporary political analysis. The popular depiction of polarization as a phenomenon principally driven by increasingly extreme elected officials and imposed on an ideologically innocent mass public ignores the extent to which conservative leaders and activists pursued a "middle-out" approach that exerted intellectual influence over elite policymakers while simultaneously building a grassroots movement. This coordinated mobilization of conservative sentiment successfully gained control of Republican organizations, articulated a philosophical and rhetorical alternative to programmatic liberalism and "establishment" centrism, and stimulated voters to participate in Republican primaries and general elections on behalf of conservative candidates.

On the Democratic side, the party's positions and priorities changed over time as its constituencies evolved—most notably, as it traded the working-class and southern electoral base of the New Deal era for a contemporary mass party increasingly led by racial and religious minorities, cultural progressives, and single and professional women. However, the collective convergence of Democratic leaders on a common set of issue positions more closely represents the emergence of a more internally compatible group coalition than it does the triumph of a broad liberal movement dedicated to a common vision of government's proper role in society. The contemporary Democratic Party therefore remains on the left, but not of the left.

CHAPTER 4

✧

The Not-So-Great Debate

As Barack Obama became the likely Democratic nominee for president in early 2008, national reporters began scrutinizing his past associations—with significant help from conservative media figures. Republicans (as well as Hillary Clinton supporters) sought to publicize Obama's ties to William Ayers, a founding member of the Weathermen (later Weather Underground), a radical leftist organization that planted bombs in government buildings in the early 1970s. After he avoided legal prosecution for his actions, Ayers abandoned violence but not left-wing politics. He became an education professor in Chicago, where he and Obama served overlapping terms on the board of directors of a charitable organization. Ayers contributed financially to Obama's 1996 state Senate campaign and hosted an fundraising event for Obama at his home.

American conservatives and British newspapers initially raised questions about Obama's association with Ayers, but several media fact checkers investigated and found little connection between the two men. In February 2008, however, *Politico* confirmed Obama's 1995 campaign function at Ayers's residence, attracting more attention from Obama critics. On their Fox News Channel (FNC) program following this revelation, Sean Hannity and Alan Colmes debated its significance with *National Review* writer Jonah Goldberg. "Why," asked Hannity, "would a presidential candidate be friendly with a man who declared war against the United States ... admits to being involved in the bombing of the Pentagon ... and that nobody in the mainstream media in this country has asked him that question?"[1] The Obama–Ayers association was then mentioned on at least 60 subsequent episodes of the *Hannity and Colmes* program before the November general election, stimulating additional coverage from

(130) Asymmetric Politics

other FNC hosts such as Bill O'Reilly and Greta Van Susteren. By the last few weeks of the 2008 campaign, FNC was discussing Ayers several times per day.

As Hannity suggested, the William Ayers story initially received far less attention from traditional reporters. Media critic Howard Kurtz noted that it was "all but ignored by the news media, other than Fox, until [ABC host George] Stephanopoulos raised it" in an April 2008 debate between Obama and Clinton.[2] Stephanopoulos, who had been a guest on Hannity's radio program the previous morning, asked Obama to explain his relationship with Ayers. Obama dismissed the significance of the issue, arguing that Ayers "is a guy who lives in my neighborhood, who's a professor of English in Chicago. . . . And the notion that somehow as a consequence of me knowing somebody who engaged in detestable acts 40 years ago, when I was 8 years old, somehow reflects on me and my values doesn't make much sense." The Obama campaign cited several mainstream news reports describing the connection as "phony, tenuous, and a stretch" but also pointed out that "Ayers is a tenured professor at the University of Illinois at Chicago and was a 'respected advisor' to Mayor Daley on school reform."[3] Obama's two-pronged response, minimizing his personal relationship with Ayers while simultaneously citing him as a credentialed policy expert, failed to deter the Clinton and McCain campaigns from repeatedly raising the matter.

Conservative rhetoric on the subject of Ayers remained elevated and impassioned. *National Review* writer Jim Geraghty suggested follow-up questions for Obama: "Do you, personally, know anyone who has ever tried to blow up the Pentagon? . . . [I]s that the sort of thing you could forgive, and/or dismiss? . . . Could you shake hands with this person? Go to a party at their house?"[4] Republican vice presidential nominee Sarah Palin argued that the Ayers connection was evidence that Obama is "someone who sees America . . . as being so imperfect that he's palling around with terrorists who would target their own country."[5] Conservative blogger Jack Cashill even claimed that Ayers had ghostwritten Obama's autobiography, *Dreams from My Father*, inspiring amateur investigations from online Obama critics and an attempt by a Republican member of Congress to prove Ayers's authorship.[6]

The 2008 campaign prompted similar controversies over Jeremiah Wright, the outspoken pastor of Obama's church in Chicago, and corrupt developer Tony Rezko, who had raised money for Obama's U.S. Senate campaign before serving a federal prison sentence on bribery and extortion charges. But Ayers's position as an academic provoked especially harsh attacks from conservative media figures such as firebrand Ann Coulter, who argued that "any other profession would have banned a person like Ayers. Universities not only accept former domestic terrorists, but also move them to the front of the line."[7] Right-wing critics portrayed Obama himself as a radical intellectual because of his former position as a professor of constitutional law at the University of Chicago and his previous experience as a community organizer.

In several respects, the Ayers controversy is a particularly revealing example of the current political information environment in the United States. The extensive conservative media ecosystem, which is a visible and increasingly influential force within American politics, is adept at publicizing claims and evidence that supposedly reveal the extremism, corruption, or incompetence of Democratic politicians. The repeated promotion of the stories themselves is usually accompanied by accusations that the facts are being ignored or suppressed by a "mainstream" media that acts as the conservative media's ubiquitous rhetorical foil; right-leaning commentators alternate condemnation of Democratic leaders with criticism of the reporters and broadcasters at major newspapers or television networks who allegedly slant their coverage in a liberal direction while maintaining the pretense of objectivity. Conservatives also frequently distrust claims of policy expertise that rely upon traditional academic or intellectual credentials, viewing universities as bastions of leftism and disparaging the views of "radical" professors. Democrats, in contrast, largely accept the authority of conventional news sources and academic institutions—thus limiting the popular appeal of an openly liberal alternative media universe of their own—and regard the conservative media as engaged in distortion, propaganda, and character assassination under the guise of journalism.

Republicans' reliance on conservative media to advance political arguments and Democrats' insistence on the importance of journalistic and expert neutrality in policing the spread of misinformation extend well beyond the 2008 campaign. The two parties have come to rely on different sources of information creation and dissemination: for Republicans, a consciously built network of media and research organizations created to spread conservative ideas to followers and counter ideologically hostile institutions; for Democrats, mainstream media outlets and scientific authorities that claim to be objective and nonpartisan. Rather than a "great debate" in which two sides engage each other over the optimal prioritization of values, identification of social problems, and evaluation of potential solutions, the American political world has developed separate partisan communities that largely talk past one another. When the parties' competing experts do interact, Democrats tend to rely on empirical evidence to select among policy alternatives in order to address societal challenges, while Republicans largely reject the premise of seeking government solutions, perceiving the constant effort by technocratic experts to find and address social problems as an ideological agenda embedded in the ostensibly "objective" realms of conventional journalism and academia.

This chapter investigates the unique influence of conservative media and the distinct uses of research evidence by party elites. We find that partisan identifiers and activists rely on different types of information sources. Republicans are more likely than Democrats to consume media that are openly aligned with their political orientation and to distrust other news outlets. The rhetoric of conservative media personalities is broadly ideological and uniquely coordinated with the aims of Republican officials and activists, producing a unified party message in both policy venues and public debate. The establishment since the 1990s of an explicitly conservative media ecosystem as a conscious alternative to "mainstream" journalism allows conservative writers and broadcasters to exert an influence over Republican officeholders and voters alike that has no true counterpart among Democrats. We also find differences in the content and impact of information sources on each side, which reinforce appeals to ideology among Republicans and policy analysis among Democrats. The two parties' voting bases and teams of officeholders collect policy information through different types of sources and employ it to advance distinct goals.

This structural imbalance in the information environment both reflects and reinforces the larger asymmetry between the parties. Republican perceptions of widespread bias in the mainstream media and academic community encourage party members to view themselves as engaged in an ideological battle with a hostile liberal establishment, turning even their choice of news sources into a conscious act of conservative self-assertion. Consumers of conservative media are exposed to a steady flow of content that further promotes this view, even warning that the Republican Party leadership is itself prone to intellectual corruption by this establishment and therefore requires vigilant ideological policing.

Democrats, in contrast, are relatively content to rely on traditional media and intellectual sources that often implicitly flatter the Democratic worldview but do not portray themselves or their consumers as combatants in a political or ideological conflict. FNC and conservative talk radio lack equally popular and influential counterparts on the left that openly advance the liberal cause or nurture ideological grievances against mainstream media outlets. Democrats therefore remain relatively unexposed to messages that encourage ideological self-identification or describe political conflict as reflecting the clash of two incompatible value systems. Instead, the information environment in which they reside claims to prize objectivity, empiricism, and policy expertise—thus remaining highly congruent with the character of the Democratic Party as a coalition of voters who demand practical solutions to social problems in the form of targeted government action.

LIBERAL DOMINANCE OF ACADEMIA AND THE MEDIA

Academia and the news media, the two social institutions traditionally responsible for creating and spreading information, are both dispropor- tionately populated by liberals and Democrats. Most journalists and pro- fessors do not view their proper role as furthering the advancement of a left-wing political agenda; their self-conception as legitimate intellectual experts instead reflects professional norms of disinterested inquiry and objectivity. Yet many conservatives have never accepted what they see as the self-appointed authority of these liberal elites; instead, they regularly portray media and academic institutions as politically biased and deserv- ing of challenge from explicitly conservative alternatives.

Both American academia and the independent media were the products of historical movements to define and elaborate systems of expertise with the aim of benefiting society. As Jonathan Ladd argues, "The existence of an independent, powerful, widely respected news media establishment is an historical anomaly. Prior to the twentieth century, such an institution had never existed in American history."[8] During the early 1900s, the American press abandoned its previously partisan and sensationalist character through journalistic professionalization. Joseph Pulitzer, a Democratic pol- itician and newspaper mogul who later established the Columbia School of Journalism (1912) and the Pulitzer Prizes (1917), personified this transfor- mation, forging a connection between modern journalistic practices and the rise of social science within universities by relying on the "scientific and apolitical notion of objectivity" and combining empiricism with expertise.[9] These ideas reflected the Progressive movement's distrust of partisan po- litical institutions: the neutral press was designed to provide citizens with an independent and accurate source of information to guide their political choices. As Don Wycliff, public editor of the *Chicago Tribune*, said much later, "[Reporters] may be liberals, but we have ideals of objectivity to which we aspire."[10]

Similarly, American universities and scientific associations established themselves during the early 20th century as venues for the independent creation of socially useful knowledge.[11] Disciplines established their own scientific processes for evaluating intellectual claims, while universities adopted norms of faculty and disciplinary self-governance. Yet academics continually faced pressure from business leaders and the public to more closely align their institutions with missions of civic education and workforce development.[12] Through some combination of conservatives' interest in other careers, active discrimination against conservative scholars, and the self-reinforcing process produced by academia's early reputation for liberalism, universities became disproportionately populated by liberals and have long inspired distrust from the conservative movement.[13]

Although an absence of comparable time-series data makes it difficult to assess changes in the extent of liberal dominance of the media and universities since the Progressive Era, more recent evidence validates conservative claims that both journalism and academia are liberal bastions. Figure 4-1 summarizes the party identification of journalists in surveys taken between 1971 and 2013. Democrats substantially outnumbered Republicans in the journalistic profession throughout this period, though the share of self-described independents increased over time. These surveys sometimes measured ideological identification as well (results not pictured), confirming that liberal journalists consistently outnumbered conservatives by substantial margins; in fact, more reporters sometimes identified as ideological liberals than as partisan Democrats.

Figure 4-2 draws upon two different surveys from 2004 and 2008 to further summarize the political ideology of journalists by type of news

Figure 4-1 Partisanship of Journalists by Year

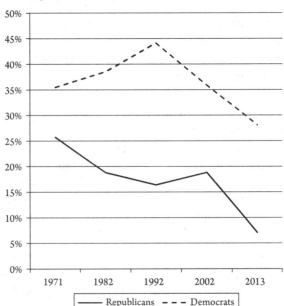

Data from Willnat and Weaver (2014).

Figure 4-2 Ideology of Journalists by Type

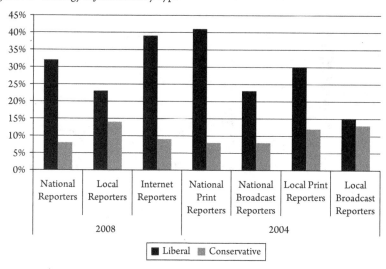

Data from Pew Research Center surveys conducted in 2004 and 2008, available at http://www.stateofthemedia. org/files/2011/01/Journalist-report-2008.pdf.

organization. Conservatives far outnumber liberals in the American public, but liberal reporters are more prevalent than conservative reporters at both the national and local levels and across print, broadcast, and Internet media. Yet the differences are less pronounced in local media and most dramatic among national print and Internet reporters. The prevalence of liberals in the journalistic profession does not itself demonstrate that news coverage is biased toward liberal viewpoints; given the clear skew of reporters' personal views, however, it is not surprising that Republicans voice more concerns than Democrats about the existence of partisan or ideological bias in the media.

Similar patterns are evident among college and university professors, especially scientists—the traditional producers of social knowledge. Figure 4-3 compares the self-reported ideological and partisan identification of professors (collected by Neil Gross in 2006) with that of the entire American public (drawn from the most proximate American National Election Studies survey). Professors are much more likely to be Democrats than Republicans (by a margin of 71 percent to 21 percent) and to identify as liberals than conservatives (52 percent to 29 percent). Strong Democrats are especially overrepresented among professors compared to the general public, while conservatives are quite underrepresented. As Gross argues, "Professors are not just garden-variety Democrats; many are extremely liberal Democrats. . . . [M]ost hold views that place them squarely to the left of most other Democrats nationally."[14]

Figure 4-3   Partisanship and Ideology Among Professors and the Public

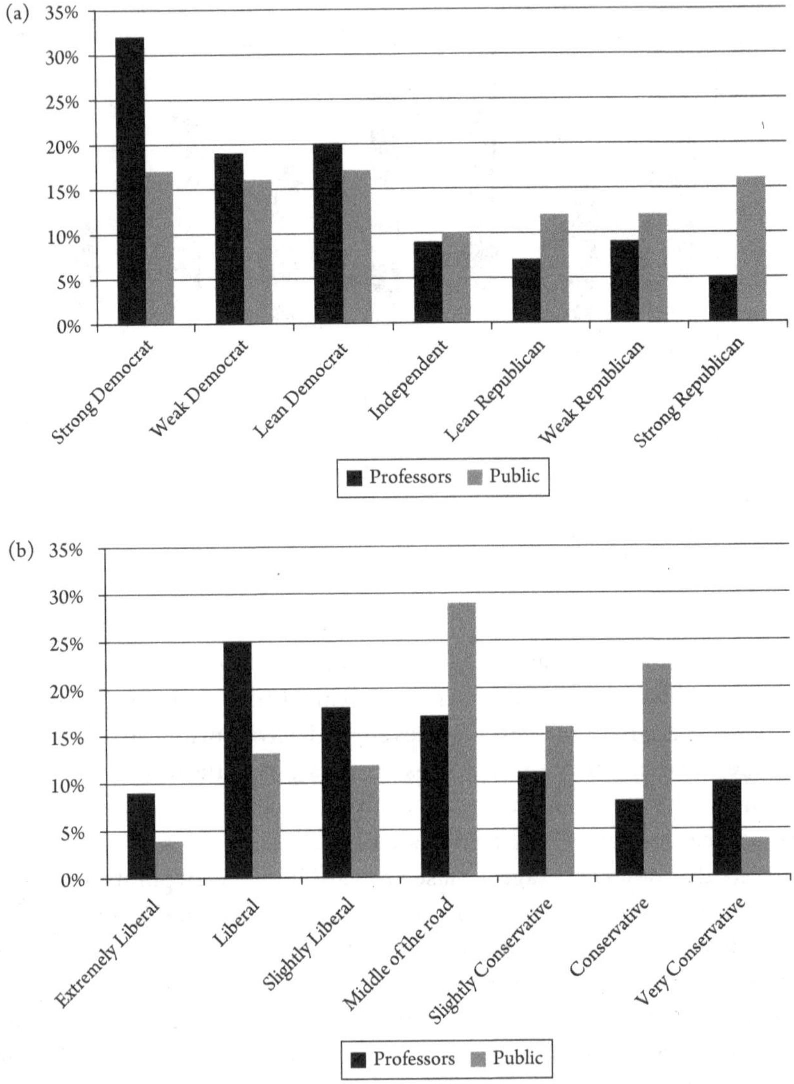

(a)

Categories (left to right): Strong Democrat, Weak Democrat, Lean Democrat, Independent, Lean Republican, Weak Republican, Strong Republican

Legend: ■ Professors   ■ Public

(b)

Categories (left to right): Extremely Liberal, Liberal, Slightly Liberal, Middle of the road, Slightly Conservative, Conservative, Very Conservative

Legend: ■ Professors   ■ Public

Data on professors from Gross (2013; data on public from ANES surveys, available at electionstudies.org.

Table 4-1 more fully distinguishes the political orientations of professors by general field of study and by some specific policy-relevant scientific disciplines. Although these data are from the same survey as those summarized for professors in Figure 4-3, they are not fully comparable because the only available measure was partisanship (with leaners classified as independents). Nonetheless, it is clear that Republican academics are much more common in applied fields like business, engineering, and health than they are in the natural and social sciences. Democrats

Table 4-1 PROFESSOR PARTISANSHIP BY FIELD AND DISCIPLINE

	Democrat	Republican
By Field of Study:		
Natural Sciences	53	14
Social Sciences	56	7
Humanities	55	11
Business	39	24
Engineering	28	23
Health Sciences	33	24
Other	59	11
By Policy-Relevant Discipline:		
Biology	51	7
Computer Science	32	10
Economics	34	28
History	78	4
Political Science	51	5
Psychology	77	8
Sociology	49	5

Data from Gross (2013.

far outnumber Republicans in some policy-relevant fields like biology, history, sociology, psychology, and political science—though economics provides a more balanced exception.

These patterns do not necessarily confirm that academic research or a university education reflect or transmit liberal or pro-Democratic views, though it is evident that conservatives have more reason to fear unfavorable political bias among scientists and professors than liberals do. It is likely that the collective left-leaning orientation of academics influences their intellectual output, even if implicitly or unconsciously. For example, social psychologists have recently amassed examples of the influence of widely shared liberal views on their discipline's findings and theories and have called for more political diversity in their field to reduce the danger of biased research, stimulating a large array of responses but provoking widespread agreement that the discipline is indeed dominated by liberals.[15] Their evidence suggests that, at least in some social sciences, political diversity is declining and liberal preeminence has become self-reinforcing over time.

Just as the conservative movement began actively critiquing academia in the 1960s, universities started to gradually shift further to the left. Any analysis of conservative suspicions of science and the media should thus begin with the acknowledgement that the right's perception of these professions as disproportionately occupied by liberals is no illusion.

Conservatives' justified skepticism of the political tenor of academia and journalism encouraged them to establish alternative institutions more conducive to their own views.

CONSERVATIVE DISTRUST OF THE MEDIA AND SCIENTIFIC RESEARCH

Although conservative elites have long viewed academia and journalism as hostile to their politics, it required a sustained effort to transmit that distrust to their public supporters and to promote alternatives. Republicans broadly perceived newspapers to be fair until the 1950s.[16] As Ladd explains, their attitudes changed because "criticism of the institutional news media was a defining characteristic" of the conservative movement that came to power with the Barry Goldwater presidential nomination in 1964; criticism of the press was "one of the basic characteristics of Goldwaterism."[17] The "attacks on the institutional media made by the Goldwater campaign and [later] the Nixon White House became a fixture of the conservative movement and Republican political strategy. Over decades, they played an important role in eroding the news media's stature."[18] Early attacks came not only from Republican elites, but also from evangelical Christian leaders and grassroots activists.[19]

In 1968, conservative political figures commissioned studies by independent academics to record and analyze nightly news broadcasts in order to demonstrate that the news media was biased against Republican politicians.[20] Activists also collected evidence that liberal guests regularly outnumbered conservatives on entertainment programs. The American Conservative Union soon created the Committee to Combat Bias in Broadcasting, while the watchdog organization Accuracy in Media was founded in 1969 to monitor the news for bias. The "white backlash" movements of the 1970s also viewed the media as part of "a liberal establishment arrayed against them," according to Ronald Formisano, even holding protests at the homes of newspaper editors.[21] Claims of a consistently unfavorable political slant in media coverage later became a dependable theme of conservative rhetoric. L. Brent Bozell III started the Media Research Center in 1987 to prove liberal media bias through research. In the presidential elections of 1988, 1992, and 1996, at least 92 percent of bias claims alleged a liberal or Democratic, rather than conservative or Republican, bias.[22] Claims of liberal bias also rose substantially from 1988 to 1996, with George H. W. Bush and his vice president Dan Quayle leading the charge. The 1992 Bush-Quayle campaign marketed a bumper sticker that

Table 4-2 MEDIA ARTICLES IN IDEOLOGICAL
JOURNALS, 1975–2005

	Positive	Negative	Neither
National Review	17	489	49
The Nation	11	239	17

Results from an analysis of data collected by Ladd (2011) and available at
http://www.jonathanmladd.com.

read "Annoy the Media, Re-elect Bush" and frequently complained about unfair coverage on the campaign trail.

Conservative media sources are particularly likely to accuse their "mainstream" counterparts of bias. Table 4-2 reports data collected by Jonathan Ladd on all articles about the media published in the conservative journal *National Review* and the liberal journal *The Nation* between 1975 and 2005. *National Review* published many more articles about the media over the period (by a margin of 555 to 267), with media coverage in *The Nation* heavily concentrated in 2003 (when many liberals viewed the media establishment as supportive of the Iraq War and the George W. Bush administration). As the table reveals, the tone of these articles was predominantly negative on both sides of the ideological spectrum.

Accusations of bias are more common in conservative broadcast media as well. One content analysis of the *Rush Limbaugh Show* conducted in 1996 discovered that Limbaugh consistently mentioned two topics, President Bill Clinton and the mainstream media, every single day during the year—with strikingly negative attitudes toward both.[23] Another study found that the media was "constantly discussed" by Limbaugh, appearing in more than 600 episode summaries between 1993 and 1995.[24] Other studies of conservative talk radio during the 2000s produced similar results.[25] Fox News Channel has long promoted itself in opposition to the liberal media, adopting "fair and balanced" and "We report, you decide" as its two most familiar marketing slogans (both of which pointedly imply a refreshing contrast with its mainstream competitors). One count found that the network used the phrase "liberal media" in more than 100 stories during 2009.[26]

Although scholars have not always found liberal bias in media content, they do consistently find that conservatives are more likely than liberals to characterize press coverage as unfair; these claims, in turn, have increased perceptions of bias in the American public.[27] As summarized by Figure 4-4, Ladd demonstrated experimentally that complaints about bias cause conservative Republicans to feel more negatively toward the news media. He presented respondents with assertions of bias by Republican

Figure 4-4 Effects of Claims of Media Bias on Feelings Toward Media

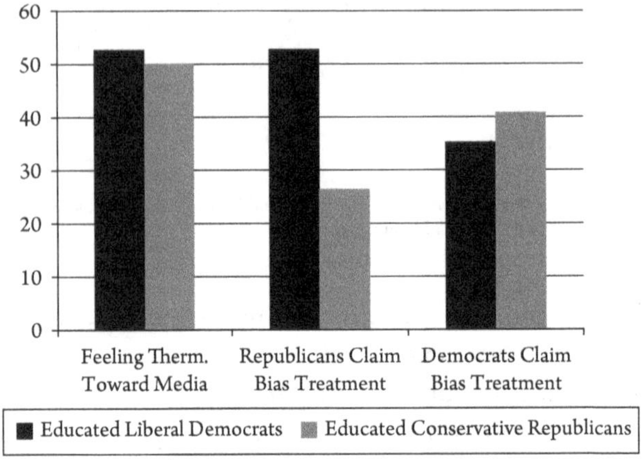

Data from Ladd (2011). Feeling thermometer toward media measured overall warm or cool attitudes.

and Democratic elites, finding that educated conservative Republicans were especially swayed by the elite messages.[28]

Natalie Stroud measured similar effects, showing that conservatives allege and perceive media bias more often than liberals, and that they adjust their candidate perceptions in response.[29] Another study found that mistrust of the news media was especially high among talk radio listeners.[30] Ladd shows that while popular confidence in the news media has decreased substantially over time among members of both parties, Democrats have long expressed more confidence in the media than Republicans, and the decline is "modestly larger among Republicans."[31] Figure 4-5 illustrates levels of reported trust in the news media among strong partisans between 1996 and 2004. Between 44 percent and 56 percent of strong Democrats trusted the news media "most of the time," whereas only 18 percent to 27 percent of strong Republicans did so. The ratio of strong Republicans to strong Democrats who "almost never" trusted the news media ranged from 2:1 to 5:1.

Republicans repeatedly voice concerns that the news media are biased against their party. Data from the Pew Charitable Trusts indicates that the belief that news organizations are "politically biased" rose from 49 percent in 1985 to 76 percent in 2011 among Republicans while only rising from 43 percent to 54 percent among Democrats.[32] Ladd's research used open-ended follow-up questions to assess the considerations that came to respondents' minds in answering generic questions about media trust. As Table 4-3 indicates, Republicans disproportionately cited political or policy biases in the mainstream media. Many Republicans, in fact, differentiate conservative media from mainstream media on this basis.

Figure 4-5 Percent Usually and Never Trusting the News Media Among Party Identifiers

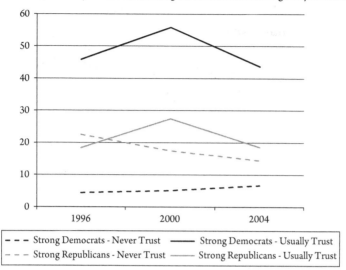

Percentage of strong party identifiers who said they trust the news media "just about always" or "most of the time" and the percentage who said they "almost never" or "never" do. Results are from American National Election Studies surveys conducted in 1996, 2000, and 2004.

Table 4-3 MENTIONS OF POLITICAL BIAS IN OPEN-ENDED
RESPONSES ON MEDIA TRUST

	Percent Citing Political/Policy Bias in Mainstream Media
Strong Republican	60%
Not Strong Republican	43%
Leans Republican	50%
Undecided/Independent	16%
Leans Democrat	30%
Not Strong Democrat	32%
Strong Democrat	29%

Percentage of each party category that reported political or policy biases in the mainstream media in an open-ended question about what came to mind when answering a question about media trust. Data originally from Ladd (2011). We collapsed his categories for Democratic bias, Republican bias, general bias, and Dan Rather into one bias category. We also re-coded the data to remove claims about biases in partisan media (e.g., "only Fox News is biased") and added responses that were coded as general negativity but consistent with specific claims about biased coverage of Bush administration policies (such as the Iraq War).

As one respondent told Ladd, "The news is very pro-liberal except Fox News," while another said that "the old mainstream media was so against President Bush. . . . I am glad there is Fox cable news."[33]

Figure 4-6 illustrates how conservative media and mainstream media inspire different degrees of trust among Republicans and Democrats,

Figure 4-6 Net Trust of News Outlets by Party

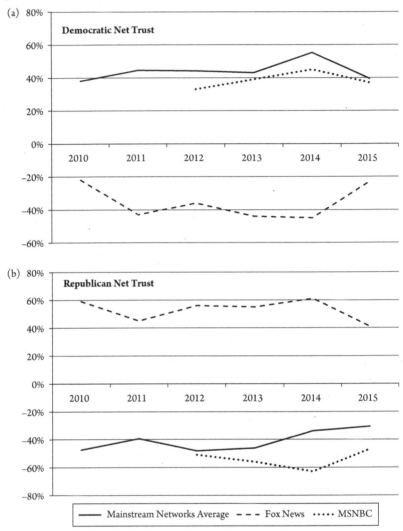

Results from Public Policy Polling surveys available at http://www.publicpolicypolling.com.

using data from a Public Policy Polling (automated) survey that has consistently asked respondents to evaluate broadcast media outlets since 2010. Figure 4-6 reports the net trust levels (percent trusting minus percent distrusting) for FNC and MSNBC along with an average of ABC, CBS, NBC, and PBS, separating Republican from Democratic respondents. Democrats consistently trust rather than distrust mainstream media outlets by a margin of approximately 40 percentage points and are slightly less trusting of MSNBC in comparison (even though it is known as a liberal network). They distrust FNC by margins ranging from 20 to 40 points. Republicans, in contrast, only trust FNC. Net trust of Fox varies from 40 to 60 points, while significantly more Republicans distrust than trust mainstream media outlets (by margins of approximately 40 points); MSNBC produces even stronger negative ratings from Republicans.

Conservatives' near-exclusive trust in Fox as a source of political information is confirmed by a broader survey of media attitudes conducted by the Pew Research Center.[34] Despite using an issue-based measure of conservatism rather than ideological self-identification, Pew found that consistent conservatives as a group trusted only 8 out of 36 possible news outlets, while consistent liberals trusted 28 of the same sources. The only outlets collectively trusted by conservatives were FNC; the *Wall Street Journal*; the radio programs of Sean Hannity, Rush Limbaugh, and Glenn Beck; *Breitbart*, the *Drudge Report*, and *TheBlaze* (Beck's website and television channel). Consistent liberals trusted a much wider range of sources, with National Public Radio, PBS, the BBC, and the *New York Times* topping the list.

Ladd shows that distrust of the news media has important political effects. Distrustful citizens are "more resistant to new information and rely more on their predispositions when forming perceptions of the world around them. As a result, they heavily weigh their partisanship when voting."[35] The availability of conservative media outlets creates a self-reinforcing cycle, increasing these differences: "At least for Republicans, alternative news outlets are an avenue through which elite rhetoric reduces trust in the institutional news media." [36] Distrusting conservatives seek out conservative news sources, which present them with more reasons to dismiss the coverage of mainstream outlets. This pattern is no accident: conservative leaders mobilized beginning in the 1950s to challenge what they considered the "liberal hegemony" of information providers, consciously developing a movement for alternatives through direct mail, talk radio, FNC, and media training programs.[37]

Similar dynamics have occurred in the domain of academia and scientific research. In a self-reinforcing process, conservatives have come to distrust ostensibly nonpartisan scientists and professors while creating an alternative research infrastructure for policy debate—providing the movement with an alternative network of policy experts that further undermines the standing of the academic community in the eyes of the right. Beginning with William F. Buckley's *God and Man at Yale* in 1951, the conservative movement has long attacked academia as excessively liberal, secular, and disrespectful of social institutions and America's exceptional history. Campus protest activity in the 1960s provoked more antagonism from the right; Ronald Reagan explicitly criticized the left-wing student protesters at the University of California, Berkeley, during his

1966 gubernatorial campaign, pledging to "clean up the mess." In a memo to the U.S. Chamber of Commerce just before his 1971 nomination to the Supreme Court by Richard Nixon, Lewis Powell Jr. argued that capitalism and the American system were under assault and that "the campus is the single most dynamic source" of these attacks.[38] He singled out social scientists and their students who proceeded to careers in the news media, academia, or government. Powell's recommendations that conservatives develop their own scholarly networks and institutions to balance faculties, demand equal time in campus speaking and media debates, and evaluate textbooks and television experts were later credited with inspiring business support for conservative think tanks.[39]

Conservatives founded Accuracy in Academia in 1985 (as an outgrowth of Accuracy in Media) to be a campus watchdog and the National Association of Scholars in 1987 to build a network of conservative academics. Conservative critics as diverse as Rush Limbaugh, Allan Bloom, and Dinesh D'Souza later found easy targets in academia, constantly poking fun at political correctness and deploring or mocking the behavior of left-wing professors.[40] Although initially focused on the humanities and social sciences, the scope of conservative attacks grew to include the hard sciences in debates over environmental regulation and issues that pitted scientists against religious authorities, such as federal funding for stem cell research.

Conservatives have especially feared the influence of liberal academic experts on public policy. Their attacks often focus on the scientific establishment, as Gordon Gauchat has noted: "Ideological challenges to the cultural authority of science cannot be reduced to left-right political polarization or to conservative religious beliefs. Instead, skepticism on the political right is multifold, involving distinct modes of thought and concerns about the institutional ties between science and the state."[41] As Jonathan Moreno concluded in a separate study, "The problem is not mistrust of science so much as it is mistrust of scientists."[42] Republican candidates sometimes seek to publicize opponents' academic ties as a means of suggesting ideological extremism or intellectual arrogance. For example, incumbent Republican Scott Brown referred to Democratic challenger Elizabeth Warren, a member of the faculty at Harvard Law School, as "the professor" throughout their 2012 campaign for a U.S. Senate seat in Massachusetts, counterattacking in one debate by remarking that "I'm not a student in your classroom."[43]

Two of the most prominent conservative critics of American academia are talk show host Glenn Beck and writer David Horowitz, who both voice alarm about leftist campus networks and organize to oppose them. But as Neil Gross argues, their attacks are part of a broader pattern:

Horowitz and Beck may be the most visible current opponents of the liberal professoriate, yet standing behind them are dozens of advocacy organizations and scores
of conservative commentators and reporters churning out a steady stream of op-eds,
articles, books, blog posts, reports, and sound bites that characterize higher education as in a time of crisis owing to the pernicious influence of the academic left.[44]

Attacks by conservative movement leaders on academic science have
successfully influenced the conservative public. Using General Social
Survey data, Gauchat demonstrated that declining public faith in science is concentrated among conservatives. He found that liberals and
conservatives expressed comparable trust in science until the late 1970s,
when it began to decline among conservatives. This decline accelerated in
the 1990s and continued through the 2000s, while there was no similar
trend among liberals.[45] Using public opinion data from National Science
Foundation (NSF) surveys between 2006 and 2012, Gauchat found stable
distrust: conservatives remain skeptical of the scientific community and
especially the role of scientific experts in policymaking.[46] This suspicion
does not extend to think tanks, which engender higher confidence overall among Republicans (especially conservative institutions such as the
American Enterprise Institute, the Heritage Foundation, and the Cato
Institute); conservative disapproval is only directed at liberal-dominated
academia.[47]

Attitudes toward scientists have become more polarized, while confidence in the role of scientists in political debates has eroded overall.
Table 4-4 summarizes contemporary evaluations of scientists, journalists, and academics by party identification. Compared to Democrats,
Republicans are significantly less likely to trust what scientists say, more
critical of political bias in academia, and less confident in colleges and
universities. Furthermore, 85 percent of Republicans believe that scientific findings are at least sometimes influenced by political ideology.
Negative attitudes toward science and the media also intersect, with one-
third of Republicans reporting no trust in journalists to accurately report
scientific studies.

Differences in trust are also apparent today among political elites in
government. Democrats and liberals, for example, are more acquiescent
to state policy research institutes designed to provide evidence to state
legislators.[48] Republican governors like Scott Walker of Wisconsin have
targeted the tenure system at state universities and presided over budget
cuts to those institutions. Congressional Republicans have sought to drastically reduce federal funding for all social science disciplines and to require all scientists to certify that their research fulfills the public interest.
Former Republican senator Tom Coburn of Oklahoma was particularly

Table 4-4 TRUST IN SCIENTISTS AND UNIVERSITIES

	Democrats	Republicans
	Trust in What Scientists Say	
A Lot	48%	20%
A Little	42%	65%
Not at All	3%	8%
	Trust in Journalists to Accurately Report Scientific Studies	
A Lot	18%	9%
A Little	63%	54%
Not at All	12%	33%
	How Often Scientific Findings Influenced by Political Ideology	
Often	16%	41%
Sometimes	52%	44%
Rarely	23%	8%
Never	4%	3%
	Confidence in Colleges and Universities	
A Lot	48%	31%
Hardly Any	7%	16%
	Critical of Political Bias in Academy	
	25%	42%

Data for first three questions are from a 2013 YouGov Poll, available at http://big.assets.huffingtonpost.com/ tabs_HP_science_20131209.pdf. Data for final two questions are from Gross and Simmons (2006).

distrustful of political science, repeatedly proposing to defund the small share of National Science Foundation grants awarded to political scientists; a limited version of this prohibition briefly took effect in 2013. Republicans have also acted to restrict the political activities of government scientists and to require additional review of scientific evidence used by government agencies. Democratic officials instead commonly defer to scientific associations and agencies. As Bruce Bimber found in an interview-based study, "When legislators talk about expertise, they almost invariably speak in terms of its origins. They do not understand analysis, policy studies, and other forms of expert information in isolation from their understanding of the people who produced it."[49] Democratic officials are open to influence from information supplied by academia, mainstream media, and government specialists, whereas Republicans seek the opinions of experts with conservative ideological credentials.

BUILDING AN ALTERNATIVE CONSERVATIVE MEDIA

Responding to the perceived leftward slant of society's main information-providing institutions, conservatives consciously constructed a separate infrastructure to distribute information more consistent with their own ideology. In the process, they reinforced their supporters' aversion to academia and mainstream journalism, forming an audience for conservative alternatives. According to media historian Nicole Hemmer, conservatives' perception of bias first stimulated the founding of alternative media sources by convincing activists to create and support conservative news outlets and to build close relationships between these outlets and political organizations.[50]

Conservative talk radio predated, but came to the fore alongside, the broader ascendancy of the conservative movement after World War II. Fulton Lewis Jr. read news and commentary on the nationwide Mutual Broadcasting System five times per week from the 1940s to the 1960s, eventually reaching millions of listeners and helping to popularize Joseph McCarthy's anticommunist campaigns.[51] According to media historian Heather Hendershot, a distinctive multimedia conservative infrastructure was burgeoning by the late 1950s and early 1960s; Table 4-5 summarizes its main participants. The print publications *National Review* and *Human Events* led the intellectual revival of conservatism and helped sell it to mass audiences (as reviewed in Chapter 3), but more popularly focused broadcast media soon joined these outlets. Key figures in this growing media landscape included Carl McIntire and Billy James Hargis, Christian fundamentalists with clear conservative political views, and H. L. Hunt and Dan Smoot, anticommunist "superpatriots" pushing a

Table 4-5 EARLY CONSERVATIVE MEDIA ORGANIZATIONS

	Media	Income:1958–1963
Reformation Hour (Carl McIntire)	Radio, Print	$4,138,500
Human Events	Print	$4,136,000
Christian Crusade (James Hargis)	Films, Radio, Print	$3,513,800
Life Line (H. L. Hunt, previously *Facts Forum*)	Radio, Print	$3,474,300
John Birch Society	Films, Radio, Print	$2,842,800
Christian Anti-Communist Crusade (Fred Schwarz)	Radio	$2,613,600
National Review	Print	$2,314,000
Manion Forum	Radio	$2,168,400
Dan Smoot	Radio, Print	$1,793,000
Christian Nationalist Crusade (Gerald Smith)	Radio, Print	$1,251,800

Data from Hendershot (2011, Table 1).

broader conservative agenda. The goals of these two groups were unified by Fred Schwarz, founder of the Christian Anti-Communist Crusade, and Gerald Smith, a leader of the Christian Nationalist Crusade. The John Birch Society spread its message via films, radio, and print media. Clarence Manion, who served on the board of both the *National Review* and the Birch Society, linked conservative elites with a mass audience. Alongside the national media, local conservatives filled the airwaves (often with businessmen as sponsors), and conservative broadcasters joined campus organizations to create media at colleges and universities.[52] In 1964, the liberal *Nation* magazine documented this conservative radio dominance—and raised alarms about it—in a cover story titled "Radio Right: Hate Clubs of the Air."[53]

Popular broadcasters had a substantial influence on the rise of American conservatism. Hunt, a rich oil executive, recruited Smoot to host a conservative economic broadcast called *Facts Forum* in the 1950s that also subsidized other radio and television programs and book publishing. It ended in 1956, to be replaced by *Life Line*, which also produced radio broadcasts and columns; Smoot went on to host a radio program that was aired on 300 stations.[54] Conservative books were sold to listeners through a network led by Henry Regnery and via bulk purchases by conservative organizations. Manion's weekly radio program became the base of the movement to draft Barry Goldwater for president.[55] Manion interviewed only conservative guests, arguing that there was "no middle of the road with communism" and "no two sides"; the political debate, in his view, placed "constitutional government" against "slavery under socialism."[56] He directly advocated electoral participation, remarking in 1962 that the "single thing that is more important than any other [was] to elect Conservatives to office." Toward this end, he created local club chapters that held regular letter-writing and public speaking events.[57] By the time the Goldwater campaign reached the 1964 convention, it had developed an entirely separate media infrastructure, as reported by Rick Perlstein:

> [T]hey built broadcast facilities. The campaign had purchased time on a local radio station every half hour, to which Goldwater delegates were to tune for general news. They tried whenever possible to interview Goldwater luminaries upon arrival, then offer them as exclusives to local TV stations, lest their words be twisted by biased reporters. They aired their televised roundup on purchased time thrice daily.[58]

Conservative talk radio remained an important part of the movement after Goldwater's loss, stimulated by openings on AM radio after the switch of most music broadcasting to the FM dial and the invention of the seven-second broadcast delay to enable live call-in programs.[59] Whereas the conservative broadcasts of the 1950s and early 1960s had often been disguised newscasts, religious programs, or short paid spots, radio hosts in the 1970s were able to interview guests and respond to callers for hours.[60] Bob Grant, who was the first radio figure to interview Ronald Reagan as a gubernatorial candidate, and Barry Farber, who later ran for mayor of New York on the Conservative Party ticket, popularized long-form conservative commentary. Marlin Maddoux and James Dobson modernized Christian conservative radio. From 1975 to 1979, Reagan recorded more than 1,000 radio commentaries to keep in touch with his conservative base. By 1986—before the rise of Rush Limbaugh—political scientist Murray Levin published *Talk Radio and the American Dream*, noting the conservative dominance of radio broadcasting and its influence on politics.[61]

By eliminating the Fairness Doctrine (which required honest, equitable, and balanced programming) in 1987, the Federal Communications Commission (FCC) removed the last remaining barrier to conservative talk ascendance. Limbaugh began national syndication in 1988, becoming the nation's leading radio figure by 1990 and the most popular and influential voice in conservative media throughout the 1990s. Limbaugh's success spawned a proliferation of other conservative hosts, creating a national network of radio stations that almost exclusively broadcast conservative talk programming all week long. Limbaugh was joined by dozens of other personalities who attracted national popularity, including former advisors and guest hosts like Mark Levin, Glenn Beck, and Sean Hannity, as well as state-level and local imitators throughout the nation. One analysis found that 90 percent of political talk radio hours are dedicated to conservative programming.[62]

Conservatives also long sought to build their own television infrastructure but did not initially achieve the same success. Hunt funded conservative television programming in the 1950s, and several radio hosts also bought television time in the 1960s. After the 1964 election, a *Manion Forum* trustee composed a memo arguing that "possibly the greatest single conservative need is control of a TV and radio network which could blanket the nation."[63] But a 1965 attempt by conservative business leaders to buy CBS through a proxy vote failed. From 1973 to 1975, conservative beer magnate Joseph Coors, Heritage Foundation co-founder Paul Weyrich, and ex-Nixon aide Roger Ailes (later the founder of Fox News Channel) helped create TVN, a video wire service that produced stories for local television networks.[64] In 1993, Weyrich founded the National Empowerment Television network, which aired programming from conservative activists, think tanks, interest groups, and politicians.[65] William F. Buckley's *Firing Line* debate program appeared from 1966 to 1999, mostly on PBS. Pat Robertson's Christian Broadcasting Network and its news program *The 700 Club* have continuously operated in various forms since the 1960s. Limbaugh found less success on television than he did on radio, hosting a syndicated late-night program between 1992 and 1996.

Conservative television efforts culminated in Ailes's effort to build the FNC. Ailes, who was made famous in the book *The Selling of the President 1968* for advising Nixon on his television appearances, turned to campaign consulting after the failure of TVN and eventually became the main force behind George H. W. Bush's 1988 advertising campaign.[66] Ailes was an effective link between politicians and conservative media; he helped Bush reconcile with Limbaugh (who had become a regular critic of his presidency) and produced Limbaugh's television series. As an executive at financial network CNBC, he developed mostly apolitical morning and afternoon discussion programming but left NBC after the announced transformation of his America's Talking network into MSNBC, joining Rupert Murdoch's effort to launch a competing channel under the Fox brand. Murdoch was known for owning conservative tabloid newspapers in the United States and elsewhere, but the Fox broadcast network—founded in 1986 and targeting a young and urban audience—had previously avoided news programming.

Murdoch and Ailes first launched *Fox News Sunday* in 1996, which aired on the broadcast network and initially featured Republican politico Tony Snow. Fox then slowly signed agreements with cable systems to air the 24-hour news channel (even offering $10 per subscriber).[67] FNC's initial sloganeering alluded to conservative displeasure with the liberal media (and relied on promotion from conservative radio hosts like Limbaugh), but its growth into a staunchly conservative network attracting like-minded viewers proceeded slowly.[68] Its programming nonetheless drew heavily on conservative radio personalities and innovated in the areas of visuals and news alerts, building a broader audience.

With FNC, conservative media gained a large national audience to unite supporters, building on a long history. As Hemmer explains, "Conservative media became the institutional and organizational nexus of the movement, transforming audiences into activists and activists into a reliable voting base."[69] Conservatives are not shy in claiming to have achieved a media revolution with the success of FNC; direct-mail magnate Richard Viguerie and author David Franke extol the rise of conservative media and even compare its influence to the role of pamphleteering in the Protestant Reformation and the American Revolution.[70]

Conservatives have never held an overwhelming advantage in print media to match their dominance of ideologically oriented broadcasting, but they did slowly build a publishing base as well. As George Nash notes,

"The publication of conservative books, essays, articles, and syndicated columns—already substantial in the 1970s—attained in the Reagan era the proportions of an avalanche."[71] In the 1990s, the conspiratorial tabloid *American Spectator* and newsy *Weekly Standard* joined more intellectually styled precursors like *Commentary* and the *Public Interest*. In 1995, the Heritage Foundation and *National Review* launched *Townhall.com* as a conservative Internet portal, presaging a wave of ideological online media outlets (a subject we will review later in the chapter). By the 2000s, 67 nationally syndicated conservative columnists maintained space in hundreds of newspapers, and five conservative opinion journals boasted circulation figures comparable to those of the *New Republic*, the leading liberal magazine.[72]

From the beginning, conservatives faced a difficult legal environment in their efforts to build ideological media outlets. In 1957, the Mutual Broadcasting System refused to air an anti-union *Manion Forum* interview with industrialist Herbert Kohler, stimulating wide news coverage and near-constant outrage from Manion while reinforcing his arguments in favor of conservative alternatives to liberal networks.[73] John F. Kennedy used the FCC to attempt to regulate conservative media, stimulating justified fear,[74] and a complaint to the FCC by the National Council of Churches and the Urban League about McIntire's radio program again produced complaints of censorship.[75] Reverend Hargis, challenged by the FCC for violations of the Fairness Doctrine (with enforcement requested by the Democratic National Committee), lost a 1969 constitutional challenge to the Doctrine in the U.S. Supreme Court.[76] In response, conservatives developed alternative legal theories and ideas that eventually undermined the basis for federal regulation of political broadcasting.[77] Reagan appointed Mark Fowler to the FCC in 1981, whose goal "was to try to strike down as much of the content regulation abridging the First Amendment [as possible]."[78] But it took until 1987 to build the legal framework that allowed past regulation to be overcome and the Fairness Doctrine overturned.[79]

THE FAILURE TO BUILD A LIBERAL MEDIA UNIVERSE

Liberal intellectual journals like the *New Republic* (*TNR*) and *The Nation* have been important voices in American political journalism for more than a century. Even in the heyday of *National Review* and *Human Events*, conservative readership failed to match that of these left-leaning magazines. In the early days of the Internet, liberal websites were more popular and more connected to the population of political activists than their conservative counterparts.[80] But these niche publications and outlets have never been accompanied by a broad liberal media apparatus designed to provide the Democratic electorate or the American left with a comprehensive set of alternatives to mainstream sources.

TNR was founded in 1914 by Herbert Croly as part of the Progressive movement and with the explicit aim of advancing social justice through strong government. Yet it was politically distant from the factionalized Democrats over its first few decades, and was even skeptical of Franklin Roosevelt. David Seideman recounts this oddity in his history of the magazine: "The vast realignment of labor, farmers, and the professional class that TNR had envisioned for so long within the framework of a third party finally occurred in the form of the New Deal coalition—and the editors missed it. Their celestial aloofness during the election distanced them further than ever from the secular world of politics."[81] After initially promoting alliance with the Soviet Union, *TNR* was forced to renounce communism in 1940. It served as an effective outlet for liberal ideas in the 1950s while also providing cultural content. In the 1980s and 1990s, it became an increasingly unreliable ally of intellectual liberalism and the policy agenda of the Democratic Party, growing particularly skeptical of identity politics and even publishing an attention-getting condemnation of Bill Clinton's health care reform plan. The more reliably left-wing magazines *The Nation* and *Mother Jones* did not maintain strong connections to the Democratic Party apparatus or an emphasis on pragmatic politics. None became the mouthpiece of a broader liberal political movement.

In broadcasting, liberals faced greater difficulties. As William Mayer observes, "The more striking reality is the complete dominance of talk radio by conservatives. . . . [T]here is scarcely any disagreement about the predominant ideology of talk radio. The most popular radio talk-show hosts in America are either openly and zealously conservative or almost entirely apolitical."[82] Liberal failure in radio was not for lack of trying. Pacifists founded the Pacifica Radio network in 1949, but its primary policy concern was conscientious objector policy, and it did not fit easily within a broader liberal agenda.[83] The network soon descended into chronic infighting over institutional control and organizational reform.[84] After the ascendance of conservative talk radio in the 1980s, liberal efforts to mimic this trend produced a variety of short-lived programs hosted by former Democratic politicians, including Jerry Brown, Gary Hart, Mario Cuomo, Jim Hightower, and Ed Koch—all of whom were touted as the "liberal Rush Limbaugh."[85]

The most famous liberal failure in recent years was the national radio network Air America, which was founded in 2004, declared bankruptcy in 2006, and went out of business for good in 2010; despite generous subsidies, the network lost money every year of its existence.[86] Its explicit goal was to balance conservative talk radio. Air America began with 100 employees and an initial $30 million budget, even though only four stations had originally signed up to carry its programming.[87] Political scientist William Mayer successfully predicted Air America's demise in 2004, noting that the "potential audience is small, fragmented, and probably not dissatisfied enough with the mainstream media."[88] Conservative activists, normally eager to spread warnings about the threat of liberal ideologues, scoffed that the failure of explicitly liberal media ventures demonstrated the limits of the left's organizational power. "There's no liberal there there," argued Viguerie and Franke in 2004. "Ambitious ideological projects like Air America require a mass ideological movement to sustain it, and if a robust liberal movement exists today, it can teach the Air Force something about stealth."[89]

The contemporary face of liberal media is MSNBC, often touted as the left-leaning equivalent of the far more popular FNC. It was founded as a technology-driven partnership with Microsoft and originally included conservative personalities like Ann Coulter and Laura Ingraham. After FNC (permanently) surpassed CNN to claim the largest primetime cable news audience in 2002, MSNBC executives considered shifting their own programming to the right in order to compete.[90] Former ESPN sportscaster and outspoken George W. Bush critic Keith Olbermann soon gave the network a liberal reputation, though former Republican congressman Joe Scarborough also hosted a conservative news show during primetime until 2007 and continues to co-host the network's morning program. It was not until 2008 that MSNBC became avowedly liberal in its marketing and primetime programming, building a lineup of multiple left-of-center hosts. Former vice president Al Gore transformed his user-generated video channel Current TV into a competing liberal network in 2011 by hiring Olbermann after his exit from MSNBC, but Olbermann departed after a year, and Current TV ceased operations in 2013. The Daily Show and The Colbert Report achieved sustained success in attracting young, left-leaning audiences, though these programs (aired on cable's Comedy Central) emphasized parody and satire of conservatives and media figures more than the overt expression of liberal ideas or support for Democratic politicians. Hosts Jon Stewart and Stephen Colbert mocked extremism and partisanship on both sides of American politics, holding a "Rally to Restore Sanity and/or Fear" on the National Mall in October 2010 as a half-serious call for a more respectful political debate.

Just as the modern conservative movement lacks a corresponding liberal counterpart of comparable influence, efforts on the left to replicate the construction of the increasingly powerful conservative media universe have largely failed—and for similar reasons. A Democratic activist population that is divided into multiple constituent groups and organizations with distinct identities and priorities is less likely to consume a single set of media sources, while the relatively high levels of trust and respect that liberals and Democrats maintain for the traditional media establishment limits the demand for more explicitly partisan alternatives. As Mayer observed, "The potential audience of liberal talk shows, already smaller than the audience for conservative programs, is further fractionalized by all of the demographic and identity-based divisions that have long posed problems for American liberalism."[91] For example, Air America was forced to compete for Democratic listeners with the liberal audiences of National Public Radio, talk radio programs hosted by African Americans like Tavis Smiley and Tom Joyner, and shows oriented toward Latinos.[92] When Air America took over a radio station in New York that had previously featured programming that appealed to black listeners, it faced a backlash and demands for broader representation.[93]

Similarly, MSNBC has regularly changed its lineup of hosts in an effort to better cater to a variety of Democratic social constituencies; its programs have included *PoliticsNation* with civil rights activist Al Sharpton and the *Ed Show* (focused on union and working-class concerns). Its current programming features the *Rachel Maddow Show* (with the liberal, feminist, and LGBT activist), a news show hosted by José Díaz-Balart (of Telemundo), and the proudly wonkish program *All In with Chris Hayes* (the former *Nation* editor). Despite these efforts, liberal broadcasting outlets continue to attract a disproportionately wealthy, white, and well-educated audience that does not resemble the popular electoral base of the Democratic Party.[94] As Mayer points out, the less-diverse Republican electorate is motivated principally by ideology and therefore more naturally unites around a shared set of media sources: "Conservative radio has largely been spared these sorts of problems, simply because identity politics plays much less of a central role on the Right than on the Left. The only thing conservatives appear to demand from their talk show hosts is that they be conservative."[95]

Unlike Republicans, Democratic supporters look to specific constituency organizations more than ideologically identified media figures to express their views, inform them about political developments, and guide their positions on issues. "Conservative media—and the habit of consuming conservative media that is so central to conservative political identity—have been something that has a half-century of history," argues Nicole Hemmer. "And liberals don't have that same history. To the extent that liberalism has a base, it doesn't come out of media, it comes out of organizations—like labor unions, or groups like MoveOn."[96]

Veteran U.S. representative and political scientist David Price of North Carolina also reports that constituent pressure on Democratic members of Congress primarily occurs via advocacy organizations, rather than contacts generated by media personalities.[97] Even the media reform movement that sought broadcast regulation and opposed corporate ownership of news media later became its own interest group sector.

There is a long history of Democratic interest groups attempting to build their own media outlets. Historian Elizabeth Fones-Wolf studied the rise and fall of union-sponsored radio programs, which were common in the 1930s and had become part of a national station network by 1949; by 1952, however, all of labor's FM stations were off the air, and their public affairs commentary declined in the 1960s.[98] Some stations did attempt a broad perspective—with one featuring a nightly "liberal look at the news"—but they also faced the same internal constituency divisions that plagued other left-of-center outlets, including ideological disagreements that led to a postwar purge of leftist commentary. Labor's radio presence included separate variety programs targeted to each trade and hours dedicated to Jewish and African American programming. By 1968, the United Auto Workers had disbanded their radio and television department, with the AFL-CIO folding most of its own media efforts soon afterward.[99]

The various social movements of the 1960s led to the development of myriad media institutions associated with the underground press. Most of these publications faded quickly, with the survivors becoming broader alternative newsweeklies funded by the sale of personal advertising.[100] *Rolling Stone* briefly served as a countercultural institution merging music and political content but soon purged its radical associations in order to gain advertisers.[101] Bob Ostertag documents the separate journals created by environmentalists, gays and lesbians, the antiwar movement (and disaffected soldiers), and the women's movement; most exhibited the same pattern of making initial forays into extreme politics before a quick fall from prominence.[102]

Another burst of liberal media building occurred in the early years of the World Wide Web. In part because the original Internet user base was disproportionately young, technologically sophisticated, and socially liberal, the first political causes to gain a significant online following involved civil liberties and free speech issues.[103] Civil libertarian interest groups, among all group sectors, benefited disproportionately from online publishers compared to other mediums.[104] Because liberal broadcast media had been less successful than its conservative counterpart, an "untapped market" was left for exploitation by online activists; in the early 2000s, when liberal frustration with the presidency of George

W. Bush and its coverage in the traditional media reached a peak, liberals were more likely than conservatives to visit political websites.[105] Howard Dean's campaign for the 2004 Democratic presidential nomination was fueled by particularly strong support among well-educated white liberals who used online tools to publicize Dean's views, make financial donations to his campaign, and organize voter outreach and mobilization efforts. This activity attracted increasing attention from traditional journalists as Dean pulled ahead in public opinion polls and the money race during the summer and fall of 2003, leading temporarily to the perception that liberals had succeeded in dominating the Internet just as conservatives had captured talk radio.[106] However, the subsequent rise of a conservative counterpart to the liberal online universe ultimately disproved this comparison.

The biggest liberal online success stories were MoveOn.org, which originated in an Internet-based effort to defend President Clinton from impeachment in 1998 and became a broader liberal interest group, and DailyKos, an online liberal blogging community that intervened in some Democratic primary elections, raising money and organizing on behalf of favored candidacies such as Ned Lamont's 2006 challenge to pro–Iraq War senator Joseph Lieberman of Connecticut. These outlets resembled advocacy organizations as much as they did media sources, however, becoming a separate "netroots" constituency that Democratic candidates sought to appease. Similarly, social movements like the antiglobalization and antiwar movements effectively used the Internet to organize and cover protests—but the media outlets only lasted as long as the movements remained in ascendance, and they inevitably faced pressure to become traditional interest groups.[107]

One medium that liberals do appear to dominate today is documentary filmmaking. Michael Moore's repeated success with films on the subjects of manufacturing decline, civil liberties, and gun control inspired other successful efforts like *An Inconvenient Truth* (on global warming) and *Waiting for Superman* (on education), both of which have been credited with spurring political activism. There is also evidence that the documentary *Gasland* has helped spread antifracking activism and led to local policy changes.[108] Liberals thus do not face uniform difficulty in distributing their political messages, but they have achieved far more success with single-issue activism or in communities they dominate. They have repeatedly failed in efforts to copy the conservative movement's success in building a broader media infrastructure that unifies and mobilizes a large population of supporters, displaces traditional media sources, and publicizes its views among a wider mass audience.

THE PARTISAN GAP IN SELECTIVE EXPOSURE

One straightforward consequence of the burgeoning of conservative media compared to liberal alternatives is that Republicans are more likely than Democrats to be disproportionately exposed to ideologically oriented media. Social scientists have been surprisingly reluctant to investigate this partisan difference, preferring instead to assess the general incidence of selective exposure: the extent to which the population as a whole is consuming political news from sources aligned with their existing viewpoint. One review of the literature finds that the evidence for selective exposure is limited, in part because citizens overreport their exposure to all media, and in part because studies of behavior have been limited by geography or technology.[109] The vast majority of citizens consume nonpartisan media, especially local television news, while the cable news audience remains small relative to the size of the national electorate.

When given the opportunity, more people prefer to watch sports or entertainment programs than to view news coverage of any kind. The highest level of public exposure to political information occurred in the 1970s, when television viewers were usually restricted to a choice of three networks that often scheduled news programming simultaneously.[110] Since that time, citizens have increasingly chosen to avoid news. Kevin Arceneaux and Martin Johnson confirm this pattern in a series of experiments that allow citizens to choose among channels: "The influence of Bill O'Reilly, Rachel Maddow, and their colleagues is limited by the fact that the audience is fragmented, diluting the reach of these shows. The evidence . . . suggests that, when people are allowed to choose what they view, the direct effects of partisan news talk shows are limited to the people who actually tune in to them."[111] The fact that ideologically flavored news coverage is watched mostly by a loyal, highly engaged, and politically sophisticated audience, however, might make its influence on political behavior and institutions *more* important than if it were instead consumed by casual, uninformed viewers—especially if the most conservative and active Republicans are more likely than equivalent Democrats to place themselves in an informational cocoon. As journalist Matt Bai argues, "A sizable portion of that paltry cable viewership comprises nearly every congressional aide, White House official, and assignment editor in Washington. . . . [E]ven more so than Limbaugh's radio broadcasts, the cable-news shows take on outsize importance, defining the hourly debate for all those political influentials who, in turn, define it for the rest of us."[112]

Social scientists have used two methods for making causal inferences about the role of selective exposure to ideological media, especially

television, in American politics: randomized controlled laboratory experiments and the "natural experiment" produced by the sequential geographic rollout of FNC. But the structure of both types of study causes
them to understate the partisan asymmetry of selective exposure. In the
first case, researchers commonly assign subjects to the consumption of
either liberal or conservative media, such as FNC or MSNBC programming, and measure the subsequent effects on their political attitudes.
Even if the two treatments produce comparably sized effects on individuals (which they often do not), relying on these findings to draw conclusions about the world outside the lab requires a recognition that FNC's
nightly viewership is, on average, about three times the size of MSNBC's
audience, generating a significantly larger impact on the aggregate opinion of the electorate.

Experimental studies also draw from pools of participants that consist
disproportionately of liberals because scholars rely on undergraduates or
paid online subjects (such as those recruited via Amazon's Mechanical
Turk website). For example, one study groups together all moderates and
conservatives into a single "conservative" group in order to make comparisons to another sizable group of self-identified liberals.[113] These subject
populations not only lack a representative proportion of the conservative
Republicans who dominate the audience for partisan media but also suffer
a shortage of the nonliberal Democrats who constitute a majority of their
party's electoral base. Likewise, when analysts make comparisons between "liberal Democrats" and "conservative Republicans," they are underreporting the actual difference between Democrats and Republicans
as a whole because they exclude the Democrats least likely to be exposed
to (and influenced by) partisan news.[114]

Alternatively, scholars can analyze the "natural experiment" associated with the gradual spread of access to FNC across the nation between
1996 and 2000; these studies have greater external validity because they
measure the actual influence of partisan media in the real world. Because
FNC was added to cable systems as a result of exogenous financial factors unrelated to the partisanship of the areas covered, scholars can use
geographic measures of FNC availability to track its influence on public
opinion or vote choice. Unfortunately, these studies also underreport the
incidence and influence of selective exposure because the FNC rollout
was complete by 2000, before two important shifts took place. First, FNC
began moving to the ideological right in 2001. Qualitative observations
confirm that the channel's programming, though always right-leaning,
became much more conservative over time, especially in the aftermath
of the 2001 terrorist attacks.[115] The FNC audience only became disproportionately Republican in 2000 (before then, more Democrats than

Figure 4-7 Median Monthly Primetime Viewership in Thousands by Year

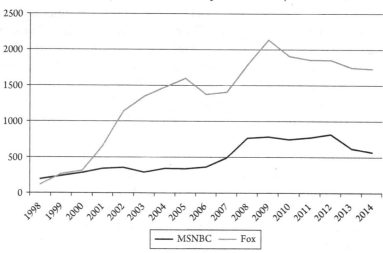

Median monthly primetime viewership in thousands by year. Data from Nielson ratings made available by the Pew Research Center.

Republicans watched the network) and only gradually became overwhelmingly Republican.[116]

More importantly, the viewership of FNC was quite small and comparable to that of MSNBC prior to 2000, as indicated by the monthly median primetime ratings displayed in Figure 4-7. Furthermore, the early years of FNC also coincided with an era in which MSNBC was both more widely available and, like FNC, lacked the clear ideological tilt that it would later adopt. Consequently, in unfortunate timing for researchers, the post-2000 surge in FNC's audience occurred just after the end of the period for which causal inferences can be made about its impact. Any analysis that found comparable effects of these two sources on public opinion in the 1990s might thus be inapplicable to the years after 2000. FNC's consistently higher ratings even after MSNBC's decisive turn to the left during the George W. Bush presidency confirm that either the selective exposure of cable news viewers is far greater among Republicans than among Democrats or that FNC is reaching a broader audience beyond the Republican base (or, what is more likely, both).

The disproportionate popularity of FNC, Republicans' exclusive trust in FNC and a handful of other conservative media outlets at the expense of traditional journalistic authorities, and the repeated claims of FNC hosts that they offer a "balanced" or "no-spin" corrective to the "liberal mainstream media" combine to create a self-reinforcing cycle that further increases Republican selective exposure.[117] As conservative activists argue, Republicans simultaneously see FNC as an alternative to biased news and as an influential arm of the conservative movement: "Conservatives will almost always defend Fox's claim to be 'fair and balanced' but they find it hard to do so without a smirk. . . . They proudly want to claim Fox as one of their own—it's one of the movement's great success stories."[118]

It is natural for scholars and commentators to treat MSNBC as simply the left-of-center equivalent of FNC, especially because it came to model itself after Fox by adopting a consistent ideological perspective across the range of its primetime programming. But MSNBC is not nearly as important or as trusted a news source for liberals as FNC is among conservatives. Table 4-6 demonstrates this asymmetry by drawing upon data from the Pew Research Center to show that nearly half of consistent conservatives name FNC as their main news source, as do nearly one-third of other conservatives, while only 12 percent of consistent liberals and 5 percent of other liberals rely primarily on MSNBC. Consistent conservatives overwhelmingly report trusting FNC (88 percent) and receiving at least some of their news from the network (84 percent), compared to 52 percent of consistent liberals who trust MSNBC and just 38 percent who watch it at least part of the time.

Republicans' increasingly restrictive dependency on FNC as a news source reflects the growth of the network's popularity after the 1990s. Between 2000 and 2010, the percent of Republicans who reported being regular Fox viewers increased from 45 percent to 69 percent.[119] By 2012, both FNC and conservative talk radio had become frequent sources of

Table 4-6 PERCENT TRUSTING AND GETTING NEWS FROM FOX NEWS AND MSNBC BY IDEOLOGY

	Fox News			MSNBC		
	Main Source	Get News From	Trust	Main Source	Get News From	Trust
Consistently Liberal		10%	6%	12%	38%	52%
Mostly Liberal	5%	24%	28%	5%	32%	48%
Mixed	8%	39%	47%		25%	39%
Mostly Conservative	31%	61%	72%		23%	26%
Consistently Conservative	47%	84%	88%		13%	7%

Percentage of respondents in each ideological category (based on a series of issue attitudes) who use each partisan media outlet as their "main source" of news, get news from the source, and trust the source. Data from Amy Mitchell, Jeffrey Gottfried, Jocelyn Kiley, and Katerina Eva Matsa, "Political Polarization and Media Habits," Pew Research Center, October 21, 2014, http://www.journalism.org/2014/10/21/political-polarization-media-habits/.

Figure 4-8 Number of Conservative Radio and Fox News Shows Mentioned by Party

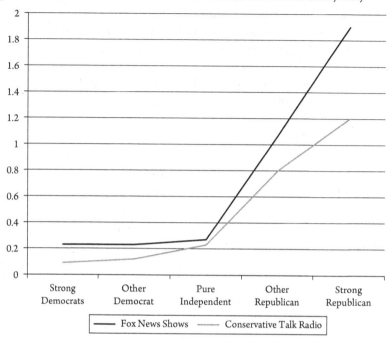

Number of conservative talk radio programs and Fox News television shows mentioned by respondents in each category of party identification. The questions asked what shows respondents watched or listened to regularly. Results are from our re-coding of show titles from the 2012 ANES. We combine leaners and weak partisans into the "other" categories.

political information for Republicans, but not for Democrats or independents. Figure 4-8 reports the number of FNC and conservative talk radio shows that respondents watched or listened to regularly, as measured by the 2012 American National Election Studies. On average, strong Republicans now regularly tune in to multiple FNC programs and more than one conservative talk radio program; other Republicans—but very few non-Republicans—also report consuming these media sources. Few ANES respondents reported regularly consuming expressly liberal radio or television programs regardless of their party identification.

This survey evidence is consistent with the easily observed conservative dominance of radio programming. In fact, the ANES found difficulty in compiling a list of liberal talk radio programs about which to ask its respondents. One analysis of the top 100 talk radio programs categorized 84 percent of political shows as conservative and only 10 percent as liberal.[120] In a wider analysis of all talk radio programs and hosts mentioned in open-ended survey responses from 2006, Natalie Stroud classified 89 hosts or programs as conservative and 32 as liberal; however, many of the liberal programs from that period—such as those produced by Air America—did not survive for long in the radio marketplace.[121]

Studies of talk radio listeners confirm a decidedly Republican composition. One study of Rush Limbaugh's audience between 1994 and 2006 found that Republican party identification and conservative ideology were the largest and most consistent factors affecting probability of listenership.[122] Stroud estimates the probability that a conservative Republican listens to conservative talk radio at .13, with the probability that a liberal Democrat listens to liberal radio equaling .08.[123]

Experimental evidence also confirms that Republicans are disproportionately likely to engage in selective exposure. One study found that adding the FNC logo to a news story increased the probability that Republicans would choose to read the story by 25 percentage points, whereas adding CNN's logo or NPR's logo reduced the chance by 10 points. No equally strong effects occurred among Democrats, who had a moderate tendency to be less likely to read the FNC article.[124] An experiment using abortion news coverage found that only Republicans are less likely to read news from another viewpoint.[125] FNC viewers also acknowledge in opinion surveys that they enjoy news that "shares their personal views," whereas respondents who watch broadcast networks and CNN prefer news with "in-depth interviews."[126]

The evidence for asymmetric selective exposure on the Internet is more limited. Most websites have ideologically diverse audiences, and most users visit nonideological media outlets.[127] While studies rarely assess party asymmetries in online news consumption, surveys by the Pew Research Center do reveal partisan differences in reported online behavior: consistent conservatives are more likely than other groups to report visiting ideologically aligned sites that are only popular among fellow ideologues.[128] Table 4-7 draws upon Pew data to show that exposure to political websites is indeed influenced by ideology. The *Huffington Post* is the most visited of these sites; its audience skews liberal along with

Table 4-7 GETTING NEWS FROM IDEOLOGICAL WEBSITES BY IDEOLOGY

	Drudge Report	Breitbart	Huffington Post	Daily Kos	Mother Jones	Think Progress
Consistently Liberal	1%	1%	29%	9%	10%	6%
Mostly Liberal	1%	1%	15%	1%	2%	1%
Mixed	2%	1%	8%	0%	1%	0%
Mostly Conservative	10%	5%	8%	0%	0%	0%
Consistently Conservative	20%	16%	10%	1%	0%	0%

Percentage of respondents in each ideological category (based on a series of issue attitudes) who get news from each online partisan media outlet. Data from Mitchell et al., "Political Polarization and Media Habits."

its political coverage, though much of its most popular content is nonpolitical (including celebrity news, self-help advice, and miscellaneous clickbait). The *Drudge Report* also offers nonpolitical subject matter, but its audience is almost exclusively conservative. All of the other political news sites draw overwhelmingly from a single ideological group.

Rather than purposely relying on a particular source for news, Internet users often read stories presented to them by social networking sites—especially Facebook. Consistent conservatives are twice as likely as other users to report seeing ideologically compatible news stories on their Facebook feeds.[129] This matches an offline pattern, in which half of all consistent conservatives (but only 31 percent of consistent liberals) name only like-minded friends as political conversation partners.[130] Facebook engineers recently confirmed that their newsfeed algorithm unintentionally provides users with news that disproportionately matches their existing political orientations, but the effects found for this relationship were modest (Facebook displays self-identified conservatives 5 percent fewer liberal hard news stories and self-identified liberals 8 percent fewer conservative stories). But conservatives are much less likely to click on liberal stories than liberals are to click on conservative stories; clicking behavior reduces exposure to cross-cutting stories by only 6 percent among liberals and 17 percent among conservatives.[131] On social media, consistent liberals mostly receive news from single-issue groups rather than parties or candidates.[132]

Liberal sites were initially more advanced in using social networks to distribute news, mirroring Democrats' greater early success in online campaign mobilization. But a new generation of conservative sites has emulated viral media and become far more popular than their older counterparts.[133] Of the 19 most popular conservative news websites identified by Calmes in 2015, seven were founded in 2012 or thereafter.[134] Table 4-8 updates this analysis using data from the web analytics firm Alexa, which measures traffic to all web domains. We reviewed the top 100 sites listed under the political and news categories, finding 35 conservative sites and 22 liberal sites that placed in the top 100 on either list. This ideological disparity is particularly strong among the most popular websites, with four times as many conservative sites in the top 25 as liberal sites. Table 4-8 also lists political Internet domains in rank order based on their web traffic, separating liberal and conservative sites into separate columns for easy comparison. The *Huffington Post* is again the most popular, followed by FoxNews.com, the *Drudge Report*, DailyKos, Breitbart, and Salon. Below that, the popular conservative sites are far more numerous and varied than their liberal counterparts.

The modern conservative media universe even includes decidedly old media such as books. Table 4-9 summarizes our efforts to categorize

Table 4-8 TOP POLITICAL WEBSITES

	Liberal	Conservative
Top 100	22	35
Top 25	4	16
Partisan Political and News Domains Ranked by Traffic, 2015	huffpost	
		foxnews
		drudge
	dailykos	
		breitbart
	salon	
	theatlantic	
		newsmax
		worldnetdaily
		infowars
		nationalreview
		townhall
		rightwingnews
		chicksontheright
		reason
		freerepublic
	newrepublic	
		weeklystandard
	thenation	
		powerline
		lucianne
		redstate
		lewrockwell
	commondreams	
	marxists	
		frontpagemag
		spectator
		mises
		marginalrevolution
	wsws	
		judicialwatch
	inthesetimes	
		gopusa

Data from the Alexa politics and news categories, categorized by the authors.

political bestsellers between 2001 and 2014 (based on the top 100 books sold each year on Amazon). During the Bush administration, conservative books were slightly less common than liberal books. During the Obama administration, conservative books were far more dominant. FNC personalities and talk radio commentators were frequently the

Table 4-9 POLITICAL BESTSELLERS PER YEAR DURING THE BUSH
AND OBAMA ADMINISTRATIONS

	Bush Administration	Obama Administration
Conservative	2.8	3.7
Other Political	3.6	0.8
Liberal	3.1	0.8

Average number of political books per year that made the Amazon top 100 from 2001–2014 in three categories: books by conservative politicians and commentators, books by liberal politicians and commentators, and other books about politics. Analysis was conducting using the annual lists available at amazon.com.

authors of these bestsellers, often outpacing Republican politicians. Conservative books have focused not only on current events, but also on philosophical and historical figures like Adam Smith, Alexis de Tocqueville, John Locke, Edmund Burke, and the American founding fathers.[135]

Democrats have often looked with frustration and envy at the rise of modern conservative media, which effectively transmits political messages from Republican elites and conservative authorities to a large mass audience of supporters. The increasingly popular array of conservative Internet sites that have emerged over the past decade has become integrated into the existing conservative network of print publications, talk radio, and cable news, creating an extensive alternative media universe. However, the disproportionate selective exposure of conservatives also carries risks and drawbacks of its own. Julian Sanchez of the Cato Institute has argued that the uniquely close connections between the new generation of online sources and more traditional media institutions on the ideological right have also worked to seal American conservatives off from exposure to unwelcome—but accurate—information. He notes:

One of the more striking features of the contemporary conservative movement is the extent to which it has been moving toward epistemic closure. Reality is defined by a multimedia array of interconnected and cross-promoting conservative blogs, radio programs, magazines and of course, Fox News. . . . Whatever conflicts with that reality can be dismissed out of hand because it comes from the liberal media, and is therefore ipso facto not to be trusted.[136]

Sanchez dismissed conservative rejoinders that this phenomenon was equally prevalent on the left, even if one considered the mainstream media to be located on the liberal end of the spectrum:

I can't pretend that, on net, I really see an equivalence at present. . . . The output may have varying degrees of liberal slant, but *The New York Times* is not fundamentally *trying* to be liberal; they're *trying* to get it right. Their conservative counterparts—your Fox News and your *Washington Times*—always seem to be trying, first and foremost, to be the conservative alternative.[137]

THE DISTINCTIVE CONTENT OF LIBERAL
AND CONSERVATIVE MEDIA

Partisan disparities in the relative degree of exposure to ideological media would have important political consequences even if the style and content of conservative and liberal news sources were similar, but differences exist on these dimensions as well. Kathleen Hall Jamieson and Joseph Capella document the key distinctive features of conservative media figures: they identify liberalism as their shared enemy, articulate a broad alternative conservative philosophy, apply their ideology to the concerns of the day, and argue that they are providing news that the liberal media is suppressing.[138] These scholars' qualitative analysis of talk radio, FNC, and the *Wall Street Journal* finds that right-leaning media sources consistently rail against liberals and "big government," guard the conservative legacy of Ronald Reagan, and criticize other media coverage as indicative of a left-leaning elite bias.[139]

Content analysis of Rush Limbaugh's program found considerable airtime devoted to Bill Clinton's scandals, "personal responsibility," and "individual efficacy," topics that were rarely discussed in mainstream media.[140] Limbaugh constantly complained about liberals and the double standard that (in his view) they applied to attack conservatives. Jamieson and Capella describe Limbaugh as "vigilantly monitoring the mainstream for bias" and nearly always characterizing his opponents as liberals.[141] A review of the content of FNC finds equivalent frames (though usually advanced with more subtlety). In a separate qualitative review of FNC content, Matthew Levendusky concludes that the channel's commentators regularly criticize liberals but are not uniformly supportive of Republican politicians; instead, FNC hosts often suggest that Republican leaders are too accommodating to liberal objectives.[142]

Former FNC commentator Bruce Bartlett, who accused the channel of damaging the Republican Party (and of banning him from appearing on it), argues that FNC and talk radio strike a philosophical pose, present themselves as outsiders, and maintain a constant level of anger.[143] A content analysis of conservative television and radio programs, columns, and blogs by Jeffrey M. Berry and Sarah Sobieraj confirms that expressions of outrage are indeed common. Table 4-10 summarizes the differences that Berry and Sobieraj found between liberal and conservative media.

Table 4-10 INCIDENTS OF OUTRAGE IN CONSERVATIVE
AND LIBERAL MEDIA PER EPISODE

	Liberal	Conservative
Claims of Ideological Extremity	0.91	1.74
Emotional Displays	0.64	1.26
Character Assassination	0.44	0.66

Average number of instances of three types of outrage per episode on conservative and liberal
television and radio programs, blogs, and columns. Data from Berry and Sobieraj (2014).

Conservative programs more commonly claim that the opposition is ideologically extreme, engage more frequently in emotional displays, and attack their opponents more often on a personal basis.

The content of conservative media may help to enable the American public's simultaneous prevailing conservatism on general symbolic values and liberalism on specific policy issues (as described in Chapter 2). Liberals are more adept than conservatives at reconciling general ideological predispositions with particular issue positions, but conservatives can still draw connections between their philosophical instincts and other political subjects. Instead of opinions on social problems or policies, they may apply their broader views to specific controversies. Jamieson and Capella note that conservative media regularly sow mistrust, but the "kind of mistrust they express is ideological."[144] Another analysis finds that the general size of government is Limbaugh's most frequently mentioned issue, with many examples of government overreach blamed on specific politicians.[145]

Conservative media discusses particular issues in ideological terms, as illustrated by Levendusky's review of the scandal over federal loans to the energy firm Solyndra, which later went bankrupt: "Obama's position on climate change is not simply wrong on its own," his critics said, "but it also represents his flawed liberal, statist approach to problems more generally; his support of Solyndra is just another example of his (and the Democrats') support of crony capitalism." Levendusky observes that liberal media figures focus instead on the groups in the party coalitions: "The Republicans' support for tax cuts for the wealthy is not only wrong on its own but also shows how Republicans are in the pocket of the rich more generally on deregulation, financial reform, and so forth."[146] Table 4-11 reports evidence from the 2004 campaign that conservative blogs also focused more on scandals than did their liberal equivalents, though the coverage in both outlets overwhelmingly concerned foreign policy (reflecting the particular salience of the Iraq War and terrorism in that year's election).

Table 4-11 STORIES PER DAY ON LIBERAL AND
CONSERVATIVE BLOGS

	Conservative	Liberal
Domestic Policy Issues	9.2	10.6
Foreign Affairs	53.0	48.1
Scandals	10.2	6.5

Average number of stories per day on major conservative and liberal blogs
during the 2004 presidential campaign. Kevin Wallsten collected and coded
the materials. We compiled the mentions he reports in Wallsten (2007).

A broader automated text analysis of ideological news websites and
chat rooms found different motivational themes among liberals and
conservatives.[147] Liberal sites focused on themes of affiliation and social
connectedness, using words like "care," "help," "intimate," "kind," and
"volunteer." Conservative sites focused on themes of power and influence, using words like "boss," "hero," "strong," and "victory." The analysis used predefined dictionaries, rather than exploring other themes, but
showed that they matched the similarly distinct rhetoric of Democratic
and Republican politicians.

We conducted an original analysis of Fox and MSNBC primetime programming since 2005 from a random sample of dates. Table 4-12 reports
data on the content of the top story for each program analyzed. Because
the MSNBC segments were significantly longer than those that aired on
FNC, we report the expected value for each party of a medium-length
statement. MSNBC programs cited significantly more sources and (surprisingly) more generic American imagery than did FNC programs;
other differences were not large or significant. Liberal and conservative
cable networks appear to create less distinctive thematic content than do
parties or politicians. MSNBC may thus serve a similar purpose for its
small audience of liberal ideologues as that which Fox serves for its larger
audience of conservatives.

For comparison, we also assessed how each party's politicians convey
their views in the mainstream media. Table 4-13 presents the results of
our content analysis of the initial newsmaker interviews since 2000 on
Meet the Press, which airs each Sunday on NBC and is a key vehicle for
communicating with Washington insiders and the most politically attentive segments of the electorate. We found that Democratic guests were
more likely than Republicans to cite particular social or interest groups,
and they referenced demographic groups more than twice as often. Other
differences were not large, though the results do confirm a familiar pattern across all of our data: Republican invocations of principle were more
likely to be consistent with conservative ideology, whereas Democratic

Table 4-12 CONTENT OF FOX/MSNBC TRANSCRIPTS

No. of Mentions Per Segment	Fox News	MSNBC
Ideology or Principle	2.64	2.78
Conservative (Republican)/Liberal (Democratic) Ideological Principles	1.73	1.12
Public Policy	1.82	1.8
New Policy Proposals	0	.18
Conservative (Republican)/Liberal (Democratic) Policy Position	.16	.12
Social Group or Interest Group	1.22	1.43
Demographic Groups (Class, Race, Religion, Gender, Age)	.51	.53
American Imagery	1.6	2.51
American Exceptionalism/Threats to Way of Life	.56	.46
Sources	3.28	4.31
n	124	122

Data from an original content analysis of the initial segments of primetime broadcasts on Fox/MSNBC programs since 2005 from a random sample of days. Because the MSNBC segments were significantly longer, we report the expected value for each party of a medium-length segment. The only statistically significant differences are for imagery and source mentions. Our data, content analysis codebook, and analyses of reliability are available online at mattg.org.

Table 4-13 *MEET THE PRESS* INTERVIEWS

No. of Mentions per Newsmaker Interview	Republicans	Democrats
Ideology or Principle	4.6	4.5
Conservative (Republican)/Liberal (Democratic) Ideological Principles	2.4	1.7
Public Policy	5.6	6.5
New Policy Proposals	.9	1.5
Conservative (Republican)/Liberal (Democratic) Policy Position	.9	1.3
Social Group or Interest Group	2.6	4.2
Demographic Groups (Class, Race, Religion, Gender, Age)	.8	1.9
American Imagery	3.1	3.5
Sources	3.5	3.8
n	769	731

Data from an original content analysis of a random sample of politician statements in the first interviews on each *Meet the Press* episode since 2000. Our data, content analysis codebook, and analyses of reliability are available online at mattg.org.

policy proposals were more likely to be consistent with liberal ideology. Unlike Republicans, Democrats rarely used media appearances to articulate broader ideological principles.

We also analyzed data collected by Hans Noel on opinion columns in liberal and conservative journals and newspapers. The two leftmost columns in Table 4-14 compare liberal to conservative opinion journals,

Table 4-14 CONTENT OF OPINION COLUMNS

No. of Mentions per Article	Conservative Journals	Liberal Journals	All Conservatives	All Liberals
Ideology or Principle	.63	.29	.62	.25
Conservative (Republican)/ Liberal (Democratic) Ideological Principles	.55	.11	.55	.11
Explicitly Political Principles	.58	.28	.58	.24
Public Policy	2.01	2.38	2.05	2.06
Specific New Policy Proposals	.13	.16	.15	.13
Social Group or Interest Group	1.06	1.31	.97	1.17
Demographic Group (Class, Race, Religion, Gender, Age)	.60	.90	.57	.82
Combined Mentions of Social or Interest Group with Public Policy	.40	.37	.37	.34
Uses of American Imagery	.31	.57	.30	.53
Claims of American Exceptionalism	.01	0	.01	.02
Threats to American Way of Life	.06	.09	.05	0
Sources	.09	.42	.08	.07
n	67	98	73	127

Data from an original content analysis of a random sample of 200 opinion columns from 1970 and 1990 found in Noel (2009). We assessed each article for the number of mentions of each type. Our data, content analysis codebook, and analyses of reliability are available online at mattg.org.

while the other columns present the results among all conservative and liberal columnists. These findings demonstrate that conservative opinion columns are much more likely to mention (conservative) ideological principles, whereas liberal columns are more likely to mention demographic groups. Generic American imagery, however, is (unexpectedly) more commonly invoked in liberal columns. The differences are not as stark as in other media, suggesting that opinion columns might be more similar in their thematic content than other partisan news sources.

THE POLITICAL VOICE OF CONSERVATIVE RADIO

Republicans disproportionately rely on ideological media, whose reach and content are unmatched by Democratic outlets. Although historians had long recognized the existence of a conservative media ecosystem, it was the unequaled rise of Rush Limbaugh that led researchers to start assessing its impact systematically. As Nicole Hemmer notes, "Limbaugh, both in good times and bad, illustrated just how different the second generation of conservative media activists were from the first: they were profitable, popular, and powerful, wielding influence that reached far beyond the conservative movement. Republican politicians began to attune themselves to right-wing media as proxies for the party's base."[148]

The political influence of conservative broadcasting became visible in the early 1990s. When Bill Clinton's 1993 health care reform initiative stalled in Congress, nearly half of legislators and staff credited talk radio as the most important media source during the debate.[149] After Republicans took control of Congress in the 1994 elections, incoming House Speaker Newt Gingrich's press secretary Tony Blankley credited Limbaugh: "After Newt, Rush was the single most important person in securing a Republican majority in the House of Representatives."[150] Gingrich invited talk radio hosts to broadcast live from Capitol Hill during the first 100 days of the new congressional session; 40 took him up on the offer.[151] Limbaugh served as Clinton's most outspoken opponent and foil for the remainder of his presidency.

The important political role of talk radio continued into the administration of George W. Bush. Conservative broadcasters urged popular support for Bush's policies, especially after the September 2001 terrorist attacks; during the build-up to the Iraq War in 2003, radio host Glenn Beck staged rallies around the country.[152] But talk radio also represented a source of pressure on Bush to remain true to the conservative cause. When Bush nominated his own aide Harriet Miers to a position on the U.S. Supreme Court in 2005, broadcaster Laura Ingraham led an opposition campaign fueled by worries that Miers would not be a forthrightly conservative justice (with several pundits arguing that Ingraham, who had clerked for Justice Clarence Thomas, was more qualified herself); Bush ultimately withdrew the nomination in response to Republican opposition in the Senate. When Bush proposed comprehensive immigration reform in 2007, Limbaugh, Hannity, Beck, Michael Savage, and Mark Levin all railed against it as an "amnesty" bill, rhetoric that played a key role in its demise.[153]

The Democratic administration of Barack Obama tried to take advantage of talk radio's reputation for extremism, tying their Republican opponents in Congress to the outspoken views of conservative media figures. For example, Democratic National Committee chair Tim Kaine and White House aides David Axelrod and Robert Gibbs regularly referred to Limbaugh as the "leader of the Republican Party."[154] While Obama advisors may have hoped to sow mischief by forcing Republicans to make a choice between embracing the controversial radio host or distancing themselves from a popular figure within their party, they also had good reason to fear his influence. One estimate suggested that Limbaugh's campaign against the Affordable Care Act led to over 40,000 calls per hour to the congressional switchboard.[155]

The power of talk radio in general, and Limbaugh in particular, within the Republican Party is sufficiently imposing that Republican elected officials who find themselves in disagreements with Limbaugh or other prominent broadcasters often end up backing down or apologizing, lest they provoke outrage among loyal radio listeners in their home constituencies. After promising to pursue compromise with President Obama in a 2010 interview with the *Wall Street Journal*, Representative Darrell Issa of California distanced himself from his own comments following Limbaugh's vociferous objection.[156] Georgia congressman Phil Gingrey publicly defended the Republican congressional leadership from attacks by conservative commentators in early 2009, remarking that "it's easy if you're Sean Hannity or Rush Limbaugh . . . to stand back and throw bricks. You don't have to try to do what's best for your people and your party." When irate Limbaugh fans responded by deluging his office with critical phone calls, Gingrey issued a statement apologizing for his comments and praising Limbaugh and Hannity as "the voices of the conservative movement's conscience. . . . [W]e are inspired by their words and their determination."[157] Even Republican National Committee chair Michael Steele acknowledged Limbaugh's influence within his party by issuing an apology after referring to the broadcaster's radio program as "entertainment" and "incendiary" in a 2009 interview with CNN.[158] It is difficult to identify any media figures on the left who would receive a comparable amount of public deference from high-ranking Democratic politicians under similar circumstances.

Radio hosts like Limbaugh often mobilize listeners to contact their members of Congress by phone or social media. One legislator observed in 2015 that overall rates of constituent contacts had more than quintupled in the previous two decades, attributing most of the increase to the influence of talk radio.[159] Conservative radio broadcasting also helped to stimulate the Tea Party movement: radio hosts helped to organize the initial protests against Obama's economic stimulus package in early 2009 that presaged the Tea Party movement and later promoted Tea Party rallies, candidates, and groups on the air. Tea Party organizations later reciprocated by sponsoring the shows of Limbaugh, Ingraham, Hannity, Beck, and Mark Levin.[160]

Talk radio also plays an important role in elections. Christian radio hosts helped to defeat Senate Democratic leader Tom Daschle in 2004.[161] In 2010, conservative radio personalities encouraged their listeners to provide electoral and financial support to Republican Scott Brown, whose upset special election victory in Massachusetts denied Democrats a filibuster-proof majority in the U.S. Senate. Libertarian broadcaster Neal Boortz was the key popularizer of the "fair tax" proposal that was adopted by several presidential candidates in 2012, including Gingrich and Herman Cain, who served as guest hosts on Boortz's program and advanced his proposals. A variety of local talk radio hosts, though less visible at the national level, can yet wield significant political influence in specific states. Melanie Morgan and Eric Hogue were the major early promoters (and signature collectors) for the 2003 recall election in California that ousted Democratic governor Gray Davis in favor of Hollywood actor Arnold Schwarzenegger. Milwaukee radio host Charlie Sykes helped propel conservative Scott Walker's popularity as he rose to the Wisconsin governorship in 2010 and defended himself against an attempted recall of his own two years later.[162]

Talk radio hosts often buck the Republican "establishment" in favor of more conservative primary challengers. Mark Levin was an early supporter of Rand Paul, who defeated party favorite Trey Grayson in the 2010 Kentucky Senate primary, and Mike Lee, who defeated incumbent senator Bob Bennett for the Republican nomination at the 2010 Utah Republican convention. Talk radio support also helped Dave Brat shock the Washington media by upsetting House Majority Leader Eric Cantor in a 2014 Republican primary election that few mainstream journalists expected to be competitive. Brat had received no major endorsements from elites or Tea Party organizations, but he was the beneficiary of multiple rallies and on-air support from Ingraham, appeared four times as a guest on Levin's program, and was promoted by Beck.[163]

Talk radio hosts also sometimes end up in Congress themselves. Republicans Jesse Helms, J. D. Hayworth, Bob Dornan, Mike Pence, Jody Hice, Markwayne Mullin, and Trey Radel all hosted radio shows before running successfully for federal office. One of the few congressional Democrats with talk show hosting experience is Minnesota senator Al Franken, an alumnus of the short-lived Air America network, though Franken was better-known for his previous career as a performer on *Saturday Night Live* and as the author of several humorous books. For other Republicans, talk radio is an attractive post-Congress career, with the roster of former members–turned-radio-hosts including Bob Barr, Peter Blute, Bob Ehrlich, Mark Foley, Thaddeus McCotter, Bob Ney, Joe Scarborough, Fred Thompson, Mike Rogers, and Joe Walsh.

Political scientists have accumulated quantitative evidence of talk radio's impact as well. One experiment found that consumption of Limbaugh's program increased listeners' perception that both

Democratic and Republican officeholders were excessively liberal.[164] Liberal talk shows did not strengthen partisan attitudes among Democratic listeners, but Limbaugh had an especially strong impact on the views of Republicans. The more that Limbaugh discussed a particular issue, the greater the likelihood that his listeners were persuaded to adopt his position. David Barker found that a few minutes of exposure to talk radio changes listener considerations and opinions; repeated listening leads conservatives to feel efficacious and participate more in many political activities.[165] An early review of opinion data concluded that talk radio listeners likely increased Republican support in the 1994 elections, or at least reinforced listener attitudes (though causality was difficult to assess).[166]

Jamieson and Capella also analyzed the evolving behavior of talk radio listeners after the founding of FNC. Although Limbaugh stoked his audience's mistrust of traditional media, they initially still consumed a broad array of other sources. After FNC was established, however, Limbaugh listeners became more selective, increasingly relying on Fox for information instead of mainstream news outlets. As Jamieson and Capella explain, these sources together created an information cocoon:

> Conservative media create a self-protective enclave hospitable to conservative beliefs. This safe haven reinforces the views of these outlets' like-minded audience members, helps maintain ideological coherence, protects them from counterpersuasion, reinforces conservative values and dispositions, holds Republican candidates and leaders accountable to conservative ideals, tightens their audience's ties to the Republican Party, and distances listeners, readers, and viewers from "liberals," in general, and Democrats, in particular.[167]

FOX NEWS CHANNEL: GOP TV

As far as Democratic critics are concerned, talk radio and FNC effectively operate as the publicity department of the national Republican Party, even coloring the political coverage of mainstream media outlets. For example, Al Gore claimed that conservative media was "injecting the daily Republican talking points into the definition of what's objective as stated by the news media. . . . Something will start at the Republican National Committee, inside the building, and it will explode the next day on the right-wing talk-show network and on Fox News."[168] Obama told the *New York Times* in 2008 that FNC's partisan role had a direct effect on voters: "I am convinced that if there were no Fox News, I might be two or three points higher in the polls."[169]

Political scientist and analyst Jonathan Bernstein also argues that FNC should be defined as part of the Republican Party because of its influence over conservative politics and connections to Republican politicians, contending that "American political parties are made up of both formal organizations (such as the RNC) and informal networks. Fox News Channel, then, is properly understood as part of the expanded Republican Party."[170] Former White House press secretary Scott McClellan acknowledged that the George W. Bush administration provided FNC hosts with coordinated talking points to discuss on air.[171] FNC and talk radio help Republicans communicate with their base and spread their ideas, and they have been effective in mobilizing voters to participate in midterm elections (as in 2010 and 2014). Yet after two decades of celebrating conservative media, some Republicans began in the Obama years to consider whether its existence has had the counterproductive effects of limiting the party's public appeal and shifting the internal Republican balance of power from elected officials to talking heads. Reformer David Frum argued in 2010 that FNC had become the tail wagging the party dog: "Republicans originally thought that Fox worked for us and now we're discovering we work for Fox."[172]

Historian Heather Cox Richardson describes the political influence of FNC as more subtle and profound than simply propagandizing on behalf of Republican politicians:

> FNC charged all other news stations with bias, forcing them to air the views of Movement Conservatives in self-defense.... [Mackinac Center Vice President Joseph Overton] came up with the idea of the Overton Window, a span of ideas the public would accept. To move that range rightward, Movement Conservatives had to promote their views aggressively, until arguments and policies that had previously been considered outrageous would become acceptable. FNC moved the Overton Window by keeping up a constant stream of media chatter charging Democrats with socialism, elitism, and anti-Americanism.[173]

Scholars have been able to demonstrate the broad influence of FNC. Using the natural experiment of its geographic expansion in the 1990s, one study found that FNC availability increased Republican voting, especially in conservative but Democratic-held districts, and may have been decisive in some Senate elections in 2000.[174] An individual-level study found that the presence of FNC increased Republican voting intention among Republican identifiers and pure independents, but did not influence others.[175] These studies are able to demonstrate causality because of the exogeneity of cable system placement in FNC's early days, but they understate the likely effects of FNC because they cover a period when the network's ratings were only one-fifth of their current level. Another study used the channel position of FNC as a possible exogenous factor driving FNC viewership (because television viewers are more likely to watch low-numbered channels), finding a more substantial increase in Republican voting intention in cable systems in which FNC had a lower number but no effect among satellite subscribers in the same areas, who served as a control group uninfluenced by cable channel order.[176] A panel study found that FNC viewership is associated with respondents changing their presidential vote from Democratic to Republican from one election to the next.[177] Other research concluded that exposure to FNC convinces subjects that they are more conservative than their issue positions would indicate.[178] FNC viewers were also more likely to expect that Mitt Romney would defeat Barack Obama in 2012[179] and are more likely to both maintain their Republican identification when threatened[180] and mislabel their own liberal issue positions as conservative.[181]

By experimentally inducing people to watch FNC and MSNBC, Levendusky confirmed many important causal effects of cable news: "Partisan media make citizens more convinced that their views are the 'right' ones . . . make citizens less willing to trust the other party and less willing to support compromise with them, thereby contributing to persistent gridlock . . . [and] influence vote choice, as well as how citizens come to understand elections."[182] Levendusky found that watching cable news programs induced more extreme attitudes and reduced support for bipartisan compromise in viewers. As demonstrated in Chapter 2, however, only Republicans have increasingly adopted anticompromise attitudes in the wider electorate. Experiments conducted by Arceneaux and Johnson have found smaller effects of cable news on public opinion because these researchers allow participants to change the channel to nonpartisan programming, but they still conclude that cable news can harden attitudes: "We find evidence that exposure to proattitudinal news can reinforce preexisting attitudes and cause people to be more resistant to opposing arguments."[183] Their experiments do not reveal whether or not FNC exerts a stronger effect than MSNBC, but even comparable individual-level effects outside the lab would produce a collective impact that was three times as large on the conservative side, given FNC's superior ratings.

Research confirms that FNC also influences the behavior of political elites. One study using the natural experiment of FNC cable availability found that FNC reduced legislator support for President Clinton's positions by 4 percent, even during the initial rollout in 1998 and 2000 (when FNC's ratings were only one-fifth their current level).[184] The relationship between the number of subscribers with access to FNC in a district and that legislator's voting record is much stronger. A separate study of the FNC rollout in the 1990s found that availability of the channel made both Republicans and Democrats in Congress more likely to support the Republican position on divided votes.[185] The research also pointed to an explanation involving a mobilized Republican base, rather than a direct effect of the members watching the channel: the effects of FNC were strongest in areas with more Republicans and increased as Election Day approached.[186]

These findings comport with qualitative judgments suggesting that FNC moves Republicans toward the right. Explaining the Republican failure to modify or block the Affordable Care Act, David Frum argued that conservative media was to blame: "There were leaders who knew better, who would have liked to deal. But they were trapped. Conservative talkers on Fox and talk radio had whipped the Republican voting base into such a frenzy that deal-making was rendered impossible."[187] Jackie Calmes, a *New York Times* journalist who took a leave of absence to write about conservative media for the Kennedy School of Government, interviewed many members of Congress and staffers who reported that conservative media act as a constraint on legislative behavior, driving waves of angry constituent calls to congressional offices.[188] Legislative insiders perceived that the influence of conservative media after the 1990s was stimulated by the emergence of FNC, talk radio, and Internet sources. Former Senate majority leader Trent Lott acknowledged that these institutions successfully pressured Republican legislators: "If you stray the slightest from the far right, you get hit by the conservative media."[189]

FNC maintains several other political roles that reinforce its power. First, it affects the coverage of other journalists; in one survey, more than half of journalists acknowledged that the channel significantly influences other coverage.[190] Second, the channel helps vet candidates. It played a role in the rise and fall of Mike Huckabee's presidential candidacy in 2008 and in encouraging conservatives' broader acceptance of John McCain's 2008 primary campaign compared to his previous bid in 2000.[191] Other figures lacking conventional political credentials, including Herman Cain, Ben Carson, and Donald Trump, have been able to reach national audiences of conservative activists via frequent appearances on FNC that allowed them to build presidential campaigns of their own.

Third, FNC institutionalizes new kinds of participants in policy debates. Many of the same policy analysts appear on multiple conservative media platforms but gain particular visibility through their roles on FNC.[192] Fourth, it promotes scandals and controversies, such as that over the relationship between Barack Obama and William Ayers, which otherwise might receive little media attention—often forcing these matters onto the agenda of the mainstream media as well. Besides the Ayers issue, repeated FNC coverage also helped raise the profile of such stories as Hillary Clinton's role in the fatal 2012 attacks on the American consulate in Benghazi, Libya; the gun-running scandal known as "Fast and Furious"; the business practices of federal loan guarantee recipient Solyndra; the past activism of Obama White House operative Van Jones; the 2004 attacks on John Kerry by the Swift Boat Veterans for Truth; the controversial sermons of Obama's Chicago pastor Jeremiah Wright; the filming of undercover videos of supposed wrongdoing by the liberal activist group ACORN; and even the "war on Christmas" supposedly waged every December by secular, multicultural liberals.[193]

FNC also helped to launch and sustain the Tea Party movement during Obama's first term in office.[194] Televised antigovernment remarks by commentator Rick Santelli in February 2009 on rival network CNBC are often credited with inspiring the movement, but the broader conservative media universe—including Hannity, Limbaugh, and Drudge—immediately promoted Santelli's comments. Hannity interviewed Newt Gingrich live from the first Tax Day rally in 2009, with several other FNC hosts later appearing live at Tea Party events and Glenn Beck organizing one himself; FoxNews.com even posted an online guide to organizing a Tea Party rally.[195]

By the 2016 election, the unique role of FNC within the world of Republican politics had become even more apparent. A Fox-produced presidential debate among Republican candidates in August 2015 raised questions about whether FNC executives were attempting to influence the outcome of the race after Donald Trump accused FNC host Megyn Kelly, one of the debate moderators, of unfairly targeting him with hostile questions. *New York* magazine reported that FNC head Roger Ailes later personally contacted Trump to make peace, motivated by a "volume of pro-Trump emails from Fox's loyal viewers."[196] Trump was temporarily assuaged, backing down from threats to boycott the network, although he renewed his feud in January 2016, refusing to appear at an Iowa debate televised by FNC and co-hosted by Kelly.

Throughout this saga, all of the actors involved—as well as the Washington community at large—operated under the common assumption that FNC is fully integrated into the modern conservative movement and the extended Republican Party network, serving as the most important vehicle by which Republican elites transmit political messages to the public. Republican candidates for elective office are particularly concerned about receiving critical coverage on FNC that might damage their popularity with the viewership that constitutes the base of their party, while FNC simultaneously takes care to maintain its positive reputation and appeal among conservative voters. Veteran Republican political consultant Alex Castellanos has argued that Fox News Channel is not merely a journalistic source of information about current events, but also "the most powerful Republican institution in contemporary American politics."[197] No media outlet maintains the same embedded role or exercises a parallel level of influence within the Democratic Party.

THE RISE OF CONSERVATIVE THINK TANKS
AS ALTERNATIVE INFORMATION SOURCES

Just as the conservative movement built a national media apparatus as an alternative to the "establishment" press, conservatives have also developed a network of policy experts outside the liberal confines of academia. A recent dispute over a prominent study on media bias can illustrate the ways in which liberals and conservatives think differently about the role of expertise in policy debates. Tim Groseclose and Jeff Milyo measured bias by comparing the citations of conservative and liberal think tanks that appeared in media content with mentions of the same organizations in Congress.[198] The analysis assumed that if a news source cited a similar group of think tanks as a member of Congress, it shared that legislator's ideological position. According to this measure, nearly all news outlets are located on the center left, with the exception of an FNC program and conservative newspaper that remained on the center right.

Brendan Nyhan raised objections to this measure, arguing that the citation patterns of Democratic officeholders reflected respect for neutral competence, not ideological affinity: "Technocratic centrist to liberal organizations like Brookings and the Center on Budget and Policy Priorities tend to have more credentialed experts with peer-reviewed publications than their conservative counterparts."[199] Groseclose and Milyo defined organizations as think tanks by looking for indicators that they considered to be signs of scholarly purpose: a lack of public membership, not being a K Street lobbying firm, and the existence of institutional staff called "fellows."[200] But Nyhan argued that these markers were flawed: "Conservative think tanks have consciously aped the tropes of the center-left establishment (such as fellows and closed memberships) while discarding their commitment to technocratic scholarship."[201]

This dispute is not simply a technical debate about a measure but represents a window into the informational infrastructure of the two political parties. From the Democratic point of view, Republicans have undermined a system of empirical expertise based in academia by establishing institutions for ideological advocacy disguised as scholarly enterprises. From the

Republican perspective, separate groups of policy specialists agree with the objectives of each party; any judgment that deviates from a balance between these two sides constitutes bias in science and journalism. This difference in interpretation does not challenge the facts as agreed upon by both sides: the conservative movement founded a series of think tanks to counteract a liberal academic establishment and expects them to be treated as equally respected participants in policy debates. Like conservative media, think tanks "tend to focus on a few conservative ideas, often in loose coordination with Republican leaders."[202] Both networks were built to counterbalance the traditional scholarly community, which collectively leans to the left but views itself as motivated by analytic accuracy rather than partisan or ideological commitments.

Sociologist Thomas Medvetz has reviewed the history of think tanks and their influence in American governance, identifying the role they sought to fill. From an international perspective, both the federal government and the two major parties suffered from comparatively low levels of internal policy expertise for much of American history. New Deal programs relied on ties to economists and other experts outside of government but avoided agency-led research programs. That vacuum left room for a "semiformal advisory structure that filled the gap left by the absence of a technocratic arm of the federal government. . . . [T]his organizational structure [of ties between government and academia] helped to institutionalize a technocratic style of production as the dominant form of intellectual engagement in American politics in the 1950s and 1960s."[203] These developments led to a brief period of government-by-expert: "By the early 1960s, a set of technocratic specialists had secured for themselves a major role in American politics, especially in matters related to foreign policy, economics, social policy, and military affairs. A group of semi-autonomous technocrats enjoyed a brief but relatively uncontested period of dominance in the field of expertise."[204] This influence could be felt even as late as the Ford administration, which drew eight Cabinet members from the ranks of the professoriate.[205]

This intellectual establishment faced its main challenge, Medvetz argues, from "an emergent group of conservative 'activist-experts' who sought to undermine the power of technocrats from a standpoint of greater intellectual openness and public engagement."[206] The key development in the rise of this rival center of power was the 1973 founding of the Heritage Foundation by ex-Republican congressional aides Paul Weyrich and Edwin Feulner. As Weyrich explained, Heritage was created to supply Congress with conservative policy expertise: "[Conservatives needed] an outside operation that could provide timely information to Members of Congress from a principled perspective [and] . . . supply witnesses for hearings and experts to privately brief senators and congress-men."[207] To provide an audience for Heritage's activities, Weyrich drew upon organized blocs of conservative officeholders: "We targeted the Hill and our niche was to be very responsive. . . . I went and helped organize the Republican Study Committee and it became a generator of requests. Likewise, [Heritage founders] organized the Senate Steering Committee, and again, it became a generator of requests."[208] Feulner became the in-stitution's first long-term leader, serving as president from 1977 to 2013.

Economist Murray Weidenbaum observed that Heritage was the "pro-totypical advocacy think tank" with "no academic pretensions" that saw itself engaged in a "war of ideas" rather than the production of scholar-ship.[209] Heritage became a central component of the conservative move-ment, holding regular meetings that fostered connections among elected officials, activists, and policy analysts.[210] Its activity has evolved along with the larger movement, extending its reach into partisan and elec-toral politics in recent years. The choice of Senator Jim DeMint of South Carolina as the foundation's president in 2013 signaled an alignment between the organization and the purist wing of the Republican Party; DeMint promptly expanded the role of Heritage Action, a 501(c)4 sister organization that actively intervenes in Republican primaries on behalf of like-minded candidates. DeMint referred to his resignation from the Senate to join Heritage as "a big promotion," arguing that he could better advance conservative principles and policy ideas from his new position than he could within the legislative branch.[211]

Medvetz associates the founding of Heritage, the Cato Institute, and the Manhattan Institute with the growth of the broader conservative movement, observing that "conservative philanthropists underwrote a multifaceted institution-building project that supported the growth of legal foundations, television programs, magazines and journals, and po-litical action committees."[212] Alongside this mobilization, the American Enterprise Institute (AEI) was transformed from a business association into a think tank. AEI was still perceived as relatively moderate as late as the 1980s, but a 1986 dispute that prompted conservative foundations to temporarily withdraw funding and the institute's president to resign ultimately caused AEI to adopt a more avowedly right-leaning align-ment.[213] The conservative scholarly universe also encompasses religious universities such as Hillsdale College, Liberty University, and Bob Jones University, as well as centers like Stanford University's Hoover Institution and the Institute for Humane Studies at George Mason University. Richard Meagher notes that business leaders like Joseph Coors joined conservative foundations—such as the Bradley, Olin, Smith Richardson, and Scaife foundations, known as the "four sisters"—in explicitly funding "not just institutions but ideas," seeking to battle liberals in public debate and offering financial prizes and strategic advice.[214]

Conservatives have also been active in the states. In 1973 Weyrich helped found the American Legislative Exchange Council, which distributes talking points and model bills to Republican state legislators across the nation. The state-level network of conservative think tanks now includes the Buckeye Center for Public Policy in Ohio, the Mackinac Center for Public Policy in Michigan, the John Locke Foundation in North Carolina, the South Carolina Policy Council, the Texas Public Policy Foundation, and the Evergreen Freedom Foundation in Washington. Among state-focused think tanks, ideologically conservative institutions outnumber their liberal counterparts by a 2:1 margin and have been growing at a much faster rate than left-leaning or nonideological institutions.[215]

Over the course of this conservative mobilization, the meaning of the phrase "think tank" itself evolved. The term referred in the early 20th century to academic organizations, became associated in the 1950s with military planning organizations such as the RAND Corporation, and only adopted its current meaning with the rise of the Heritage Foundation in the 1970s. After Heritage and AEI became associated with conservative expertise, Progressive Era organizations like the Brookings Institution, the Council on Foreign Relations, and the Carnegie Endowment for International Peace also became commonly classified as "think tanks."[216] Although these latter organizations traditionally maintained more ties to academia and government than the later conservative institutions and were seen as "universities without students," they eventually became known as the center-left equivalents to Heritage and AEI. They served as conservative institutions' official adversaries and debating partners, often collaborating in events and producing "policy briefs" and "presidential transition manuals" (originally Heritage innovations).[217] Some observers describe a broad "Heritage-ization" of think tanks, perceiving a shift in emphasis from academic research toward advocacy in response to donor and legislator demand.[218]

Andrew Rich argues that ideologically aligned institutions, especially on the right, have come to dominate the think tank universe: "As the number of think tanks has grown in recent decades, well more than half of those that have emerged have represented identifiable ideological proclivities in their missions and research. The overwhelming majority of these ideological think tanks have been broadly conservative, producing work that favors limited government, free enterprise, and personal freedom."[219] Another study found that the five most influential think tanks now include one identified as liberal (Brookings), one perceived as neutral (the Center for Strategic and International Studies, or CSIS), and three viewed as conservative (AEI, Heritage, and Cato); other liberal think tanks are more specialized in their policy scope and more closely tied to particular issues and constituencies.[220] While members of Congress from both parties cite Brookings and CSIS at comparable rates, Republicans refer to AEI, Heritage, and Cato much more often than do Democrats.[221]

By 1988, Ronald Reagan could argue that "today the most important American scholarship comes out of our think tanks" in a speech at AEI, which he singled out as the most influential organization in "a revolution of ideas" and as a model representing "the triumph of the think tank."[222] Reagan argued that the conservative embrace of think tanks was born of necessity: "Our ideas were greeted with varying degrees of scorn and hostility by what we used to call the establishment institutions. The universities, once the only real home for American scholarship, had been particularly unresponsive. And so, it became necessary to create our own research institutions."[223] Indeed, more than half of Reagan's highest-level appointments to his 1981 campaign policy task forces were drawn from think tanks, and nearly 200 think tankers joined or advised his administration during its eight years in office.[224]

Medvetz cites the prominent intellectual Charles Murray as an illustrative example of the rise of conservative policy experts estranged from the academy. Heritage, AEI, and the Manhattan Institute, Medvetz argues, "helped catapult Murray from marginality into the mainstream despite persistent doubts from social scientists about the tenability of his claims."[225] *Losing Ground*, Murray's 1984 analysis of the failure of social welfare policy, received largely positive reviews from general interest publications and a much more negative response from social science specialists. After several contrary studies, some academics concluded that his theses had been "substantially undermined," but they continued to have influence among policymakers of both parties; Bill Clinton declared the analysis "essentially right," and its conclusions greatly influenced subsequent efforts to reform federal welfare programs.[226] This pattern recurred with Murray's 1994 book *The Bell Curve* (written with Richard J. Herrnstein) on the role of intelligence in social achievement; this work's conclusion that genetics could partially account for racial differences in intelligence tests was rejected by social scientists, this time with more popular agreement. Yet Murray gained publicity and a broader audience as a result of attacks on his scholarship from liberals, following up in 2012 with *Coming Apart*, an influential book on social inequality.

Think tanks played an important role in the welfare reform debate of the 1990s. House and Senate hearings on welfare reform between 1993 and 1996 included 27 appearances by representatives of conservative think tanks and 18 appearances by individuals from liberal think tanks;

overall, think tank experts outnumbered those based at universities.[227] They also played significant roles in other policy debates, such as those over the rise of low-tolerance "broken windows" policing, the 2001 Bush tax cut proposals, and the Iraq War deliberations of 2002–2003. Think tanks have also been active in congressional reform: all of the reform provisions proposed in the House Republican Party's Contract with America (1994) had appeared earlier in a Heritage Foundation study.[228] Conservative think tank studies and associated legislation also regularly inspire stories in conservative media.[229]

The conservative think tank movement succeeded not only through direct policy influence, but also by undermining the case for independent elite experts who assess policy choices and arbitrate evidentiary disputes. Conservatives created an alternative coalition to coordinate policy expertise, undermining ostensibly nonpartisan advocacy for technocratic government by academic and public sector experts (as well as existing research institutes).[230] As Frank Fischer explains, "Instead of merely dismissing experts and intellectuals as wrong-headed academics, conservatives' leaders began to . . . reach out to their own—often forgotten— conservative brethren in the intellectual world. . . . Seeking to counter liberal policy expertise on its own terms, the strategy was essentially to politicize the process of expert advice-giving." [231]

In the process, conservatives were able to create two-sided debates over policy research in areas where right-of-center voices were outliers in the broader academic community. Most prominently, conservative think tanks have played an important role in promoting skepticism about environmental policy; one study found that more than 90 percent of 110 books questioning the scientific consensus on environmental regulation were tied to conservative think tanks.[232] Media reporting on climate change shifted as a result, with more than half of news stories giving "roughly equal attention" after 1990 to the liberal-endorsed scientific consensus in favor of human-caused global warming patterns and to conservative dissent.[233] Conservative think tanks have also dominated public debate over education policy, eclipsing the role of university-based education research organizations and centrist think tanks in providing material to media organizations.[234] Additionally, think tanks have been more active than other groups in congressional hearings because legislators seek to build panels of witnesses who represent the opposing positions in policy debates, relying on think tanks to supply experts for each side.[235]

Conservative organizations and activists have also sought to combat the prevailing liberalism of many college campuses by funding efforts to popularize conservative thought among undergraduates. Young America's Foundation reprints books, organizes conferences for conservative student leaders, and funds campus appearances by conservative speakers. Its National Journalism Center connects students with conservative media figures, seeking to create new generations of journalists and activists. Think tank leaders often run summer programs, such as those conducted by the Hertog Foundation; many graduates of these youth education programs go on to lead conservative intellectual and media organizations.[236] This movement, Jean Stefancic and Richard Delgado have found, offers "cradle to grave" education and employment opportunities for educated conservatives.[237]

THE MANY ROLES OF LIBERAL THINK TANKS

In the view of their founders, conservative think tanks served the purpose of challenging the liberal orthodoxy of policy research, including that generated by academia and by long-standing research organizations such as the Brookings Institution. Although most Progressive Era think tanks are properly placed on the center left, they do not serve as proper equivalents to those on the conservative side. For example, Brookings' founders believed that the institution's credibility rested on its identity as an objective arbiter of academic research that remained independent of political parties.[238] The Carnegie Endowment and other organizations continue to maintain similar postures. The 1960s saw a rise in engaged liberal think tanks like the Urban Institute, but these institutions' activity included both research and administration of related government programs.

Leftists critiqued this technocratic planning, especially within security-focused organizations like the RAND Corporation. Yet liberal think tanks such as the Institute for Policy Studies failed to gain comparable influence to those positioned in the political center or right. In response to these critiques, most liberal intellectuals became either "activist-experts" dedicated to particular causes or inward-looking and professionalized social scientists. [239] Left-leaning technocrats eventually founded the Center on Budget and Policy Priorities (1981), which serves as the main liberal source of information on fiscal policy. The Economic Policy Institute (EPI), founded in 1986, maintains strong ties to unions and advances liberal views on labor and economic policy. The Progressive Policy Institute, founded in 1989 as a branch of the (moderate) Democratic Leadership Council, gained influence during the administration of Bill Clinton. The Center for American Progress (CAP), founded in 2003, was explicitly created as a liberal counterpart to the Heritage Foundation and has achieved more success. Yet CAP has had to develop a curriculum in the "progressive tradition" on its own in order to counter long-standing conservative efforts.

A CAP report finds that the conservative network of student organizations, constructed and funded to combat the generally liberal environment of academia, lacks a left-leaning parallel. In addition to the College Republicans (a much better-financed and nationally active organization than the College Democrats), the right has a set of ideological organizations "centered on conservative or libertarian values", as compared to an array of groups on the left devoted to single issues such as gay rights, the environment, and immigration.[240] Conservative groups, they find, are oriented toward sustaining an ideological movement:

> [The right] prefers to focus on broader topics, including limited government and fiscal conservatism. . . . [C]onservative organizations have built core competencies in broad programmatic areas geared toward ingraining conservative values in young people, followed by trainings on activism and journalism to ensure that young people have the skills needed to implement their values. . . . Meanwhile, most progressive organizations are narrowly focused on either a specific group among Millennial youth, such as immigrants, or a specific issue area. [241]

The report also found significant differences in scale, as summarized in Table 4-15. Conservative student organizations, though fewer in number, boast substantially more staff and resources than do liberal groups.

Scholars have attempted to explain this imbalance in educational and research infrastructure. Richard Meagher emphasizes the priorities of financial donors: "Liberal foundations . . . have often aspired to political neutrality and a more programmatic agenda; funding for them was philanthropy, the doing of public good, rather than building an alliance. As a result, they were not able to compete with the Right's 'movement consciousness.' "[242] Liberal scholars Jean Stefancic and Richard Delgado similarly cite liberal foundations' commitment to immediate action over slower movement building, yet they add that liberal scholars,

Table 4-15 STUDENT-ORIENTED LIBERAL AND CONSERVATIVE GROUPS

	Conservative Youth Groups	Liberal Youth Groups
No. of Organizations	25	38
No. of Youth-Oriented Staff	355	275
Youth Engagement Budget (2008–2010)	$247 million	$88 million
Building and Land Assets	$43 million	0

Characteristics of conservative and liberal organizations designed to organize students or young people. Some recent organizations or those that are components of a larger organization are not included in the budgets because no data were available from their tax returns. Data from Johnson and Van Ostern (2012).

especially specialists in identity politics, have also settled more easily in academia.[243] Medvetz explains conservative dominance of think tanks in part as a product of the move of liberal activist-experts into the university: "Numerous biographical and autobiographical accounts, in fact, have documented every step along the path from 1960s student-activist to 1980s professor. And while these accounts vary in their details, they tend to converge on one particular theme: namely, the process of turning away from one's activist ideals in favor of a new set of professional obligations and incentives."[244]

One of the most important factors in the failure to build a broad liberal movement in the United States was the left's traditional division into a variety of distinct issue agendas and constituencies—a pattern that extends to the intellectual realm. A survey of 294 university catalogs found 114 African American studies programs, 41 Latino studies programs, 24 American Indian studies programs, 17 Asian American studies programs, 215 environmental studies programs, 99 urban studies programs, 192 women's studies programs, and 5 sexuality studies programs in 2000.[245] Nearly all of these disciplines have doubled in size since 1975, and most are still growing. These networks developed in response to student protest movements and soon became associated with sectors of advocacy organizations.[246] They also drew financial support from liberal foundations interested in aiding civil rights advocacy, especially the channeling of protest movements into academic research.[247] Battles were mostly waged on campus rather than in the political arena and focused on the program's status as a department, an interdisciplinary major or minor, or a part of a larger ethnic studies initiative.[248] The legacy of multiculturalism in academia includes not only these "studies" programs but also a broadening of traditional disciplines to include identity-based subdivisions and canons of established research—a trend that has stimulated conservative concerns about excessive fragmentation and declining standards of intellectual rigor.[249]

Similar diversity in program goals and constituencies is evident among liberal think tanks, as Medvetz explains:

> [E]ach of the major progressive movements of the past half-century has at least one think tank tied visibly to its cause. The Worldwatch Institute, for example, describes itself as playing a "pivotal role in the global environmental movement," while the Joint Center for Political and Economic Studies has dedicated itself to the struggle for civil rights. Likewise, the Institute for Women's Policy Research . . . is often described as the main think tank of the women's movement.[250]

In comparison, the think tanks on the right tend to be "all-purpose conservative torchbearers," although some key organizations reflect distinct ideological traditions (such as the libertarian Cato Institute and the neoconservative Project for the New American Century).[251] Libertarians in the Republican Party are somewhat analogous to the left wing of the Democratic Party: they form an ideological faction that does not dominate the broader party but is attached to important elite institutions. Nonetheless, most liberal think tanks lack a broad ideological scope. A count by Andrew Rich finds that 69 percent of national liberal think tanks are focused on specific issue domains, compared to only 34 percent of conservative think tanks.[252] Individual liberal researchers active in policymaking, according to Stefancic and Delgado, also tend to engage as single-issue specialists:

> A liberal scholar is likely to spend an entire career on one issue. . . . Conservatives have no such limitation . . . [reminding] the key player that he or she is part of the larger conservative agenda. A liberal working on a single issue is likely to view himself or herself [more] in terms of that issue than of liberalism as a whole.[253]

We further investigated the content of advocacy by liberal and conservative think tanks by analyzing the content of executive summaries of reports from a random sample of publication days. Table 4-16 summarizes the results, classifying AEI and the Heritage Foundation as conservative and CAP and the Brookings Institution as liberal. Liberal think tanks mention far more public policies and more than three times as many

Table 4-16 CONTENT OF THINK TANK REPORTS

No. of Mentions Per Executive Summary	Heritage/ AEI	CAP/ Brookings
Ideology or Principle	1.3	1.5
Conservative (Republican)/Liberal (Democratic) Ideological Principles	.9	.7
Public Policy	3.2	6.1
New Policy Proposals	.7	1.6
Conservative (Republican)/Liberal (Democratic) Policy Position	.5	.8
Social Group or Interest Group	.7	2.4
Demographic Groups (Class, Race, Religion, Gender, Age)	.3	1.5
American Imagery	1	1.3
American Exceptionalism/Threats to Way of Life	.4	.4
n	100	100

Data from an original content analysis of think tank reports from the American Enterprise Institute (AEI), the Heritage Foundation, the Center for American Progress (CAP), and the Brookings Institution from a random sample of days. We group Heritage and AEI as conservative think tanks and Brookings and CAP as liberal think tanks. Our data, content analysis codebook, and analyses of reliability are available online at mattg.org.

Table 4-17 SOURCES IN THINK TANK REPORTS

	Heritage/ AEI	CAP/Brookings
Sources per Report	25.2	63.2
No. of each type of source in first 10 citations		
Academic Research	1.1	1.6
Government Report	1.9	1.7
Media	1.8	1.2
Interest Group	1.3	1.5
Think Tank	1.4	2.3
No. of Each Type of Citation in First 10 Citations		
Broad Principles	3.6	3.4
Evaluates Social Problem	1.7	2.6
Assesses Effectiveness	2.3	1.9
No. Citing Specific Data in First 10 Citations	1.9	2.7
n	100	100

Data from an original content analysis of think tank reports from the American Enterprise Institute (AEI), the Heritage Foundation, the Center for American Progress (CAP), and the Brookings Institution from a random sample of days. We group Heritage and AEI as conservative think tanks and Brookings and CAP as liberal think tanks. Our data, content analysis codebook, and analyses of reliability are available online at mattg.org.

social groups in their reports compared to conservative institutions. The differences between ideological mentions and uses of American imagery are small and insignificant, however, suggesting that conservative think tanks are not compensating for limited policy or social group content by adding additional symbolic verbiage.

Table 4-17 summarizes the use of sources in each think tank report. Liberal think tanks cite more than twice as many sources as conservative think tanks, more closely following academic norms. Based on an analysis of the first 10 citations in each report, we find that liberal think tanks are more likely to cite academic research and studies by other think tanks (including self-citations), while conservative think tanks rely more on media citations. Liberal think tanks are slightly more likely to use sources to evaluate the extent of social problems and more likely to cite particular data as opposed to broad claims or quotes taken from elsewhere. Again, liberal think tanks more closely mirror academic practice.

Both liberal and conservative think tanks attempt to attract attention to their research from reporters and legislators, but they may not have equal success. Table 4-18 displays the citations of liberal and conservative think tanks in television news coverage, newspapers and magazines, and congressional debates, along with appearances from their representatives before congressional committees between 1999 and 2008. Liberal

Table 4-18 PROMINENCE AND INVOLVEMENT OF THINK TANKS IN MEDIA
AND CONGRESS

	Television Citations	Print Media Citations	Citations in Congress	Testimony Appearances
Liberal Total	373	12,094	756	197
Conservative Total	266	16,905	1,198	739
Liberal Percent of Ideological Total	58%	42%	39%	21%
Top Think Tanks	1. Brookings	1. Brookings	1. Heritage	1. AEI
	2. Heritage	2. AEI	2. Brookings	2. Heritage
	3. AEI	3. Heritage	3. Urban	3. Cato

Mentions of top think tanks in media reports and congressional publications and the number of testimony appearances by representatives from the same think tanks from 1999–2008 (print media citations also include 1998). Several think tanks, including CSIS and RAND, are not categorized as liberal or conservative and are not included in the liberal percent of the total. Data from Abelson (2009).

think tanks, especially the Brookings Institution, were more successful in stimulating media coverage than in receiving attention from Congress. Heritage was especially prominent in informing congressional debate, with AEI slightly more active in committee testimony. Although liberal institutions became more frequently cited by legislators and their representatives were more often invited to committee hearings after Democrats took control of Congress in the 2006 midterm elections, representatives of AEI and Heritage still testified more often than experts from other think tanks. Evidence from a prior study found that Brookings had ranked first among think tanks in supplying testimony until Republicans gained a congressional majority in 1995.[254] A survey of congressional staff and reporters from 1997 found that 72 percent believed conservative think tanks to be more influential than liberal think tanks, with only 4 percent citing liberal institutions as holding more sway on Capitol Hill.[255]

The conservative movement has invested substantial resources in creating an alternative research infrastructure to counter academic science, but that hardly means that traditional research no longer plays an important role in policymaking. Table 4-19 summarizes the research-related factors that historians credit with bringing about significant policy change. This analysis classifies the most significant federal policy changes since 1945 based on whether they expanded the scope of government (liberal), contracted it (conservative), or fell somewhere in between (mixed). Within each category, Table 4-19 indicates the share of policy changes that included involvement by think tanks or academics (as identified by at least one policy historian), as well as the proportion of changes influenced by a key report issued by a government agency or nongovernmental organization (such as an advocacy group).

Table 4-19 RESEARCH-RELATED FACTORS IN EXPLANATIONS
FOR POLICY CHANGE

	Liberal Policy Changes	Mixed Policy Changes	Conservative Policy Changes
Think Tank Involvement	2.0%	0.7%	5.7%
Academic Involvement	12.6%	8.0%	8.6%
Influential Government Report	21.8%	11.7%	21.4%
Influential NGO Report	12.8%	4.7%	2.9%

Percentage of liberal, conservative, and ideologically mixed federal policy changes since 1945 that involved each factor, based on the explanations offered by policy historians. Data from Grossmann (2014).vn

The results show that academic experts are more often credited with influencing policy change than are think tanks, though liberal policy shifts are especially likely to be associated with academics, while conservative shifts draw disproportionately from think tanks. Government reports more commonly influence policy changes in both ideological directions. Interest group reports are more than four times as influential for liberal policy changes compared to conservative changes; the preponderance of single-issue advocacy groups on the left may overwhelm conservatives' slight advantage among think tanks (despite the research focus of the latter). Research on congressional testimony confirms that think tanks compete with other experts: in hearings involving think tanks, 15 percent of other witnesses come from universities, 15 percent come from government, and 40 percent are supplied by interest groups, and when think tank reports are cited in Congress, they are likewise less often prominently cited than are reports by government agencies.[256]

Academics are hardly absent from policymaking. The President's Council of Economic Advisors and the President's Council of Advisors on Science and Technology draw from academic experts. Scientific bodies like the National Academy of Sciences also maintain quasi-official roles in policymaking. More economists work for the Department of Commerce than for all Washington think tanks combined.[257] Interest groups often use academic policy analysis and evaluation to gain legitimacy and modify their proposals in response to the results of scientific research.[258] Despite the challenges from avowedly conservative research enterprises, the scientific establishment is still well represented in government and influential in policymaking.

Compared to other Western democracies, however, policy research in the United States is more likely to be generated by private, ideologically aligned organizations; a comparison with three European nations revealed less influence by semi-public, partisan, or university research organizations in the United States and far more influence by think tanks engaging in political advocacy (though the United States still stood out for its strong legislative research organizations).[259] According to this study, however, both sides of the American think tank divide are relatively conservative in international terms:

> There are no truly left-wing political parties in America by European standards. Similarly, there are very few truly leftist policy research organizations in the United States. EPI is the only one in our sample that even comes close ... [and] organizations like Heritage and Cato are oriented further to the right than [conservative think tanks in Europe]. ... The center-left in America is comparable to what Europeans would call a centrist and more likely a center-right position.[260]

DIFFERENCES IN APPROACH TO RESEARCH

Journalist Chris Mooney has charged that the contemporary Republican Party systematically ignores or undermines nonpartisan science and research evidence. His two books, *The Republican War on Science* (2005) and *The Republican Brain: The Science of Why They Deny Science—and Reality* (2012), argue that conservative activists and policymakers are blinded by ideological devotion, seeking to undermine scientific findings that conflict with their existing beliefs—a phenomenon that was particularly characteristic of the George W. Bush administration.[261] Although Mooney is hardly a neutral observer, his research provides a useful summary of relevant historical developments that would be uncontested by Republican critics. Conservatives formed organizations like the George C. Marshall Institute, the Competitive Enterprise Institute, and the Heartland Institute (all founded in 1984) to challenge scientific orthodoxy. Under Republican rule, Congress later held "scientific integrity" hearings to dispute various unwelcome findings. Senator James Inhofe of Oklahoma has led the Republican opposition to government regulations designed to combat climate change, denying the validity of scientific research on the subject. "The claim that global warming is caused by manmade emissions is simply untrue," claimed Inhofe in a 2003 floor debate, "and not based on sound science. ... [With] all of the phony science, could it be that manmade global warming is the greatest hoax ever perpetrated on the American people? It sure sounds like it."[262] Inhofe later published a book entitled *The Greatest Hoax* and even brought a snowball onto the floor of the Senate in February 2015 as supposed evidence that the Earth was not in fact growing warmer.

After gaining control of Congress in 1995, Republicans substantially reduced government research capacity, though mostly for budgetary reasons.[263] They eliminated Congress's main scientific arm, the Office of Technology Assessment (OTA), while reducing the staff and research capacity of the Government Accountability Office and Congressional Research Service.[264] Committee staff also declined by one-third in both the House and the Senate.[265] Newly empowered Republican congressional leaders implemented these cuts in order to demonstrate their commitment to a smaller government even within their own institution, but they also remained less interested than their Democratic predecessors had been in maintaining a research infrastructure for the development of public policies. Before OTA began operations in 1974, it was attacked in National Review as a potential "political weapon" for Democrats, and it continued to withstand attacks from conservative critics throughout its history (especially when it was led by liberals).[266]

Because Republicans are more skeptical than Democrats about the benefits of government regulation, they also favor tighter standards of evidence to justify action in administrative agencies. To Mooney, Republican invocations of "sound science" are disingenuous, but he acknowledges that liberals naturally prefer lower burdens of proof before government is permitted or compelled to act (since scientific evidence is always indefinite). Republicans passed the Data Quality Act in 2001 to restrict the use of research by executive agencies, proposing new review practices to include nonacademic scientists. The Center for Regulatory Effectiveness, established in 1996, employs these tools to object to dependency on scientific expertise in the development of new environmental and health regulations. Many scientists—especially those working on environmental issues—endorse the view that conservatives have distorted science. One review catalogs examples of obfuscating and misrepresenting results, intimidating scientists, invoking political rules to suppress unwanted findings, and invoking media biases to balance scientific findings with conservative alternatives.[267]

Mooney believes that the conservative resistance to science stems from a distinctive psychological makeup. He cites research showing that conservatives are less likely to recognize inconsistency and more likely to react with defensiveness to uncertainty and ambiguity.[268] He argues that these findings mirror political science research that has found that conservatives defend their political positions more aggressively[269] and have historically used simple declarative language rather than complexly integrated thoughts.[270]

But recent studies suggest a more complex picture. Joshua Blank and Daron Shaw presented survey respondents with a long list of topics on which scientific experts agree; in some cases, the consensus disfavored conservatives (such as stem cell research and climate change), while in others, liberals would be more likely to object (such as biotechnology and nuclear power). They found that conservative ideology was negatively associated with deference to science across all issues, whereas Democratic party identification was positively associated with deference across all domains.[271] Independent of ideology, however, Republican respondents were more deferential in those cases in which science supported their policy position. Other studies, however, have found that both conservatives and liberals reduce their trust in the scientific community when presented with findings inconsistent with their beliefs[272] and that prior findings of conservative distrust in climate science are sensitive to changes in survey ordering and question wording.[273]

It seems likely that partisans on both sides engage in motivated reasoning when it comes to the use of scientific evidence in political controversies—seeking information in support of their existing views and discounting contrary evidence. But conservatives more often reject the role of the scientific community in arbitrating disputes and are more likely to perceive scientific findings as inconsistent with their beliefs. One recent study offers something of a resolution: Troy Campbell and Aaron Kay find that conservatives are averse to the common solutions associated with scientific consensus, which usually involve more governmental intervention. When confronted with market-based or nongovernmental solutions to environmental problems, they are far more willing to accept scientific expertise.[274] If the scientific consensus suggests that government will not solve a problem, in contrast, liberals can be more skeptical. Liberals often assume that if conservatives believed the scientific evidence for problems like global warming, they would accept the necessity of their proposed regulatory solutions. The evidence suggests otherwise: conservatives oppose the solutions on ideological grounds and therefore work backward to reject the evidence supposedly justifying them.

Since liberals believe that government should accept responsibility for identifying social problems and evaluating potential policy responses, they tend to accept scientific evidence that advances either cause. To avoid creeping government expansion, conservatives tend to minimize evidence of problems that might be solved by government and may distrust the motives of those who seek to emphasize problems in order to provoke government activity. There is little evidence that distinctive conservative personality traits produce a unique attitude toward science itself. But conservative movement leaders certainly maintain an incentive to raise the standards of evidence required for government action and to sow mistrust of researchers who view their job as raising problems that require an active response from the public sector.

INTERPRETING HISTORY ON THE LEFT AND RIGHT

The network of conservative experts from think tanks and academic associations is at a considerable numerical disadvantage compared to their liberal colleagues. Because conservatives have formed an explicitly ideological counter-establishment, however, they are often able to critique the liberal majority and obtain more equal time in public debate. The same policy experts often appear regularly across the conservative media, allowing a small number of scholars to effectively act as informed spokespersons for the conservative side of policy disputes.[275]

One recent example, the controversy over the College Board's new standards for the teaching of advanced placement classes in U.S. history, helps illustrate how both sides view their opponents. As the *Washington Post* reported in 2015:

> Conservatives, including the Republican National Committee and 2016 GOP presidential hopeful Ben Carson, slammed the 2014 Advanced Placement history course, saying it overemphasized negative aspects of U.S. history, portrayed historical events as "identity politics"—a series of conflicts between groups of people as opposed to explaining historical events through shared ideals—and did not fully explore the unique and positive values of the U.S. system.[276]

The president of the American Historical Association defended the standards, saying that conservatives offered only "a more comfortable national history" over "a more unsettling one." But a conservative think tank leader argued that "the College Board continues to be under the influence of leftist historians."[277]

In response to the initial guidelines, the Republican National Committee issued an official resolution complaining that "the Framework includes little or no discussion of the Founding Fathers, the principles of the Declaration of Independence, [or] the religious influences on our nation's history."[278] They requested state legislative action, a congressional investigation, and an effort to defund the College Board. In response, Texas, Oklahoma, and Georgia proposed legislation to change the standards.[279] The National Association of Scholars presented an open letter from 100 conservative historians protesting the new guidelines.

The College Board revised the guidelines in 2015, adding a new section on American identity and dampening the emphasis on Japanese internment, segregation, and atomic weapon use. But this did not satisfy critics; one conservative wrote, "I give the College Board credit for reducing the overt emphasis in [the 2014 standards] on identity group politics and for reintroducing in [the new version] the theme of 'national identity,' but the sub-group emphasis is merely less conspicuous."[280] They complained that the document should instead emphasize "the idea that America was and is a new kind of nation, one founded on the philosophical principles named in the Declaration of Independence."[281]

This example is but one skirmish in the many ongoing battles over politics, ideology, and identity in educational curricula, but it fittingly encapsulates the role of intellectuals on each side. Leaders of institutions like the American Historical Association and the College Board are disproportionately drawn from the left; although these organizations are (and perceive themselves to be) nonpartisan and deferential to neutral expertise, their intellectual perspective also tends to reflect the prevailing political values of their academic disciplines, including a distinctive and growing emphasis on cultural and demographic diversity. To conservatives, claims of deference to the prevailing scholarly consensus by the traditional academic establishment are a misleading guise for the imposition of a "leftist" or even "un-American" ideological agenda, necessitating the construction of an alternative network of openly right-of-center alternative institutions and policy experts to dispute this consensus—which in turn are viewed by their opponents as a politically motivated movement seeking to attack scientific merit. In the intellectual arena, as in the media world, an asymmetric pattern thus endures.

THE INFORMATIONAL MISMATCH
OF AMERICAN POLITICS

The Democratic and Republican parties each rely on research and expertise in policy debates and use the news media to convey their ideas to the public. Yet there are substantial differences in their sources of information as well as the networks on which they rely for communication. Democrats are more trusting of scientists and more reliant on their scholarly output to supply the research base for public policy. Fearing the biases of liberal academics, Republicans have established think tanks that provide research consistent with conservative ideology. Republicans want their experts to be treated as equivalent to those preferred by Democrats, even though they are collectively less academically credentialed.

Likewise, Democrats rely primarily on mainstream media outlets to report on problems and debates over potential solutions; they look to these same sources to police the information presented by each side. Republicans instead depend on avowedly conservative media to spread their message, perceiving mainstream media outlets as biased toward liberal ideas. Because their movement has long distrusted academic and journalistic experts, conservatives built a distinct ecosystem of information providers and disseminators. Since the rise of more popular talk radio programs in the 1990s and FNC in the 2000s, the Republican Party has become increasingly influenced by conservative media.

Today, the same patterns of information use and dissemination are repeated in every election and each policy dispute, producing a political conversation that is less a "great debate" over principles and policies than it is an asymmetric dialogue between combatants who do not share each other's rules or styles. Conservative media—and the experts they rely on—spread stories such as that concerning Barack Obama's ties to William Ayers that they believe mainstream institutions are ignoring as a result of political bias. Democrats accuse Republicans of dismissing scientific evidence and cocooning themselves in an alternative media universe—criticisms that have some merit but understate conservatives' legitimate aversion to trusting institutions overwhelmingly composed of liberals to fairly adjudicate information on the public's behalf.

Democrats depend on an extensive array of advocacy groups tied to party constituencies—in which each sector maintains its own intellectual research base and specialized media—to generate policy proposals and arguments. Yet they are also comfortable with mainstream media and academic experts, trusting them to provide information about how best to achieve substantive goals. Republicans instead rely on a conservative media and research ecosystem created to advance their ideological movement. The success of this conservative effort to delegitimize mainstream outlets and to construct a network of alternative authorities means that when the two sides intersect, Democrats and Republicans more often talk past each other, engaged as they are in separate conversations.

CHAPTER 5

ᐧᐧᐧ

Campaigning in Poetry and Prose

MSNBC political reporter Benjy Sarlin covered the large field of Republican candidates seeking the nomination of their party for a full year before the Iowa caucuses marked the formal start of the 2016 presidential race, while his colleague Alex Seitz-Wald likewise followed the campaign activities of the Democratic contenders over the same period. In an experiment designed to give each reporter a fresh perspective on the campaign, MSNBC asked them to temporarily exchange journalistic beats in January 2016 and describe the differences that they noticed after switching to cover the other party. Sarlin spent a week reporting on the Democratic race in Iowa, while Seitz-Wald attended Republican campaign events in New Hampshire and Massachusetts before heading to Iowa to follow a cross-state bus tour organized by Texas senator Ted Cruz, who ultimately won the state's first-in-the-nation presidential caucus on February 1.

When asked what he had learned by observing the opposite party with fresh eyes, Sarlin responded:

> I was caught off guard by how specific and personal Democratic voters' issues tended to be. One woman told me she had lost a job because she had to take care of a sick relative and wanted paid family leave. Another woman told me her insurance stopped covering a certain medication that had grown too expensive and she liked how [Hillary] Clinton and [Bernie] Sanders talked about lowering drug prices. . . . By contrast, Republican voters tend to be excited by more abstract issues: One of the most common answers I get from Cruz voters when I ask about their leading concern is "the Constitution." There are fewer "I have a specific problem in my own life, and I'd like the government to do x about it" responses.

Seitz-Wald agreed that "the two parties are operating in different parallel universes," adding that, in his own experience, Democrats also care more than Republicans about choosing a nominee who will be formidable in a general election:

> [W]hile electability has become a major issue in the Democratic primary, Republican voters I talked to said it was more important to pick someone who represents their values than to try to guess who can beat the Democrat in November. The candidates likewise didn't spend much time making their case in electability terms. Meanwhile, Bernie Sanders is reading his general election match-up poll numbers on stage at rallies, and Clinton is running ads saying only she can beat the GOP.[1]

The impressions formed by these reporters after a few days on the campaign trail reveal how the fundamental differences between the parties extend to the realm of political campaigns. Democratic candidates appeal to voters by invoking group interest and pledging practical solutions to their problems, while Republicans prefer to emphasize more abstract themes that draw upon larger principles. Because Democratic constituencies prioritize concrete policy change, Democratic candidates tout their ability to win elections and, once in power, to work within the political system in pursuit of tangible accomplishments. Republicans, in contrast, resist viewing the electorate as an assortment of specific separable interests, instead seeking support by presenting themselves as champions of an ideological cause.

This partisan difference extends to general elections as well as party primaries. Attempting to make sense of his unexpectedly unsuccessful 2012 challenge to incumbent Barack Obama, Republican nominee Mitt Romney told a conference call of top financial donors a week after the election that "what the president's campaign did was focus on certain members of his base coalition . . . following the old playbook of giving a lot of stuff to groups," while his own campaign had instead been "talking about big issues for the whole country."[2] Romney aides expressed amazement in retrospect at how Obama's advisors had at regular intervals over the course of the campaign "rolled out a new policy for a different segment of their coalition they hoped to attract." These policies included federal student loan reforms designed to appeal to college students and recent graduates, support for same-sex marriage (popular among gay and lesbian voters and the nonreligious), and liberalized immigration initiatives of particular interest to Latinos, methodically assembling a large enough base of popular support to win reelection despite the middling performance of the national economy.[3]

Romney's comments were largely dismissed by Democrats as the rationalization of a sore loser, and even some Republicans distanced themselves from the implication that Obama had traded government-bestowed "gifts" to key electoral constituencies in exchange for their votes.[4] (All of the policy proposals were part of a programmatic agenda, after all, not selective benefits provided by Democratic officeholders.) Yet his remarks likewise reflected an enduring difference between the voter persuasion and mobilization strategies adopted by Democrats and Republicans. Aware that the bulk of their electoral support is supplied by a coalition of discrete social groups primarily attracted to the party on the basis of shared interests or identities, Democratic candidates tend to campaign for office by priming voters' group identification and promoting specific policy positions and proposals that promise to benefit members of these particular groups. Because Republican voters are a more socially homogeneous bloc principally motivated by their affinity with the conservative cause, Republican candidates prefer to emphasize broader ideological commitments over detailed policy proposals while largely eschewing explicit group-based appeals. Romney was hardly the first presidential candidate to recognize this distinction. According to the election chronicler Theodore White, Richard Nixon noted during his successful 1972 reelection campaign that he "wasn't putting groups together in a coalition the way [Democratic president Franklin D.] Roosevelt had—he was trying to cut across groups, binding people in every group who had the same ideas."[5]

Candidates battling for the nomination of either party face an obvious strategic incentive to adopt the most effective means of stimulating popular appeal among their fellow partisans, which might be expected to carry over into elevated enthusiasm within the loyal party base once a successful nominee turns to face the opposition in the fall campaign. But the tendency of Democrats to emphasize policy specifics and group benefits and the corresponding Republican penchant for stressing more abstract ideological themes are both further reinforced by the broader American public's simultaneous preference for operational liberalism and symbolic conservatism. Democratic and Republican candidates compete for the support of persuadable voters in general elections by battling to establish their preferred frame of partisan conflict: Democrats gain an advantage by portraying the differences between the candidates as primarily defined by distinct policy positions, while Republicans benefit when voters instead view their electoral options as representing a choice between contrasting philosophical commitments. As William Mayer observes, "Democrats do think—very frequently—about gaining the votes of particular groups in the population by appealing to relatively narrow group interests. Indeed, group-based appeals have long been a central preoccupation of Democratic presidential campaigns."[6]

Although campaigns are waged for the purpose of electing specific candidates, the collective accumulation of campaign messages from election to election inevitably shapes the mass public's more general perceptions of the two parties. The ideas and rhetoric espoused by individual office-seeking politicians—within a unique American system featuring lengthy campaign seasons, frequent electoral contests, voter-controlled nomination processes, and permissive campaign finance laws—can provide citizens with the informational basis on which to select a favored party while simultaneously reinforcing and strengthening the attitudes, beliefs, and allegiances of existing partisans. Indeed, it would be quite surprising if the asymmetric nature of American party politics did not extend to campaigns, in which Democratic and Republican elites are compelled to craft appeals to party loyalists and swing voters alike in order to gain or maintain political power.

This chapter explores the nature of party asymmetry in campaigns for both the presidency and lower offices in party primaries as well as general elections. It begins by examining the distinct nature of nomination politics in each major party, focusing especially on presidential nominations. The final section of the chapter concentrates on electoral competition between the two parties, confirming that Democratic and Republican candidates continue to differ systematically in their preferred strategic approach to winning popular support once they advance to the general election. Ambitious Republicans have concluded that an emphasis on broad ideology in their communications with voters breeds success in both electoral stages, while Democrats consistently prefer to emphasize group ties and policy specifics.

PRESIDENTIAL NOMINATIONS: AN OVERVIEW

Party asymmetry is evident in how candidates position themselves in front of party leaders and voters during the presidential nomination process. Table 5-1 lists the winners of contested nominations in both parties since 1948, indicating whether eventual nominees differentiated themselves from their chief rival or rivals with a clear ideological appeal to the left (for the Democrats) or the right (for the Republicans), presented themselves as more moderate than the competition, or either made no clear ideological appeal or portrayed themselves as a compromise between competing candidates. Only one Democratic nominee won by avowedly making an appeal to the ideological left, whereas three Republicans won by running to the right of their opponents; other Republicans tried but failed to differentiate themselves from fellow conservatives in their field. Over the same time period, six Democratic nominees won by making a pitch for electability from the center, whereas only incumbent Republican

Table 5-1 CONTESTED NOMINATION BATTLES

	Democratic Nomination Winner Differentiation			Republican Nomination Winner Differentiation		
	Liberal Ideological Appeal	No Clear Ideological Appeal or Compromise	Moderate Appeal	Moderate Appeal	No Clear Ideological Appeal or Compromise	Conservative Ideological Appeal
1948		**Truman***		Dewey		
1952		Stevenson		**Eisenhower**		
1956		Stevenson				
1960		**Kennedy**			Nixon	
1964						Goldwater
1968			Humphrey	**Nixon**		
1972	McGovern			**Nixon***		
1976			**Carter**	Ford*		
1980			Carter*			**Reagan**
1984		Mondale				
1988		Dukakis			**H.W. Bush**	
1992			**Clinton**	H.W. Bush*		
1996					Dole	
2000			Gore			**W. Bush**
2004			Kerry			
2008		**Obama**			McCain	
2012					Romney	

Winners of all contested nomination battles in both parties, classified based on whether the winner differentiated himself as a more ideologically extreme (conservative or liberal) or more moderate candidate compared to his opponents. The default category of "not clear or missed" is used if ideological differentiation was not a clear strategy of the candidate or if his positioning was mixed (such as a win by a compromise candidate).

General election winners are in bold; *denotes the incumbent.

presidents have recently used that strategy (and more out of necessity than by design).

The reforms to the presidential nomination process enacted by the national Democratic Party after its disastrous 1968 convention in Chicago ultimately precipitated fundamental change in both parties. By requiring most convention delegates from 1972 onward to be selected via a process open to any eligible voter belonging to the party, Democrats encouraged many state governments to implement presidential primary elections as the standard means of delegate selection—a measure that effectively reformed the Republican Party as well.[7] The once-common practice among state parties of choosing an uncommitted slate of delegates—or a delegation claiming nominal affiliation with a home-state "favorite son"—as a prelude to negotiation and dealmaking by organizational leaders at the convention itself, was already in decline after the 1950s and died out within the first decade of the post-reform era.

Because voters attending state primaries and caucuses now cast ballots for delegates who have pledged in advance to support a particular national presidential candidate at the convention, would-be Democratic and Republican nominees must build an expansive national campaign apparatus devoted to persuading and mobilizing party voters to choose them over what can be a large field of rival contenders. Whereas nominations were once contested mostly among networks of political elites, who corresponded privately in advance of the convention and cut deals with each other in smoke-filled rooms, competition among candidates now occurs openly in front of a mass party electorate.

Despite major institutional changes, the distinctive natures of the two parties are still apparent. The Democratic nomination process has evolved from a bargain among constituency representatives to an open competition to assemble voting blocs. The conservative movement has proven effective at guiding both Republican elites and voters. The ideological nature of the Republican Party remains on public display throughout the quadrennial process of selecting a presidential standard-bearer.

REPUBLICAN PRESIDENTIAL NOMINATIONS BEFORE REAGAN

The temporary eclipse of the Republican Party's conservative wing in the wake of the New Deal was especially visible in the presidential nomination battles of the 1940s and 1950s. In 1948, Senator Robert Taft of Ohio, the unofficial leader of the Republican right wing, sought the presidential office earlier held by his father William Howard Taft but proved unable to defeat more moderate competitors, losing to New York governor Thomas E. Dewey (who had also been nominated in 1944) on the first convention ballot by a margin of 434–224. Taft also fell short four years later to Dwight D. Eisenhower by a vote of 595–500 (although Taft did win more popular votes and state primaries that year despite running against a popular war hero). Eisenhower's vice president, Richard Nixon, prevailed in 1960 despite an active campaign to draft Barry Goldwater, whose candidacy represented the first stirrings of the resurgent conservative movement's attempt to assert influence over Republican presidential politics. Goldwater ultimately delivered a speech at the 1960 Republican convention that removed his name from consideration while simultaneously urging conservatives to await the next opportunity to take control of the party.

That opportunity presented itself four years later, when Goldwater's successful nomination demonstrated the considerable institutional power within the GOP now held by ideologically motivated activists aligned with the modern conservative movement. Goldwater's campaign was bolstered by his strong performance in several state primaries that year (especially those in California and Texas), but accumulating the overall majority of delegates needed to win the nomination in the pre-reform era still required him to attract substantial support from delegations controlled by the leadership of state party organizations. Benefiting from the conservative movement's ascendancy within the Republican Party apparatus in many southern and western states, Goldwater prevailed on the first ballot at the Republican convention. His landslide defeat in the November election at the hands of Democratic incumbent Lyndon B. Johnson merely vindicated the fears of many pragmatic Republican politicians from the East and Midwest that a "movement conservative" like Goldwater was far too ideologically extreme to be elected president in an era of broad public support for New Deal and Great Society policymaking.

Seeking to avoid another electoral calamity, a number of Republican officials coordinated more effectively in 1968 to deliver the nomination to Richard Nixon for a second time. Nixon had carefully positioned himself as a unifying candidate within the party, appealing to a broad cross-section of Republican leaders and voters alike. While conservative activists found Nixon more ideologically tolerable than either New York governor Nelson Rockefeller (the de facto leader of the moderate Republican faction) or Rockefeller's ally George Romney, the victory-starved Republican mainstream also viewed Nixon, who had nearly captured the presidency eight years before, as far more electable than Goldwater had been. Nixon "had the support of the regular Republicans and of most of the important figures on the party's right, while still maintaining his ties to the liberals in the eastern states," observed Nicol Rae. "As the organization candidate, Nixon was acceptable to the pragmatists in both liberal and conservative camps, who valued his ability to prevent the leaders of their ideological opponents from securing the nomination."[8] Nixon received 692 votes in the first round of balloting at the Republican National Convention in Miami Beach, enough to immediately secure the nomination, with Rockefeller the runner-up at 277 delegates and Ronald Reagan, running to Nixon's right, placing third with 182 votes—a promising performance for the new governor of California, who had yet to serve two full years in elective office.

Because Nixon was elected president in 1968 and faced only token opposition for renomination four years later, the procedural reforms that caused an abrupt upheaval in the Democratic Party by enabling the insurgent candidacy of George McGovern did not affect the Republican side as immediately. In 1976, however, the newly central role of state primaries and caucuses in selecting convention delegates convinced Reagan, now out of office after two terms as governor, that he could successfully challenge incumbent president Gerald R. Ford for the Republican presidential nomination. As Reagan's campaign manager John Sears later explained, the nomination process had "changed drastically. . . . Republicans could afford to disregard the obligations which the party leaders felt to the man in office. It was now possible to run against an incumbent and win."[9]

Ford, the former minority leader of the House of Representatives, had been appointed to the vice presidency by Nixon upon the resignation of Spiro T. Agnew in 1973; when Nixon himself resigned the following year amid the Watergate scandal, Ford ascended to the White House without ever having received the nomination of his party for either national office. A middle-of-the-road Republican in the pragmatic midwestern tradition, Ford did not inspire broadly enthusiastic support within the modern conservative movement. Instead, many conservatives defected to a Reagan candidacy that was well positioned to capitalize on the ability of ideologically motivated activists to take advantage of the additional power handed to them by the new party reforms. "There can be little doubt that the new dynamics of presidential nominations were a godsend to the militant right," concluded Rae. "Their ever-expanding network of pressure groups, campaigning organizations, and single-issue activists could be effectively mobilized for primary elections or open caucuses, where the total turnout of registered Republicans was likely to be low."[10] This pattern of conflict—in which rebellious conservatives fueled a formidable "outsider" challenge to "establishment" Republicanism, with a veteran incumbent officeholder often facing accusations of having drifted away from the party's ideological principles over time—would come to be reenacted many times in Republican primary elections at all levels of public office over the succeeding forty years, steadily increasing pressure on the Republican Party in government to make significant concessions to the preferences of the activist right.

Anticipating that conservative mobilization on Reagan's behalf would pose a significant threat to his own ability to win the nomination, Ford took preparatory measures to bolster his appeal among the increasingly restive Republican popular base. Nelson Rockefeller, the long-time nemesis of party conservatives whom Ford had appointed to succeed himself in the vice presidency, acquiesced to Ford's wishes by withdrawing from consideration for a place on the 1976 party ticket. "Because of the challenge from Reagan on the right, Ford had to throw off some ballast, and

Rockefeller was the biggest piece of ballast that he could throw aside," recalled Rockefeller aide Peter Wallison.[11]

At the same time, Ford was concerned that a nomination fight would pull him too far away from the ideological center, leaving him in a weakened position to contest a general election in an era when Republican presidential candidates needed to attract significant support from independents and Democratic voters in order to compensate for the overall Democratic plurality in the national electorate. Like other Republicans who became targets of an intra-party challenge from the right, Ford responded largely by making the case for his own candidacy on the grounds of political practicality instead of disputing the ideological precepts of his opponent. He argued that while the hearts of conservative Republicans might be with Reagan, the former California governor was simply too far to the right to win the presidency—as the Goldwater debacle had proven 12 years before—and that the Republican cause could best be advanced by electoral victory, not internal debates over ideological purity. "I think [evidence shows] beyond any doubt that I am the most electable Republican candidate," Ford told the press. "If I am the most electable Republican candidate and can help elect members of the House and Senate on our side of the aisle, plus state legislatures, I think I am the candidate that is in the best interest of the philosophy of the Republican Party."[12]

The rationale for Reagan's presidential candidacy employed the arguments that had by then come to define modern conservatism: the American state was both far too powerful at home and far too weak abroad. In the domestic realm, Reagan held excessive federal activism responsible for rising inflation, a growing budget deficit, and rampant bureaucratic incompetence. "The truth is, Washington has taken over functions that don't belong to it. In almost every case it has been a failure," Reagan argued, citing welfare programs, energy policy, and "federal interference" in public education (including school busing mandates intended to achieve racial integration).[13] Turning to foreign affairs, Reagan sounded similarly dire warnings. "Our nation is in danger," he claimed, "and the danger grows greater with each passing day." He charged the incumbent administration with mishandling Cold War conflicts in Angola, Vietnam, and Cuba; with meekly "yielding to demands" by the Chinese; and with projecting weakness worldwide by pursuing an agreement with the Panamanian government to relinquish control of the Panama Canal. "We should end those negotiations," said Reagan, "and tell the General [Omar Torrijos, the Panamanian leader]: We bought it, we paid for it, we built it, and we intend to keep it."[14]

Reagan justified his challenge to Ford by sounding familiar conservative themes about the corrupting influence of Washington and the inferior virtue of career politicians, turning Ford's more extensive experience in office against the sitting president:

> An effort has been made in this campaign to suggest that there aren't any real differences between Mr. Ford and myself. Well, I believe there are and these differences are fundamental. One of them has to do with our approach to government. Before Richard Nixon appointed him Vice President, Mr. Ford was a Congressman for 25 years. His concern, of necessity, was the welfare of his congressional district. For most of his adult life he has been a part of the Washington Establishment. Most of my adult life has been spent outside of government. My experience in government was the eight years I served as governor of California. . . . I had never in my life thought of seeking or holding public office and I'm still not quite sure how it all happened. In my own mind, I was a citizen representing my fellow citizens against the institution of government.[15]

In the end, Ford was able to hold off the Reagan challenge, though by a strikingly narrow margin for an incumbent president. Reagan's considerable popularity among the Republican electorates of the expanding South and West—he defeated Ford by margins of 65 percent to 35 percent in the California primary, 66 percent to 33 percent in Texas, and 68 percent to 32 percent in Georgia—propelled him to within a few dozen delegates of the nomination, though Ford ultimately prevailed on the first ballot at the national convention by a tally of 1,187 to 1,070. Some observers believed in retrospect that Reagan's choice of moderate Pennsylvania senator Richard Schweiker as his vice presidential running mate, designed to broaden his appeal within the party and signal a more pragmatic approach to a potential general election, backfired by dampening conservative enthusiasm for his candidacy among a few key state delegations.[16]

Ford's defeat by Democratic nominee Jimmy Carter in November 1976 left Reagan as the clear favorite for the 1980 Republican presidential nomination. In that contest, former representative George H. W. Bush, who had served the Nixon and Ford administrations as director of the Central Intelligence Agency, ambassador to China, and chairman of the Republican National Committee, occupied an ideological space immediately to Reagan's left, while Representative John Anderson of Illinois led the party's increasingly moribund moderate-liberal wing. Bush's campaign, like that of Ford four years before, attempted to counteract Reagan's strong ideological and personal appeal among Republican primary voters by raising questions about his electability. After an overly cautious and disengaged initial campaign strategy led to an unexpected defeat at Bush's hands in the Iowa caucus, however, Reagan quickly regrouped and marched easily to the nomination, choosing Bush as his vice presidential running mate as a gesture of rapprochement with what remained of the old-time eastern Republican establishment. Unreconciled to Reagan's ascendance, Anderson abandoned the Republican Party to contest the general election as an independent, symbolically marking the end of moderate Republicanism as a nationally viable party faction.

Reagan's decisive victory over Carter in the 1980 general election (he received 51 percent of the national popular vote to 41 percent for Carter and 7 percent for Anderson, winning 489 of 538 electoral votes), followed by an even more lopsided triumph in his 1984 reelection campaign (in which he defeated Democratic nominee Walter Mondale by a popular margin of 58 percent to 41 percent, carrying every state in the nation except Mondale's native Minnesota), cemented the Republican Party's identity as an electoral vehicle for the modern conservative movement. The strongest argument that moderate and establishment Republicans had advanced for nearly 50 years against a party-wide embrace of unalloyed conservatism—that such an ideological shift would render national victory impossible in a post–New Deal America that had become accustomed to an expanded federal government—was decisively contradicted by Reagan's two landslide victories.

By the time he left office in January 1989, the GOP had become the party of Reagan. No major Republican faction remained that did not claim adherence to conservative principles as Reagan had defined them. A memorable line from Reagan's first inaugural address—"In this present crisis, government is not the solution to our problem; government is the problem"—became the motto of post-Reagan Republicanism, usually stripped of its conditional first four words and applied rhetorically to nearly any aspect of domestic policy. In foreign affairs, Reagan's sizable defense buildup and symbolic demonstrations of strength against the Soviet Union were credited by fellow party members with precipitating the fall of the communist regimes of Eastern Europe (1989) and the dissolution of the Soviet Union itself (1991) during the presidency of his successor George H. W. Bush.

To be sure, Reagan the president was not averse to compromise, which was often necessary to achieve legislative success in a separation-of-powers system in which the opposition Democrats controlled at least one house of Congress for all eight years of his administration. The large-scale income tax cuts of 1981 were succeeded by more modest increases in later years, while Reagan's presidency was also marked by bipartisan agreements to reform the federal tax code, Social Security, and immigration policy. Likewise, Reagan's get-tough stance with respect to the Soviet Union softened during his second term, most notably illustrated by his negotiation of a treaty with Soviet premier Mikhail Gorbachev to ban intermediate-range ballistic missiles in 1987—an act that provoked considerable criticism from committed Cold Warriors on the American right.[17]

As Reagan's presidency drew to a close, however, the actual record of his tenure in office—replete, just like that of any other presidential administration, with compromises, failures, and practical deviations from stated doctrine, as well as major accomplishments—became eclipsed in the Republican imagination by a symbolic Reagan, who came to represent not only a triumph of Republican governance but also a shining lodestar of unblemished conservative purity. All subsequent major Republican presidential candidates, as well as innumerable aspirants for lower office, have pledged loyalty to this conception of Reagan, citing it as their primary model for both electoral and governing success. More than 35 years after Reagan's election to the presidency, Republican candidates running for the 2016 presidential nomination continued to claim his mantle. Florida senator Marco Rubio referred to Reagan as a "great president . . . [because] he understood that America was a unique nation . . . founded on universal principles"[18]; Texas senator Ted Cruz claimed that "in 1980, we saw the Reagan Revolution . . . a grassroots movement that turned this country around, [and] the same thing is happening today"[19]; and Ohio governor John Kasich bragged that "in 1976, I . . . worked with Ronald Reagan and I got to travel with Ronald Reagan. Yes, I actually knew the real guy, not [just] from the history book."[20] Even developer Donald Trump, who had been regularly critical of Reagan during the 1980s, told Sean Hannity that Ronald Reagan was the president he most admired because he "represented something very special for this country."[21] The Republican Party's nature as an ideological movement has been further reinforced since the 1980s by Reagan's unique mythical status within the party—a phenomenon with no true counterpart on the Democratic side.

While Republicans today are united in admiration for a common hero who is viewed in retrospect as standing, above all, for unwavering devotion to conservative principles, the presence of the towering Reagan legend also makes it difficult for later generations of Republican politicians to appear equally faithful to the conservative cause—thus rendering them vulnerable, as Gerald Ford was in 1976, to fierce intra-party competition from a primary challenger claiming to carry the banner of ideological purity. As conservative movement pioneer Richard Viguerie remarked in 2007, "For at least 15, 20, maybe more years, every conservative I know has been looking for [another] Ronald Reagan. Is he around that corner over there? Maybe he's behind that door, down the street. . . . We just keep looking for Ronald Reagan."[22]

REPUBLICAN NOMINATIONS IN THE POST-REAGAN ERA

Since Reagan's departure from office, Republican nomination contests have continued to be dominated by ideological conflict, with the various contenders competing to convince donors, activists, and voters of their superior devotion to conservative principles. Compared to Democratic presidential candidates, Republicans are less likely to direct specific appeals to discrete social groups or to present themselves as incremental problem-solvers rather than committed members of an ideological movement. In addition, while Democrats often perceive the existence of an inevitable trade-off between philosophical purity and electoral formidability, Reagan's two coast-to-coast victories convinced many Republicans that it is not necessary to trim the party's ideological sails in order to win broad appeal within the national electorate.

George H. W. Bush, nominated to succeed Reagan in 1988, was not a natural leader of the modern conservative movement. His father, Prescott Bush, a Wall Street banker by profession, had represented Connecticut between 1952 and 1963 in the U.S. Senate, where he was an ally of Dwight D. Eisenhower and Nelson Rockefeller. The younger Bush moved to Texas after graduating from Yale University in 1948, prospering in the oil business before entering Republican politics. After two terms in the House of Representatives and two unsuccessful campaigns for the Senate, Bush held several positions in the Nixon and Ford administrations before seeking the Republican presidential nomination in 1980. Bush accepted the vice presidency after placing a distant second to Reagan in the primaries, shifting rightward on social issues such as abortion and abandoning his former opposition to Reagan's supply-side economic policies, which he had previously mocked as "voodoo economics."

After eight years as vice president, Bush sought the presidency once again in 1988—now as Reagan's political protégé. His most formidable rival for the Republican nomination was Senate minority leader Bob Dole of Kansas. Recognizing that the path to victory in the Republican Party now ran in a decidedly rightward direction, the Bush campaign mined Dole's long congressional voting record for evidence of insufficient devotion to conservative principles, especially on the issue of taxes. After Dole won the Iowa caucus, relegating Bush to a third-place finish behind evangelical Christian broadcaster Pat Robertson, Bush aides Lee Atwater and Roger Ailes initiated a sharp attack on Dole's past legislative support for several tax increases. As Niall A. Palmer recounted, New Hampshire governor John H. Sununu, a co-chair of Bush's state campaign, persuaded the state's sole commercial television station to "bend its normal regulations regarding campaign commercials and to air a last-minute attack ad

against Dole. Entitled Senator Straddle, it purported to show Dole's reversal of position on various key issues, notably taxation. This final wave of
negative advertising may have contributed to Bush's margin of victory."[23]
"I think if it hadn't been for [Bush's] false advertising the last three days,
we would have beaten him," lamented Dole on the night of the primary.[24]
Bush also benefited from an endorsement from Barry Goldwater just
before the New Hampshire vote.[25]

Dole was incensed at the tactics of the Bush campaign: when asked
on camera after his loss in New Hampshire if he had a message for his
opponent, the senator snapped, "Stop lying about my record." But Bush
had discovered the unique effectiveness of the tax issue as an indicator of
ideological orthodoxy in the post-Reagan Republican Party. As Grover
Norquist, chief enforcer of the antitax philosophy within Republican politics, later recalled:

> Remember in 1988, even after Reagan passed tax reform, Dole refused to take the
> pledge [to oppose all tax increases]. He won Iowa, but then during a debate in New
> Hampshire, [former Delaware governor] Pete DuPont handed him the pledge, and
> he reacted like someone had thrown the cross in the lap of a vampire. George Bush
> took the pledge and won.[26]

Bush defeated Dole for the Republican nomination, building on his
key success in the New Hampshire primary to achieve a sweeping victory in subsequent states. He went on to win the general election over
Democratic nominee Michael Dukakis on an antitax message that had
become distilled by the summer of 1988 into a six-word catchphrase repeated in every stump speech: "Read my lips: no new taxes!" Once in
office, however, Bush decided to address the growing federal deficit by
negotiating a budget agreement with congressional Democrats that included tax increases as well as spending cuts. This violation of his campaign pledge provoked an intra-party challenge to Bush in 1992 from Pat
Buchanan, a conservative opinion columnist who had served in the Nixon
and Reagan administrations. Buchanan, with no experience in elected
office and little campaign infrastructure, did not pose a realistic threat
to Bush's renomination, but his success at attracting a significant protest
vote—in his best performance, Buchanan received 38 percent of the vote
in the New Hampshire primary, holding the incumbent to a narrow majority of 53 percent—suggested that Bush's broken promise on taxes had
alienated a substantial fraction of conservatives.

With his popularity deeply damaged by the national economic recession of 1991–1992, Bush was defeated in the general election by
Democratic challenger Bill Clinton. Many conservative activists chose to

interpret Bush's loss to Clinton as powerful evidence that straying from the antitax position severely endangered Republican chances in general elections as well as party primaries, reinforcing the view that the defense of low-tax and small-government principles represents the central purpose of modern Republicanism. "Bush broke his pledge in 1990," argued Norquist 25 years later, "and broke the Republican Party. It cost him the presidency. Well, no one's life is a complete waste; some people serve as bad examples to others. We haven't had someone break the pledge since Bush."[27] Conservative newspaper columnist Robert Novak quipped that "God put the Republican Party on earth to cut taxes. If [Republicans] don't do that, they have no useful function."[28]

Bob Dole, who became majority leader of the Senate after the Republican congressional victories of 1994, sought the presidency once again two years later. Like Bush before him, Dole responded to a previous second-place finish in the Republican nomination race by moving to the ideological right in preparation for another presidential bid. Dole abandoned his former refusal to sign a no-new-taxes pledge, instead promising to implement an across-the-board income tax cut of 15 percent. He even touted his vote from 30 years earlier against the creation of the federal Medicare program, remarking in a speech to the American Conservative Union on October 24, 1995, that he "knew it wouldn't work" at the time.[29]

Most of Dole's opponents for the nomination openly questioned the front-runner's conservative bona fides. Texas senator Phil Gramm criticized Dole for negotiating a budget compromise with Bill Clinton, even sponsoring an advertising campaign that resurrected the "Senator Straddle" attack successfully employed by Bush eight years before. Magazine publisher Steve Forbes attacked Dole for supporting a raise in congressional pensions and for demonstrating insufficient zeal for instituting term limits in the House and Senate. Dole attempted to rebut Forbes from the right, arguing that Forbes's signature flat-tax proposal would actually raise the tax rates of middle-class citizens. Ultimately, Dole's rightward turn on taxes, claims of superior experience in office, and compelling biography as a wounded veteran of World War II proved sufficiently appealing to defeat a relatively weak field of competitors for the Republican presidential nomination.

The 2000 Republican nomination contest serves as a particularly illustrative example of the importance of conservative ideology as the party's defining characteristic. Front-runner George W. Bush, the governor of Texas and son of the former president, faced an unexpectedly serious challenge for the nomination from Arizona senator John McCain. While McCain had amassed a strongly conservative voting record during his 14 years in the Senate, his presidential campaign did not emphasize his adherence to ideological doctrine. Instead, McCain ran openly to Bush's left, presenting himself to voters as a political "maverick" dedicated to battling ideological extremists and powerful special interests in both parties. He emphasized his support for stricter campaign finance regulations and accused Bush of pandering to "agents of intolerance" such as Pat Robertson and Jerry Falwell, both leaders of the Religious Right.

By distancing himself from his party's most divisive national figures, McCain explicitly sought to "bring about a new Republican Party" with an inclusive message that could appeal to "Republicans, Democrats, libertarians, and vegetarians."[30] He argued that his unique ability to attract support from outside the party would make him a stronger candidate in the general election than his primary opponent. "I am a Reagan Republican who will defeat [likely Democratic nominee] Al Gore," declared McCain. "Unfortunately, Governor Bush is a Pat Robertson Republican who will lose to Al Gore."[31]

McCain's claim that he could unite a broader coalition of voters than could Bush was corroborated by evidence from election results and surveys of public opinion. McCain attracted high favorability ratings from American voters at large, and self-identified independents and Democrats preferred McCain to Bush, suggesting that a McCain nomination would give Republicans their best shot at reclaiming the White House. McCain benefited in New Hampshire from its primary election law allowing participation by registered independents. According to exit polls, Bush and McCain ran roughly even among self-identified Republicans, but independent voters preferred McCain by a margin of 61 percent to 18 percent, boosting him to an unexpectedly wide overall victory over Bush of 49 percent to 30 percent.[32] In addition, more than 3,000 of the 150,000 participants in the Democratic primary that day wrote in McCain's name rather than choosing either Gore or his opponent Bill Bradley, giving the Republican senator a third-place finish in the opposition party contest as well.[33]

McCain's well-publicized New Hampshire victory stunned the Bush campaign, which immediately began planning a counterattack in South Carolina, the site of the next Republican primary. Rather than attempting to match McCain's electability argument, Bush instead appealed to Republican voters by claiming superior ideological fidelity. "Emphasizing his belief in limited government, Bush offered himself as 'the conservative candidate,' using the word 'conservative' seven times in one short speech the day after [the] New Hampshire [primary]," observed Andrew E. Busch and James W. Ceasar. "Bush also received the endorsement of [flat-tax advocate] Steve Forbes and stepped up accusations that McCain's tax cut plan was Clintonesquely small. Independent groups supporting Bush also attacked McCain for alleged ambiguity on abortion."[34]

Because South Carolina does not officially register voters by party, independents and even self-identified Democrats were eligible to participate in the state's primary; according to exit polls, nearly 40 percent of the electorate consisted of non-Republicans. As in New Hampshire, these voters broke heavily for McCain, who won 60 percent of the independent vote and 79 percent of the Democratic vote, as well as majority support among self-described moderates. However, Bush's campaign succeeded in capturing the Republican vote by a lopsided margin of 69 percent to 26 percent, more than overcoming McCain's strength among non-Republicans and giving Bush a crucial 53 percent to 42 percent statewide victory.[35] With his campaign righted, Bush proceeded to consolidate Republican popular support in subsequent state primaries, many of which were closed to independents and Democrats. By early March, Bush had essentially wrapped up the Republican presidential nomination.

The failure of McCain's first presidential campaign in 2000 demonstrated that Republican voters choosing a presidential nominee are unlikely to weigh broad personal popularity and cross-party appeal more heavily than visible devotion to the conservative cause. McCain was not particularly moderate in his substantive policy views, but his campaign's strategy of largely eschewing ideological rhetoric while openly picking fights with prominent conservative figures ultimately provoked considerable suspicion among Republican partisans that he was simply not a conservative. As McCain's campaign was beginning to fade in early March, Mark J. Rozell observed:

> Pleas of electability won't do. McCain has to make a convincing case that his socially conservative views and voting record in Congress make him the stronger candidate for the Christian right. His record clearly makes him credible in that regard. But his rhetoric in the campaign has not. Until recently, McCain almost seemed to be going out of his way to alienate the most conservative GOP activists.[36]

Bush, elected president in 2000, faced no opposition to his renomination four years later. He benefited from an overwhelming degree of popularity among Republicans and conservatives, reinforced further by his response to the terrorist attacks of September 11, 2001, and the subsequent invasions of Afghanistan and Iraq. But Vice President Dick Cheney declined to run for the presidential office himself at the end of Bush's second term, leaving Republicans without an identifiable heir apparent to Bush's political legacy once his presidency was complete.

McCain launched another presidential campaign in 2008, though he did not initially appear to enjoy front-runner status within the party despite his second-place finish eight years before. Although McCain had personally reconciled with Bush after several years of intermittent political conflict between the two men, many conservative leaders and media personalities remained largely suspicious of McCain's devotion to Republican principles. Concluding from his defeat in 2000 that he needed to prove acceptable to the activist right in order to win the nomination, McCain no longer distanced himself from social conservatives and other elements of the Republican base, even delivering the 2006 commencement address at the Jerry Falwell–founded Liberty University.

Even so, McCain's campaign struggled to gain traction through the summer of 2007, suffering a series of debilitating shake-ups of senior staff amid substantial internal dissension over the extent to which the candidate needed to present himself as a orthodox Republican. Fortunately for McCain, he soon found an issue on which he could portray himself as a proponent of Bush-style conservatism, becoming the chief defender in the party of Bush's "surge" policy increasing the number of U.S. troops in Iraq. Inscribing the words "No Surrender" on the side of his campaign bus, McCain increasingly emphasized his hawkish positions on foreign policy and military affairs—an issue domain in which his views fell in line with conventional conservative precepts. When former Massachusetts governor Mitt Romney suggested setting a deadline for the withdrawal of American forces from Iraq, McCain pounced at the opportunity to position himself on Romney's ideological right. Romney remarked in a September 2007 debate that "the surge is apparently working," which prompted an interrupting McCain to insist that "the surge *is* working, sir . . . not 'apparently'—it's *working!*"[37]

McCain also maneuvered to reshape his "maverick reformer" persona into an image that would be more palatable to conservative Republicans. With campaign finance reform fading as a national issue—the Bipartisan Campaign Reform Act, co-sponsored by McCain, had been enacted in 2002, reducing the demand for further legislative action—McCain boasted instead about his record of opposition to congressional earmarks, an issue likely to find a more sympathetic hearing on the right. "Give me the pen, and I'll veto every single pork-barrel bill Congress sends me, and if they keep sending them to me, I'll use the bully pulpit to make the people who are wasting your money famous," McCain told an audience of Michigan businesspeople.[38]

McCain also benefited from comparison with the two other leading Republicans in the 2008 nomination race. Romney had originally won the governorship of the traditionally Democratic state of Massachusetts in 2002 as a moderate Republican, only shifting to the right as he prepared to seek the presidency, while former New York City mayor Rudy Giuliani maintained liberal positions on abortion and gay rights that rendered him unacceptable to religious conservatives. By early 2008, McCain's reconciliation with his party's right wing was sufficiently complete to earn him the endorsement of the conservative *Union Leader*, the largest-circulation newspaper in New Hampshire, which had played a key role in the state's Republican presidential primaries in 1976 and 1980 as an enthusiastic booster of Ronald Reagan. McCain scored his second New Hampshire victory in eight years, defeating Romney by a margin of 37 percent to 32 percent. After achieving follow-up victories in South Carolina and Florida later in the month, McCain's political comeback was complete, and by early February he had effectively captured the Republican nomination.

Like McCain, Dole, and George H. W. Bush before him, Mitt Romney responded to a previous loss in the Republican primaries by moving rightward when he embarked upon a second presidential campaign in 2012, while looking for opportunities to attack his opponents for holding insufficiently conservative beliefs themselves. Romney's chief policy accomplishment as governor of Massachusetts had been the implementation of a universal health care program in the state, but the parallels between the structure of the plan enacted by Romney and the Obama-endorsed Affordable Care Act, which had become a conservative *bête noire* during its development and passage in 2009–2010, forced him to distance himself from his own governing record. Romney also proposed a tax cut initiative that would move federal tax policy far to the right of the position advocated by George W. Bush, calling for an across-the-board 20 percent cut in personal income tax rates from their Bush-era levels, as well as a repeal of the federal estate tax and alternative minimum tax.[39]

Romney criticized each of his chief rivals for the 2012 Republican nomination from a conservative direction. He attacked former House Speaker Newt Gingrich for having previously supported a bipartisan proposal to impose regulations on industry in order to combat climate change. Former senator Rick Santorum of Pennsylvania's record of supporting legislative earmarks and raises in the federal debt ceiling while in Congress similarly served as grist for Romney's attacks. When Texas governor Rick Perry belatedly entered the race in the late summer of 2011, the Romney campaign—concerned that Perry's reputation as a staunch southern conservative represented a potentially serious threat to their chances in a Republican nomination race—recognized a rare area of ideological vulnerability in Perry's relatively moderate stance on immigration. In a September 2011 debate, Romney charged that the Texas policy of offering discounted state university tuition rates to state residents regardless of immigration status created a "magnet" for illegal immigrants. Perry's defensive reply—"If you say we should not educate children who come into our state ... I don't think you have a heart"—damaged his standing among many conservatives, who resented the implication that depriving illegal immigrants of state benefits amounted to cruelty.[40]

Romney's opponents struck back at his attacks by similarly accusing him of holding ideologically impure views. Santorum described Romney's record in office as "not conservative," Perry mocked Romney as a "conservative of convenience," and an advertisement sponsored by the Gingrich campaign referred to Romney as a "Massachusetts moderate."[41] Romney responded by claiming that he had "worked very hard to promote a conservative agenda" as governor: "We cut taxes 19 times. We balanced the budget every year.... That kind of conservative model in a [normally left-of-center] state like Massachusetts was a model in many respects that other states could look at and say, 'OK, conservative principles work.'"[42] The only Republican candidate in 2012 who did not seek to participate in this more-conservative-than-thou competition was Jon Huntsman, a former governor of Utah who had resigned his post to serve as ambassador to China in the Obama administration. Huntsman ran as a pragmatic, bipartisan figure à la John McCain in 2000 but fared even worse than McCain had, winning less than 1 percent of the vote in Iowa and only 17 percent in New Hampshire before folding his campaign.

Romney emerged from the 2012 primaries as the Republican nominee, benefiting from a hastily launched, gaffe-riddled Perry campaign and from the limited organizational strength and personal appeal of Santorum and Gingrich. But the policy commitments that Romney made during the nomination contest in order to satisfy Republican concerns about his dedication to conservative principles may have reduced his appeal in the general election race against Obama. Romney's tax cut plan served as a primary target of attack for the Obama campaign, which accused him of seeking to benefit the wealthy and corporate interests at the expense of middle-class Americans. In addition, Romney's aggressive position on immigration—memorably described by the candidate during one Republican debate as amounting to a policy of "self-deportation" for unauthorized residents of the country—may well have contributed to his particularly poor showing among Latinos. After the election, Republican strategist Ana Navarro lamented that the candidates "were trying to outright-wing each other.... [W]e had a terrible discussion that haunted Governor Romney all along about immigration ... that I think just made it more difficult" to win the general election.[43]

A few leading voices within the Republican Party concluded in the wake of Romney's defeat that the party needed to moderate its positions and rhetoric on a few key issues in order to increase its appeal as the national electorate became more demographically diverse and increasingly dominated by post-Reagan generations of voters. Republican National Committee chair Reince Priebus agreed that a more centrist policy and a softer tone on the issue of immigration were necessary to win future presidential contests, producing a post-election report under the imprimatur of the RNC that called for Republican candidates to make a more concerted effort to attract the votes of Latinos and racially liberal young people. A set of younger intellectuals dubbed "reform conservatives," including Reihan Salam of *National Review* and Ross Douthat of the *New York Times*, also questioned whether large income tax cuts disproportionately benefiting the wealthy should remain at the heart of the Republican Party's economic program in an era of rising inequality and stagnant wage growth.[44] These reformers were careful to insist that they remained conservatives in good standing, preferring to speak of "growing," "modernizing," and "reinventing" the Republican Party rather than moving it leftward, and they seldom criticized other Republicans by name. They expressed the hope that the approaching 2016 nomination contest would allow a politician sympathetic to their positions to grasp the reins of the Republican Party and lead it in a less doctrinaire direction.

By 2015, however, it had become clear that the presidential nomination race would only push the party away from pragmatic coalition building and toward more extreme positions. Celebrity real estate developer Donald Trump vaulted into a persistent lead in national polls while running on a strongly anti-immigration platform that included the construction of a wall across the entire Mexican border and the forcible ejection of all 11 million illegal immigrants then residing in the United States. Retired neurosurgeon Ben Carson temporarily attracted significant support by proposing a flat income tax; arguing that the presidency should be closed to Muslims; and condemning abortion, homosexuality, and "political correctness." Texas senator Ted Cruz presented himself as an ideological purist who had relentlessly battled his own party's leadership in Washington in defense of conservative principles. Even Florida senator Marco Rubio, the most "establishment-friendly" of the leading candidates, disavowed his own previous efforts on behalf of bipartisan immigration reform in the Senate, expressed his support for a total ban on abortion regardless of circumstance, and proposed an economic plan that would eliminate all federal taxes on capital gains and dividend income. The candidates that offered the highest probability of embracing a more pragmatic style of politics—former Florida governor Jeb Bush and Ohio governor John Kasich—languished in the polls by comparison, indicating that a Republican electorate stirred to anger by eight years of the Obama presidency was in no mood to alter its long-term trajectory toward rewarding partisan pugnaciousness and punishing conciliation.

Trump, who by the spring of 2016 had become the unexpected front-runner in the Republican delegate count, did not rely as heavily as other Republican candidates on rhetoric extolling constitutional principles and the virtues of small government—prompting some intellectual leaders of the American right, such as the editors of *National Review,* to deny that he was a true conservative.[45] Trump was more reliant on explicit nativist appeals (including negative comments about ethnic and religious minorities), drawing ethnocentric voters including those who do not traditionally participate in Republican primaries. But the themes of Trump's campaign otherwise conformed to the familiar conservative principles of American nationalism and cultural traditionalism, and he hardly resembled a pragmatic, consensus-building moderate in substance, tone, or style. In a more belligerent manner, he echoed Republicans' long-standing projection of American international strength, but adopted the traditional rhetoric of "America First."

Trump's specific policy positions (including the largest tax cut proposal among the candidates) mostly respected conservative orthodoxy. Exceptions included his opposition to entitlement reform and his support for Planned Parenthood funding, issues on which many symbolic conservatives in the electorate maintain operationally liberal views. Claiming the mantle of unblemished conservatism, Cruz emerged as Trump's main competitor for primary votes despite limited support from his fellow Republican members of Congress, who viewed him as an opportunistic grandstander prone to publicly criticizing his colleagues for his own political benefit.[46] The electoral success of both leading Republican presidential candidates in 2016 represented a dramatic expression of popular disaffection with the party's leadership in Washington, disdained by an increasing share of the Republican electorate for supposedly failing to provide effective opposition to the policies of the Obama administration.

While each quadrennial Republican presidential primary race features a distinctive set of candidates, issues, and events, retrospective analysis reveals the presence of a larger repetitive pattern that governs most nomination contests within the party. Major contenders for the nomination proudly and insistently adopt the "conservative" label and devote a great deal of effort to the twin goals of establishing their own qualifications as conservatives in good standing and disputing the ideological credentials of their major opponents. Most successful Republican presidential nominees since 1980 have run to the ideological right of their chief rivals, and the series of second-place finishers who have returned to successfully capture the nomination in a subsequent election—including George H. W. Bush, Bob Dole, John McCain, and Mitt Romney—have all shifted their issue positions in a conservative direction during the interim.

It is rare for a major Republican candidate to claim that a relatively moderate or bipartisan style of governing represents a significant asset in a general election and should therefore be an attractive attribute to the party faithful. McCain attempted to convince Republican voters of this argument when he first ran for president in 2000, but his well-chronicled appeal to independents and Democrats—and attacks on several long-standing conservative leaders—merely raised the suspicions of conservatives. With Reagan serving as a historical exemplar of both ideological fidelity and electoral dominance, would-be Republican reformers of younger generations have found it difficult to convince their fellow partisans of the political advantages that might accrue from party "modernization." As Ted Cruz argued in a November 2015 Republican presidential debate, "We [Republicans] will win by following Reagan's admonition to paint in bold colors, not pale pastels."[47]

Though they may disagree on the details, Republican candidates, activists, and primary election voters appear to maintain a long-standing consensus that the advancement of conservatism is the central purpose of their party. Successful candidates for the Republican presidential nomination rarely speak extensively of their eagerness to work with partisan opponents in pursuit of problem-solving compromises and incremental progress, or to transcend the ideological differences that divide the nation by appealing to a broad cross-section of voting blocs; they prefer instead to emphasize their determination to defend conservative principles and policies. (When, for example, the moderator of an August 2011 presidential debate asked the assembled field of candidates whether they would accept a budget agreement that contained tax increases but cut $10 of spending for every dollar it raised in revenues, not one Republican responded in its favor.[48]) In the Republican mind, political success is realized by standing true to the ideals of limited government, foreign policy hawkishness, and cultural traditionalism espoused by the modern conservative movement.

DEMOCRATIC PRESIDENTIAL NOMINATIONS BEFORE CLINTON

The Democratic presidential nomination process has often exposed ideological and group-centered rifts within the party. In 1948, for example, incumbent president Harry Truman—characterized by Nelson Lichtenstein as a "border-state Democrat" and "a party centrist whose political skill would lie in successfully presiding over an increasingly factionalized party coalition"—was nominated and reelected despite the desertion of southern segregationists in favor of Strom Thurmond's States'

Rights Party and leftist defections to the Progressive Party, led by ex–vice president Henry Wallace.[49] The 1960s-era dispute over American involvement in the Vietnam War, which was being prosecuted by the Democratic administration of Lyndon Johnson, not only divided the party but ultimately precipitated fundamental changes in the nomination process itself.

Internal party conflict over Vietnam came to define Democratic presidential nomination politics in 1968, when it ultimately erupted in an explosion of chaos and violence during the August national convention in Chicago. While the Democratic primaries had been dominated after Johnson's withdrawal from the race in March 1968 by antiwar candidates Eugene McCarthy and Robert Kennedy (who was assassinated immediately after winning the California primary on June 4), Vice President Hubert Humphrey emerged with the nomination by cultivating broad support within the state party organizations, which still controlled a majority of convention delegates at the time. Unlike the movement conservatives in the Republican Party, who had managed to achieve sufficient organizational influence to engineer the 1964 nomination of Barry Goldwater prior to the implementation of party reform, the antiwar left lacked the institutional power within Democratic ranks to block Humphrey's nomination on the first ballot.

The procedural innovations that followed sought to bolster the popular legitimacy of the Democratic presidential nominee by requiring most convention delegates to be pledged to specific candidates and chosen by party voters. The capacity of these reforms to revolutionize the Democratic nomination process became immediately apparent upon the nomination of South Dakota senator George McGovern in 1972. McGovern not only resided at the left edge of the party's ideological spectrum but also maintained poor relations with most of the Democratic congressional and organizational leadership. His nomination for president would have been unthinkable prior to the enactment of reform and was a product of a combination of unique circumstances that would never again arise. McGovern alone recognized the disproportionate importance of early states Iowa and New Hampshire in the new, post-reform strategic environment, which other candidates had yet to grasp; this insight allowed him to perform well in both states against limited competition, thus gaining crucial early momentum for his campaign, while also benefiting from a "dirty tricks" operation run by Richard Nixon staffers to sabotage the candidacy of McGovern's more moderate rival Edmund Muskie.

The McGovern coalition of ideological liberals, young professionals, and Vietnam War opponents was sufficiently sizable and active in the Democratic primary elections to deliver him the nomination even though he won just 25 percent of the total popular vote.[50] But McGovern proved unable to unify his own party behind his candidacy, much less build a wider electoral appeal. McGovern did not get along well with organized labor, a key element of the Democratic coalition, and union leaders were further alienated by the conspicuous cultural liberalism of his strongest supporters. Surveying the national convention that nominated McGovern, AFL-CIO president George Meany asked in amazement, "What kind of delegation is this? They've got six open [homosexuals] and only three AFL-CIO people on that delegation!" Another labor leader complained that "there is too much hair and not enough cigars at this convention."[51] The AFL-CIO ultimately refused to endorse McGovern in the general election—a remarkable snub for any post–New Deal Democrat to suffer—and his candidacy suffered massive defections among several large groups that had traditionally delivered millions of votes to the Democratic Party, including white southerners, union members, blue-collar northerners, and Catholics. According to findings from the National Election Studies, about 40 percent of self-identified Democrats and Democratic-leaning independents crossed party lines to support Nixon's reelection.[52]

The 1976 election also resulted in the nomination of an "outsider" candidate who would have stood little chance of success in the pre-reform Democratic Party. But the eventual nominee, former Georgia governor Jimmy Carter, was not a liberal crusader like McGovern; rather, he portrayed himself as a relatively moderate or conservative Democrat who, uncorrupted by any previous service in Washington, could clean up the federal government and restore public trust in the wake of the Watergate scandal and Gerald Ford's unpopular pardon of Nixon. Like McGovern, Carter took advantage of a superior campaign strategy that emphasized the importance of strong performances in Iowa and New Hampshire, while his less adept opponents waited too long to jump in the race. He also benefited early in the process from a division of the more liberal vote in the northern states among several rival candidates (including Arizona representative Mo Udall, Indiana senator Birch Bayh, Oklahoma senator Fred Harris, and 1972 vice presidential nominee Sargent Shriver). In the South, Carter ran as a centrist, pious native son who was also a supporter of the civil rights movement, an identification that allowed him to defeat his chief regional rival, George Wallace, in the key early primaries of North Carolina and Florida on a wave of African American votes. As Carter pulled ahead in the delegate count over the course of the spring, a bloc of dissatisfied liberals led by California governor Jerry Brown and Idaho senator Frank Church attempted to organize an "anybody-but-Carter" campaign, but this last-minute attempt to block his nomination fizzled well before the convention.

After one tumultuous term as president, Carter faced opposition for renomination in 1980 from Massachusetts senator Edward Kennedy.

The Kennedy challenge was partially ideological in nature, supported by liberals who viewed Carter as excessively moderate and timid in his policy positions. Yet Kennedy did not simply run a left-wing version of Ronald Reagan's 1976 campaign against Gerald Ford. His primary line of attack was not that Carter was insufficiently liberal, but that the incumbent lacked the competence, vision, and leadership skills to effectively govern the nation and achieve policy success during a period of widespread economic distress. Kennedy's campaign voiced the frustration of many Democratic politicians and interest group leaders who perceived the Carter administration as stubborn, insular, and unwilling or unable to work productively with the Democratic majority in Congress during its first term in office to pursue the policy objectives sought by the party's various constituencies. Kennedy dwelled on this point when declaring his candidacy in a November 1979 speech at Boston's Faneuil Hall:

> I have learned to deal with the continental diversity of interests that my colleagues [in Congress] have been elected to represent: fishermen in Massachusetts and farmers in Iowa, construction workers in California and small businessmen and women in Pennsylvania, oil workers in Texas and timber workers in Alabama. . . . [But only] the president can inspire the common will to reach our goals. . . . I question no man's intentions, but I have a different view of the highest office in the land—a view of a forceful, effective presidency in the thick of the action, at the center of all the great concerns our people share.[53]

As Kennedy prepared his entry into the race, he appeared to represent a very serious threat to Carter's nomination; most national polls of Democratic voters found him leading the incumbent, sometimes by wide margins, while Carter's low job approval ratings suggested to pragmatic Democratic regulars that the party might be better served by nominating a new candidate in 1980. But after Iranian revolutionaries seized 52 hostages at the American embassy in Tehran on November 4, 1979, followed by the Soviet invasion of Afghanistan the following month, Americans— especially partisan Democrats—rallied around their president, allowing him to successfully fight back against what turned out to be a flawed Kennedy challenge in the 1980 presidential primaries. Kennedy regained strength late in the primary season after Carter's popularity was damaged by the failure of an April 1980 mission sent to rescue the hostages, but he had by that time fallen hopelessly behind in the delegate count, and even a persistent campaign that lasted until the summer convention itself did not succeed in preventing the incumbent's renomination.

The dynamics of the 1980 nomination contest suggest that Democratic voters' initial dissatisfaction with Carter reflected his performance in office more than any perceived ideological impurity. Kennedy's early lead in the race coincided with a more widespread popular disapproval of Carter's presidency—the incumbent's job approval rating sank to 28 percent in one poll during the summer of 1979—that was due primarily to a weak national economy. Little evidence existed of a mass revolt among Democratic partisans against Carter's issue positions or ideological views. Even Kennedy's reputation as a committed liberal, while well established in Washington, did not extend equally into the public at large; Gallup found in October 1979 that while Kennedy was the favorite over Carter among Democratic identifiers, only 44 percent of Democrats viewed Kennedy's politics as "left-of-center," compared with 36 percent who perceived him as "right-of-center."[54]

The 1984 Democratic nomination contest produced a highly competitive race that is nonetheless difficult to interpret in strictly ideological terms. Former vice president Walter Mondale ran as a standard-issue New Dealer in the style of his political mentor Hubert Humphrey on a platform that was strongly attuned to the various policy demands of the party's discrete social constituencies. His most formidable opposition came, somewhat unexpectedly, from Colorado senator Gary Hart. Hart's ideological position was to Mondale's right on trade and other economic matters, but to his left on issues important to white-collar liberals, such as environmentalism and foreign policy. Overall, the competition between Mondale and Hart turned less on ideological conflict than on stylistic and generational differences. Mondale pledged to further the interests of the traditional groups that had supplied the Democratic Party with the bulk of its popular support since the era of Franklin D. Roosevelt—labor, African Americans, the poor, and the working class—while Hart promised "new ideas" for a "new generation" that came of age in or after the 1960s and viewed the party's devotion to further expansion of the federal welfare state as increasingly obsolete.

Unsurprisingly, the two candidates attracted popular support from different voting blocs in the 1984 Democratic primaries. Hart became the favorite of "voters who were younger, more educated, more affluent, whiter, and disenchanted with the orthodoxies of the Democratic Party," in the words of political analyst Jeff Greenfield, who noted that many of these voters "had backed Eugene McCarthy in 1968 and George McGovern in 1972."[55] But Hart's electoral appeal was ultimately not large enough to outweigh Mondale's greater strength among blue-collar voters, southern and midwestern whites, and African Americans (though some black voters defected to the candidacy of civil rights leader Jesse Jackson, to Hart's temporary strategic advantage). The Mondale–Hart race, though closely fought and often personally rancorous, was less a battle over large philosophical differences than a schism between two factions within the broader Democratic coalition.

In 1988, eventual Democratic presidential nominee Michael Dukakis, the three-term governor of Massachusetts, prevailed over a large field of rivals arrayed across the ideological spectrum, from Jesse Jackson and Illinois senator Paul Simon on the party's left wing to southern moderate Al Gore and labor champion Dick Gephardt. Though a conventional liberal in most respects, Dukakis portrayed himself as an experienced, dependable, budget-balancing technocrat rather than as the idealistic leader of an ideological movement. Dukakis also employed his fluency in Spanish and personal biography as the son of immigrants to successfully court Latino voters in the key states of Florida, Texas, and California. Jackson, who ultimately became Dukakis's chief rival in the race, expanded upon his 1984 success in the heavily African American Deep South, running strongly among young white liberals in such states as Vermont, Michigan, and Colorado. Compared to Jackson, Dukakis was the overwhelming choice of strategic-minded Democrats, who viewed him as far more electable in a national contest.

In the end, Dukakis was not elected president in 1988. Like Mondale four years before, he fell victim in the general election to politically effective Republican attacks that portrayed him as a tax-and-spend, soft-on-crime, weak-on-defense liberal who could not be trusted with the American treasury, military, or moral culture. Despite a national popular plurality in the electorate and a durable majority in Congress and state offices, the Democratic Party had become, according to conventional wisdom, out of touch with the average voter in presidential elections during the 1980s. For many figures in the party, the prospect of making further concessions on policy matters in exchange for a key to the White House became increasingly attractive.

DEMOCRATIC NOMINATIONS IN THE 1990S AND BEYOND

The 1992 election serves as a particularly revealing example of the limited role of ideology as a force structuring Democratic presidential nomination politics. Governor Bill Clinton of Arkansas, the eventual nominee, eschewed the liberal label entirely, instead publicizing his identity as a centrist "New Democrat." The New Democrats sought to move beyond Great Society–era policies and rhetoric, arguing that national Democratic leaders needed to reestablish the party's popularity among a white middle class that had become suspicious of big-government activism in the era of Nixon and Reagan. Clinton had co-founded the Democratic Leadership Council, the organizational home of the New Democrats, and served as its president in 1990 and 1991. His October 1991 speech formally entering the presidential race emphasized a desire to transcend, rather than represent, ideological commitment:

> Today, as we stand on the threshold of a new era, a new millennium, I believe we need a new kind of leadership: leadership committed to change, leadership not mired in the politics of the past, not limited by old ideologies. Proven leadership that knows how to reinvent government to help solve the real problems of real people. . . . The change we must make isn't liberal or conservative. It's both, and it's different. The small towns and main streets of America aren't like the corridors and back rooms of Washington. People out here don't care about the idle rhetoric of "left" and "right" and "liberal" and "conservative" and all the other words that have made our politics a substitute for action.[56]

Clinton constructed a political profile as a "different kind of Democrat," one who supported the death penalty, proposed a tax cut for the middle class, and advocated reforms to federal welfare programs that would impose time limits and work requirements on beneficiaries. Many liberal Democrats disagreed with these policies, but the experience of three consecutive landslide defeats in presidential elections had increased the appeal within the party of a more moderate candidate who could expand the Democratic electoral coalition. As George J. Church reported in *Time*, "Many Democrats did not need the media to tell them that their standard-bearer should be someone who cannot be attacked as a McGovernite liberal. Reporters on the early campaign trail have been struck by the number of party activists who volunteer that this time around they are looking for 'electability' far more than liberal purity in a nominee."[57]

In any event, the 1992 Democratic presidential field did not provide conventional liberals with a viable champion of their views. New York governor Mario Cuomo belatedly decided not to enter the race in December 1991, and other prominent liberal Democrats had ruled themselves out of the running earlier in the year, when incumbent president George H. W. Bush appeared to be a strong favorite for reelection. Only Iowa senator Tom Harkin ran as a traditional New Deal Democrat, but he quickly faded from contention after a poor performance in the New Hampshire primary.

Former Massachusetts senator Paul Tsongas and former California governor Jerry Brown soon emerged as Clinton's chief competitors for the nomination. Tsongas presented himself as a socially liberal but business-friendly candidate who accused other Democrats, especially Clinton, of pandering to voters by promising tax cuts for the middle class and ignoring the painful sacrifices necessary to reduce the federal budget deficit. Brown claimed the mantle of an anti-establishment insurgent, arguing as he entered the race that "our democratic system has been the object of a hostile takeover engineered by a confederacy of corruption, careerism, and campaign consulting. . . . In reality, there is only one party: it's the Incumbent Party. . . . [Democrats and Republicans] share the same worldview and serve the same private interests which, in return, finance the campaigns of both."[58] While Brown's campaign sounded many themes that appealed to the ideological left—campaign finance reform, a single-payer national health care plan, the reduction of mass hunger and nuclear weapons around the world—he advocated a quirky and inconsistent liberalism that also encompassed a flat federal income tax and mandatory term limits for members of Congress.

Clinton's wobbly front-runner status, which was due largely to accusations and rumors about his personal life that raised Democratic concerns about his character, kept Tsongas and Brown in contention for most of the 1992 nomination race. In the end, however, both candidates failed to expand their electoral appeal beyond Tsongas's popular base of affluent white suburbanites and Brown's coalition of left-wingers, students, and anti–free trade workers. Clinton particularly benefited from the regional loyalty of southern voters, who preferred him to the other candidates by overwhelming margins, but he sealed the nomination by winning key primaries in the northern states of Illinois, Michigan, New York, and Pennsylvania thanks to heavy support from African Americans, Latinos, union members, and non-college-educated whites.[59] For the mass membership of the Democratic Party, neither Brown's idiosyncratic insurgency nor Tsongas's prescription of pro-business austerity proved as attractive as Clinton's message of middle-class moderation.

Clinton's victory in the 1992 general election, followed by his reelection in 1996, seemed to vindicate his visible efforts to separate himself from the left wing of his own party. Vice President Al Gore ran to succeed him in 2000 on a platform of continuing Clinton's policies (though not his personal foibles). Gore faced a single challenge for the Democratic nomination from former New Jersey senator Bill Bradley, who presented himself as a more principled alternative to the Clinton–Gore regime. Bradley took positions to Gore's left on welfare reform, health care, and gun control, nearly upending the vice president in the New Hampshire primary by winning majorities among college graduates (who voted 54 percent Bradley to 45 percent Gore), voters under the age of 30 (who split 58 percent Bradley to 41 percent Gore), and voters making more than $100,000 a year (who voted 54 percent Bradley to 45 percent Gore).[60] Once the primary calendar moved on to states where many of these groups constituted a smaller share of the total Democratic electorate, Gore seized an overwhelming lead, soon forcing Bradley from the race. Like Clinton, Gore particularly enjoyed strong support from African Americans and Latinos, who collectively cast a growing proportion of the Democratic primary vote.[61]

In 2004, former Vermont governor Howard Dean filled the role of "idealistic liberal outsider" in the Democratic presidential field. While Bradley had been cerebral and reserved, Dean was fiery and sharp-elbowed, incessantly blasting his main rivals for their votes in favor of authorizing the 2003 invasion of Iraq by the George W. Bush administration. Dean's repeated attacks on fellow Democrats attracted a great deal of media attention, and he gained a devoted following over the summer and fall of 2003 from many liberals who were frustrated with the perceived reluctance of their own party's leaders to provide effective opposition to Bush's policies. Dean found particular success in raising money and recruiting campaign volunteers from among the ranks of the Internet-based "netroots" activists on the left, who were especially attracted to his antiwar message.

By the beginning of 2004, Washington consensus had declared Dean the favorite in the race. Dean's campaign was well financed—unlike those of most previous insurgent candidates—and he began to win endorsements from a number of liberal officeholders, interest groups, and celebrities. But Dean finished a distant third in the Iowa caucus, behind Massachusetts senator John Kerry and North Carolina senator John Edwards, and then promptly lost his lead in the New Hampshire polls to Kerry, the eventual nominee, who defeated him there by 12 points. Dean's share of the popular vote did not exceed 16 percent in any of the seven state primaries and caucuses held on February 7, and he withdrew from the race 11 days later after a final disappointing performance in the Wisconsin primary.

Public opinion surveys indicated that most Democrats agreed with Dean in opposing the invasion of Iraq: entrance and exit polls in Iowa and New Hampshire, for example, found that 75 percent of Iowa caucus-goers and 63 percent of New Hampshire primary participants disapproved of the war.[62] But these antiwar voters still opted for Kerry (who had voted to authorize the war in the Senate) over Dean by a 10-point margin (34 percent to 24 percent) in Iowa and by 11 points (41 percent to 30 percent) in New Hampshire. The Democratic popular base seemed less interested in rewarding Dean for his stance on Iraq than in choosing a candidate who could claim superior experience in foreign and military affairs and thus represent a potentially strong challenger to Bush in the general election.

Kerry relentlessly touted his service as a decorated Navy lieutenant in the Vietnam War, suggesting that he would be uniquely insulated from the usual Republican accusations characterizing Democratic candidates as weak on national security. His campaign portrayed the nomination race as offering Democrats a choice between either symbolically expressing their opposition to Bush or actually removing him from office. "We need to offer answers, not just anger; solutions, not just slogans," Kerry told Iowa Democrats at the state party's annual Jefferson-Jackson dinner in November 2003, in an unmistakable reference to Dean. "So, Iowa, don't just send them a message next January. Send them a president."[63] Like Bill Clinton before him, Kerry successfully played upon Democratic voters' collective preference for electability and pragmatism over rhetorical devotion to liberal principles.

The 2008 election produced a Democratic nomination race that was highly competitive and hard-fought, resulting in a narrow victory for Illinois senator Barack Obama over former First Lady and New York senator Hillary Clinton. Clinton began the race as the strong favorite, but Obama's first-place finish in the Iowa caucus provided his campaign with valuable publicity that allowed him to keep pace with her throughout a long nomination contest. Obama's strategy for defeating Clinton recognized two vulnerabilities in the front-runner: many Democrats viewed her as overly calculating and hawkish on foreign policy, while others worried that she was a polarizing figure among the broader electorate.

Obama presented himself not as a pugnacious liberal leading an ideological movement into battle with the conservative opposition but rather as a unifying figure who, free of the baggage of the Clintons' 1990s-era partisan battles, could attract broad support, work productively with Republicans, and heal the nation's political divisions. "I think the country is at a crossroads right now," Obama remarked at a September 2007 debate. "Number one, it needs someone who can bring the country together, and that's the kind of experience that I bring to this office."[64]

The Clinton campaign responded by portraying Obama as too inexperienced and naive to achieve success in enacting the Democratic policy agenda. "Now, I could stand up here and say, 'Let's just get everybody together, let's get unified, the sky will open, the light will come down, celestial choirs will be singing, and everyone will know we should do the right thing and the world will be perfect,'" Clinton told a Rhode Island rally in February 2008, mocking the consciously idealistic themes of Obama's campaign rhetoric. "Maybe I've just lived a little [too] long, but I have no illusions about how hard this is going to be."[65]

In truth, the conflict between Obama and Clinton masked a strong underlying consensus on policy matters, with few substantive differences separating the candidates, except in foreign affairs. Both took more moderate positions than former North Carolina senator John Edwards, the most liberal major candidate in the race, who ran a campaign based primarily on the theme of ending poverty in America but dropped out after placing a distant third in the South Carolina primary. The contrast between Obama and Clinton centered instead upon rhetorical style and preferred approach to governing. As George Packer of the *New Yorker* observed in early 2008:

> [P]erhaps the most important difference between these politicians—whose policy views, after all, are almost indistinguishable—lies in their rival conceptions of the Presidency. Obama offers himself as a catalyst by which disenchanted Americans can overcome two decades of vicious partisanship, energize our democracy, and restore faith in government. Clinton presents politics as the art of the possible, with change coming incrementally through good governance, a skill that she has honed in her career as advocate, First Lady, and senator.[66]

As Patrick Fisher observed, the "race between Obama and Clinton [was] especially noteworthy because of the distinctiveness of the candidates' bases of support despite the lack of major ideological differences between the candidates."[67] Like Gary Hart, Jerry Brown, Bill Bradley, and Howard Dean before him, Obama invoked a sense of idealism and promised to transcend the normal messy give-and-take of politics, stimulating strong enthusiasm among the young, the wealthy, and the well-educated. In the New Hampshire primary, Obama defeated Clinton among voters under the age of 25 by a margin of 60 percent to 22 percent, among voters with a postgraduate education by 43 percent to 31 percent, and among voters who earned more than $100,000 a year by 41 percent to 36 percent.[68] Yet Clinton still won the primary by three percentage points (39 percent to 36 percent), benefiting from the support of older voters, white women, and less-educated and less-prosperous Democrats. Apparently, her emphasis on political realism and the value of experience still held strong appeal among the Democratic electorate.

Obama ultimately succeeded in narrowly capturing the presidential nomination that had eluded Hart, Brown, Bradley, Dean, and similarly styled candidates before him, critically as a result of his membership in an electorally pivotal constituency group. Obama received support from 79 percent of his fellow African American Democrats in South Carolina, the second primary of the season, allowing him to defeat Clinton by nearly 30 points despite polling just 24 percent among whites.[69] In the 33 states that held primaries after New Hampshire, Obama captured 40 percent of the white vote but 83 percent of the black vote, providing his campaign with landslide popular margins across the Deep South and allowing him to limit the magnitude (and delegate-count advantage) of Clinton's victories in northern and western states such as California, New Jersey, and Pennsylvania. Though committed liberals slightly preferred Obama to Clinton in 2008, the decisive factor in the race was not ideology, but social group affinity.[70]

After Obama's unopposed renomination in 2012, Hillary Clinton mounted a second bid for the Democratic nomination in 2016, immediately becoming the prohibitive favorite in the field. Clinton faced a challenge on her left flank from Vermont senator Bernie Sanders, a self-described socialist who criticized her for being insufficiently bold in addressing economic inequality, and toured college campuses promising tuition-free higher education. Sanders's appeal within the party was, like previous liberal insurgencies, concentrated among highly educated, left-wing whites and young voters attracted to an "outsider" candidacy. Clinton again stressed her superior expertise and pragmatic approach, which, she argued, would make her a better choice to address the kitchen-table concerns of the Democratic electorate. When asked by a debate moderator if she was "a progressive or a moderate," Clinton replied that she was "a progressive, but I'm a progressive who likes to get things done." As Stephen Stromberg of the *Washington Post* noted, Clinton built her campaign on the rationale that "the way to advance progressive goals is not to toss off an ideologically satisfying wish-list of grandiose government programs and expect the country to suddenly fall into agreement, it is to admit that policymaking demands a sense of nuance and of the possible."[71]

Clinton also responded to Sanders's singular focus on attacking unfettered capitalism and the federal campaign finance system by arguing that many serious social problems faced by various Democratic constituencies did not stem from a common source. As she told a debate audience in Milwaukee on February 11, "Wall Street and big financial interests, along with drug companies, insurance companies, big oil, all of it, [have] too much influence. . . . But if we were to stop that tomorrow, we would still . . . have racism holding people back. We would still have sexism preventing women from getting equal pay. We would still have LGBT people who get married on Saturday and get fired on Monday. And we would still have governors like [Wisconsin's] Scott Walker and others trying to rip out the heart of the middle class by making it impossible to organize and stand up for better wages and working conditions." Clinton contrasted herself with Sanders by appealing to the group interests of the traditional Democratic coalition, pledging to "keep talking about tearing down *all* the barriers that stand in the way of Americans fulfilling their potential."[72]

The results of Democratic primaries soon vindicated this strategy. Clinton established a decisive lead over Sanders in the national delegate count on March 1, when she scored strong victories in a number of populous southern states. Clinton's electoral success was especially fueled by overwhelming support from African American and Latino voters, who preferred her to Sanders by lopsided margins.[73] Sanders then shifted his message to incorporate more Democratic constituencies, arguing that his campaign was "listening to" African-Americans, Native Americans, Latinos, young people, and women, and methodically reviewing the particular problems and policy concerns of each group that he sought to address. Sanders benefited from rising liberalism among young white voters, but still fell short of assembling a winning coalition.

With the unique exception of George McGovern, successful candidates for the Democratic presidential nomination have, like Hillary Clinton, emphasized the importance of working within real-world political constraints in order to pursue the party's concrete policy agenda, prizing incremental progress in lieu of revolutionary transformation. (Even Obama, with his idealistic rhetorical bent and campaign theme of "change," presented himself as an inclusive figure who could escape rather than exacerbate partisan and ideological conflict, and who was eager to compromise with Republicans in order to achieve practical goals.) While Democratic candidates sometimes accuse each other of insufficient loyalty to the party, Democratic nomination contests are seldom dominated by debates over, or competing proclamations of devotion to, liberal ideology as such. Democrats seek to prove themselves acceptable to the major constituent groups within the party—labor unions, racial minorities, feminists, environmentalists—but also work to convince voters of their superior potential strength in a general election campaign against the Republican opposition, which often involves visible separation from the political left.

To be sure, liberal ideologues remain a significant share of the party base, and nearly all contested nomination races include one or more candidates who claim to be their champion. But the majority of the Democratic primary vote is still cast by members of groups who are not particularly motivated by liberal ideological reasoning, including African Americans and Latinos, blue-collar whites, and self-identified moderates or conservatives. These groups appear less devoted to using the nomination process to enforce an ideological litmus test on candidates than they are committed to choosing a nominee who persuades them of his or her ability to win office against Republican opposition and to achieve real-world policy successes on their behalf.

The contrasting appeals invoked by Democratic and Republican presidential candidates are revealed in a systematic analysis of campaign

Table 5-2 RHETORICAL ASYMMETRY IN PRESIDENTIAL PRIMARY DEBATES

No. of Mentions per Debate Answer	Republicans	Democrats
Ideology or Principle	.56	.26
Conservative (Republican)/Liberal (Democratic) Ideological Principles	.48	.18
Public Policy	.58	.59
New Policy Proposals	.08	.1
Conservative (Republican)/Liberal (Democratic) Policy Position	.07	.09
Social Group or Interest Group	.15	.24
Demographic Groups (Class, Race, Religion, Gender, Age)	.06	.12
American Imagery	.32	.23
n	731	769

Data from an original content analysis of a random sample of candidate responses from first and last presidential primary debates since 1999. Our data, content analysis codebook, and analyses of reliability are available online at mattg.org.

rhetoric. Table 5-2 summarizes the results of a content analysis of candidate responses delivered during presidential primary debates between 1996 and 2012. Republican presidential candidates were more than twice as likely as Democrats to mention ideology or principles in their debate statements and were nearly three times as likely to invoke conservative principles as Democrats were to invoke liberal principles. Republicans also more frequently drew upon American imagery than did Democrats. By comparison, Democrats cited social, demographic, and interest groups at markedly higher rates than Republicans and mentioned new policy proposals at a slightly higher frequency.

PARTY ASYMMETRY IN CONGRESSIONAL PRIMARIES

The role of ideology in defining the contours of candidate competition in Republican primary elections has increasingly extended beyond the presidency. Since the 1990s, several well-funded national conservative organizations, including the Club for Growth, FreedomWorks, and Heritage Action, have come to play an influential role in congressional nomination politics, regularly intervening in open-seat contests and boldly supporting primary challengers to incumbent Republican members of Congress who are deemed to be insufficiently devoted to conservative principles. By the Obama era, these groups had combined with the conservative activists mobilized under the banner of the Tea Party movement to form a powerful weapon of ideological enforcement aimed directly at the ranks of Republican officeholders in Washington. Republican primary voters have repeatedly proved to be quite open to being persuaded that their sitting representatives—even those with decades of service and broad appeal to general electorates—have betrayed the conservative cause and deserve to be replaced by more principled challengers.

Three incumbent Republican members of the U.S. Senate were denied renomination in 2010 or 2012, in all cases by opponents who ran to their ideological right. Three-term senator Robert Bennett of Utah, whose father, Wallace F. Bennett, had served four terms of his own in the same seat between 1951 and 1974, failed even to qualify for the primary ballot after placing behind two Tea Party–backed challengers at the 2010 Utah Republican convention. Lisa Murkowski of Alaska, whose father, Frank Murkowski, also preceded her in the Senate, lost her 2010 primary to Tea Party challenger Joe Miller, though she successfully retained her seat by waging a write-in campaign in the general election that attracted substantial crossover support from Democrats. In 2012, Indiana state treasurer Richard Mourdock defeated six-term incumbent Richard Lugar by a 20-point margin in the Republican primary after Lugar angered conservative activists by supporting immigration reform, congressional earmarks, and Barack Obama's nominees to the U.S. Supreme Court.

Several other Republican senators faced significant primary challenges during the Obama years, including former presidential nominee John McCain of Arizona (2010), Senate Republican leader Mitch McConnell of Kentucky (2014), Thad Cochran of Mississippi (2014), Pat Roberts of Kansas (2014), and Lamar Alexander of Tennessee (2014). Of the 31 Republican incumbents who sought reelection between 2010 and 2014, 10—or 32 percent—were held to 60 percent of the vote or less in their state's Republican nomination primary or convention, with three losing outright. In every case, the incumbent's most serious challenger or challengers attacked him or her from the ideological right, accusing the sitting senator of betraying conservative principles or failing to provide sufficiently strong opposition to the policies of the Democratic Party.

Competition among non-incumbent Republicans is also often defined by ideological considerations. In several politically competitive constituencies, Republican primary voters have preferred to nominate a staunch conservative rather than a more moderate candidate who would be a stronger contender in the general election, ultimately benefiting the Democratic opposition. Recent examples of this trend include political neophyte Christine O'Donnell's upset primary defeat of moderate nine-term U.S. representative and former governor Mike Castle of Delaware (2010), former Nevada state legislator Sharron Angle's successful bid for the Republican nomination to oppose Senate Democratic leader Harry Reid of Nevada (2010), Representative Todd Akin's victory over two more highly-touted contenders in the contest to run against Democratic senator Claire McCaskill of Missouri (2012), and former World Wrestling Entertainment CEO Linda McMahon's victory over veteran congressman Chris Shays of Connecticut (2012). Each of these primary winners was defeated by his or her Democratic opponent in the general election.

In strongly Republican states where nearly any candidate nominated by the party enters the general election as the prohibitive favorite, the growing success of conservative purists in Republican primaries has not endangered the GOP's electoral prospects. Instead, it has resulted in the election of Republicans who frequently attack fellow party members from the ideological right once they arrive in Congress. Senator Rand Paul of Kentucky won a Republican primary in 2010 as a Tea Party–backed outsider candidate over Kentucky secretary of state Trey Grayson, who was the favored candidate of Mitch McConnell and most of the national Republican leadership; during his time in the Senate, Paul has pursued a libertarian ideology that often places him in opposition to other Republicans. Similarly, Texas senator Ted Cruz captured the 2012 Republican nomination in an upset over Lieutenant Governor David Dewhurst, a more conventional business-class Republican whom Cruz accused of being too hesitant to fight for conservative principles. Cruz has likewise devoted his Senate career to engaging in sharp debates not only with Democrats but with the leadership of his own party, regularly accusing them of failing to stand for conservative values and even accusing McConnell, the leader of his own party, of telling a "flat-out lie" on the Senate floor. Within a year of Cruz's election, John Dickerson of *Slate* observed that "no senator has created as many enemies in his party in as short a time as the junior senator from Texas."[74]

No remotely comparable mechanism of ideological enforcement exists in Democratic Party primaries. The extensive network of activists, donors, and interest group organizations exerting visible pressure on Republican candidates to maintain their conservative credentials lacks a true counterpart on the Democratic side. Congressional Democrats remain relatively insulated from the threat of primary challenges fueled by accusations of insufficient ideological loyalty; even the moderate "Blue Dogs" who regularly distance themselves from the more liberal national leadership of their party are rarely punished by Democratic primary voters for their independent ways. Since 2008, only two incumbent Democratic senators have faced a strong primary challenger who attacked them from the ideological left: Blanche Lincoln of Arkansas, who narrowly won renomination in 2010 over a more liberal rival before losing her seat in the general election to Republican John Boozman; and Arlen Specter of Pennsylvania, who was defeated in the 2010 Democratic primary by challenger Joe Sestak.

Specter, however, was a long-time moderate Republican who had opportunistically switched parties in 2009 rather than risk likely defeat in the Republican primary and could thus be criticized for his long record of opposition to the Democratic Party.

Intra-party competition among Democratic candidates for elective office is often defined not by ideological distinctions but by differing social group affiliations. For example, Hawaii senator Brian Schatz faced serious opposition in the 2014 Democratic primary from two-term U.S. representative Colleen Hanabusa. Unlike most challengers to sitting Republican members of Congress, Hanabusa did not attack the incumbent for insufficient ideological devotion—if anything, Schatz was the more liberal of the two candidates—but instead emphasized her personal background as a fourth-generation Hawaiian of Japanese ancestry (in contrast to Schatz, a Jewish Caucasian who was born in Michigan). Schatz barely defeated Hanabusa by a margin of 49 percent to 48 percent, despite boasting the endorsement of Democratic president (and Hawaii native) Barack Obama. Preelection polls indicated that the Democratic primary electorate was sharply divided along racial lines: white voters overwhelmingly supported Schatz, while Japanese Americans and native Hawaiians strongly preferred Hanabusa.[75]

A comparison of the 2014 primary campaigns to represent Michigan's 8th Congressional District provides a useful partisan contrast. On the Republican side, Mike Bishop, who had served in the Michigan Senate between 2007 and 2010, faced off against Tom McMillin, who had served in the state House from 2009 to 2014. McMillin criticized Bishop's pre-2009 legislative accomplishments, all of which had required the support of the state's Democratic governor, as revealing his insufficient conservatism. Bishop, in turn, attacked most of the post-2010 legislation that had passed with McMillin's support (even though it had been signed by the Republican governor). Both candidates had accumulated similar legislative records, so they attacked each other by citing laws that had passed in the short windows when only their opponent was serving in the legislature. Both ran on opposition to typical governing, not on their legislative achievements.

The Democratic contest was far different. The four Democratic candidates (an economist, a professor of social work, an attorney known for his sponsorship of marijuana legalization, and a county treasurer) decided to hold a joint press conference to publicize their candidacies. They then agreed to hold a series of joint candidate forums (being careful not to label them debates) sponsored by various advocacy groups. They each emphasized unique signature concerns but went out of their way to express their agreement with other candidates. The low-key primary was partially a product of the Democrats' slim likelihood of a general election victory, even for an open seat in a state that Obama had won by 7 percent in 2008 and lost by only 3 percent in 2012. The top Democratic candidates did compete against one another behind the scenes, but mostly for the endorsements of local unions and advocacy groups.

Most congressional primary campaigns in both parties, of course, are foregone conclusions, as the incumbent or party favorite generally cruises to victory. When contested, however, the parties exhibit distinct forms of competition. The difference between the nomination politics of the two parties—with ideology playing a larger role in Republican primaries and social group membership weighing more heavily among Democrats—is confirmed by more systematic analysis of primaries. Figure 5-1 demonstrates that between 1970 and 2014, Republican primary challenges to congressional incumbents were consistently more likely than Democratic challenges to be based on ideology.[76] By the 2010s, nearly half of all Republican challenges were ideological in nature—a rate nearly four times as high as that of Democratic challenges. Democratic primary challenges, in contrast, were much more likely to be based on race (11 percent to 0.3 percent) and were slightly more likely to be invited by the incumbent's involvement in public scandal. While the proliferation of well-funded, ideologically motivated challenges to Republican members of Congress in recent years has captured a great deal of media attention and exerted an increasingly visible

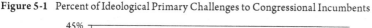

Figure 5-1 Percent of Ideological Primary Challenges to Congressional Incumbents

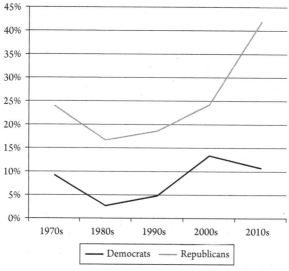

Percentage of primary challenges to congressional incumbents that were mounted on the basis of ideology (with the challenger avowedly more extreme than the legislator) in each party from 1970–2014. Data from Boatright (2013, 2014).

Table 5-3 DISTRICTS WHERE MINORITY CANDIDATES RUN AND HOLD
OFFICE BY PARTISANSHIP

	2000 State Legislative Officeholders Nationwide		2012 Candidates in States with High Minority Populations	
	Democratic Minorities	Republican Minorities	Democratic Minorities	Republican Minorivties
Minority Districts	82.3%	40.6%	59.8%	43.6%
Mixed Districts	14.5%	25.0%	35.7%	46.4%
White Districts	3.2%	34.4%	4.5%	10.0%

Percentage of minority candidates and officeholders who represent majority-minority districts, mixed districts (< 75 percent white), and white districts. Data are from coding by Eric Gonzales Juenke.

effect on the behavior of sitting officeholders in the GOP, this development represents an intensification of an existing asymmetry between the parties rather than a dramatic break with the past.

The parties are also distinct in the extent to which they nominate candidates who share descriptive characteristics with the bulk of the population within their electoral constituency. Table 5-3 demonstrates this difference based on data from state legislative officeholders and candidates.[77] The vast majority of Democratic officeholders who are members of racial minority groups represent majority-minority constituencies; Democratic minority candidates are also more likely to seek office in these districts than to mount campaigns in districts that are heavily white. Republican minority officeholders, however, are much more likely to represent majority-white districts, and a majority of nonwhite Republican candidates have sought office in mostly or heavily white constituencies. Descriptive representation of racial groups among both candidates and officeholders thus occurs more frequently in the Democratic Party, reinforcing the bonds of social identity connecting Democratic voters to their representatives.

In both presidential and nonpresidential nomination contests, Democratic and Republican candidates exhibit differences in campaign style and message that reflect the distinctive character of each party's base of popular support. Democratic primaries usually produce efforts by candidates to construct a coalition of supporters among the party's constituent social groups (often with the aid of elite organizational endorsements). In contrast, Republican primaries tend to inspire battles among contenders for the mantle of conservatism; the campaigns do not always address the same issues, and the most conservative candidate may not succeed, but serious candidates must convince Republican voters that they are sufficiently faithful members of the conservative movement.

TWO STYLES OF CAMPAIGNING IN GENERAL ELECTIONS

The distinctive campaign approaches of Democratic and Republican candidates endure once the nomination stage gives way to the general election. Democrats remain more likely to explicitly emphasize group ties and interests, and more frequently explain how their specific policy positions are designed to benefit these groups. Republicans prefer to cite more general themes, especially conservative ideas about limited government, as well as attributes of personal character such as strong leadership and moral qualities. These contrasting styles not only work to mobilize each party's loyal electoral base but also maximize the relative persuasive capacity of each side in response to the American public's simultaneous preference for symbolic conservatism and operational liberalism.

The persistence of this rhetorical difference is apparent in a content analysis of general election presidential debates summarized in Table 5-4, which parallels the nomination-stage analysis presented in Table 5-2. Since 1960, Republican presidential nominees have been slightly more likely than Democrats to invoke either ideology or principle, but especially more likely to cite principles consistent with their party's dominant ideology. Many references to principle by Democratic nominees, in contrast, are generic, apolitical, or even conservative. Democrats have maintained their relative penchant for mentioning social and demographic groups in their general election debate responses and are particularly fond of connecting policy

Table 5-4 RHETORICAL ASYMMETRY IN GENERAL
ELECTION PRESIDENTIAL DEBATES

No. of Mentions per Debate Answer	Republicans	Democrats
Ideology or Principle	.76	.69
Conservative (Republican)/Liberal (Democratic) Ideological Principles	.45	.27
Public Policy	.75	.86
New Policy Proposals	.18	.23
Conservative (Republican)/Liberal (Democratic) Policy Position	.15	.20
Social Group or Interest Group	.34	.48
Demographic Groups (Class, Race, Religion, Gender, Age)	.18	.31
Policy with Target Group	.18	.29
American Imagery	.26	.27
American Exceptionalism/Threats to Way of Life	.09	.07
Sources	.14	.18
n	509	491

Data from an original content analysis of a random sample of candidate responses from presidential debates since 1960. Our data, content analysis codebook, and analyses of reliability are available online at mattg.org.

proposals to the target group or groups that represent the intended beneficiaries (such as women and racial minorities). However, the partisan gap
in the invocation of American imagery is not replicated in general election
debates, perhaps because Democratic nominees consciously attempt to use
the platform of nationally televised events to insist upon the patriotic fervor
of their party in the face of Republican suggestions to the contrary.

Partisan rhetorical differences endure once the election is over and the
victor prepares to assume office. According to an analysis by Julia Azari,
Republican presidents are more likely to employ "responsible party" rhetoric (i.e., assertions that the electorate has placed political power in the
hands of a single party in order to enact its agenda) but less likely to claim
that the electorate endorsed specific policy proposals.[78] These findings
suggest that Republicans are likely to publicly interpret—and perhaps
privately view—elections as constituting referendums on general orientations toward government, whereas Democrats are likely to treat them
as policy debates.

Other researchers also find partisan rhetorical differences. As Figure 5-2
demonstrates, Democratic presidential candidates are slightly more likely
than Republicans to refer to parties and voters in their campaign speeches.[79]
Republicans, however, are significantly more likely to employ less specific
language invoking the concepts of liberty and patriotism. General conservative rhetoric is not limited to explicit references to ideology but also

Figure 5-2 References to Campaign Actors and Themes in Presidential Campaign Speeches

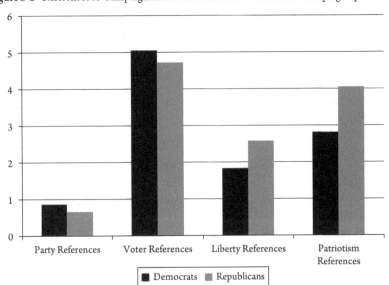

Number of references to specific actors and themes in presidential campaign speeches from 1948–2000. Data from
Jarvis (2004).

Figure 5-3 References to Class Groups in Presidential Campaign Speeches

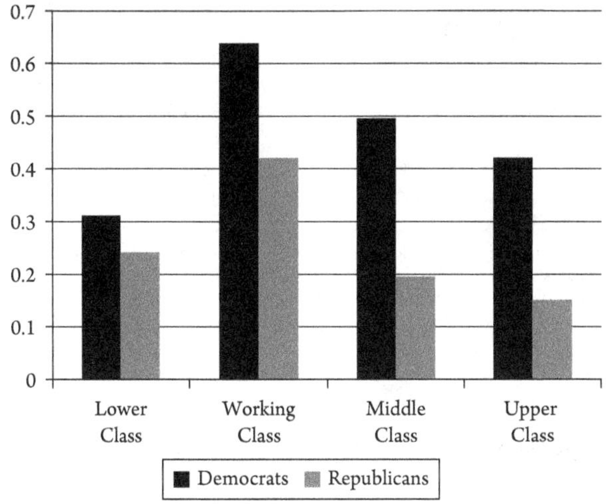

Average number of references to each class within presidential campaign speeches from 1952–2012 (no results available for Goldwater or Romney). Data from Rhodes and Johnson (2015).

extends to broader themes that encompass the symbolic and value-laden principles of limited government and American exceptionalism.

The presidential nominees of the two parties also exhibit an imbalance in their propensity to refer to economic class in public speeches. As Figure 5-3 shows, Democrats are much more likely than Republicans to invoke class identity, and this gap between the parties increases in magnitude as one moves from the lower to the upper class. Democrats often attempt to win public support by describing their policy program as furthering the interests of the middle class or "working men and women" while assailing Republican policies for supposedly benefiting the wealthy few. Candidates in both parties have increasingly adopted class-based rhetoric over time, but Republicans tend to remain largely silent about the rich, and Democrats have consistently referred to all classes more, demonstrating the party's distinctive preference for discussing public policy in terms of concrete interests.[80]

Paid advertising sponsored by candidates for presidential and congressional office also exhibits asymmetry. Table 5-5 summarizes two indicators of ideological content in federal campaign advertising: from 2000 to 2004, candidates' relative emphasis on ideology, personal values, and policy issues were measured; from 2010 to 2012, mentions of liberal and conservative ideological labels in campaign advertisements were counted.[81] Republican candidates not only consistently used the terms "liberal" and "conservative" in their advertising far more than Democratic candidates but also disproportionately stressed ideology in general rather than specific issues.

Table 5-5 IDEOLOGICAL EMPHASIS IN CAMPAIGN ADVERTISING

	Focus on Ideology or Personal Values			2010 Mentions		2012 Mentions	
	2000	2002	2004	Liberal	Conservative	Liberal	Conservative
Democrats	5%	20%	18%	1%	2%	0%	0%
Republicans	10%	26%	23%	9%	11%	4%	8%

Percentage of advertising that mentioned ideology or personal values in federal elections from 2000–2004. Data from the Campaign Media Analysis Group, coded by the Wisconsin Advertising Project and the Wesleyan Advertising Project. The 2010 and 2012 data only include explicit mentions of liberal or conservative ideological labels. Data descriptions and analysis from Fowler, Franz, and Ridout (2016). Cross-tabulations for 2012 were provided by Erika Franklin Fowler.

Figure 5-4   Congressional Candidate Advertising, 1968–2008

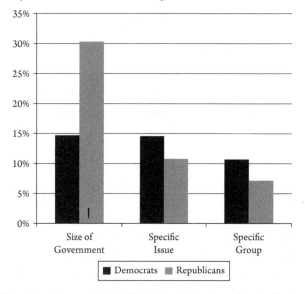

Average chance that each party's congressional candidate ad would cover three categories of topics: references to the size and scope of government (budget, taxes, big government), specific issue areas (entitlements, environment, health, education, crime, inflation, welfare, drugs, the economy, defense, trade, guns, and transportation) and specific groups (big business, small business, police, children, the middle class, and the elderly). Data from Henderson (2013).

Systematic differences in the messages of the two parties' commercial advertisements, though seldom previously noted, have in fact endured for decades. Based on a large sample spanning 40 years of television advertisements in congressional campaigns, John Henderson found that Republican candidates were, on average, more than twice as likely as Democrats to emphasize issues concerning the general size of government (see Figure 5-4). In particular, the proportion of Republican ads that attacked excessive government power or spending doubled between 1976 and 2008.[82] Democratic advertising, in contrast, was more likely during this period to discuss specific policy problems, with Figure 5-4 indicating the average emphasis across 13 issues (entitlements, environment, health, education, crime, inflation, welfare, drugs, the economy, defense, trade, guns, and transportation).[83] Even though Republicans maintained an advantage in public assessments of performance on national security, Republican ads were not significantly more likely than Democratic ads to focus on foreign policy. Democratic advertising also mentioned specific social groups at higher rates than Republican ads; Figure 5-4 reports the average citation rate of big business, small business, police, children, the middle class, and the elderly. Democrats emphasized both their own social group ties and those attributed to Republicans.

Comparable partisan differences are apparent in presidential campaign advertising as well. Figure 5-5 summarizes citations of social, political, and ideological groups in candidate advertising in the 2008 presidential election.[84] As the figure reveals, Barack Obama's advertising was much more likely to contain references to groups—especially social groups— than were ads sponsored by the John McCain campaign. Obama was also more likely to cite political groups, such as lobbyists or corporations, in a negative context, reflecting the common Democratic strategy

Figure 5-5   References to Groups in Presidential Advertisements in 2008

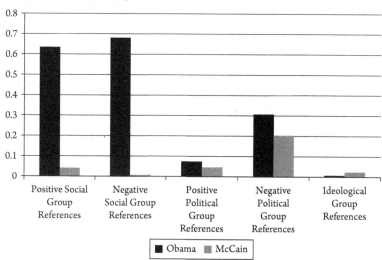

Proportion of airings that included positive and negative references to social, political, and ideological groups. Social group references incorporated references to class, race, gender, taxpayer, senior, economic, occupational, patriotic, family, religious, sexual, and vulnerable groups. Political group references were identified as references to specific or general classes of interest groups, campaign donors, organizations, or lobbyists. Ideological group references were identified as direct references to liberals and conservatives. Data from Rhodes and Johnson (2014). We present the totals across all references within each category.

of portraying political conflict as a battle of competing interests. For example, Obama's television ad entitled "Real Change," which first aired on September 12, 2008, featured the candidate himself stating that "to me, change is a government that doesn't let banks and oil companies rip off the American people. . . . Change is giving tax breaks to middle-class families instead of companies that send jobs overseas."[85]

The distinct images that each party presents to voters also appear in the design of candidate websites. Table 5-6 reports several characteristics of the typical website maintained by Republican and Democratic candidates for Congress.[86] On average, Democratic websites include more policy positions, actions, and legislation than Republican websites, though the differences are slight. They present issue content more prominently on the front page but are less likely to refer to general sentiments toward government or the need for broad reform. Bigger differences emerge in the candidates' relationships to groups; Democratic candidates highlight 50 percent more endorsements on their campaign websites than Republicans and are much more likely to emphasize their advocacy for social groups and constituencies. Even the websites maintained by the national party organizations exhibit a similar degree of asymmetry. As of early 2016, the front page of the Democratic National Committee's website included a list of links designed to appeal to 17 different social and demographic groups (compared to just seven group links on the corresponding page of the Republican National Committee), while the RNC website included a prominent link to "Eleven Principles for American Renewal" (in contrast, the word "principle" was entirely absent from the DNC's front page).[87]

The content of the 2008 and 2012 presidential campaigns provides a useful illustration of how the parties rely on distinct political strengths,

Table 5-6 MENTIONS ON CANDIDATE WEBSITES

	Democrats	Republicans
Policy Positions	1.88	1.77
Policy Actions	0.88	0.83
Legislation	1.03	0.99
Issues on Front Page	1.87	1.46
Endorsements	14.3	9.5
Group Advocacy	0.35	0.25
General Sentiments	0.06	0.07
Government Reform	0.08	0.09

Average number of mentions of each item on U.S. House and Senate candidate campaign websites in 2002, 2004, and 2006. We created aggregate indicators from data from Druckman, Kifer, and Parkin (2009).

grounded in their unique compositions, to appeal to voters. In 2008, Barack Obama's victorious campaign combined the (traditional out-party) message of change, attacks on George W. Bush's economic record, and identity-based appeals invoking new generational leadership and the historic chance to elect the first African American president. He also offered more targeted issue appeals based on a claim of policy moderation than did his Republican opponent, with one television ad even including a graphic depicting an actual issue spectrum that placed Obama's own health care plan in the median position between two extremes. In contrast, John McCain chose as his running mate conservative agitator Sarah Palin, who repeatedly attacked Obama in ideological terms for exhibiting insufficient patriotism and harboring a desire to transform America's traditional character. After Obama told an Ohio voter on camera that "when you spread the wealth around, it's good for everybody," McCain criticized his opponent's remarks as revealing a commitment to socialism, repeatedly invoking the constituent (whom he named "Joe the Plumber") and assailing Obama for advocating a redistributionist agenda.

Obama's campaign against Mitt Romney in 2012 attempted to convince middle- and working-class voters that their interests would be best served by a Romney defeat. Obama's speeches and advertisements repeatedly invoked Romney's personal wealth and career in the field of private equity while accusing him of demonstrating a lack of empathy with average Americans; the incumbent's most heavily run ads criticized his opponent's foreign bank accounts and portrayed him as a heartless corporate raider who had enriched himself by laying off workers. Romney made Obama's task easier by committing a series of verbal gaffes, stating that he was "not concerned about the very poor,"[88] characterizing 47 percent of Americans as "dependent on government,"[89] and suggesting that young people who wished to go to college or start a business should simply "borrow money if you have to from your parents."[90] Obama's positive campaign messages stressed his long list of policy achievements and proposals—universal health care, same-sex marriage rights, support for legalized abortion, liberalized immigration policies, and the 2009 auto industry bailout—with at least one achievement targeted at every party constituency. The best-received speech of the 2012 Democratic National Convention was delivered by Bill Clinton, who made a case for Obama's reelection by methodically comparing each Obama policy with a more extreme Republican position and arguing that "cooperation [in government] works better than constant conflict."[91]

Romney attacked Obama in ideological terms, characterizing his opponent's policies as a failed attempt at a government takeover of the economy (especially in the realm of health care). Rather than match Obama's extensive agenda of specific policy proposals, Romney focused on his own record of economic management. On foreign policy, Romney attacked Obama for going on an international "apology tour," criticizing America, and showing "weakness" in front of the nation's adversaries. Republicans extended symbolic critiques to domestic issues, dedicating an entire night of their convention to publicizing Obama's statement that business owners rely on society, rather than only individual initiative ("you didn't build that"), as evidence of his belief in government power and collectivism.

The distinct strategies pursued by party nominees in general elections are further reinforced by enduring differences in the reputations of the parties among the American public. Figure 5-6 demonstrates that Democratic and Republican presidential candidates routinely differ in their perceived personal traits.[92] Voters perennially view Democratic candidates as caring more than Republicans about regular people; Republican candidates are usually, but less consistently, rated as being stronger leaders. Republicans are also usually perceived as more moral than Democrats, while Democratic candidates usually hold an advantage in perceptions of relative compassion.[93]

As Chapter 2 demonstrated, the specific policy positions of Democratic candidates are consistently more popular than those of Republican candidates, but the Republicans also maintain some issue-based advantages. On consensus issues, they are viewed as better able to manage national security matters. Table 5-7 indicates the party's average relative "issue

Figure 5-6 Republican Party Advantage (and Disadvantage) in Candidate Traits

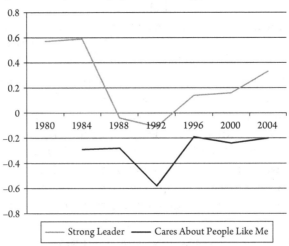

Difference in average ratings (on a scale of 1 to 4) of whether the Republican and Democratic presidential candidates are "strong leaders" and "care about people like you." Data from the American National Elections Studies and summarized in Hayes (2005).

Table 5-7 REPUBLICAN PARTY
ADVANTAGE (AND DISADVANTAGE)
ON CONSENSUS ISSUE AREAS

	Republican Advantage
Domestic Security	14.5%
Military	13.9%
Immigration	8.5%
Inflation	8.5%
Crime	6.6%
Foreign Affairs	6%
Education	−10.4%
Jobs	−12%
Health Care	−12.4%
Social Security	−14.4%
Environment	−17.8%
Poverty	−18.1%

Average percent Republican Party advantage on dealing
with each issue from the 1970s–2000s as estimated by
Egan (2013).

ownership" advantages across 12 policy domains, measuring public belief
in the parties' competencies rather than agreement with their policy positions.[94] The Republican advantages are concentrated in domestic and international security, whereas the Democratic advantages are more widespread across domestic policy issues.

Both parties thus have significant strengths on which they can draw
in their pursuit of electoral majorities, but the Democratic Party benefits
from emphasizing shared identity, interests, and specific issues, whereas
Republican candidates are aided by the party's broader ideological orientation and public perceptions of its strength in handling national security. Of
course, both parties could also decide to pursue strategies oriented toward
mobilizing their base rather than those that aim to persuade independent
voters. Since the 1930s, Democrats have been able to win presidential elections simply by capitalizing on an overall numeric advantage in partisan
identifiers, a strategy that allowed Obama to defeat Romney in 2012 despite Romney's victory among independent voters. However, Republicans
maintain a structural advantage in congressional and state legislative races
as a result of the more efficient distribution of their supporters across geographic constituencies, which allows them to assemble national majorities
without winning a substantial share of votes from Democrats.

The ideological homogeneity of Republicans provides the party with inherent advantages in employing a strategy of base mobilization. Republican identifiers consistently turn out to vote at higher rates and defect less often to Democratic candidates; they are also more likely to report engaging in all forms of political activism, including influencing others, attending meetings, working for candidates, displaying campaign paraphernalia, and contributing money.[95] Recent evidence also suggests that implicit Republican partisan identity is stronger, contributing to greater information processing and behavioral biases in favor of their party.[96] Gregory Shufeldt finds that Republicans' disproportionate activism is a product of lower levels of ambivalence between their group and partisan identities; Democrats experience much higher levels of internal conflict between their partisanship and their ideological and social group identities, dampening their partisan activism.[97]

Even in general elections, in which both parties have incentives to reach the same voters, the two sides employ distinct strategies. Republicans focus on their broader (more popular) values and ideology, rather than their specific (less popular) policy proposals. Republican elites tend to reject the idea that candidates are competing to attract the median voter on a spectrum of aggregate issue positions.[98] They instead prefer models that emphasize directional choices between liberal and conservative poles and believe that voters reward a consistent and broad viewpoint, especially one based on limited government. When Republicans do discuss specific policies, they disproportionately portray their record as more centrist than it is; Democrats demonstrate only slight tendencies to exaggerate the moderation of their issue positions.[99] Democrats face less difficulty in matching the issue positions of their constituency groups with those of the broader electorate, but they encounter more opposition to their broader vision of government.

ELECTORAL COMPETITION BETWEEN UNMATCHED SIDES

The ideological focus of the Republican Party and the social group coalition structure of the Democratic Party are manifested over the course of election campaigns. Democrats' relative emphases on group-based and specific issue appeals tied to their organized constituencies are apparent in both pre- and post-nomination campaign activity. Battles for Republican Party nominations are instead fought over ideological commitment, and Republican candidates prefer broader, more symbolic messages advocating small-government principles in general elections as well. Both parties are able to match the focus of their party members with that of the wider electorate. Democrats can provide specialized messages to party constituencies while appealing to the public on the basis of rhetorical identification with the common people over more privileged groups, as well as the popularity of their specific positions. Republicans can both mobilize their base and take advantage of voters' prevailing right-of-center general sentiments by relying upon appeals to broad conservative values linked to symbolic American imagery.

The extended Republican Party has developed and popularized a broadly defined ideology that unites its electoral and activist bases. Its core tendencies have only been enhanced by decades-long trends in partisan and ideological polarization among politicians, activists, interest groups, and voters. Republicans see politics as a battle between left and right over the size and scope of government in which the conservative side can effectively draw upon traditional American suspicion of state authority to mobilize popular support. Both their internal conflicts and their public presentations in general elections reflect their existential and strategic focus on this conflict of visions.

The extended network of the Democratic Party is shaped by its internal diversity, matching organized activists and interest groups with each party constituency. Democrats not only perceive politics as a battle between social groups but also seek to enact their vision by assembling discrete minorities into a unified coalition to oppose powerful interests allied with Republicans. Ideological liberals have always represented one group among many in the Democratic fold (in the New Deal coalition, they were viewed as the small social group of intellectuals). It is possible that partisan and ideological polarization will enhance liberals' role in their party, but their influence is limited both by Democrats' objective electoral incentives and by their subjective view that extremism endangers the party's electability.

American elections are closely fought contests between only two parties—the most limited competitive landscape in the developed world. Both sides must therefore seek broad popular support, but they use different methods to do so. Democrats and Republicans hold distinct advantages—and disadvantages—in mobilizing their loyal supporters and appealing to the wider electorate, producing an enduring difference in the nature and style of their electoral campaigns.

CHAPTER 6

ᴄᴠᴏ

Policymaking in Red and Blue

When John Boehner stepped up to a Capitol Hill podium to address the news media on September 25, 2015, he began his remarks with the same conservative rhetoric that he had employed throughout his turbulent five-year tenure as Speaker of the House of Representatives. "My mission every day," declared Boehner, "is to fight for a smaller, less costly and more accountable government." But this was no ordinary press briefing. With a characteristic display of open emotion, Boehner proceeded to announce that he was resigning the Speakership and his Ohio congressional seat to avoid "prolonged leadership turmoil [that] would do irreparable harm to the institution."[1] Boehner added that he had considered leaving Congress the previous year but had temporarily postponed retirement because his heir apparent, former majority leader Eric Cantor of Virginia, was unexpectedly defeated in a 2014 primary election.

While it is common for congressional leaders to retire in the wake of unfavorable electoral results for their party—Dennis Hastert, the previous Republican Speaker, had left the House immediately after the GOP lost its majority in the 2006 midterms—Boehner's record in this arena was marked by unmatched success. House Republicans gained 63 seats in 2010 (the biggest net partisan swing in a single election since 1948), firmly regaining control of the chamber after four years in the minority. Further victories in 2014 left the party with a 247–188 advantage over the opposition Democrats. Republicans had not won so many House seats since the election of 1928.

Explaining a Speaker's sudden departure from the House at the apex of his majority's electoral dominance—and why the Washington community responded to his announcement with something less than total shock—requires a recognition of the distinctive character of the congressional Republican Party. Internal battles over its strategic direction had roiled the GOP for nearly Boehner's entire tenure as the presiding officer of the House, severely complicating his efforts to lead the institution. A hard-line faction of purist backbenchers had become alienated from the bulk of the House Republican Conference, increasingly aiming rhetorical and even procedural fire at Boehner himself. The series of Republican electoral victories during his Speakership failed to satisfy Boehner's detractors, and rumors of his impending departure had circulated around Capitol Hill for at least a year before they were publicly confirmed.

Both sides of this intra-party conflict identified themselves as conservatives and agreed much more than they differed on policy matters, but each adopted a very distinct approach to governing. To the dissenters, most of whom had become identified by the time of Boehner's resignation with an organization dubbed the "House Freedom Caucus," Boehner had failed to defend conservative principles with sufficient vigor when drafting legislation and negotiating with the Obama-led Democrats. "Grassroots conservatives across America . . . voted in 2010, 2012, and 2014 for a conservative counterweight to the White House," argued Representative Tim Huelskamp of Kansas, a leading Boehner critic, in the fall of 2015. "And for those entire four-and-a-half years since then, all we've heard from John Boehner and the establishment is [that] we can't do it. You know, there's a difference between winning [or] losing, and not trying at all."[2]

Boehner had responded to the hard-liners with a mix of tactics ranging from punitive discipline (he engineered the removal of Huelskamp and several other members of the rump faction from their favored committee assignments in December 2012) to weary, have-it-your-way acquiescence (he reluctantly supported a purist-led effort to shut down the government in October 2013 as an ultimately unsuccessful means of forcing the repeal of the Affordable Care Act). But none of these approaches had dampened the rebellion in the Republican ranks. Representative Mark Meadows of North Carolina took the notable step in July 2015 of formally filing a notice to vacate the chair, a procedure unused since 1910 that allows House members to call for a vote to oust the Speaker at any point during a legislative session. Even if Boehner managed to survive this particular challenge (which might have forced him to seek support from Democrats to remain in his position, since the Speaker, uniquely among congressional leaders, is subject to a majority vote of the entire House membership), the disaffected Republicans could depose him by withholding their votes in the next regular election for Speaker in January 2017.[3] Calculating that his time would soon be up, Boehner opted to depart on his own terms rather than risk an embarrassing public defenestration.

The dissension in the Republican Conference initially extended to the question of Boehner's successor. Majority Leader Kevin McCarthy of California quickly gained broad support among Republican members, only to withdraw abruptly from the competition after about 40 hard-liners threatened to block his ascension. Paul Ryan of Wisconsin, chairman of the House Ways and Means Committee and a former Republican nominee for vice president, reluctantly agreed to stand for Speaker after several days of maneuvering and negotiation. Ryan, whose reputation and voting record placed him to the ideological right of both Boehner and McCarthy, was widely viewed as the only prospective Speaker who could unify the House Republican Party. He accepted the position after demanding, and receiving, the support of most members of the Freedom Caucus.[4]

While Boehner's hasty exit from the Speakership was an unusually dramatic development, it fell within a long-standing historical pattern in which Republican congressional leaders, especially in the House, have regularly faced criticism and even public opposition from party members who accuse them of exhibiting insufficient devotion to the conservative cause. No comparable dynamic exists among congressional Democrats in either chamber of Congress. In the past, Democratic leadership fights have occasionally exposed the differing policy preferences of liberals and moderates within the party, but a series of Democratic leaders have demonstrated the ability to successfully manage the varying demands of their diverse constituencies without facing charges of ideological treason from their membership.

The distinctive characters of the two congressional parties extend to the policy process itself. Many Republicans in Congress have long preferred taking principled stands to pursuing incremental policy achievements. Elected Democrats tend to treat policymaking as an attempt to address a catalog of social problems, each requiring a corresponding government action, whereas Republicans view policy disputes as battlegrounds in a broader philosophical conflict. Because realistic new policy alternatives usually expand rather than contract the role of government, Democrats are more likely to prioritize policy change. Democrats propose major legislation more often and are more amenable to practical compromises that result in the partial accomplishment of their goals. Republicans, in contrast, prefer a confrontational approach that relies more on procedural brinkmanship in pursuit of total victory—which is often defined as the successful blockade of Democratic initiatives. The behavior of congressional Republicans, though more unyielding today than in the past, reflects a long-standing preference among their party's supporters for allegiance to ideological principles rather than a commitment to pragmatic governance.

This chapter documents the remarkable persistence of these differences over the past several decades of congressional history, even as the ideological gap between the parties has widened significantly and Republicans have ascended from perennial minority status to become frequent rulers of the legislative branch. Historical studies often treat the institutional reforms of the mid-1970s as a pivotal moment at which the decentralized, ideologically incoherent, and committee-governed congressional Democrats transformed into a much more unified, disciplined, and liberal-dominated party, yet these developments in fact coincided with the close of an epoch of left-of-center policy change that reached its peak in the 1960s and early 1970s. While the Democratic Party in Congress has collectively moved modestly to the left since that era, principally as a result of the electoral attrition of its relatively conservative southern wing, congressional Republicans have shifted much more decisively to the right while simultaneously capturing a growing proportion of seats in both chambers. Democrats have retained the structure of a group coalition—though the composition and relative importance of the constituent groups has evolved over time—as their Republican counterparts have demonstrated increasing dedication to conservative ideological doctrine, thus preserving and even strengthening the foundational difference between the parties.

The two sides' asymmetric approaches to governance are grounded in the distinctive demands of their respective constituencies and the bifurcated preferences of the American public for operational liberalism and symbolic conservatism, with significant implications for the nature of public policy. The popular influence achieved by conservative critiques of "big government" has exerted an observable effect on the behavior of Democratic legislators, who often attempt to satisfy the programmatic goals of their party coalition by enacting policies that incorporate markets, build incrementally on existing institutions, and decentralize responsibility. As a result, American public policy frequently uses the tax code to incentivize behavior; subsidizes employers to provide public goods; and relies on private contractors, subnational governments, and nonprofits in order to avoid "bureaucratic" or "top-down" programs that might attract criticism from small-government Republicans and symbolically conservative voters.

Republican officeholders face their own set of challenges. The party has succeeded in limiting visible expansions of government's size but not in reducing the breadth of national policy goals, while popular support for reducing the existing scope of public programs usually declines once the debate moves from generalities to specifics. Though the commitment of Republican leaders to conservative principles has become stronger over time, with many GOP candidates publicly advocating a revolution-ary reduction in the size and responsibilities of the federal government, party officeholders have proven more adept at obstructing or scaling back Democratic initiatives than at achieving significant rightward shifts in national policy. This widening gap between the rhetoric and record of the Republican Party in government has provided fodder for the series of in-ternal rebellions against Republican officials that have divided the party in recent years, claiming, among a growing list of political casualties, the Speakership of John Boehner.

PARTISAN ASYMMETRY AND AMERICAN POLICYMAKING

Most theories of Congress and policymaking are designed to apply equally to Democrats and Republicans. Whether scholars treat members of Congress as single-minded seekers of reelection or grant them broader and more varied motives, legislators' incentives are normally deemed to be similar regardless of party.[5] Models of congressional parties commonly assume symmetry in the goals and styles of Democrats and Republicans, even as they differ over whether parties are best understood as strong leg-islative cartels, as coalitions dependent on internal unity, or as secondary players in congressional organization.[6] All analyses allow for party behav-ior to vary based on exogenous conditions—such as whether the party is in the majority or minority, or in the lower or upper chamber—but tend to assume that similar changes or differences in the institutional environ-ment are likely to produce comparable effects on each party.

This scholarship should be considered in its historical context. Many influential studies of Congress, and most theories of American policy-making, were developed during the long period between the 1950s and the 1980s when Congress was dominated by an internally factionalized Democratic Party, circumstances that potentially render them less ap-plicable to other eras and parties. The post-1980s growth of partisan po-larization, now at its highest level in more than a century and driven by a more powerful and ideologically conservative Republican Party, has changed the operation of Congress considerably, challenging a number of previous assumptions and conclusions.[7]

Political scientists not only built institutional theories from observa-tion of the less polarized and overwhelmingly Democratic era in Congress but actively encouraged reform of its perceived deficiencies. The 1950 report "Toward a More Responsible Two-Party System," produced by the American Political Science Association (APSA) Committee on Political

Parties under the leadership of E. E. Schattschneider, advocated the creation of two internally united and externally distinct parties that would present a clear choice of policy programs to voters; the winning party would then hold a popular mandate for enacting its stated platform.[8] Like many liberals, these scholars objected to the substantial institutional power held at the time by conservative southern "Dixiecrats," who often exercised their influence to block legislation favored by the national leaders of their own party, and were frustrated by the tendency of the midcentury party system to offer what they viewed as insufficient policy alternatives to the electorate.

In a prophetic response to the APSA report, Austin Ranney warned that a sharply majoritarian party system was incompatible with the American constitutional structure. The existence of two competing ideologically oriented parties might indeed give voters a greater range of policy choices. But Ranney predicted that staggered terms of office, supermajoritarian vote requirements, and separated branches of government would produce frequent procedural gridlock in practice.[9] Contemporary scholars agree that a combination of intentional reforms and wider political change (including the regional realignment of the South, the decline of patronage-based political machines, and the rise of the modern conservative movement) caused the American party system to evolve in the direction envisioned by the APSA report over the second half of the 20th century. Today, however, many analysts express concern that the rise of polarized parties in a decentralized institutional framework has rendered Congress a "broken branch" of government.[10]

Public policy scholarship presents a different view than that offered by congressional research but also ignores how party asymmetry might influence theory and outcomes. Paul Sabatier's volume summarizing theories of the policy process, for example, includes only one reference to Republicans (in an aside referring to their similarity with Democrats).[11] The three dominant theories of policymaking, developed by Sabatier and Hank Jenkins-Smith, Frank Baumgartner and Bryan Jones, and John Kingdon, all cite partisan trends in institutions or public opinion as potential sources of instability but treat leftward and rightward trends equivalently as instigators of policy change.[12] The view that policy solutions are, or at least should be, a response to social problems historically justified the study of policy as an independent field of inquiry. In contemporary Washington, however, only one major party—the Democrats—conforms to this baseline view of policymaking as an effort to solve social problems through legislative or administrative action.

The two parties engage in distinct styles of policy development, reflecting the different nature of each major party's popular base. Because the

Democratic Party is composed of a coalition of social groups making specific programmatic demands on government, Democratic officeholders seek to appease this diverse set of interests by initiating large-scale legislative and administrative programs to address a variety of social problems. Democrats tend to divide public policy into specific issue areas, which are often associated with discrete party constituencies, and to enlist experts to develop potential solutions, aiming for a high rate of productivity and policy change and thus fulfilling the ideal-typical model of policymaking.

Conversely, as agents of an ideological movement united by conservative values and skeptical of the assumption that government action can ameliorate social problems, Republican officials treat policymaking as a broader fight over the proper size and scope of government. Republicans tend to evaluate policy in general terms and to be guided by widely accessible principles; they are less likely than Democrats to rely on separate issue networks composed of trusted policy professionals. Because policy debates in American politics are often initiated by ambitious Democratic proposals for change to which Republicans respond with opposition, Republican officeholders are more content than Democrats with inaction or legislative gridlock. Existing theories of policymaking are therefore less successful at accounting for Republican approaches to governance.

These party differences are tendencies, rather than absolute and unconditional characteristics of each side. Republican politicians do at times pragmatically seek concrete policy change, though moderate representatives who remain open to compromise in order to achieve legislative success are disappearing from their party, and some Democrats are likewise more rigidly liberal and less motivated by the goal of legislative productivity than others. Yet the distinct approaches of each party to policymaking are long-standing, reflecting the relatively stable preferences of their respective coalitions.

This partisan mismatch can help account for an otherwise puzzling divergence between the historical accounts contained in the scholarly literatures devoted to Congress and to public policy. Congressional studies describe the House of Representatives as mostly ruled by a "conservative coalition" of Republicans and southern Democrats from the late 1930s until the rules reforms of the mid-1970s, which marked the end of committee government and vested institutional power in the left-of-center leadership of the ruling Democratic Party. In contrast, most policy scholars characterize the pre-reform 1960s and early 1970s as "the high tide of liberalism" or "the liberal hour," perceiving a broad rightward shift in the direction of federal policy beginning in the late 1970s.[13] Both accounts agree that the resulting policy outcomes resembled stasis more than revolution; the growing electoral strength of conservatism in the Reagan

era inhibited the further policymaking productivity of liberal officeholders but failed to actually reduce the scope of government activity to any
significant degree. As historian Julian Zelizer noted, the rise of party
government in Congress often failed to deliver on the promise that pro-
reform liberals saw it as holding, although conservatives faced obstacles
of their own:

> America's Congress underwent significant reform in the 1970s at the hands of liber
> als who hoped to make the institution more progressive and accountable. But . . .
> conservative Republicans proved to be extremely adept at operating in the new in
> stitutions to achieve political power. A new generation of Republicans who entered
> Congress in the 1970s and maintained close ties to the conservative movement, mas
> tered the post-committee legislative process—both the decentralizing features that
> benefited the minority or mavericks, as well as the centralizing features that favored
> the majority leadership—and used the process to achieve influence in national poli
> tics. But the political success of conservatism in Congress did not slay the dragon of
> the American state. Republicans watched as the state proved to be extremely durable
> in the conservative era.[14]

Party reforms implemented by liberals gave neither side what it wanted
but did reinforce existing differences in the priorities and governing style
of congressional Democrats and Republicans.

ASYMMETRIC POLARIZATION IN CONGRESS

Although most theories of Congress and policymaking treat the parties as
mirror images, some scholars have noted that the phenomenon of ideological polarization, arguably the most consequential development in the last
30 years of American party politics, has not progressed equally on both
sides. A few noteworthy studies have identified Republicans as mostly
responsible for the growing ideological divergence between the congressional parties—and thus, for those who view polarization as an undesirable
phenomenon, as the political actors who should largely shoulder the associated culpability. Jacob Hacker and Paul Pierson argue that Republicans
have tilted far "off center" and face little incentive to moderate their policy
positions: "Today's governing Republican majority . . . [has] overseen a
major transformation of America's governing priorities. . . . It has strayed
dramatically from the moderate middle of public opinion and yet faced
little public backlash."[15] Thomas E. Mann and Norman J. Ornstein condemn the GOP even more harshly for its dramatic shift to the right: "[T]he

Republican Party has become an insurgent outlier—ideologically extreme; contemptuous of the inherited social and economic policy regime; scornful of compromise; unpersuaded by conventional understanding of facts, evidence, and science; and dismissive of the legitimacy of its political opposition."[16]

The most influential finding in favor of asymmetric polarization is supplied by the quantitative DW-NOMINATE analysis of congressional roll-call votes conducted by Keith T. Poole and Howard Rosenthal. Figure 6-1 displays each party's mean value on this ideological measure in the House and Senate between 1945 and 2013, as well as the values for non-southern Democrats only in each chamber over the same period. The results are unequivocal: the Republican Party has collectively moved swiftly toward the conservative pole in both houses of Congress since the late 1970s, accounting for the vast majority of the widening ideological gap between the parties. The comparatively modest leftward shift among congressional Democrats over the same period is almost entirely explained by the decline of the party's historically atypical southern conservative faction; northern Democrats have collectively remained ideologically stable since the 1970s.

As Mann and Ornstein explain, this quantitative evidence matches the qualitative histories of each party (previously reviewed in Chapter 3):

> The center of gravity within the Republican Party has shifted sharply to the right. Its legendary moderate legislators in the House and Senate are virtually extinct.... The post-McGovern Democratic Party, while losing the bulk of its conservative Dixiecrat contingent, has retained a more diverse constituency base, and ... has hewed to the center-left.... Anyone who has reviewed the voluminous literature on the intellectual and organizational developments within the conservative movement and Republican Party since the 1970s will find that an unremarkable assertion.[17]

It is striking that the obvious congruence between the congressional voting data and the qualitative histories of each political party has not attracted more attention from scholars and commentators investigating the causes and dynamics of party polarization.

According to Hacker and Pierson, Mann and Ornstein, and other critics who do recognize—and lament—the asymmetric nature of party polarization, the modern Republican Party displays a troubling combination of ideological extremity, procedural belligerence, and indifference to the policy preferences of the wider American electorate. While these observers express well-founded concerns about the difficulties introduced by an ideologically charged and procedurally ruthless style of politics, Republican leaders' relative aversion to compromise is, in our

Figure 6-1 Mean Ideological Positions of the Political Parties in Congress

(a) House of Representatives:

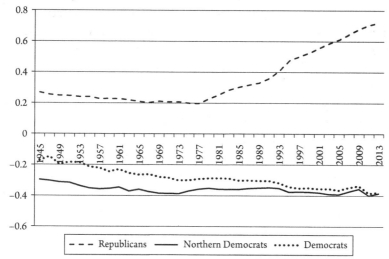

(b) Senate:

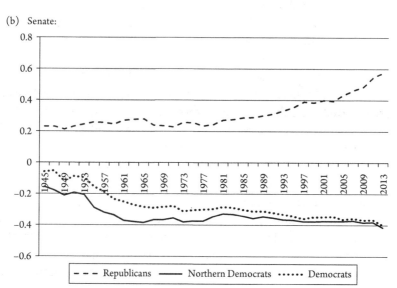

Mean DW-Nominate scores from voteview.com.

view, not irrational or pathological in nature. Rather, it is an understand-
able consequence of the ambitious objective adopted by the modern
conservative movement of combating the expansion of federal responsibilities over time. Pursuing their substantive goals with the best available tools, Republican politicians naturally prefer stalemate to episodes
of bipartisan cooperation that would likely further increase the scope of
government.

POLICY DIRECTION AND THE CONSERVATIVE DILEMMA

Significant laws are enacted more frequently during Democratic presidential administrations and congressional majorities than under Republican leadership.[18] There is a good reason for this pattern: Democrats are more likely than Republicans to focus on policymaking, because any change that occurs is much more likely to move policy to the left than to the right. New policies usually expand the scope of government responsibility, funding, or regulation. Conservatives occasionally achieve policy successes as well, but they are less frequent and are usually accompanied by the expansion of government responsibility in other areas.[19] The distinct governing styles of the two parties thus reflect an asymmetry in the ideological direction of new policy: historically, policy change has more frequently expanded the scope of government than contracted it.

Figure 6-2 illustrates the comparative infrequency of conservative policy change, drawing upon data from a content analysis of 268 policy area histories that describe the most significant policy changes in each branch of government across domestic policy areas between 1945 and 2004.[20] On average, liberal policy changes occurred more than three times as frequently as conservative policy changes during this period. As a rule, policymakers debate which additional actions the federal government should take, not whether government should maintain its existing reach. Reducing the scope of government is difficult because policies create beneficiaries who subsequently act as constituencies for those policies' continuation and expansion. Conservative policy changes in the executive branch, made via presidential directives or agency rule, are even less common. This pattern is not a product of historians' judgments; it is confirmed by other measures.[21]

Because many more policy changes expand government than contract it, increased legislative activity does not tend to satisfy conservative goals. As rates of policymaking increase, outcomes usually move in a liberal direction. Figure 6-2 reveals the association over time between the total number of significant policy changes in each biennium (represented by the black line) and the number of net liberal policy changes (liberal changes minus conservative changes, represented by the gray dotted line). These trends generally rise and fall together, but this tendency became less prevalent after the 1970s. In the wake of the massive growth of government activity that occurred in the 1960s, efforts to reduce the government's scope or exchange expansions in one area for contractions in another subsequently found occasional success. Nevertheless, there has been only one period of both active and conservative governance: the two years following the Republican takeover of Congress in 1994.

Figure 6-2 Trends in Policymaking Productivity and Ideological Direction

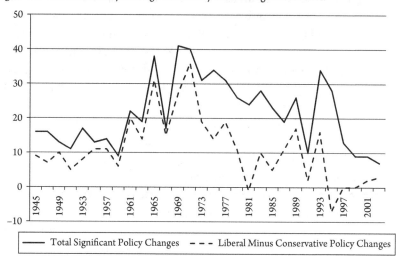

Number of significant policy changes and the difference between the number of liberal and conservative policy changes per biennium. Liberal changes are those that expand the scope of government regulation, funding, or responsibility. Conservative changes are those that contract the scope of government regulation, funding, or responsibility. Other changes have no or mixed ideological content. Data from Grossmann (2014).

Table 6-1 POLITICIANS AND INTEREST GROUPS CREDITED
WITH SIGNIFICANT POLICY CHANGES

	Democratic Politicians	Republican Politicians	Liberal Groups	Conservative Groups
Credited with a Policy Change	277	204	101	46
Credited with >1 Policy Changes	118	69	38	17
Credited in >1 Issue Areas	91	54	27	6
Of 100 Most Often Credited	39	26	14	3

Number of actors credited with significant policy changes in the legislative, executive, and judicial branches of the federal government since 1945. The identification of significant changes and the actors credited with those changes come from policy area histories, compiled and analyzed in Grossmann (2014). A politician or interest group is credited when any policy historian views that actor's involvement as instrumental in bringing about a policy change; most policy changes are credited to more than one actor.

As a result, Republican politicians and conservative interest groups are less involved in significant policymaking. Table 6-1 reports the number of actors in each category that policy historians have credited with bringing about policy change.[22] Democratic politicians have been more active than Republicans, especially when it comes to involvement in multiple policy changes across issue areas. The most active Republicans—Richard Nixon, Jacob Javits, and Bob Dole—were open to the expansion of government power; Javits, who represented New York in the Senate between 1957 and 1981, was a leader of the now-defunct liberal wing of the GOP, while Nixon and Dole (though self-identified conservatives) pragmatically pursued policy goals in ways that regularly drew criticism from ideological purists within their own party.

This historical analysis confirms the existence of a long-standing dilemma that is unique to Republican officeholders. Even after decisive electoral victories, Republicans achieve limited success at rolling back previous expansions of federal authority, in large part because the public's preference for smaller government in the abstract rarely translates into support for specific proposals to reduce or abolish existing government programs, regulations, and benefits. Yet failing to deliver on prior rhetorical commitments to achieve significant reductions in the scope of government's reach risks alienating a Republican popular base that remains devoted to conservative principles.

Conservatives are left in a political bind: they want to reduce the size of government but have difficulty achieving this goal without suffering popular rejection. As Pierson notes in his study of Reagan's attempted reversal of welfare state expansion in the 1980s, "There are two distinct reasons that retrenchment is usually an exercise in blame avoidance rather than credit claiming. First, the costs of retrenchment are concentrated, whereas the benefits are not. Second, there is considerable evidence that voters exhibit a 'negativity bias,' remembering losses more than gains."[23]

As a result, most policy proposals (whether enacted or not) constitute expansions of government responsibility. Figure 6-3 illustrates a measure of the ideological direction of policy proposals in six different policy areas. We identified all proposals mentioned in *Congressional Quarterly* since 1981 and described them to panels of experts in each policy area, asking them to rate each proposal on a seven-point scale from most liberal (+3) to most conservative (−3) based on how much it expanded or contracted the scope of government. We also measured whether each proposal was enacted and whether it was endorsed by the Democratic or Republican party leadership. The average proposal in all issue areas slightly expanded the scope of government, as did the subset of proposals that were ultimately enacted. Republicans, on average, endorsed proposals that were slightly more conservative than those endorsed by Democrats. Strikingly, however, even Republican-endorsed proposals were more likely to increase than to decrease government's size.

Republicans often acknowledge that maximizing legislative productivity is not their goal. Then-Speaker John Boehner remarked in July 2013

Figure 6-3 Average Ideological Position of Major Policy Proposals and Laws by Issue Area

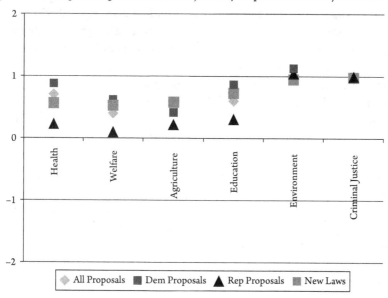

Average ideological position of major legislative proposals (as identified by *Congressional Quarterly*) on a seven-point scale from most liberal (+3) to most conservative (−3). Ratings were determined by expert and online public surveys conducted by Matt Grossmann.

on the CBS public affairs program *Face the Nation* that Congress "should not be judged on how many new laws we create. We ought to be judged on how many laws we repeal."[24] Conservative leaders have a long tradition of making similar statements. "My aim is not to pass laws, but to repeal them," wrote Barry Goldwater in his 1960 manifesto *The Conscience of a Conservative*. "It is not to inaugurate new programs, but to cancel old ones that do violence to the Constitution, or that have failed in their purpose."[25] Since successful repeals of existing measures are much less common than the enactment of new laws, an important implication of this view is that inaction might be preferable to legislative productivity of any kind. John H. Sununu, the former New Hampshire governor who served as White House chief of staff during the presidential administration of George H. W. Bush, brazenly expressed this view when addressing a conservative group in November 1990, at the midpoint of Bush's presidential term: "There's not a single piece of legislation that needs to be passed in the next two years for this president. In fact, if Congress wants to come together, adjourn, and leave, it's all right with us. We don't need them."[26]

The international historical record suggests that the scope of government grows over time, even during attempted periods of deregulation and retrenchment.[27] In the domain of moral and cultural issues, conservatives—as defenders of traditional values and opponents of social change—also tend to be fighting against a strong historical tide.[28] Because conservatism is a broad predisposition rather than a stable set of issue positions, it can evolve to oppose new areas of government expansion and express wariness about emerging social trends while accepting previous instances of change. But Republican officials experience difficulties in compiling a governing record that fulfills their conservative ambitions. They face a quandary: as society evolves, government takes on additional responsibilities. With reason, conservative activists view these developments with alarm, often directing their frustration and anger not only at Democrats but also toward the leadership of their own party for failing to stop, or even encouraging, the increasing power of government. Republican politicians are often much more effective at fomenting popular backlash to the perceived overreach of Democrats than they are in dismantling Democratic policies.

As Zelizer observes, Republicans habitually find it easier to rail against big government when serving in the minority than to grapple with these dilemmas once installed in power:

> [I]nternal tensions would become more pronounced when conservatives were forced to switch from being an opposition movement to becoming office holders dealing with the challenges of governance. It was one thing for conservatives to demand that the federal government should disappear when they were primarily working on the campaign trail and at the grassroots level, but it was quite another to make this demand when they were the ones in charge. . . . Conservatives in positions of governance had to contend with the durability of public policy.[29]

The repeated failure of elected Republicans to achieve an enduring reversal of federal policy's general leftward trajectory, despite perennial rhetorical attacks on "out-of-control government" and promises on the campaign trail to lead a conservative revolution, is not a myth propagated by misinformed Tea Party activists. Rather, it is an enduring characteristic of the policymaking process that provides Republican leaders with very different governing challenges than those faced by their Democratic counterparts.

CONGRESSIONAL PARTIES AND POLICY PRODUCTIVITY

Congress operates very differently under the leadership of each party. Democratic control of the House or Senate is associated with higher rates of legislative productivity and a more active policymaking process. To

Table 6-2 BILLS AND COMMITTEE MEETINGS UNDER DEMOCRATIC AND
REPUBLICAN CONTROL

	Bills Introduced	Bills Passed	Committee Meetings
Democratic House	12,215	1,066	5,011
Republican House	5,742	727	2,941
Democratic Senate	3,867	1,004	
Republican Senate	3,226	754	

Average number of bills introduced and passed and the average number of committee and subcommittee meetings held in years that the Democrats and Republicans had a majority in each house of Congress from 1961–2012. Data from Ornstein et al. (2013).

provide a general summary of the effects of party control, Table 6-2 reports characteristics of the average session of Congress under each party's leadership between 1961 and 2012. On average, more than twice as many bills were introduced, and nearly 50 percent more passed, under Democratic House majorities (though the legislative success rate was therefore correspondingly lower during periods of Democratic rule). Committees also met significantly more often under Democratic leadership. Restricting the analysis to the period after Jim Wright's elevation to the Speakership in 1987 does not significantly change the results: the average rate of bill introductions under Democrats has been approximately 6,600 per year since 1987, while the rate of committee meetings has declined to 4,100 per year. The Senate was also more active in terms of bills introduced (and, especially, bills enacted) under Democratic control during the same period.

Frank Baumgartner and Bryan Jones argue that the shift to Republican governance was part of a wholesale change in congressional information gathering and the process of discovery of new social problems.[30] Indeed, these scholars' measures of legislative activity, based on the breadth of policy topics considered, confirm that Congress investigates and acts with a broader scope during periods of Democratic control. Table 6-3 shows that Democratic-led Congresses cover more topics in legislative hearings, pass more laws, and consider more major initiatives (as identified by *Congressional Quarterly*). Democratic majorities also consider the creation of more new federal agencies. Since these data cover few eras of unified Republican rule, these results should be interpreted with caution, but it is notable that policymaking has become less broad in the period since 1995, during which Republicans have often held partial or total control of the legislative branch.

Similar differences appear only to a modest degree in comparisons of the activities of Democratic and Republican legislators serving simultaneously. Table 6-4 reports the average number of bills sponsored and

Table 6-3 LEGISLATIVE ACTIVITY UNDER DEMOCRATIC AND REPUBLICAN CONGRESSES, 1949–2010

	Legislative Hearing Subtopics	Legislative Hearings Total	New Laws Subtopics	*Congressional Quarterly* Subtopics	New Agency Hearings
Unified Democratic	155	1187	131	139	41
Divided/Mixed Government	160	1098	128	123	52
Unified Republican	123	768	114	77	6

Average number of legislative hearings and hearings dedicated to consideration of new agencies during Congresses of unified Democratic and Republican governance as well as the number of policy agenda project subtopics covered in legislative hearings, in new laws, and in *Congressional Quarterly* summaries of legislative activity. When the House, Senate, and presidency are not all controlled by the same party, we place the Congress in the mixed category. There have only been a small number of periods of unified Republican control in 1949–2010, but the same differences hold if periods when Republicans controlled two of the three forums are included.

Table 6-4 AVERAGE BILL SPONSORSHIP PER MEMBER BY PARTY SINCE 1981

	Democrats	Republicans
House Bills Sponsored	13.9	12.1
Senate Bills Sponsored	32.2	29.0
House Bills Co-Sponsored	159.9	140.8
Senate Bills Co-Sponsored	75.8	71.1
Average Word Count of Bills	1781.7	1669.9

Average number of bills sponsored and co-sponsored by members of each political party in the U.S. House and Senate since 1981. Data from Adler and Wilkerson (2014) and Fowler (2010). Word count only includes bills from the 112th Congress.

co-sponsored by members of each party in the House and Senate between 1981 and 2012. Democrats sponsored and co-sponsored slightly more bills than did Republicans in both legislative chambers. Calculating the average word count of bills by party (only available for the 112th Congress of 2011–2012) reveals that bills sponsored by Democrats are somewhat longer than those introduced by their Republican counterparts. Yet the differences between Democratic and Republican representatives serving in the same legislative sessions are not as large as the differences between Congresses controlled by opposite parties.

Craig Volden and Alan Wiseman have created the most comprehensive measure of legislator productivity.[31] They calculate a legislative effectiveness score based on how far each member's bills proceed through the legislative process, with scores normalized to a mean of 1 for each congressional session (thus controlling for aggregate productivity differences over time). Volden and Wiseman find equivalent majority-party advantages in productivity for Democratic and Republican legislators when each party holds the majority, but they identify two important differences between the parties: (1) Democrats are more successful in producing significant legislation, while Republicans are more successful in passing less significant (but nonceremonial) legislation; and (2) Democratic legislative effectiveness is mostly led by party leaders and committee chairs, whereas junior members make a greater contribution to party productivity on the Republican side. Figure 6-4 illustrates these patterns by summarizing one key measure: the average number of bills passing the House that were authored by majority party leaders, committee chairs, and backbenchers between 1985 and 2013.

Democratic presidents are also more active than Republicans in driving the congressional agenda. Table 6-5 displays the average number of total legislative proposals (and the subset devoted to domestic policy) made by Democratic and Republican presidents per two-year session of Congress since 1945. Democratic presidents made 39 percent more proposals than Republicans overall and 62 percent more domestic policy proposals, while a higher share of Republican proposals was dedicated to foreign policy or government reorganization. Presidential legislative activity has declined since its peak in the 1960s, but the differences between Democrats and

Figure 6-4 Sponsored Bills Passing the House by Majority Partisanship and Role

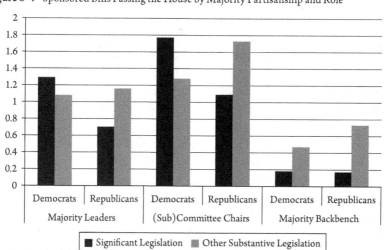

Average number of bills passing the House of Representatives that were authored by majority-party members in the leadership, in committee or subcommittee chairmanships, or in neither from 1985–2013. Data from Volden and Wiseman (2014). The dataset is available at thelawmakers.org.

Table 6-5 AVERAGE PRESIDENTIAL LEGISLATIVE PROPOSALS PER
CONGRESS

	Democrats	Republicans	Carter/ Clinton	Reagan/ H.W. Bush
All Legislative Proposals	366	264	339	205
Domestic Policy Proposals	273	169	216	119
Percent Domestic Policy	75	64	65	58

Total number of legislative proposals made by the presidents and the number concerning domestic policy.
Democratic and Republican averages are for all presidents from 1945–2012. The last two columns provide
a more contemporary comparison between two 12-year periods. Averages calculated from data in Cohen
(2012).

Republicans remain equally stark. Jeffrey Cohen (who collected these
data) finds these patterns to be unexpected and striking.[32] Using a more
restrictive methodology, David Mayhew identified major legislative proposals by presidents from Harry Truman to George W. Bush, finding that
Democratic presidents averaged 15.5 proposals per administration compared to 10.1 proposals made by Republicans.[33]

In addition to these numerical differences, Democratic and Republican
congressional majorities exhibit qualitatively distinct behavior. Congressional
activity during periods of Republican control is often dominated by symbolic
acts demonstrating support for conservative ideology rather than practical
efforts to enact substantive legislation. Between 2011 and 2014, for example, the Republican-led House held more than 50 votes to repeal all or part
of the Affordable Care Act—all of which had no chance of success in the
Democratic-controlled Senate—even as the rate of bills enacted into law
sank to the lowest level in decades. While congressional Republicans maintain aggressive oversight of the executive branch during Democratic presidencies, other types of committee activity, such as markup sessions or hearings
to choose among competing bills, tend to recede under Republican rule.[34]
Republican rhetoric often endorses a fundamental redefinition of the role
of government in American society, but this commitment is not commonly
translated into an extensive roster of concrete legislation. After Paul Ryan
became Speaker in late 2015, he announced that the House would spend
the following year developing a series of conservative policy proposals but
acknowledged that this agenda would not necessarily be introduced by holding floor votes on specific legislative initiatives.

The pressure placed on Republican officeholders by party activists to communicate philosophical loyalty—rather than deliver practical legislative
accomplishments—sharply distinguishes the contemporary Republican
Party from its Democratic counterpart. In the next section, we explain how
the congressional parties developed these distinctive characteristics.

THE UNFULFILLED LIBERAL PROMISE
OF PARTY REFORM

The Democratic Party controlled the House of Representatives for all but four years between 1933 and 1995 and the U.S. Senate for all but four years from 1933 to 1981. Yet these Democratic majorities were seldom liberal majorities. From the late 1930s to the early 1970s, a "conservative coalition" of Republicans and (largely southern) conservative Democrats often allied to gain effective control of committee business and floor voting.[35] As Nelson W. Polsby explains, the coalition exercised its authority in the House through the effective use of chamber rules and norms:

> By 1937, most of the elements of the conservative coalition power that became familiar over the next two decades had emerged: (1) entrenchment of the coalition in the House Rules Committee, which provided an all-important strategic bottleneck; (2) the enfeeblement of the caucus as a device to mobilize the majority of the majority party; and (3) the cloak of seniority that protected conservative committee chairmen.[36]

With often-sizable Democratic chamber majorities, this cross-party alliance required significant Democratic defections to retain its numerical strength; up to 1961, "southern Democrats supplied one-third of the conservative coalition's hard-core members and just over 40 percent of the coalition at least half the time."[37]

Although its power was broader in the House, the coalition also emerged in the Senate. From the 1940s to the 1960s, as David Mayhew notes, "the stances of the Senate as the negative outlier on civil rights and the House as the conservative outlier on domestic policy in general were available for all to see."[38] Traditionally, the Senate has been informally governed by six norms that impede swift action and enhance the power of seniority: apprenticeship, the prioritization of legislative work, specialization, courtesy, reciprocity, and institutional patriotism.[39] The Senate's weak partisan institutions and procedural complexity provided copious opportunities for conservatives to delay, block, or scale back legislation.[40]

Conservatives did not succeed in rolling back the New Deal–era growth of the federal government, but they were much more effective in thwarting further legislative measures introduced and supported by mainstream Democrats. "The conservative coalition was mostly obstructionist in character, preventing action on a variety of issues," notes Polsby. "The list of liberal complaints from 1937 to 1957 was very long."[41] By the 1950s, a number of frustrated northern Democrats had begun to press for institutional reforms designed to attack the procedural power wielded by the conservative coalition. These reforms were part of a broader agenda focused on internal processes within the Democratic Party, reflecting the belief that substantive gains for liberal causes were being systematically blocked by "undemocratic" rules and practices.

Democratic congressional majorities during the 1960s did succeed in enacting wide-ranging legislation, reaching a peak of productivity during the Great Society Congress of 1965–1966 (made possible by the national Democratic landslide of 1964, which swept enough northern and western Democrats into Congress to outnumber the conservative coalition in both chambers). But Republican gains in the 1966 congressional midterms and Richard Nixon's victory in the 1968 presidential election limited the extent of liberal policymaking success, and some old-line liberals were ultimately disappointed in the results. Theodore Lowi argued in *The End of Liberalism* (1969) that "the expansion of government that helped produce sustained prosperity also produced a crisis of public authority" that gave rise to "a set of sentiments that elevate[d] a particular view of the political process above everything else" and dispensed with justifications for government expansion.[42] Within this environment, Lowi argued, traditional, ideologically motivated liberalism was replaced with "interest group liberalism," which recognized the legitimacy of groups representing each social interest and provided procedural access for them to influence and compete over legislation.

This progressive vision pretended not to employ government to achieve broad ends but focused instead on creating a "fair process." The policy results were important but ineffective: departments focused on constituency interests (e.g., agriculture, labor, and commerce) were vaguely empowered but lacked sufficient policymaking authority. More goals were delegated, while the means to achieve them were limited. According to Lowi, both the policy results and the political reforms required too much constituency responsiveness without broader support for federal intervention.

This triumph of interest group liberalism reflected the long-lived preoccupation of mainstream Democratic officeholders with questions of governmental process. In the late 1950s, an informal group of legislators met with academics and interest groups engaged in studying potential institutional reforms. After the sizable national Democratic congressional victories of 1958 failed to advance the prospects of liberal legislation in Congress, an alliance of House liberals and moderates created an internal Democratic caucus called the Congressional Study Group, soon renamed the Democratic Study Group (DSG). According to Edwin Feulner, "The name was consciously noncontroversial for fear a more ideological name might carry a tinge of insurgency. . . . The newly appointed Executive

Committee avoided controversial words like liberal and action, and stressed party loyalty."[43] DSG members maintained many different policy objectives, but a lack of consensus on goals restricted their attention to curbing the institutional clout of the conservative coalition.[44]

In addition to members of Congress, more than 40 Democratic-aligned interest groups united around the cause of reform. As Zelizer reports:

> With representatives from civil rights organizations, unions, academia, foundations, and the Democratic party, this [reform] coalition . . . invested their resources into convincing the public that process had a monumental impact on what government could or could not do. . . . The coalition swelled by the 1960s to include public interest groups such as Common Cause and individuals like Ralph Nader, who . . . demanded government reform as an end in itself rather than merely as an avenue to obtain policies.[45]

In 1961, Speaker Sam Rayburn acceded to the wishes of the DSG by expanding the liberal membership of the House Rules Committee in order to help pass the Kennedy administration's legislative program.

The 1960s also began a dramatic expansion in cross-branch policymaking—much of it leading to liberal-backed policies that expanded the scope of government (see Figure 6-2 for a quantitative measure). During the "Long Great Society" period from 1961 to 1976, Congress averaged 11 additional landmark liberal laws each session, with the executive branch adding three liberal policy changes and the courts four liberal policy changes per biennium.[46] Liberal policy change continued under the Nixon administration (peaking with a series of landmark environmental statutes), although observers at the time perceived a loss of legislative momentum. According to Norman J. Ornstein, "The period of 1967–1970 was one of maximum frustration, both substantive and procedural, for the Democratic liberals: Much was tried and little was accomplished."[47]

Still, the liberal coalition maintained its emphasis on process, seeking to reform Congress further in order to enhance its legislative power. As political scientist David Rohde explains, "The leadership of the DSG . . . wanted to create a situation in which liberal policy proposals would win more often. What is more, they told everyone, allies and adversaries alike, that that was what they wanted to do."[48] The 1970 Committee on Organization, Study and Review drafted reform proposals in consultation with liberal interest groups and academics. This group pursued three related tracks for reform: reducing the autonomy of chairs over the structure and business of their committees and component subcommittees, enabling the Democratic caucus to approve the assignment of chairmanships, and strengthening the power of the party leadership.[49]

In 1970, John Gardner, a Johnson administration veteran, founded Common Cause, an interest group ironically seeking "to curtail the power of interest groups," according to Zelizer: "The Common Cause founders believed that interest-group liberalism, which had promised that the struggle between organized interests would balance each other out for the public good, had not worked as planned."[50] Their efforts met resistance among other party constituencies: "Democrats had to strike a delicate balance between Common Cause, which insisted on the broadest reforms, and organized labor, which opposed many reforms (such as campaign finance limitations) since they did not want to risk losing their hard-earned political influence."[51] Another conflict emerged between legislative reformers seeking stronger parties and good-government interest groups that, following the Progressive tradition, viewed party power unfavorably: "deeply suspicious of political parties," good-government groups "attacked the organizational mechanisms of parties that had traditionally served as intermediaries between voters and elected officials."[52]

Despite these tensions, the reform movement found new momentum in the early 1970s as a result of the political fallout produced by the failure of the Vietnam War and the revelation of the Watergate scandal. Congress centralized its budget process, opened its committees and procedures to more scrutiny, recorded committee and floor amendment votes, created a bill of rights for its subcommittees, changed the committee assignment process, created select committees, and enabled the referral of bills to multiple committees. Democrats also abandoned the automatic seniority system used to determine committee chairmanships, requiring approval of candidates by a secret-ballot majority vote of the full party caucus.

The electoral backlash against Watergate in 1974 produced a freshman class of 75 new Democratic House members who were particularly lacking in deference to the traditional ways of Washington. These "Watergate babies" helped to depose three sitting committee chairs (a fourth, Ways and Means chairman Wilbur Mills of Arkansas, resigned because of personal scandal), backed new Democratic bylaws allowing the Speaker to appoint the majority party's representatives on the House Rules Committee, and supported rules changes that granted committee assignment powers to the Steering and Policy Committee. The cumulative effect of these reforms on the operation of the House was momentous, shifting institutional power from committees to party leaders and significantly increasing the incentives for committee chairs and prospective chairs to build voting records demonstrating their party loyalty and to eschew collaboration with Republicans. As political scientist Barbara Sinclair explained, "The committee government system was dead and a very different House was in the process of emerging. Committee chairs' powers and control over scarce resources had been severely curtailed; the basis of committee autonomy had been undermined."[53]

The passage of these procedural reforms is often treated by scholars as a pivotal moment in the ascendancy of the congressional Democratic Party's liberal wing. In practice, however, limiting the power of House committee chairs did not automatically advance the substantive goals of left-leaning members. As Sinclair observes, the reforms failed to produce the intended policy results:

> The Democratic party was too ideologically heterogeneous to make successful policy leadership possible.... Successful policy leadership requires that legislative preferences be broadly shared over a range of issues within the party, a condition that did not hold in the mid- and late 1970s.... Having multiplied opportunities and incentives for rank-and-file participation, the reforms exacerbated the collective-action problem inherent in the passing of legislation.... In the 1980s, House Democrats would have to grapple with the problem in a political environment much more hostile to their policy, reelection, and influence goals. [54]

Party leaders became slowly more involved in major agenda items from 1969 to the 1980s, but the reforms incentivized broad constituency support and legislator involvement. Referral of legislation to multiple committees often required leaders to broker agreements among Democratic constituencies aligned with different committee jurisdictions. As liberals increasingly occupied committee chairs, their individual resources undermined the necessity for wider liberal organizing (even though chairmanships now provided less legislative power).[55] The reforms did enable the introduction of more legislative initiatives at the subcommittee level and more policy specialization by junior Democratic members.[56] But their main long-term impact was to expand the influence of the party leadership, with each new post-reform Speaker, eventually including the Republicans elected after 1994, being more likely to grasp and exercise procedural power.[57]

In the 1960s, liberal northern senators similarly destabilized the policymaking system, changing committee leadership positions and reducing the power of seniority.[58] In 1970, they further reduced the role of committee chairs.[59] In 1975, a liberal-backed rule change attempted to reduce the rate of Senate filibusters by lowering the threshold to end debate from two-thirds of senators present to three-fifths of all senators (60 votes). Again, however, the reforms did not produce the leftward change in policy outcomes that supporters had expected. A group of more conservative senators in the 1970s, including Jesse Helms and James Buckley, became the chamber's most active faction in legislating and amending legislation, and eventually the minority party became more aggressive in blocking majority legislation via the filibuster.[60] The evolution of Senate procedures occurred less through organized caucus activity and more through informal changes in norms, according to Sinclair:

> [T]he cumulative effect of various changes on how the institution functions was even greater in the Senate than in the House. In a body with rules as permissive as those of the Senate, norms are a critical determinant of how the institution actually functions. . . . [O]nce Senate norms specifying restraint lost their hold, Senate rules allowed unrestrained floor activity by any senator so inclined.[61]

The sustained era of liberal policymaking came to an end in the mid-1970s despite the success of congressional reformers (see Figure 6-2). The institutional empowerment of party leaders and the majority caucus at the expense of committee chairs could not compensate for the limited support for additional large-scale liberal policy initiatives within Congress as a whole. Although the faction of southern conservative "Dixiecrats" had entered a period of rapid electoral decline after the mid-1960s, most of its members were succeeded in office not by party liberals but by either moderate Democrats or conservative Republicans. The rise of the southern Republican Party rendered many Democratic members vulnerable for the first time to serious challenges from the ideological right in general elections. In addition, the increasing popular success of Republican presidential candidates in many congressional Democrats' home states and districts during the 1970s and 1980s, especially in the South, signaled to these members that their constituents had grown weary of liberal policies.

Democrats from other regions of the nation also became more likely to challenge New Deal–style government activism during this era. Factions dubbed "Atari Democrats" and "New Democrats" emerged within congressional ranks, composed of members who argued that their party needed to modernize its policy platform in order to maintain its appeal to middle-class voters and effectively address newly salient national challenges such as growing federal budget deficits, more stringent international economic competition, accelerating technological change, and rising rates of violent crime, drug abuse, and teen pregnancy. Many of these Democrats represented burgeoning suburban constituencies where sensitivity to taxation levels ran high while faith in the effectiveness of government-run programs ran low, encouraging them to propose minimally bureaucratic solutions to social problems. Consequently, they simultaneously expanded the number of issues on the legislative agenda and sought to shed the electoral baggage of big-government liberalism.

The persistence of ideological factionalism continued to hinder the congressional Democratic Party in the years after reform. "Fragmented and decentralized governance—where strong subcommittees, caucuses, and mavericks could wield significant influence—had been institutionalized at the same time that congressional parties were strengthened," notes Zelizer. "This made things difficult for Democrats. . . . They found that internal divisions were making it challenging to legislate. New divisions among northerners, rather than ideological unity, had replaced the party's old regional split. A cadre of young Republicans, moreover, started to make use of the new procedural tools to stifle business."[62] In addition, the more frequent Republican control of the executive branch in this era (and, from 1981 to 1986, the Senate) decreased the probability that liberal policies would become law.

The task of managing an unruly party fell to the Democratic leadership. Throughout the 1980s, enacted legislation declined in sheer number but increased in average length, reflecting its growing complexity.[63] House Speakers, beginning in 1977, steadily increased their reliance upon restrictive rules designed by the Rules Committee to limit floor amendments. These trends led to larger party differences in floor voting, especially on amendments proposed by the minority.[64]

Progressive reformers had concentrated on opening up the process of congressional governance, which they assumed would remove artificial obstructions to the enactment of liberal policies—but instead they found that these changes made compromise more difficult. The reformers underestimated how Democrats had benefited from the old system. Distributive politics had allowed party leaders to buy off recalcitrant members and reach broader deals. Committee government enabled giant logrolling arrangements, which worked well for a party composed of multiple constituencies with different policy concerns. Zelizer judges the movement largely a failure: "[T]he institutional changes of the 1970s did not produce many of the outcomes that proponents of reform had hoped for. Congress has not emerged as the dominant branch of government, it is not an icon of efficiency, it has not regained public favor, and it has certainly not become a factory of progressive policies." [65] Rohde evaluates the reforms more positively, arguing that they helped produce party unity.[66] The revised rules did increase party-line voting and contribute to polarization, but they did not succeed in uniting the heterogeneous Democratic coalition.

SOCIAL IDENTITY AND DEMOCRATIC POLICYMAKING

The Democratic Party has long been a popular coalition of social minorities, although the party in government has not always reflected the diversity of the party in the electorate. But after the expansion of voting rights and the social changes of the 1960s, more racial minorities were elected to Congress—overwhelmingly as Democrats. African American representatives were accompanied within the party ranks by members of other racial and ethnic groups, women, and non-Christians.

Minority legislators organized institutionally, founding the Congressional Black Caucus (CBC) in 1971 and the Congressional Hispanic Caucus in 1976. Expert Robert Singh notes that the CBC "initiated a new era in black congressional politics."[67] The CBC increased African American representation on key committees, improved these members' access to party leaders, and influenced Democratic legislative priorities. CBC membership rose from 5 percent of the Democratic caucus in 1971 to 19 percent of the caucus in 1995.[68] By 1992, three committee chairs and sixteen subcommittee chairs were CBC members. As the CBC grew as a force in Democratic politics, it became a critical component of the congressional party. But Singh argues that the group was most successful in winning symbolic appointments and shaping minor policies rather than uniting around a cohesive agenda.[69]

Figure 6-5 illustrates the dramatic increase in the demographic diversity of House Democrats since the 1970s. The black line in the figure

Figure 6-5 Increasing Diversity in the Democratic Caucus

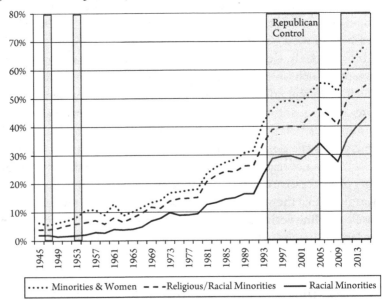

Percentage of the Democratic caucus that is made up of racial minorities (African American, Hispanic, or Asian) plus the percentage who are religious minorities not already included in this total (white members who are Jewish, Buddhist, Muslim, or Hindu) and the percentage who are white Christian women. The percentages are of all those who served in the House of Representatives during some part of each Congress.

represents the share of Democrats serving during each Congress who were members of racial minority groups, which rose from 1 percent in 1945 to 43 percent in 2015. The gray dashed line also incorporates Jews and other non-Christians not included in the racial minority total. Until 1969, religious and racial minorities together accounted for less than 10 percent of the Democratic caucus. Today, they constitute a majority of the party. The gray dotted line represents the total proportion of women or minorities among House Democrats by adding white Christian women to the prior total. The remaining demographic category—white Christian men—accounted for a solid majority of the House Democratic caucus until 1995 but now represents less than one-third of the party. Today, the Democratic caucus contains several openly gay representatives, along with Native Americans, Asian Americans, Buddhists, Muslims, and one Hindu member. The 247 House Republicans serving in the 2015–2016 Congress, in contrast, included only one non-Christian, 22 women, and 11 nonwhite members.

Democratic leadership has also diversified. By the 1990s, according to Sinclair, the whip system was "highly diverse, including members from all segments of the party. Northerners and southerners, conservatives and moderates as well as liberals, women, African-Americans, Latinos, and Asians are all represented." [70] The rise in minority representation among Democrats reflects greater diversity in the population at large and within the Democratic electorate. Yet the share of nonwhite and female elected officials has risen faster than the corresponding proportion of the electorate because it started at such a low level (with minorities once severely underrepresented both in Congress and among Democrats). Racial minorities also gained representation in the party as Democrats lost seats in Congress over time. Figure 6-5 shades the eras of Republican control to illustrate this relationship. When 54 House seats and majority status in the chamber shifted from Democrats to Republicans in the 1994 election, Democratic losses were concentrated among white members. The 31-seat Democratic gain in 2006 and 63-seat Democratic loss in 2010 also disproportionately affected the party's white representatives.

Nearly all nonwhite members represent safe Democratic seats in part because minority voting populations are geographically concentrated, but there are also institutional reasons why Republican electoral gains tend to occur at the expense of white Democrats. The creation of majority-minority seats has tended to pack a supermajority of Democratic voters into those districts, tilting neighboring seats toward the Republicans. Republican presidents interpreted the 1982 Voting Rights Act amendments as favoring majority-minority districts and used the Justice Department and the courts to explicitly pursue them. [71] As political scientist Thomas Schaller argues, "Republicans now had a strategic interest in colluding with minority politicians to create more such districts."[72] The large gains in minority representation within the House began in 1992, which Schaller claims was the product of a key alliance: "The 1992 results also confirmed the wisdom of the GOP's decision to broker the deal with the Congressional Black Caucus to draw an unprecedented number of new majority-minority districts that packed Democratic voters into fewer districts, improving Republican competitiveness elsewhere."[73] Whether or not Republican help was needed, the party benefited. David Lublin and Stephen Voss found that conservative Republicans gained 10 extra seats after the 1990 census as a result of mapmakers shifting nonwhite voters into adjacent districts drawn to ensure the election of minorities.[74]

Nevertheless, racial minority groups have benefited from their increased numerical strength in Congress. As Paul Frymer notes, "Increased numbers of African-Americans in the Democratic Party's legislative branch made a difference. The institutional presence of the Caucus transcends changes in party voting scores. The visibility corresponds to a powerful role in setting the legislative agenda and a much more powerful veto voice."[75] The effects of minority representation are confirmed by quantitative metrics. According to one analysis, African American House members "represent group interests more vociferously than non-Black members, including liberal non-Black Democrats from similar districts."[76] Their roll-call voting records reflect African American interest group positions, their floor speeches promote African American ideas, and their bill sponsorship and co-sponsorship concentrates on African American welfare and the promotion of African American history and culture. The existence of minority legislators also increases minority voter turnout both in those legislators' districts and statewide.[77]

African American members of Congress are also more engaged on substantive bills in committees that focus on African American interests and concerns.[78] African Americans and Latinos are even more active in congressional oversight on issues of interest to minorities: they write more letters in support of civil rights policy enforcement, spend more time asking agencies to address minority concerns, and produce more committee deliberation on minority issues.[79] African American legislators allocate more resources to minority constituency service and succeed in providing more federal dollars and attention to African American voters—even when representing mostly white constituents.[80] Latino and African American legislators have more liberal voting records than other legislators, even those whose districts have large minority populations.[81] Notably, these effects are only present among black and Latino Democrats—not Republicans—even though the racial identity of representatives in both parties are influenced by district demographics.[82]

One review of pertinent scholarly analyses notes near-unanimous findings that minority legislators better represent the views of minority populations than their nonminority counterparts and often succeed in enacting policies designed to address their issue concerns.[83] Nearly every study also recognizes, however, that the creation of concentrated majority-minority districts has tended to (at least slightly) reduce the total number of elected Democrats.[84] A rise in minority representation thus coincided with the increasing importance of identity-based concerns in the Democratic Party, the internal differentiation of issue agendas across Democratic members, and the rise of southern conservative Republicans.

Although research on other issue priority divisions in the Democratic Party is limited, there is evidence that the influence of Democratic constituency politics extends to issues unrelated to identity. For example, among Democrats, voting on environmental policy issues is a product of district-level interest group membership and economic interests; among Republicans, environmental votes are instead determined by cross-issue ideological position.[85]

Indeed, the prevalence of Democratic organizations defined by social identity is part of a broader pattern. Democratic members of Congress join more caucuses than Republicans, especially those with a specialized role in policymaking. Table 6-6 displays the average number of caucus memberships for Democrats and Republicans across three recent sessions of Congress, based on data compiled by Jennifer Nicoll Victor.[86] Democratic legislators, on average, hold more memberships in constituency caucuses like the CBC, but the Democratic overrepresentation is equally strong in caucuses organized around specific policy areas.

Ideological caucus membership rates are more equal across the parties, but this apparent partisan balance masks a key asymmetry, as depicted in Figure 6-6. Most House Democrats belong to one of three internal organizations corresponding to their ideological identity: the Congressional Progressive Caucus (representing the party's left wing), the Blue Dog Coalition (representing southern and rural moderates), and the New

Table 6-6 TYPE OF CAUCUS MEMBERSHIP BY PARTY

	Specific Policy Area	Constituency Group	Ideological	Other
Democrats	11.5	3.9	0.8	3.6
Republicans	7.6	2.5	0.7	3.5

Average number of caucus memberships for each legislator in each party in the 109th, 110th, and 111th Congresses. These data were provided directly by Jennifer Nicoll Victor. Her broader data on congressional caucuses is analyzed in Ringe and Victor (2013).

Figure 6-6 Ideological Caucus Growth

(a) Democratic Caucuses

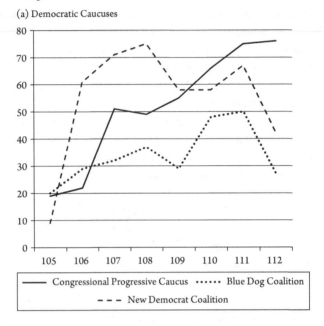

(b) Republican Caucuses

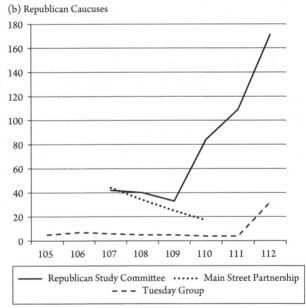

Number of members whose membership in each caucus is reported in their individual member biographies in the winter *Yellow Book* of even-numbered years. These data were provided directly by Jennifer Nicoll Victor. Her broader data on congressional caucuses is analyzed in Ringe and Victor (2013).

Democrat Coalition (representing northern suburban moderates). While the Progressive Caucus has gained membership over the past 20 years, it still contains a minority of House Democrats; the two centrist organizations, though declining in size, together represent a significant share of Democratic members. On the Republican side, in contrast, the vast majority of House members belong to the Republican Study Committee (RSC), the organizational home of party conservatives. A smaller bloc of right-wing Republicans who characterize the Study Committee as exhibiting insufficient ideological purity recently founded the House Freedom Caucus as an alternative vehicle for their views. A small proportion of Republicans belong to the Tuesday Group, which represents party moderates. Under Democratic control, the Rules Committee is more likely to allow amendments by members of the party's centrist groups, whereas Republicans tend to marginalize their moderates (based on available data over three Congresses).[87]

This imbalance reflects a long history of differences in ideological organization. Even when the DSG was active, it had a mean conservative coalition support score of 42 (meaning it supported a significant share of conservative initiatives), whereas the Conservative Democratic Forum and Republican Study Committee produced average scores of 86 and 84, respectively.[88] By 1995, the DSG had reorganized as part of the Democratic caucus. Whereas moderate Democrats are active in policy compromises, moderate Republican organizations serve mainly to discuss issues and organize electoral politics.[89]

Republicans have been less supportive of the congressional caucus system as a whole, reflecting the party's relative aversion to group-interest politics. Under Democratic rule prior to 1995, House caucuses could hire staff and pay for office space in House buildings. (Caucuses in the Senate developed later and were less organized).[90] Republicans officially eliminated the role of these service organizations after gaining the majority in 1995, forcing member caucuses to rely on externally funded foundations or advisory groups. In the succeeding years, the most successful caucuses have been those based on ideology or identity.[91] Leaders consult with both types of caucuses on floor action and negotiate with them for votes.[92] Both the CBC and Democratic ideological caucuses were active, for example, in last-minute legislative maneuvering over the ACA in 2010.

Despite substantial enduring diversity within the party ranks, contemporary Democrats have recently demonstrated increased success in reconciling the demands of their various internal factions. During the Speakership of Nancy Pelosi (2007–2010), House Democrats pursued an ambitious programmatic agenda, attempting to satisfy various party constituencies favoring specific policy initiatives: an equal-pay bill for women's rights organizations, a raise in the minimum wage for labor unions, a climate change bill for environmentalists, repeal of the military's "don't ask, don't tell" policy for gay rights groups, financial services regulation for consumer advocates, and so forth. The 2009 economic stimulus bill signed by Barack Obama combined aid to urban areas, environmental initiatives, education and health services funding, and tax cuts, attempting to simultaneously satisfy interests across the breadth of the party membership.

This burst of legislative productivity reflected a lessening over time of tensions among the groups that constitute the Democratic coalition. Since the 1970s and 1980s, the American labor movement has become more accepting of positions held by other Democratic constituencies on issues like immigration and environmental regulation, while the waning influence of moral traditionalists within the party membership at both the mass and elite levels has reduced internal conflict over cultural issues such as abortion and gay rights. From the other ideological direction, many liberal Democrats have become more broadly skeptical of New Deal–style domestic policy proposals that would result in the expansion of federal bureaucracies or require raising taxes on nonwealthy citizens. The ACA, for example, relied on the expansion of the Medicaid program and the creation of regulated private individual insurance markets rather than direct government provision funded by broad-based taxation.

Yet significant divisions remain within Democratic ranks. During the party's most recent turn in the majority, the congressional Democratic Party's relative lack of ideological unity often made passage of legislation challenging (some proposals favored by liberals, such as "card check" provisions for labor unions, were ultimately blocked by party moderates, while others, such as the ACA, passed narrowly and precariously because of significant moderate defection). Despite these limitations, the party membership's widespread visible engagement in policy details and willingness to compromise in order to improve the prospects of enactment—illustrated by the extensive revisions and concessions made during the ACA's year-long journey though the legislative process—reflected the preferences of constituencies prizing substantive achievements over philosophical purity. Republican officeholders, in contrast, usually govern quite differently.

THE CONSERVATIVE MOVEMENT IN CONGRESS

Conservatives have long been the dominant group among House and Senate Republicans. During the 1960s, they further consolidated their influence within the congressional party, reducing the power of moderates and liberals. In some cases, these changes mirrored Democratic reforms, such as the procedural maneuvering employed by Republican leaders to bolster conservative representation on the House Foreign Affairs Committee in 1963.[93] Since Republicans were habitually relegated to the minority during this era, ideological divisions were relatively less consequential for the development of a party agenda. Some conservatives complained that their partisan colleagues were too willing to work with Democrats, but cross-party collaboration allowed Republicans to exert some policy influence despite their long-lived minority status. Republicans blamed Democratic presidents for the increase in liberal policymaking in the 1960s.

But conservatives within and outside Congress became increasingly frustrated with the Republican congressional leadership during the Nixon years. Feulner describes the impetus behind the founding of the Republican Study Committee, the primary conservative caucus, in 1973:

> [B]eginning with the Nixon administration, policies were propounded which many Republicans found objectionable and against which conservatives felt the need to unify. This was especially so since senior Republicans, the "regular conservatives" . . . became the chief contact with high-level officials in the Nixon administration. Their touch with power softened their ideological beliefs and they soon altered their legislative objectives to accommodate the administration.[94]

The DSG was the obvious model for the RSC, but there were two key differences between the two groups. First, while the DSG concentrated on advocating procedural reforms and civil rights, the members of the RSC voiced broad substantive disagreements with Republican leaders across a range of domestic and foreign issues. Second, the DSG was formed during a period of frustration with an administration of the opposite party (the presidency of Dwight D. Eisenhower), whereas the RSC's founding represented conservative dissatisfaction with a fellow Republican president.[95] During the Nixon administration, Feulner notes, conservatives "awoke to the fact that working on the theory of voting right by voting no was fruitless. Jolted by the Nixon administration's move to the left, conservative Republicans decided to cut loose from the formal Republican House leadership."[96]

In the view of conservative critics, the policy apostasies committed by Republican leaders included support for a guaranteed income (the Family Assistance Plan, or FAP) and federal funding for a national network of child care centers (the Comprehensive Child Development Act). The FAP passed the House Ways and Means Committee in March 1970 with a bipartisan vote but was denounced by conservative leaders. It was defeated in the Senate Finance Committee the following November, which, Feulner says, emboldened conservatives: "The FAP battle gave proof of this: A handful of Republican conservatives were able to stop their own administration, which had the original support of the most powerful committee in the House of Representatives, as well as the formal leadership of both parties in the House."[97] The Comprehensive Child Development Act passed Congress with substantial bipartisan support in 1971 but was somewhat unexpectedly vetoed by Nixon, who acquiesced to pressure from conservatives communicated through sympathetic White House aide Pat Buchanan and Vice President Spiro T. Agnew.[98]

These victories provided an opening for the RSC, which explicitly mobilized against the Republican leadership. The group took positions on taxes, a balanced budget amendment, land use, and legal services, but won only a few concessions. In the mid-1970s, the RSC expanded its offerings to include a research directory and guide, campaign activities, and promotion of welfare reform. Minority Whip Bob Michel of Illinois joined the caucus in 1974 and was elected to the RSC executive committee. By 1976, the RSC had assembled a staff of 11 and produced more than 100 reports on pending bills. Phil Crane of Illinois and Jack Kemp of New York led the group's outreach to academics and think tanks. The RSC helped promote Kemp's supply-side tax policies, which eventually served as the blueprint for Reagan's 1981 tax cuts. Though Kemp failed to convince President Ford to endorse them in 1976, he built a slow Republican consensus over five votes. When offered as an alternative to the Humphrey-Hawkins full employment bill in 1978, Reagan endorsed the policy in a national radio address.[99] After RSC staff director Feulner became the president of the Heritage Foundation, the RSC solidified its strong connections with conservative movement groups.

The equivalent conservative Senate organization, the Senate Steering Committee, evolved out of a lunch club in the 1960s and the Senate Whip Group in 1973. Heritage co-founder Paul Weyrich was a primary staff mover in this group, but senators Bob Dole of Kansas and Strom Thurmond of South Carolina were early influential members. Though the Senate contained a visible faction of moderate Republicans, the party in that chamber was less divided by ideology than its Democratic opponents. One count found a majority of conservatives in the Republican Party in the Senate in every decade, with liberals absent after the 1970s.[100]

Conservatives did not need to seize internal power from another dominant group in the party, but they did seek to maintain pressure on Republican leaders to push policy further rightward. Rohde describes traditional conservatives as the "largest and most durable faction within the Republican party" during this period. By 1976, the Republican Study Committee included over half of the House Republican Conference and was often referred to as the "Reaganite wing."[101] As Zelizer argues, "There was a cohort of young Republicans who entered Congress between 1972 and 1982 who were closely linked to the conservative movement. Many were southern, southwestern, or western conservatives who came into Congress with a strong ideological mission, yet they were simultaneously committed to playing hardball politics so that they were not relegated to the margins."[102] Conservatives ran against "Washington" and the entire political system, portraying themselves as defending their principles against threats in both parties. Establishment-friendly Republican leaders were surprised by the purist right's ability to organize and its success in identifying issues that mobilized the Republican popular base, such as opposition to the Equal Rights Amendment and treaties with Panama and the Soviet Union.

The congressional reforms of the mid-1970s, as well as the electoral decline of the Democratic wing of the conservative coalition, further worked to the advantage of the younger generation of conservative Republicans. Reforms removed previously existing opportunities for bipartisan cooperation and reduced the incentive for Democratic committee chairs to work productively with Republicans, leaving the minority party without a stake in committee operations and undercutting the case for a go-along approach.[103] Soon, a new generation of conservatives mobilized to thoroughly discredit Democratic rule—setting their sights on winning a majority of their own.

NEWT GINGRICH AND THE RISE OF COMBATIVE CONSERVATISM

Republican gains in the 1978 elections brought reinforcements to the conservative wing of the congressional GOP, initiating the long rightward shift that continues to the present (see Figure 6-1). In the wake of Reagan's narrow loss to Ford in the 1976 Republican presidential nomination race, conservatives mobilized to challenge moderate incumbents within the party (with Jeffrey Bell defeating four-term senator Clifford Case in the New Jersey Senate primary). Citizens for the Republic, a PAC holding funds left over from supporting the 1976 Reagan campaign, contributed to 25 Senate candidates and 234 House candidates.[104] The Committee for the Survival of a Free Congress and the National Conservative Political Action Committee ran two successful Senate campaigns against liberal Democrats. In California, Proposition 13 was enacted, leading to nationwide tax limitation amendments.

Georgia history professor Newt Gingrich, after attempting to gain moderate support in two prior campaigns for Congress, successfully ran as a movement conservative in 1978.[105] In a speech to the College Republicans,

Gingrich argued that Republican leaders were too timid: "[O]ne of the great problems we have in the Republican Party is that we don't encourage you to be nasty. We encourage you to be neat, obedient, and loyal." He recommended a different approach: "Raise hell all the time. . . . This party does not need another generation of cautious, prudent, careful, bland, irrelevant, quasi-leaders. . . . What we really need are people who are . . . willing to stand up in a . . . slug fest and match it out with their opponent."[106]

Gingrich followed his own advice resolutely when he came to Washington. Thomas Mann and Norman Ornstein, who met regularly with Gingrich and other freshmen, later recalled that he pursued a clear plan from the beginning:

> The core strategy was to destroy the institution in order to save it, to so intensify public hatred of Congress that voters would buy into the notion of the need for sweeping change and throw the majority bums out. His method? To unite his Republicans in refusing to cooperate with Democrats in committee and on the floor, while publicly attacking them as a permanent majority presiding over and benefiting from a thoroughly corrupt institution.[107]

Polsby identifies Gingrich as "a self-identified bomb thrower, leader of a group that believed that his colleagues had been too acquiescent in their minority status and needed to pursue a strategy of overt obstreperousness with the ends in view of discrediting Democratic stewardship."[108] Before 1980, Gingrich had already tried to expel a Democratic legislator against the wishes of the Republican leadership. He helped the freshmen organize, and they held at least 40 meetings.[109]

Reagan's 1980 victory topped off another banner year for conservatives. Javits—the last of the liberal Republicans with a national reputation—was defeated in his Senate primary. Liberal icons George McGovern of South Dakota and Gaylord Nelson of Wisconsin lost their seats as Republicans gained control of the Senate for the first time since 1954. But inside the House, the more aggressive generation of conservatives would take longer to ascend. Bob Michel, a mild-mannered conservative known for his mastery of House procedure and friendly relationships with Democrats, narrowly beat Guy Vander Jagt (who was supported by Gingrich) in an election for minority leader.

Gingrich and his allies began using one-minute floor speeches to promote their views; the number of such speeches increased from 110 in 1977 to 344 in 1981.[110] Their inspiration was the 1979 founding of C-SPAN, a cable channel providing live coverage of congressional proceedings. Despite modest viewership in the early days of cable,

Gingrich saw C-SPAN as an important tool: "How far would you go to speak to five thousand people? The average politician would go around the planet."[111] Tip O'Neill, the Democratic Speaker, did not disguise his contempt, grousing that "as far as they were concerned, the House was no more than a pulpit, a sound stage from which to reach the people at home. If the TV cameras were facing the city dump, that's where they'd be speaking."[112]

In 1983, Gingrich founded the Conservative Opportunity Society (COS) to provide a formal organization for the hard-charging conservative members of the House Republican Conference.[113] Vin Weber of Minnesota explained that it was designed to promote a new strategic approach: "[We've] been too reluctant to confront. . . . I'm hard-pressed to see where compromise has advanced the Republican agenda." Even Reagan's policies were not immune from criticism; Gingrich remarked that the administration was "feeding the liberal welfare state instead of changing it."[114] House Republican leaders referred to the COS as the "Gingrich Guerillas," expressing annoyance at the upstarts' gestures of disaffection (including voting against approval of the House journal, normally a routine matter).[115] But the Gingrich Republicans also advanced substantive goals: the COS drafted its own budget in 1984, including cuts in Medicare growth and domestic spending.

In a May 1984 tactical eruption, COS members attacked Democrats while giving floor speeches to an otherwise unpopulated House chamber. O'Neill ordered C-SPAN to pan the normally stationary cameras to reveal the empty seats to the home audience, calling the speeches "the lowest thing I've ever seen in my 32 years in Congress." O'Neill's remarks violated the rules of House decorum, and his words were taken down (after requests by Gingrich allies Bob Walker and Trent Lott), making him the first Speaker to be rebuked in this way since the 18th century.[116] Having drawn blood, COS redoubled its assault on the Democratic leadership, leading a walkout and all-night session in 1985 over a disputed Indiana election.[117] As political scientists William F. Connelly and John J. Pitney noted, "Over time, GOP frustration mounted, the apparent benefits of cooperation decreased, and Gingrich's gospel of rebellion became more and more persuasive."[118]

In 1986, former Delaware governor Pete du Pont gave Gingrich control of GOPAC, an electoral fund for Republican candidates. Gingrich substantially broadened GOPAC's mission, recruiting and training conservative candidates across the nation and mailing them audiotapes of messaging advice that were long remembered by their recipients. His efforts won over true believers, built a finance operation, and developed a common conservative language for candidates.

Gingrich's ascent from junior gadfly to leading figure in the House Republican Party was complete by 1989, when he called for an investigation into a book deal offered to O'Neill's successor Jim Wright that ultimately led to Wright's resignation. In the midst of the controversy, Gingrich ran for and won the office of minority whip, the number-two leadership position, narrowly defeating Michel's ally and Illinois colleague Ed Madigan.[119] From this perch, Gingrich pressured other party leaders to resist compromising with Democrats, even leading most House Republicans to oppose the 1990 tax-raising budget deal signed by President George H. W. Bush (Gingrich referred to the agreement as "the fiscal equivalent of Yalta").[120] By this time, as political scientist Sean M. Theriault explained, "The Republican Conference in the House, and the entire House of Representatives, had been transformed into an image very much like that personified by Newt Gingrich and his supporters in the COS, who even a dozen short years prior constituted a tiny minority of a minority party."[121] This included a shift not only toward the ideological right but also toward a persistently confrontational style of politics. Theriault found that COS members and others who received GOPAC money led this ideological and tactical charge.

The transformation of the House Republican Party was also reflected in leadership contests. COS won three such races in 1988, with Duncan Hunter becoming research chair, Bill McCollum becoming conference vice chair, and Vin Weber becoming conference secretary. Consensus conservatives Jack Kemp and Dick Cheney had served as conference chairs in the 1980s, working as liaisons between COS and the leadership.[122] Kemp left to run for president, eventually becoming the secretary of housing and urban development under George H. W. Bush; Cheney became whip and then secretary of defense. Gingrich's 1989 victory to succeed Cheney as whip was followed by the 1992 election of COS affiliates Dick Armey and Tom DeLay to the positions of conference chair and secretary; both later served as majority leader after Republicans captured House control.

During this period, ties strengthened between Republicans in Congress and the wider conservative movement. Grover Norquist, the president of Americans for Tax Reform, created the Taxpayer Protection Pledge in 1986, convincing more than 90 percent of House Republicans to publicly oppose tax increases.[123] Norquist's antitax pledge has been renewed in every subsequent election, committing candidates to refuse support for any rate hike or revenue increase. The pledge continues to be a critical element of Republican policymaking, with party leaders regularly seeking Norquist's personal assurance that any proposed tax reform legislation would conform to its requirements, and successfully constrains candidates, with any violations resulting in a public backlash.[124]

After George H. W. Bush broke his no-new-taxes promise and suffered defeat in the 1992 presidential election, the stage was set for Gingrich's final ascendance. The easygoing Michel announced his retirement from Congress rather than face what would likely have been a successful Gingrich challenge for the office of Republican leader in 1994. Taking control of his party's national electoral strategy to a greater extent than any congressional leader had done before or since, Gingrich worked to raise money, recruit candidates, and develop an enumerated list of popular reform measures dubbed the "Contract with America" that he encouraged all Republican congressional candidates to endorse; more than 300 ultimately appeared with Gingrich to sign the contract on the steps of the U.S. Capitol.

The landslide Republican victories of 1994 swept the GOP into the majority and Gingrich into the Speaker's office. Gingrich further consolidated institutional power in his new position. Polsby noted that "Republicans [had been] running a far more ideologically compact and hierarchical operation [than House Democrats]. Committee assignments, for example, had been more successfully monitored by ranking members of key committees than the divided Democrats had done. . . . Gingrich and his leadership team took centralized control a step or two further."[125]

Democrats had seldom violated seniority when assigning committee chairmanships after the initial "purge" of 1974, despite the right of the caucus to do so. But Gingrich ignored seniority in multiple cases, installing loyalists in committee chairmanships and creating task forces (and a "Speaker's Advisory Group") to develop policy outside the committee system. He also instituted term limits for committee chairs, leading Senate Republicans to do the same. Gingrich himself observed that he was not merely acting like a Republican version of his Democratic predecessors. "There were enormous differences between the role of the previous Democratic speakers and my role," he argued. "They had been essentially legislative leaders . . . [while I] was essentially a political leader . . . seeking to do nothing less than reshape the federal government along with the political culture of the nation."[126]

Gingrich's influence was felt well beyond his own legislative chamber. Senators who had previously served in the House and entered the Senate after Gingrich was elected, dubbed the "Gingrich Senators" by Theriault, were the driving force behind the polarization of the upper body. The first such senator was Phil Gramm of Texas, elected in 1984; he was followed by John McCain of Arizona and COS members Connie Mack of Florida and Dan Coats of Indiana (and, later, Jon Kyl of Arizona); Rick Santorum of Pennsylvania and Jim DeMint of South Carolina moved further right in the same trajectory. Throughout the 1990s, Republican

Senate challengers with House experience received financial help from Gingrich. Theriault's research demonstrates that the closer a senator was to Gingrich in the House, the more extreme he or she was in the Senate.

Figure 6-7 reveals the "Gingrich effect" by summarizing the ideological extremity of senators from both parties over time, based on data collected by Theriault. Among Democrats, prior House experience was not associated with ideological extremity in the Senate. Republicans, however, demonstrated a marked shift after 1978: former House members before Gingrich were more moderate than their Democratic counterparts; afterwards, they were far more extreme. The Gingrich senators accounted for nearly all of the increase over time in the ideological polarization of the Senate and were as distinct from other Republicans as southern Democrats were from northerners.

Theriault identifies a variety of ways in which the Gingrich senators transformed the institution. They often acted as a group to depose leaders and vote on amendments. They led the first partisan votes on debt limit extensions and opposed bipartisan budget agreements. They voted against previously uncontroversial unemployment benefit extensions and executive nominations. Under the Gingrich senators, filibuster use

Figure 6-7   Average Ideological Extremism of U.S. Senators, 1973–2010

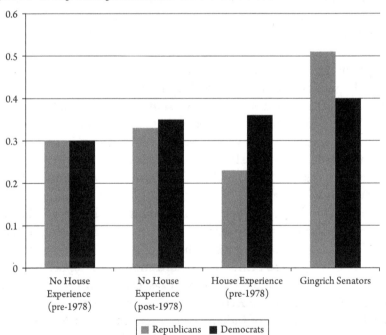

Average extremism (distance from zero) according to DW-Nominate scores of U.S. senators based on their prior experience in the U.S. House of Representatives. Data from Theriault (2013).

increased and cloture voting became more ideological. Gingrich senators demanded more roll calls on amendments and were more likely to
appear on Sunday talk shows. Overall, Republican senators were more
likely to place holds on legislative business, especially among Senate
Steering Committee members (who placed twice as many as other senators).[127] When the Senate was under Democratic control, one-third of the
bills reported by committees were subject to an outright hold by a Senate
Republican. Although Republicans use holds more often in the minority, they are more influential in blocking legislation when they are in the
majority.[128]

The most conservative senators even sought to depose their Republican
brethren. When Republican leader Mitch McConnell told DeMint that
"you can't change the Senate," DeMint responded, "If the people in the
Senate wouldn't change their minds, then I should try to change the
people in the Senate."[129] In 2004, House member Pat Toomey challenged
veteran moderate Arlen Specter in the Republican primary, losing narrowly despite help from DeMint; he was later elected to the seat when
Specter lost the 2010 Democratic primary after switching parties in anticipation of another Toomey challenge. Overall, Gingrich senators founded
more leadership PACs than their colleagues, helping them elect even
more ideologically conservative Tea Party classes in 2010 and 2012.

Tea Party–affiliated senators like Rand Paul of Kentucky, Mike Lee of
Utah, Jeff Flake of Arizona, and Ted Cruz of Texas, often elected with the
help of the Gingrich senators, are even more conservative than their senior
colleagues. The average ideological extremity of Tea Party senators was
.8 on the DW-NOMINATE scale in 2011, significantly higher even than
the rating for the Gingrich senators and twice that of other Republicans.
They offer more amendments and engage in more procedural warfare
than their Republican peers. As of 2016, Gingrich senators serve as conference chair and vice chair, and as chairs of the Agriculture, Armed
Services, Commerce, Environment, Rules, Small Business, Veterans, and
Intelligence Committees. But in the Tea Party era, even they have become
the (relatively moderate) old guard of their party.

Gingrich's distinctive combination of ideological commitment, procedural acumen, partisan and personal combativeness, and emphasis on
courting publicity had a transformational effect on the Republican Party.
More than any other single figure, Gingrich is responsible for popularizing the view that federal institutions, especially Congress, are fundamentally hostile to conservative values and deserve sustained attacks
from a mobilized public. Though he served as Speaker for just four years,
his influence is still visible across the breadth of American politics. "It is
Gingrich," argues Thomas Schaller, "not the lionized Ronald Reagan, who

should be remembered as the most significant Republican politician of the late twentieth century."[130] No Democratic leader in the modern Congress is a comparable figure.

THE ACTIVIST RIGHT AND GOVERNING DYSFUNCTION

The increasingly conservative Republican Party has now spent considerable time in the congressional majority—holding the House for 18 and the Senate for more than 12 of the 22 years between 1995 and 2017—while retaining much of the hard-edged character that it developed as a minority party. Congressional scholar Richard Fenno noticed this pattern immediately upon the advent of the "Republican Revolution" in 1994 but perceived it to be a peculiarity of the freshman class elected that year. As Fenno reported:

> The newcomers styled themselves "the conscience of the congressional Republicans," and as such they injected a dose of inflexibility into budget making. Listen, for example, to three of the ringleaders describe their view of the impending conflict [with president Bill Clinton]: "We're not going to give in. If there has to be a train wreck, there will be a train wreck." "We're going to stand for principle. The consequences be damned." . . . "[Most] of us don't care if we're reelected if we fold on the balanced budget." . . . Their posture crippled the Speaker in negotiations and compounded the governing problems of the new majority.[131]

But this aggressive style turned out to be emblematic of Republican governance, rather than exceptional; members of the Tea Party Congress, elected 16 years later, uttered many similar remarks.

The 1995 freshman class helped transform the House, moving to the ideological right rather than responding to constituency preferences; one study found that this class offered "part of the explanation for the increased polarization and partisan conflict in the House during the period of Republican control [and] . . . the dominance of conservative preferences in agenda setting and policy formation."[132] Older members also helped lead the charge. Budget Committee chairman John Kasich declared a goal of balancing the budget within seven years, setting the party's budgetary agenda for the remainder of the 1990s.[133] Majority Whip (later Majority Leader) Tom DeLay, known as "the Hammer," developed broader institutional connections to the business sector, conservative activists, and financial supporters, initiating the "K Street Project" that encouraged corporations and other interests to hire Republican lobbyists in order to bolster their influence on legislation.

Gingrich ushered in the contemporary era of government shutdown threats, expressing his philosophy as: "Work to keep the government open unless it requires breaking your word to the American people or giving up your principles."[134] A standoff with the Clinton administration over cuts to entitlement programs led to 5-day and 21-day shutdowns in 1995 and 1996. Gingrich admitted misjudgment after opinion polls revealed that his hardball tactics had weakened the popularity of Republicans: "[The public wants] these disagreements to be settled in constructive ways. That is not, of course, what our own activists were telling us. They were all gung ho for a brutal fight over spending and taxes. We mistook their enthusiasm for the views of the American people."[135] Gingrich also initiated the use of the necessary periodic statutory recalibration of the federal debt limit as a bargaining chip, reversing the Gephardt Rule that automatically raised the ceiling whenever a budget resolution increased the total debt obligation. He perceived the threat of a debt default as an opportunity to rein in government spending. This approach did not work at first, but it reemerged as an important Republican tactic during the Obama years.

Gingrich ultimately became a victim of his own brand of politics. His sharp-elbowed approach to governing and penchant for controversial remarks led to a steep decline in his public approval rating beginning in late 1995, and his attempts to address this problem by cutting bipartisan agreements with Clinton raised discontent among a faction of disaffected conservatives, who plotted an abortive coup against him in 1997. One year later, Gingrich and DeLay led the House in approving articles of impeachment against Clinton over the Monica Lewinsky affair— the first Congress to impeach a president since 1868—demanding that Republicans vote to impeach and threatening primary challenges for defectors.[136] But the impeachment, too, was unpopular with the public, and Republican losses in the 1998 elections prompted Gingrich's departure from the House in the face of a certain leadership challenge from within his party.

The election of George W. Bush in 2000 placed the Republican Congress in the new position of responding to the legislative agenda of a fellow partisan in the White House. Bush found success in working with Congress, including a number of Democrats, to pass several key priorities—two large tax cuts, increased defense spending, and authorization of military operations in Afghanistan and Iraq—though some conservatives complained that the party had drifted from its small-government values by expanding Medicare benefits and increasing federal aid to public education. At the end of Bush's first term, according to Zelizer, a number of conservatives were quietly disappointed with their party's legislative record: "Most of the talk was about what had gone wrong and why so many 'revolutionaries' had compromised their principles. . . . The new Republicans in 2005 promised that things would be different."[137] After his 2005 attempt to push for the partial privatization of Social Security quickly foundered, Bush retreated from promoting a broader conservative agenda, and House Republicans blocked the president's attempts to enact immigration reform. As the president's approval ratings tumbled in response to military setbacks in Iraq, the botched federal response to Hurricane Katrina, and a weakening economy, some Republicans instead preferred to blame the "big-government conservatism" of the Bush presidency.[138] After losing the majority in the 2006 midterms, congressional Republicans increasingly asserted independence from Bush. House conservatives even helped defeat the administration's 2008 financial bailout measure when it was first brought to a vote, although the bill passed on a revote days later after a precipitous drop in the financial markets.

On the day of Obama's presidential inauguration in January 2009, Republican congressional leaders met with Newt Gingrich and consultant Frank Luntz to plan a strategy of legislative obstruction and rhetorical attack.[139] Obama's first major legislative priority—an economic stimulus package—drew united opposition from Republican leaders and conservative activists. The Tea Party movement emerged during Obama's first few months in office and was on full public display during the summer 2009 fight over the president's health care plan. Unlike in 1995, the Senate largely followed the House in its tactical aggressiveness. Some Senate Republicans, for example, began blocking Obama's nominations to executive agencies in order to obstruct the operations of the agencies themselves rather than to force him to choose different nominees. Jim DeMint argued that the fight over "Obamacare" would define Obama's presidency: "If we are able to stop Obama on [health care], it will be his Waterloo. It will break him."[140]

Though Republicans failed to block the ACA by a single vote in the Senate, the 2010 elections fulfilled their political hopes, returning the party to power in the House with a 63-seat gain. The new Republican majority banned the use of earmarks, eschewing district-based distributive politics for a more national and ideological style of governing. Budget Committee chair Paul Ryan developed a Republican budget that called for significant cuts in entitlement spending. Ryan and his fellow "Young Guns" Eric Cantor and Kevin McCarthy had helped to stoke this conservative revival, according to Mann and Ornstein: "They planned to recruit a new generation of highly ideological and uncompromising conservative candidates for the 2010 elections . . . decreasing—by any means necessary—the size of government to pre-1960s Great Society levels."[141]

Amid the Republican euphoria produced by the 2010 election results, a more troubling dynamic emerged that recalled the difficulties of the 1990s. Once again, a large, boisterous, and ideologically uncompromising freshman class who came to Washington in order to achieve dramatic reductions in the role of government simultaneously elevated Republican leaders into majority status and pressured them relentlessly to advance conservative principles or else face a rebellion of their own. A member retreat held at the Reagan Library in early 2011, organized with support from the Heritage Foundation and the RSC, helped set the tone. Conservative freshmen decided to demand immediate spending cuts of $100 billion—what some viewed as a modest goal.[142] Republican leaders attempted to negotiate with the freshmen, asking them to be satisfied with a smaller amount. Soon, conservative purists were expressing feelings of betrayal when promised cuts failed to materialize and were associated with hidden spending increases. The RSC even developed its own budget proposal, which cut spending much more dramatically than the Ryan budget.

The Tea Party Congress also proved willing to use a potential default on the national debt as leverage to demand budgetary concessions from Democrats. Mann and Ornstein have described the debt ceiling standoff of 2011 as a culmination of the era of broken government:

> The Republican Party leaders did not have guaranteed votes to pull out just in time, nor were they playing the usual political games to gain more traction on the argument for greater fealty to fiscal discipline. For the first time, major political figures, including top congressional leaders and serious presidential candidates, openly called for default or demanded dramatic and unilateral policy changes in return for preserving the full faith and credit of the United States.[143]

The last-minute agreement narrowly avoiding default led to a decline in the U.S. credit rating, but it also achieved the Republican goals of restraining spending and avoiding tax increases, leading Republicans to believe they could gain more concessions with additional threats of shutdowns and debt ceiling breaches. The strategy failed only after Democrats adopted a strategy in 2013 of refusing to negotiate over other items when discussing the debt ceiling, insisting instead on a "clean" bill.

The activist right attained considerable influence over congressional politics in the Obama years by applying intense electoral pressure to Republican incumbents. An increasingly well-funded set of national conservative organizations, including the Club for Growth, FreedomWorks, and Heritage Action, emerged as a significant force in Republican primary elections, leading to the defeat of three sitting senators for renomination in 2010 and 2012 as well as the nomination in open-seat races of outsider candidates such as Paul and Cruz over establishment Republicans. The language of abstract ideology suffuses the rhetorical arguments made on behalf of this internal partisan revolt. Matt Kibbe, president of FreedomWorks, wrote in 2013 that he perceived "a hostile takeover happening within the Republican Party. The senior management of the GOP has failed its key shareholders, abandoning the founding vision of individual freedom, fiscal responsibility, and constitutionally limited government. . . . The GOP is freedom's party, and we're taking it back."[144] Heritage Action CEO Michael A. Needham similarly stated in 2011 that "with each vote cast in Congress, freedom either advances or recedes"; the remark was made upon the introduction of a legislative scorecard designed to "empower Americans to hold their Members of Congress accountable to conservative principles."[145] Such scorecards are increasingly monitored and publicized by conservative activists as quantitative indicators of Republican officeholders' ideological fidelity, and considerations of how a particular vote might affect their personal score regularly influence members' behavior on the floor of Congress.[146]

The growing strength of the mobilized conservative movement has severely complicated Republican congressional leaders' approach to governing. Defiant blocs of members have repeatedly frustrated the efforts of party leaders to unite behind legislation, especially if it is the result of compromise with Democratic leaders. From the perspective of many Republican officeholders, exacerbating procedural confrontation with Democrats serves as an intentional strategy to inspire support (or relieve pressure) from an otherwise suspicious party base. In January 2013, a House leadership aide told *Politico* that Republicans "may need a [government] shutdown just to get it out of their system. We might need to do that for member management purposes, so they have an endgame and can show their constituents they're fighting."[147] The following October, a standoff with Obama and Senate Democrats forced by conservative purists indeed resulted in a 16-day partial government shutdown and came within days of triggering a default on federal debt repayments. Republican leaders ultimately relented, bringing a bill to the House floor that reopened the government and raised the debt ceiling without conditions; even so, a majority of House Republicans voted against the legislation out of fear of retribution from party activists.

For many Republican members of Congress, "no" has often become the safest vote—even on legislation that is broadly popular or prevents national crisis. The hard-line wing of the party often chooses to demonstrate its independence from the Republican leadership by opposing appropriations and omnibus spending bills, while other legislation that once commanded strong bipartisan support—such as federal aid to rebuild local communities after natural disasters—has attracted increasing conservative disapproval on small-government grounds. The growing Republican preoccupation with visible demonstrations of ideological purity has forced important shifts in the strategic behavior of party leaders. During his tenure as speaker, John Boehner was forced to dispense with the "Hastert Rule," an unofficial norm associated with former Speaker Dennis Hastert that allowed floor votes only on legislation that attracted majority support from House Republicans. Boehner was repeatedly compelled to bring measures to the House floor that were publicly opposed by most members of his party but were supported by a coalition of Democrats and pragmatic Republicans, including reauthorization of the Violence Against Women Act, financial assistance to the victims of Hurricane Sandy, and several critical spending and budget measures.

To some extent, this was merely an exercise in political theater; many Republicans wished these bills to pass but preferred, once approval was numerically assured, to register official opposition in order to preserve their own personal ideological credentials (leading some observers to dub them the "Vote No, Hope Yes" coalition). But Boehner's maneuvering still came with a cost, as conservative purists felt increasingly marginalized by their own party's leadership. Boehner's repeated reliance on bipartisan coalitions to enact major legislation constituted one of the grievances cited by Freedom Caucus members in their efforts to depose him in 2015.

Moreover, the tendency of many Republicans to publicly oppose major spending bills was in some ways counterproductive to the goal of maximizing the conservative character of public policy. Every vote that the Republican leadership lost from among its own ranks on "must-pass" legislation like government appropriations needed to be replaced by a vote from the other side of the partisan aisle; once minority Democrats were required to supply most of the necessary support, they were able to exercise substantial influence over legislative provisions. Efforts by Republican congressional leaders to achieve party unity in order to strengthen their negotiating position were undercut by members who wished to preserve their own conservative bona fides by voting against the party "establishment."

One illustrative example of this dynamic occurred in December 2012 amid bargaining over the imminent expiration of George W. Bush's tax cuts, popularly dubbed the "fiscal cliff." Republicans initially pushed for full renewal of the cuts, while the Obama administration supported extending them only for taxpayers with annual incomes below $200,000. After the failure of Obama and Boehner to strike a "grand bargain" exchanging a few tax increases for entitlement cuts, the Speaker proceeded to what he called "Plan B": pledging to bring up legislation before the

House that would make the tax cuts permanent for all but the upper 0.2 percent of earners. Boehner believed that the passage of such a bill would strengthen his negotiating hand by portraying House Republicans as the only party with a viable plan to avert the cliff, increasing pressure on the White House and Senate Democrats to back down from their own more ambitious demands.

In an embarrassing defeat for Boehner, he was forced to pull the Plan B legislation off the floor after finding that it lacked sufficient support from his own party. Many Republican members, worried about criticism from conservative interest groups and potential primary challenges in the next election (which was nearly two years away), refused to cast votes in favor of a bill that raised taxes on millionaires, even as a strategic ploy to shift the ultimate agreement to the ideological right—and even though a failure to act by Congress would, under existing law, lead to an even bigger tax increase for those citizens once the new year began (a state of affairs that convinced Grover Norquist to assure Republicans that voting for Plan B would not violate their antitax pledge). "I think that there were members that are so gun shy about primaries that they weren't willing to take a risk," explained Mike Coffman of Colorado. Asked why Plan B lacked the necessary votes, Mike Conaway of Texas, a member of the leadership's whip operation, responded, "You've got to ask Club for Growth, Heritage Action and all those guys who bullied members of Congress into voting against their own best interests."[148] The "fiscal cliff" was ultimately averted on New Year's Day by an agreement struck between Vice President Joe Biden and Senate Minority Leader Mitch McConnell, which passed the House with support from 91 percent of Democrats and just 36 percent of Republicans.

For decades, the institutional influence of the congressional leadership grew stronger as the congressional parties became more polarized. The theory of conditional party government developed by David Rohde suggests a logical link between these trends: as the parties become more internally unified and externally distinct, legislators choose to invest procedural power in a strong leadership to advance their common partisan agenda, rather than distribute authority more widely within a decentralized committee system.[149] Although the parties remain sharply differentiated on the ideological spectrum—the moderate wing of the Republican Party has only continued to decline in recent years—a new set of divisions has emerged within the ranks of conservative Republicans between pragmatists and purists. These tensions are particularly strong when a Republican congressional majority serves alongside a Democratic president, since the need for party leaders to cooperate with the opposition (if only to achieve the two elementary requirements of funding the government and avoiding default on the national debt) inevitably exposes them to criticism from junior members, conservative activists, and primary challengers that they have made excessive concessions to the Democratic side of the aisle. Remarkably, two of the last three Republicans to serve as Speaker have been forced from office by their own party even as it retained majority status.

Frequently, and increasingly, Republican leaders are judged by their perceived devotion to ideological principles rather than their strategic skill, legislative productivity, or ability to deliver concrete policy outcomes. The unique dynamics that have come to govern the behavior of the congressional GOP over the past three decades have no true counterpart on the Democratic side. The churning internecine disputes that pose a perennial threat to the security of Republican leaders make the traditionally "divided" Democrats appear in comparison like the picture of placidity.

According to the conventional view in Washington, widely shared among many of the city's professional Republicans as well as Democrats, conservative hard-liners in Congress are either cynical grandstanders or extremist "wacko birds" (in the memorable phrase of purist critic John McCain). Yet these members' repeated complaints that the rhetoric of Republican campaigns often fails to match the reality of Republican governance contain an unavoidable truth. On the night of the Republican midterm landslide of 2010, for example, one victorious candidate vowed to "take a new approach that hasn't been tried before in Washington by either party. It starts with cutting spending instead of increasing it, reducing the size of government instead of expanding it, reforming the way Congress works and giving government back to the people." He promised that the new Republican majority would represent the will of the voters by "standing on principle, checking Washington's power, and leading the drive for a smaller, less costly, and accountable government . . . that honors our Constitution and stands up for the values that have made America America."[150]

This orator was not a Tea Party–backed political amateur swept into office in the Republican wave, but the party's leader and incoming Speaker, John Boehner. Despite Boehner's verbal commitments to achieving a pivotal change in the role of government in American society, he found it very difficult to fulfill this goal in practice. This failure not only contributed to the end of his political career but also fueled the chronic frustration of conservative activists with the governing record of the Republican Party.

HOW DEMOCRATS AND REPUBLICANS DISCUSS POLICY

Like the above quote from Boehner, the political rhetoric of many Republicans often draws upon abstract concepts such as principles and values, reflecting the ideological character of their party and the symbolic

Table 6-7 PARTY DIFFERENCES IN CONGRESSIONAL HEARING OPENING
STATEMENTS SINCE 1981

	Democrats	Republicans
Ideology or Principle	0.26	0.28
Explicitly Political Principles	0.16	0.20
Public Policy	1.99	1.89
New Policy Proposals	0.20	0.18
Social Problems Needing Action	0.23	0.19
Broad Policy Goals or Tools	0.89	0.97
Conservative (Republican)/Liberal (Democratic) Policy Position	0.22	0.04
Social or Interest Groups	0.52	0.44
Demographic Groups (Class, Race, Religion, Gender, Age)	0.28	0.16
Sources	0.84	0.74
Specific Data Cited	0.44	0.36

Average number of mentions of each type in congressional hearing opening statements since 1981. Our data, content analysis codebook, and analyses of reliability are available at mattg.org.

conservatism of the American electorate; Democrats, in contrast, tend to speak more concretely about particular issues, programs, and groups, in keeping with their party's coalitional nature and popular advantage with respect to most specific policies. Table 6-7 reviews the results of our analysis of a random sample of opening statements in congressional hearings since 1981.[151] These statements, usually made by the committee chair and ranking minority member before any witnesses testify, have been common since the 1980s. The results reveal that Republicans rely more often on articulating political principles and broad policy goals, whereas Democrats discuss social problems in need of action, particular social or interest groups that serve as the targets of public policy, and specific data that assess the size and scope of problems or analyze potential solutions. As they do on the campaign trail, Republicans in government speak in broader terms than Democrats.

Committee hearings serve as both an internal process of communication and a public display of position-taking by members. In Table 6-8, we use recent Dear Colleague letter content to assess whether the same differences appear in solely internal policymaking discussions. These private letters are usually used to recruit co-sponsors for legislation and were released by an anonymous congressional staffer.[152] Here we divide the results into three categories, because a large share of the letters came from a bipartisan group of bill sponsors. Note that Republicans send fewer of these letters (only half as many as Democrats), even when they hold majority control and thus have a greater chance of legislative success. The results show that Republican letters are more concerned with ideology,

Table 6-8 CONTENT OF DEAR COLLEAGUE LETTERS IN CONGRESS

No. of Mentions per Letter	From Democrats	From Republicans	From Bipartisan Groups
Ideology or Principle	.31	.37	.26
Conservative (Republican)/Liberal (Democratic) Ideological Principles	.23	.27	.11L/.09C
Explicitly Political Principles	.22	.36	.21
Public Policies	.94	1.04	.88
New Policy Proposals	.68	.7	.64
Oppose New Policy	.02	.06	.01
Support Existing Policy	.04	.01	.02
Oppose Existing Policy	.07	.16	.07
Conservative (Republican)/Liberal (Democratic) Policy Position	.52	.3	.37L/.17C
Social Groups or Interest Groups	.77	.53	.59
Demographic Groups (Class, Race, Religion, Gender, Age)	.42	.19	.17
Sources	.28	.22	.18
Specific Data Cited	.13	.09	.11
n	188	90	138

Data from an original content analysis of all Dear Colleague letters sent from 2013–2015. Our data, content analysis codebook, and analyses of reliability are available online at mattg.org.

and Democratic letters are more concerned with constituency groups and sourced evidence. In this context, both parties are most concerned with public policy, though Republicans often express support for the repeal of existing policies. Tables 6-7 and 6-8 also both reveal the difficulty for Republicans in translating principles into policy proposals: the proposals that are mentioned in hearings or letters, even by Republicans, rarely limit the size and scope of government.

Somewhat greater party differences emerge in presidential State of the Union speeches, as indicated by Table 6-9. These speeches help set the agenda for the year and are often treated as laundry lists of policy proposals—although that form is more often used by Democratic presidents. Republican chief executives are more likely than Democrats to cite ideology or principles—especially those consistent with their party's dominant ideology—while Democrats more frequently discuss specific policies and social or interest groups. Republican presidents also employ nationalist themes more often than Democrats.

B. Dan Wood found similar patterns in a broader analysis of presidential speeches, summarized in Figure 6-8.[153] Wood analyzed the average

Table 6-9 PARTY DIFFERENCES IN STATE OF THE UNION RHETORIC

No. of Mentions per Sentence	Republican Party	Democratic Party
Ideology or Principle	.43	.26
Conservative (Republican)/Liberal (Democratic) Ideological Principles	.26	.11
Public Policy	.49	.56
New Policy Proposals	.11	.13
Conservative (Republican)/Liberal (Democratic) Policy Position	.05	.08
Social Group or Interest Group	.14	.21
Demographic Groups (Class, Race, Gender, Age)	.06	.10
American Imagery	.39	.27
American Exceptionalism/Threats to Way of Life	.13	.11
Sources	.03	.05
n	506	787

Data from an original content analysis of all State of the Union addresses since 1948. Our data, content analysis codebook, and analyses of reliability are available online at mattg.org.

Figure 6-8 Liberal Minus Conservative Statements in Papers of the Presidents, 1953–2000

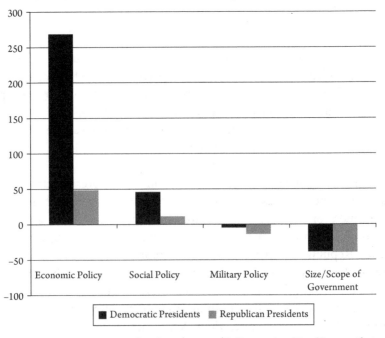

Liberal minus conservative statements made each year (on average) by Democratic and Republican presidents from 1953–2000. Economic policy areas include education, environment, health, urban, and welfare. Social policy areas include race and crime. Data from Wood (2009).

number of liberal and conservative statements made by Democratic and Republican presidents every year between 1953 and 2000, dividing the statements into policy topics. Democratic presidents made overwhelmingly left-leaning domestic policy statements, but even Republican presidential policy statements were more liberal than conservative (because most specific policy proposals expand the size or scope of government). In military policy, there were no major ideological trends or differences between the parties; the speeches were more idiosyncratic and driven by events. But when it came to broader statements about the scope of government, Wood confirmed that presidents in both parties made more conservative statements. Reflecting American public opinion, both parties used conservative rhetoric in describing their broad view of government even as they made specific policy proposals that collectively leaned leftward. The rhetoric of Democratic presidents was particularly inconsistent in this regard.

RED AND BLUE POLICYMAKING IN THE EXECUTIVE BRANCH

The individuality of presidents makes it more difficult to identify systematic partisan asymmetry in the executive branch. The differences between Democrats and Republicans in policy emphasis and productivity do extend to presidential administrations, but Republican presidents face difficulty adhering to conservative ideology because they are also under pressure to produce some new policies. Nixon, for example, said his own conservative advisors thought "we basically had sold out all of our Republican conservative policies in our 'move to the left.'"[154] The Nixon administration used polls to measure the overall level of conservatism in the American electorate, finding that "there are twice as many conservatives as Republicans," but, according to a systematic analysis of Nixon's internal polling by James Druckman and Larry Jacobs, Nixon "took the more opportunistic approach of using his polling to pinpoint openings of voter disinterest to stake out conservative positions that quieted his restless base."[155]

Democratic presidents, while habitually endorsing an extensive array of left-of-center domestic policy proposals, have also tended to remain conscious of conservative resistance to government spending, according to Zelizer:

> Liberal Democratic presidents never felt that they could or should exclude fiscal conservatism from their agenda. Harry Truman, for example, fought with the military establishment to balance the budget, while John Kennedy and Lyndon Johnson

adhered to modest levels of spending and only hesitantly accepted temporary deficits. Jimmy Carter emphasized deficit reduction more than a decade before [Bill] Clinton championed the issue. . . . [They all] encountered great pressure to demonstrate a commitment to fiscal responsibility to refute conservative warnings that their policies would result in economic instability and limitless government expansion.[156]

Ronald Reagan was the first president to try to match conservative rhetoric with retrenchment in government, but he did so carefully. As Druckman and Jacobs report:

> Reagan aggressively sought out conservative positions while ducking land mines for swing voters, while Nixon was more hesitant about pursuing a conservative agenda. . . . [D]ata on the public's general ideology were extensively collected by both presidents. When Reagan possessed only data on Ideological Identification, he moved his statements toward greater conservatism [but modified them, often leftward, when he had access to specific issue opinion data].[157]

Reagan had very limited success when he actively sought to constrain entitlement spending, according to Paul Pierson: "Reagan administration attempts to go on the offensive against this extensive system of retirement provision collapsed in the face of massive and unified resistance. . . . Although some cutbacks resulted from trust-fund pressures, the Social Security program survived—indeed almost flourished—through a decade of budgetary austerity."[158] Pierson notes some success in housing policy retrenchment and efforts to shift the administration of federal policies to the states, but less success in wider social welfare curtailment and decentralization.[159]

Among Democrats, Bill Clinton was especially concerned with conveying moderation. As a "New Democrat" who was careful to distinguish himself from the liberal wing of his party, Clinton hoped to "reinvent government" to address Democratic priorities without the need for massive public sector expansion. John Harris summarizes how Clinton put this goal into action in an ideologically confused presidency: "All these diverse aims were in the spirit of a governing philosophy that, as Clinton announced at his nomination, was not liberal, not conservative, but both."[160] For example, his administration included deficit hawks like Robert Rubin, Leon Panetta, Lloyd Bentsen, and Alice Rivlin along with liberals like Robert Reich. Clinton jokingly complained to his advisors that "we're all Eisenhower Republicans here, and we are fighting the Reagan Republicans. We stand for lower deficits and free trade and the bond market."[161]

After his party suffered massive defeat in the 1994 elections, Clinton heeded suggestions from his long-time political advisor Dick Morris, a Republican, who recommended adopting conservative rhetoric and led

Clinton to emphasize policies like night curfews and school uniforms alongside deficit reduction and welfare reform (the passage of which in 1996 caused three liberal advisors to resign). According to Harris, the 1994 elections set the terms for Clinton's tenure in office: "There were no more pitched battles to define the ideological direction of the Clinton presidency. The Gingrich challenge of 1995 and 1996, and Clinton's survival of it, had set the president securely on a centrist course from which he had no interest in deviating."[162]

The George W. Bush administration, Harris argued in 2005, was more ideologically oriented than its predecessor: "Clinton made it preeminently his task to capture the center while trying to tame the more ideological elements of his party. Bush has celebrated ideology, and has worried less about placating the center than about rallying the enthusiasm of his party base."[163] Yet Bush ended up substantially expanding the scope of government, in part because of his national security goals.

One unique constraint of Republican presidents is that most federal workers are Democrats and liberals, which they view as a habitual obstacle to a smaller government. Table 6-10 illustrates this pattern, with data comparing senior careerists and presidential appointees in the Bush and Obama administrations. Republican presidents share ideology only with their appointees and not with their civil service employees.

The rate of total policymaking in the bureaucracy nonetheless differs between Democratic and Republican administrations, but the pattern is complex because of a substantial linear time trend: as government has expanded, executive agencies have produced more rules in general. Table 6-11 reports the average number of pages in the *Federal Register* (the official docket of regulatory and rulemaking announcements) per year under each president since 1968. For more recent presidents, the Government Accountability Office (GAO) provides better data on the number of final rules published

Table 6-10 FEDERAL OFFICIAL PARTISANSHIP AND IDEOLOGY

	Senior Careerists			Presidential Appointees		
	2004	2007	2014	2004	2007	2014
Republican	14%	20%	16%	37%	75%	5%
Democrat	32%	40%	44%	49%	11%	79%
Conservative	14%	11%	10%	27%	37%	2%
Liberal	22%	17%	21%	25%	5%	39%

Results of a 2004–2005 Princeton Research Associates survey of federal officials for the Annenberg Foundation Trust and the research conducted for the Survey on the Future of Government Service from Princeton University and Vanderbilt University's Center for the Study of Democratic Institutions in 2007 and 2014. We thank David Lewis and Mark Richardson for providing these data.

Table 6-11 FEDERAL AGENCY RULES PER YEAR BY PRESIDENTIAL
ADMINISTRATION

	Pages in *Federal Register*	Final Rules Published	Major Rules Published
Nixon	31,167		
Ford	58,647		
Carter	72,350		
Reagan	54,334		
H. W. Bush	59,518		
Clinton	71,641	4,183	66
W. Bush	76,784	3,429	65
Obama	78,479	3,522	82

Average number of pages in the *Federal Register* (the publication of agency rules), number of final agency rules, and number of major rules published per year by presidential administration. Pages data are from Ornstein et al. (2013). Rules data are from the Government Accountability Office.

and the subset of these identified as major rules. Bureaucratic policymaking was low under Nixon, moderate under Ford, and high under Carter. It abruptly reversed trend under Reagan but then started growing again, especially after the transition from George H. W. Bush to Clinton. George W. Bush oversaw a longer register, but with fewer final or major rules.

The differences in how Democratic and Republican presidents discuss policy are thus reflected in their policymaking records. Democrats seek to make more policy across branches of government, whereas Republicans send fewer proposals to Congress and make less policy administratively. Despite Democrats' relative prioritization of policy action, however, conservative views are reflected in American public policy design. Many of the most distinctive features of American policy are a product of interactions between two parties with asymmetric policy goals.

THE AMERICAN STATE: SUBMERGED, DIVIDED, AND DELEGATED

Though often producing gridlock, party asymmetry also fundamentally affects the public policies that do manage to be enacted. Since the creation of the modern state in the 1930s, American government has never resembled the small-government ideal of conservative Republicans, even as it remains distinct from the social democratic systems operating in most of the industrialized world. Zelizer notes that the United States has long used "nongovernmental partners instead of more overt, bureaucratic and visible interventions into the political economy."[164]

This approach grew more distinct as the parties differentiated themselves and came to compete on a more equal electoral footing. Democrats sought to solve the social problems of their constituencies, which often entailed new government functions. But Republicans succeeded in blocking most broad bureaucratic interventions in the economy. Over time, both parties have contributed to building a state that reflects the preferences of the American public for a limited government (at least in terms of its workforce) but also addresses a growing catalog of specific responsibilities. The satisfaction of these potentially contradictory demands has resulted in complex policy arrangements that combine the substantive goals of Democrats with the forms of administration more acceptable to Republicans.

Figure 6-9 displays the number of federal employees (the black line) and state or local employees (the dotted gray line) since 1946. Federal employment has remained remarkably steady (even falling on a per capita basis), whereas state and local employment has grown dramatically. Some of the new state and local employment has followed greater tax collection through increasing population and tax rates, but a large share has been driven by pass-through dollars from the federal government to the states. New state and local jobs have also been brought about by federal mandates, which cost cities and counties millions of dollars in compliance costs. Paul Light estimates that mandates created up to 4.6 million

Figure 6-9 Federal Employees Versus State/Local Employees, in Thousands

Total number of federal and state and local government employees (full-time and part-time). Historical data are from Baumgartner and Jones (1993) and were updated with U.S. Census Bureau Annual Survey of Government Employment and Payroll data since 1999.

Figure 6-10 Federal Employees, Contractors, and Grantees, in Millions

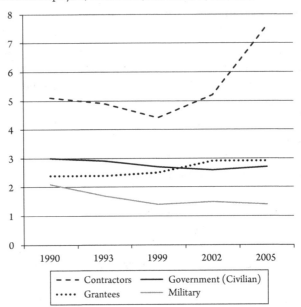

Number of federal government employees and full-time employees supported by federal contracts and grants. Data from Light (1999).

full-time-equivalent positions in state and local government, though he was skeptical of the accuracy of such a specific figure.[165]

Another key trend is the rise in government contracting and grant-funded work, which accelerated after September 11, 2001. The results, shown in Figure 6-10, indicate that substantially more people now work as federal contractors than as direct government employees. The number of grantees has also now eclipsed the civilian workforce, while the level of military personnel has declined since the end of the Cold War. These data are based on Light's analysis, which he acknowledges "tends to undercount the total number of jobs created through contracts and grants" as a result of underreporting.[166]

Grant-funded, contract-funded, and mandated workers combined now carry out substantially more federal policy than bureaucrats. These combined efforts have been politically successful. As Kimberly J. Morgan and Andrea Louise Campbell note, "Through the contracting out of public functions to private actors, and the heaping of mandates and program responsibilities upon state and local governments, politicians were able to square the circle: to claim they were addressing a wide array of public needs and demands without increasing the size of government."[167] Light agrees that this shadow government has generated broad support: "[K]eeping government looking small is the work force that satisfies almost every political preference. It is also the policy that caters to the public's core ambivalence about the size of government."[168] The government has used head-count ceilings, hiring freezes, and rounds of downsizing to limit the number of federal employees, with these strategies often implemented by both parties in restructuring initiatives.[169]

Scholars have coined several terms for this style of administration: "the delegated state" for the practice of mandating and contracting responsibilities to state and local governments, "the hollow state" for the practice of giving federal agencies more goals without providing increased staff, and "the hidden welfare state" or "submerged state" for the execution of policies via the tax code. Democrats pursue these strategies to solve new problems without triggering conservative backlash, and Republicans are more likely to accept policies that are administered by state governments or the private sector.[170]

These strategies emerged in response to the conservative movement's attacks on government-run health care in response to the founding of Medicare and Medicaid in the 1960s. Even then, proponents adapted the policies to satisfy criticism from the right, with House Ways and Means chair Wilbur Mills structuring the programs to include state governments and providers. Conservative policymakers in the 1970s sought to privatize and voucherize welfare and health benefits, relying on a concerted campaign by think tanks.[171] Conservatives found that direct cuts to most existing programs were unpopular with the public, so they produced similar reform proposals for Social Security in the early 1980s and for Medicare and Medicaid in the 1990s that aimed to simultaneously increase decentralization and reduce overall spending levels.

For Republicans, delegation to the private sector renders reforms "market-friendly" rather than government-controlled.[172] Democrats can address constituency problems without provoking a broader backlash through the same means. As Morgan and Campbell find, "Faced with the seeming wall of opposition to an expanded federal bureaucracy, and sometimes their own ambivalence about government authority, even liberal policy-makers have repeatedly chosen to delegate governing power to private actors." [173] The ACA, for example, included state governments and private insurance companies as key benefit-delivery mechanisms.

Unfortunately, these approaches have resulted in serious defects in the development and administration of public policy. Indirect mechanisms and private actors help create a Rube Goldberg apparatus of interacting policies[174] that often build on themselves and are impossible to reverse, a process Steven Teles terms "kludgeocracy."[175] Legislators are confronted with a layered mosaic of previous policies that are the product of competing interests and goals, and usually add new layers without implementing more fundamental reform. The results increase the responsibilities of citizens as well as their need for information, transferring risk from the government to individuals and the private sector. In the long term, the process may not satisfy the goals of either party. Democrats face an added problem: citizens come to believe that they are independent from government even as they unknowingly depend on more state-initiated programs, furthering popular hostility to left-of-center policy activism.

These distinctive policy choices cause the United States to stand out in international comparison. Figure 6-11 compares public and subsidized private social welfare spending across developed countries, based on data from Jacob Hacker.[176] The United States spends nearly as much in total on social welfare as Scandinavian countries, but a significant share of American social welfare provision comes from the private sector subsidized by government. As Hacker reports, "[In no rich country] does private social welfare spending comprise even half as large a share of total social spending as it does in the United States." [177] Hacker finds that the United States is also distinctive for the growth of its private welfare spending and its limited supervision of private providers.

The United States increased its share of social spending from the private sector from 1975 onward, even though that spending was already

Figure 6-11 Public and Private Welfare Expenditure in Comparative Perspective

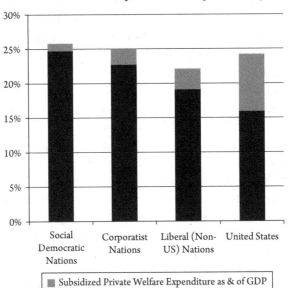

Total social welfare expenditure by the government and by private entities subsidized and regulated by the government, based on Organisation for Economic Co-operation and Development data summarized by Hacker (2002).

high by international standards.[178] As Hacker argues, conservatives were often open to the use of private actors to provide services, an approach to which liberals acquiesced.[179] American gridlock also allowed nondecisions or drift (the lack of new policies) to build-in expansion in dollars spent as new beneficiaries and providers signed on to previously legislated benefits. According to Hacker, liberal public interest groups institutionalized indirect retirement policies in the 1970s, increasing the private share of pensions. Institutional fragmentation and "rival factions within the Democratic Party" also held back the postwar expansion of health care provision.[180] Voluntary private sector proposals held up better in Congress against the conservative coalition, creating an array of private interests that became active participants in policy debates in later decades.

Today, the United States also stands out internationally in its growing use of tax expenditures (credits, deductions, or exclusions) to carry out public policies. Conservative support for particular policy goals often increases if they are packaged as economic incentives rather than government subsidies.[181] Tax expenditures can be created at a particular moment, even without agency support, and continue to grow over time, facing less political backlash than conventional spending programs.

The result of the growth in tax expenditures is a large and increasing bill of foregone revenue. Although it is hard to calculate the totals, the GAO attempts to summarize the combined costs (but does not analyze interactions, likely producing an overestimate). Figure 6-12 shows the results, compared with a measure of discretionary spending (federal nonentitlement expenditures). The total amount of revenue lost to tax expenditures (such as the home mortgage deduction and exclusion of employer-provided health insurance) now equals the total amount spent on discretionary spending. The government thus provides more benefits via the tax code than through direct expenditures.

The use of the tax code to confer benefits, the subsidization of employers to provide services, the mandating of service provision by state and local governments, the use of grants to incentivize work, and the contracting out of a significant share of government services all combine to render the American government uniquely complex and less reliant on the federal workforce. Conservatives can (accurately) complain that the state is growing in scope and producing more complex regulatory schemes, while liberals can (accurately) respond that government retrenchment is well underway and benefits are distributed unequally. The policy scholarship that analyzes these measures nonetheless treats them as a product of compromises between the parties, with scholars describing this trend of policymaking as an attempt to meet both sides' policy objectives by avoiding scrutiny from a symbolically conservative and operationally liberal electorate.

Figure 6-12   Federal Tax Expenditures and Discretionary Spending, in Billions (2014 $s)

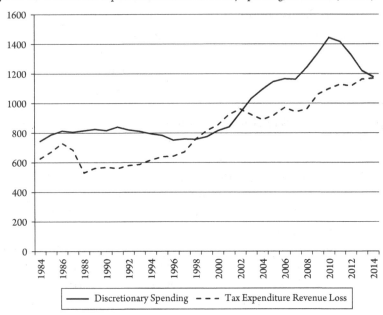

Total discretionary federal spending and the sum of revenue loss estimates associated with tax expenditures, as summarized by the Government Accountability Office. Tax expenditure estimates do not take account of interactions among tax expenditures.

ASYMMETRIC GOVERNANCE AND AMERICAN POLICYMAKING

The asymmetric American party system helps produce complex public policy that often satisfies neither side. Democrats seek concrete benefits to address the problems identified by their constituency groups, whereas Republicans seek a broad redefinition of the role of government in society. As a result, Democrats are more supportive of compromises that move policy incrementally forward and are more open to approaches that pursue liberal ends via conservative means, such as privatization, decentralization, and market competition. Republicans usually do not succeed in overturning prior policy commitments but regularly persuade citizens that additional proposals for state expansion will result in failure. Democratic officeholders face the difficulty of satisfying many competing demands without igniting a voter backlash over big government but face little pressure from their party base to move the country "leftward" in a broad sense. Republican leaders must choose among policy options that often violate conservative principles (at least according to some of their own supporters) in order to offer an agenda that addresses the specific national problems of the moment, but their attempts to compromise with the opposition often provoke accusations of ideological betrayal among conservative activists.

The dilemmas faced by each party have remained consistent for decades, but the parties themselves have evolved over time. The Democrats no longer contain their once-formidable dissident faction of southern conservatives, though they retain a significant population of moderates and a striking array of demographic constituencies—now matched by a socially diverse leadership with equally disparate issue priorities. The Republicans, though long the partisan instrument of American conservatism, have undergone a series of rightward shifts as newly arising insurgents have characterized previous generations of revolutionaries as having drifted away from party principles. The 2015 ousting of John Boehner from the Speakership is only the latest in a long line of conservative revolts fed by activist frustration with the limited success of Republican leaders in achieving a sustained rightward shift in federal policy.

Political scientists initially mistook the growing prevalence of obstruction and brinkmanship after the 1970s as the product of congressional Republicans' frustration with their party's long-term minority status, but it has become clear that these characteristics represent stable features of contemporary Republican governance, especially during Democratic presidential administrations. Unlike some critics, we view Republican actions as representing a strategic adaptation to the demands of the party's popular base and the broader conservative policymaking dilemma in the age of the modern state. Similarly, Democrats respond to their diverse constituency by pursuing multiple issue priorities and adjusting to political realities by accepting many half-measures instead of a broad vision of government expansion. Both strategies are rational even as the parties are dissimilar in nature. Polarization has not proceeded symmetrically in each party: Democrats excised their large conservative faction by the 1980s and slowly shed most of their remaining southern moderates; Republicans, though always mostly conservative, initiated a steady rightward shift beginning in the late 1970s. Increasing Republican ideological extremity largely reflected the institutionalization of the conservative movement within the national party, whereas congressional Democrats' more modest leftward trend was caused by changes in their electoral constituencies.

The specific historical developments that brought the parties to their contemporary positions match broader indicators of each side's consistent areas of emphasis. Liberals successfully pursued institutional reforms that weakened conservative committee chairs, but their triumph coincided with a decline in active liberal policymaking. Conservatives reacted to perceived betrayals by Republican presidents and congressional leaders by pursuing confrontation and committing to fewer realistic policy goals. The Democratic Party in government became more diverse in its aims over time while retaining its role as a big tent satisfying the interests of multiple constituencies. The Republican Party in government has instead been remade in the image of its conservative activist base.

CHAPTER 7

༺༻

Conclusion

American Politics Out of Balance

Human beings tend to regard symmetry as inherently pleasing. Psychological studies confirm, for example, that experimental subjects judge visually symmetrical faces to be more physically attractive than others.[1] This predisposition extends to the intellectual as well as the aesthetic realm. Scholars of politics seek to develop theories of party identification, ideology, media influence, party organizations, legislative politics, interest groups, policymaking, and other subjects that apply equally across party lines—especially in the United States, where only two parties compete for power. For journalists and other political commentators, treating the Democrats and Republicans as mirror-image equivalents not only allows for more parsimonious analysis but guards against potential accusations of subjectivity, as accounts claiming that any characteristic is unevenly distributed on both sides of the partisan divide might be interpreted as conveying a biased view of the political world.

Yet a complete understanding of American politics, past and present, requires acknowledgment of the important differences in composition, objectives, and character separating the Republican Party from its Democratic opposition. For several decades in the mid-20th century, many scholars recognized that the parties maintained distinct forms of organizational structure and governing style while exhibiting unequal levels of internal unity. Some of these specific disparities faded as national circumstances changed, but the relatively group-oriented nature of the Democrats and the ideological orientation of the Republicans remained fully intact, causing new manifestations of asymmetry to emerge as the political environment evolved. Many noteworthy recent occurrences in American politics—including the construction of the conservative media universe, the growing demographic diversity of the Democratic electorate, the procedural intransigence of congressional Republicans, and the rise of the Tea Party movement—superficially appear to be wholly novel developments. But closer examination reveals that they have deep roots in the enduring imbalance between the two parties.

These differences do not render one party more democratic, legitimate, or superior to the other; rather, each party's distinctive essence provides it with a unique set of strengths and weaknesses. But the existence of a durable mismatch in the central purpose and behavior of the two parties contributes to the contemporary challenges faced by both sides in achieving their substantive goals, while also exerting a visible and often-detrimental effect on the health of the larger political system. In today's heavily partisan and polarized era, Democrats and Republicans are not merely separated by philosophical, compositional, and policy-related differences. The parties also suffer from a deficit of mutual understanding among leaders and supporters alike that further alienates each side from the other and is reinforced by the chronic collective ambivalence of the American public toward the proper role and responsibilities of their nation's government.

THE CONTEMPORARY REPUBLICANS: PRACTICE BETRAYS PRINCIPLE

The consecutive victories of Barack Obama in 2008 and 2012 convinced many political pundits that the 21st-century Republican Party faced a serious and worsening disadvantage in national elections. The leadership of the Republican National Committee shared this interpretation, producing a posthumous "autopsy report" after Obama's reelection that warned of continued defeat in presidential contests unless the party took steps to increase its appeal among young voters, women, and racial minorities. This advice was largely ignored by subsequent Republican candidates, who worried more about the risk of alienating the party's existing popular base than about the benefits of attracting new supporters. With the important exception of the White House, however, the Republican Party had in fact reached its strongest electoral position in generations by the final years of Obama's presidency. As of early 2016, the GOP controlled Congress by margins of 247–188 in the House of Representatives and

54–44 in the Senate (with two Democratic-leaning independents) while holding 31 of 50 governorships and 64 of 98 partisan state legislative chambers. Republicans exercised unified control of 23 state governments, compared to just 7 states governed solely by Democrats.

The strong rightward shift of Republican officeholders over the past three decades has not prevented the party from receiving strong and even growing support among the American voting public in nonpresidential races—especially in midterm elections, in which Republican voters are often more likely than Democrats to participate. After the national Democratic victories of 2008, Republican leaders in Congress adopted a strategy of firm obstructionism, based on the belief that any collaboration with Obama would work to his political advantage by assisting the new president in amassing a record of legislative accomplishment for which he could claim bipartisan support. "If you act like you're the minority, you're going to stay in the minority," argued Representative Kevin McCarthy of California, a member of the Republican House leadership.[2] Explaining the united Republican opposition to Obama's health care reform legislation, Senate Minority Leader Mitch McConnell argued that "it was absolutely critical that everybody be together because if the proponents of the bill were able to say it was bipartisan, it tended to convey to the public that this is O.K., they must have figured [the issue] out. It's either bipartisan or it's not."[3] Weeks before the 2010 midterm elections, McConnell remarked that "the single most important thing we [Republicans] want to achieve is for President Obama to be a one-term president."[4]

Republicans failed to accomplish that particular goal, but their strategy was otherwise vindicated by the party's electoral victories in 2010 and thereafter. The symbolic conservatism and suspicion of government power that prevails in the American public at large, and is particularly concentrated among Republican-leaning voters, guaranteed that attacks on the Democratic legislative program as constituting an infringement of liberty, an imposition of leftist or socialist ideas, and a violation of traditional American values would find deep popular resonance. As they had previously done in response to the Democratic presidencies of Bill Clinton, Jimmy Carter, Lyndon Johnson, and Harry Truman, Republicans successfully encouraged a popular backlash to Obama's policies by framing them in unpalatable ideological terms.

This confrontational response was endorsed by the larger conservative movement to which Republican officeholders pledge loyalty. After Obama took office, conservative interest groups and movement leaders did not encourage Republicans in government to make compromises or horse-trading deals with the Democratic majority in order to win partial achievement of concrete policy goals sought by their constituencies. In the early weeks of his presidency, for example, Obama offered to support the imposition of statutory caps on medical malpractice awards—a proposal favored by business interests but opposed by the mostly Democratic-leaning trial lawyer profession—in exchange for a comparable concession from congressional Republicans, only to find that his partisan opponents were unwilling to offer him anything in return.[5] Even if Republican members of Congress had themselves wished to bargain with the new president, the intense pressure immediately directed at party leaders from conservative activists and news media figures to oppose the Democratic legislative agenda or face retribution in future primary elections bolstered their resolve to pursue an obstructionist approach.

The electoral success that followed demonstrates the political benefits that can accrue to a party organized as the vehicle of an ideological movement. Sharp, disciplined rhetorical attacks on Obama's entire legislative program, and especially the Affordable Care Act, as the product of big-government liberalism convinced the voting public to reduce its support of the president, his policies, and his fellow Democratic partisans within months of his inauguration while effectively stoking anger and fear within the Republican popular base. At the elite level, conservative think tanks and legal scholars worked energetically to develop a constitutional challenge to the ACA that very nearly succeeded in overturning the law (the U.S. Supreme Court upheld the ACA's individual mandate penalty by a 5–4 decision announced in June 2012, although the Court dealt the Obama administration a smaller blow by effectively allowing states to opt out of the law's Medicaid expansion provisions). The extensive network of influential conservative media sources publicized Republican criticisms of Obama, assisted in promoting the Tea Party movement, and mobilized voters to participate in Republican primaries and off-year general elections, to the further advantage of conservative candidates. The collective influence of these efforts deprived congressional Democrats of their House majority just two years after Obama took office, curtailing the president's ability to enact his legislative agenda. Throughout the remaining years of his presidency, unyielding pressure from the activist right also prevented the achievement of bipartisan agreements pursued by Obama in the areas of deficit reduction, gun control, and comprehensive immigration reform.

Yet the same ideological character that helped to unite Republicans in opposition worked to divide them once they returned to power. Many Republican officials, most notably House Speaker John Boehner, were judged by activists, primary voters, and fellow officeholders against strict standards of ideological purity and found wanting; the resulting internal purges of Republican incumbents and members of the congressional leadership served as constant distractions and severely complicated the party's ability to govern effectively. The conservative media ecosystem, despite its undoubtedly beneficial role in transmitting Republican political messages and stoking energetic popular opposition to Democratic candidates, also threatened to seal Republican politicians and voters alike in an informational bubble that excluded ideologically inconvenient facts. Frightened by the prospect of well-funded primary challengers, Republican incumbents have increasingly sought opportunities to demonstrate their symbolic adherence to conservative doctrine instead of devoting time and energy to the creation and enactment of realistic legislative initiatives. Republican members' frequent practice of voting against government funding legislation in Congress has, by procedurally empowering the Democratic minority, even proven counterproductive at times to the substantive advancement of conservative policy.

The Republican Party's oft-stated commitment to the tenets of limited government, American nationalism, and traditional morality has inhibited its ability to develop an extensive policy program that satisfies its ideologically identified activist base without alienating the operationally liberal general electorate. Despite frequent campaign pledges to achieve dramatic reductions in the scope of federal responsibilities and to popularize conservative cultural values in American society, the Republican Party has, when restored to power, proven much more effective at obstructing Democratic initiatives than at shrinking the size of government or reversing leftward social trends.

The Republican record on health care during the Obama presidency effectively illustrates its central dilemma. Between 2011 and 2016, congressional Republicans attempted to fulfill the demands of conservative activists by holding dozens of symbolic votes to repeal all or part of the Affordable Care Act, yet party leaders also realized that a majority of the wider electorate strongly supported specific provisions of the legislation (such as the more stringent regulation of insurance company practices) and opposed simply revoking benefits from the millions of Americans who had gained insurance and other forms of assistance under the law. Congressional Republicans had promised as early as 2009 to develop and introduce their own detailed reform plan as an alternative to the ACA, but repeated delays in fulfilling this goal suggest that the leadership of the GOP understood the significant challenge—if not outright impossibility—of devising a health care policy that would satisfy conservative demands for a small-government, free-market approach without depriving many citizens of their existing coverage.

Republican leaders and candidates adopted the slogan "repeal and replace" to describe their health care position to voters, but the lack of specific policy proposals buttressing the "replace" component of this pledge reflected the difficulty of translating conservative ideology into policy details while simultaneously protecting the party against a backlash from the American electorate. Caught between a philosophical antipathy to "Obamacare" and a sensitivity to the practical and political implications of repealing popular public benefits, the contemporary Republican Party has struggled to articulate its own specific, realistic vision for the American health care system, and (increasingly justified) fears of ideologically-motivated primary election challenges discourage Republican officeholders from pursuing legislative compromises—resulting in frequent policy paralysis. When House Majority Leader Eric Cantor attempted in April 2013 to advance legislation creating publicly funded high-risk pools for hard-to-insure Americans, a common component of reform plans proposed by right-of-center health policy experts, he was forced to withdraw his bill in the face of opposition from conservative activists and members of Congress who criticized it as "further extend[ing] the federal government's role in health care," in the words of a press release from the Club for Growth.[6]

The presidency of George W. Bush represents one recent model of Republican governance that attempted to successfully navigate the narrow straits separating the demands of party activists from the wider public's aversion to operational conservatism. While in office, Bush hewed to the conservative line on taxes and foreign policy, two issues on which public support for Republican positions was relatively robust. He also prioritized the appointment of conservatives to the executive branch and federal judiciary, satisfying movement leaders who pressed for greater representation in positions of government authority. But aside from a brief, unsuccessful attempt in early 2005 to create a partially privatized component of Social Security, Bush showed little interest once elected in reforming entitlement programs, cutting federal spending, or reducing the overall reach of the federal government in domestic affairs. His self-identified adherence to "compassionate conservatism" even encompassed the creation of a new prescription drug benefit for Medicare recipients; a significant expansion of federal funding of primary and secondary education under the No Child Left Behind initiative (which increased aid to public school districts in exchange for the imposition of performance standards); and an immigration reform proposal, ultimately blocked in Congress by Republican opposition, that would have granted legal status and a path to citizenship for undocumented residents of the United States.

Conservatives were happy to claim Bush as one of their own while he remained popular with voters and the national issue agenda was dominated by the War on Terror and the U.S. invasions of Iraq and Afghanistan. As Bush's approval ratings fell during his second term, however, some activists began to voice dissatisfaction with the president and his fellow Republicans in Congress for failing to advance small-government principles—a frustration that helped prevent Bush from joining Ronald Reagan in the pantheon of conservative movement heroes and soon boiled over into outright rebellion against a number of party leaders after he left office. As political analyst Sean Trende explained in the wake of Cantor's unexpected defeat in the 2014 Virginia congressional primary at the hands of Tea Party–supported challenger Dave Brat:

> From the point of view of conservatives I've spoken with, the early to mid-2000s look like this: Voters gave Republicans control of Congress and the presidency for the longest stretch since the 1920s. And what do Republicans have to show for it? Temporary tax cuts, No Child Left Behind, the Medicare prescription drug benefit, a new Cabinet department [of Homeland Security], increased federal spending, TARP [the Troubled Asset Relief Program, an emergency response to the 2008 financial crisis in which the federal government purchased equity in private financial institutions in order to prevent their collapse], and repeated attempts at immigration reform. Basically, despite a historic opportunity to shrink government, almost everything that the GOP establishment achieved during that time moved the needle leftward on domestic policy.... You don't have to sympathize with this view, but if you don't understand it, you will never understand the Tea Party.[7]

Growing conservative impatience with Republican politicians' lack of success in placing federal policy on a sustained right-of-center trajectory may also account for the resurgent popularity in some conservative legal circles of the belief that much of the current regulation of economic activity by government authority is in fact prohibited by the Constitution. This new libertarian-influenced intellectual movement seeks to rehabilitate the Supreme Court's long-disavowed 1905 decision in *Lochner v. New York* overturning state labor laws as violating individual freedom of contract and prescribes much less judicial deference to the judgment of democratic institutions than did previous traditions of conservative thought.[8] With faltering confidence that future Republican presidents and congressional majorities will successfully roll back the modern welfare and regulatory state, some conservatives are increasingly investing their hopes in an active federal judiciary to accomplish the central policy goal of their ideological movement.

The Republican Party has become trapped in a troubling, and even dangerous, cycle in which conservative hopes, dashed by a disappointing Republican governing record, grow into even more vociferous demands for sweeping policy change, encouraging increasingly desperate promises by Republican leaders that are in turn even more difficult to satisfy. As Jonah Goldberg of *National Review* observed several months after hard-line conservatives forced Boehner's departure from the Speakership, "All of the various [Republican] establishments and counter-establishments overpromised and underdelivered in recent years. Congressional leaders talked a big game while campaigning but played small ball once reelected."[9] By 2016, the inability or unwillingness of incumbent Republican leaders to fulfill their repeated pledges to secure a conservative transformation of government policy while restoring traditional morality and ensuring American international supremacy had inspired sufficiently widespread frustration among activists and primary voters that Tea Party–style rebellion spread to presidential nomination politics as well, fueling the outsider candidacies of Donald Trump and Ted Cruz while forcing other candidates in the race to adopt more fervently conservative issue positions and more intemperate campaign rhetoric. Candidate promises grew even more outlandish—exemplified by Trump's famous vow to combat illegal immigration by building a wall along the southern U.S. border that would be paid for by the Mexican government—producing a sideshow atmosphere that bore little connection to the sober realities of governing.

To any observer who recalled the Republican Party's former reputation for maintaining internal discipline and rewarding deference to authority, the spectacle of a broad popular uprising against a party "establishment" denounced as corrupted by power and co-opted by liberal ideas seemed like a remarkable development. Yet both sides of this Republican civil war continued to share a common conception of the GOP as properly standing for the cause of American conservatism. The fault lines that divide the contemporary Republican Party, and often interrupt the smooth workings of the federal government, represent the uncontained political energy generated by the collision between the party's steadfast commitment to conservative tenets in the abstract and its chronically limited success at putting those ideals into practice.

THE CONTEMPORARY DEMOCRATS: POLICIES SEEKING PURPOSE

The Democratic Party has never lacked for policy proposals, even if internal tensions and disagreements of its own have complicated the task of building sufficient unity to successfully enact an ambitious legislative agenda over often-fervent opposition. In the years since its southern conservative bloc departed for the Republican side of the aisle, the remaining groups within the Democratic coalition have increasingly demonstrated the ability to cooperate productively—though a sizable moderate faction continues to distinguish itself ideologically from the left wing of the party, regularly limiting the ability of Democratic leaders to implement liberal-backed initiatives. Regardless of their ideological persuasion, most Democrats emphasize practical achievements over doctrinal devotion, and the concrete priorities of the party's constituencies encourage Democratic politicians to emphasize real-world outcomes when judging the success or desirability of public policy.

The limited influence of ideological purity within the Democratic Party also allows policymakers flexibility in responding to the various demands of their supporters and the changing political environment. The pragmatic attitude of most Democratic elected officials is widely shared by the activists, interest groups, and voters within the expanded party network. Whether in or out of government, Democratic actors tend to remain respectful of empiricism and expertise, open to incrementalism and compromise, and mindful of political and managerial feasibility. The absence of a formidable leftist movement within the party, a well-funded set of outside organizations ready to punish Democratic incumbents in primary elections for any deviations from left-wing doctrine, or an extensive liberal media apparatus devoted to policing ideological orthodoxy allows Democrats in government more freedom than their Republican counterparts to maneuver without fear of retribution from within their own ranks. No recent Democratic leader in Congress has faced organized opposition or procedural challenges from junior members of the party caucus, in marked contrast to the internal leadership battles that have repeatedly divided congressional Republicans.

The Democratic Party's character as a group coalition also allows it to benefit from an increasingly heterogeneous national electorate. Nonwhite and non-Christian Americans, who represent a growing proportion of the population, routinely support Democratic candidates by sizable and widening margins. In 2012, Barack Obama won reelection to the presidency by four percentage points over Republican challenger Mitt Romney despite losing the white vote by a margin of 59 percent to 39 percent, according to national exit polls. Obama compensated for his disadvantage among whites by attracting 80 percent of the vote among racial minorities, who constituted 44 percent of his supporters nationwide.[10]

Yet the Democrats perennially confront serious political difficulties of their own. Popular support for many specific Democratic policy positions is dependably accompanied by general suspicion of government power, aversion to new taxes and expanded bureaucracies, and anxiety about broad social change—predispositions that render many citizens open to persuasion by Republican warnings about the dangers of Democratic policy activism. A decentralized constitutional structure with multiple veto points controlled by independent actors provides a powerful inherent advantage in any political conflict to the side favoring the status quo, which systematically works against the ambitions of the more legislatively prolific party. Policies and programs that manage to survive this procedural gauntlet are often diluted in strength or reduced in scope in order to gain passage, diminishing their potential impact and even contributing further to popular skepticism about the effectiveness of government.

In addition, the diverse coalition of the Democratic Party is not united by devotion to a common political creed. Its activist population is composed of a wide variety of separate groups and movements that each serve as the basis of party identification and political mobilization for a discrete sector of the party base. Democrats do not unite behind shared principles or view themselves as collectively engaged in a single political cause. Republican leaders can rally their party's supporters by calling on them to defend the conservative faith in a global battle of ideas, but Democrats lack the capacity to join this ideological fight on an equal footing.

Recognizing the symbolic conservatism of the American electorate at large, and aware that a large proportion of their own party's supporters decline to identify as liberals, Democratic leaders often avoid abstract rhetoric that describes their policy positions as deriving from a larger, more comprehensive belief system. Sharing the view that their party enters political combat on behalf of the many against the powerful few, Democratic politicians conclude that they can better achieve success by appealing to the self-interest of multiple discrete voting blocs that collectively add up to an electoral majority. They promise higher wages to the poor, affordable health insurance to the working class, a reduced debt burden to college students, secure government benefits to the elderly, protections against discrimination to social minorities, and so forth. Even issues that involve attitudes about moral values are often understood by Democrats in terms of group interest. For example, Democratic politicians and citizens commonly frame their support for legalized abortion as a defense of the particular rights of women rather than as an advancement of the universal principles of civil libertarianism or cultural progressivism, which often leads them to overstate the extent to which women in the wider electorate uniformly sympathize with the party's pro-choice position.

In response to the Republican Party's anti-intellectual tinge and growing popular identification with organized Christianity, Democrats portray themselves as motivated by science, reason, evidence, and common sense rather than traditional authorities or dogmas. This approach both reflects and encourages the pro-Democratic loyalties of academics and other members of the "creative class," religious minorities, secular voters, and gays and lesbians. Democrats prefer to confront their political opponents on empirical grounds, viewing their party as defending objective truth against perceived threats from the forces of ignorance, myth, and misinformation rather than allowing themselves to be drawn into a debate over competing philosophies or values.

This tendency can put Democrats at a disadvantage when attacked on the basis of ideology. Republicans often effectively characterize the Democrats' extensive array of detailed proposals for government action as collectively representing infringements on liberty, suggest that their policies reflect adherence to a leftist belief system that is unconstitutional or un-American, and propose as a remedy that the nation return to the (conservative, in their view) principles upon which it was founded. Democrats routinely struggle to rebut these charges, in part because they lack an easily invoked alternative set of concepts and values that provide coherence to their wide assortment of specific policy goals. Well-informed symbolic liberals often understand how their positions on individual political issues can be derived from a set of larger ideals, such as egalitarianism or multiculturalism, but Democratic leaders seldom emphasize such reasoning in their communications with voters. They prefer instead to engage with the Republican opposition on what they see as the firmer political grounds of group interest, policy specificity, and empirical practicality.

The two most recent Democratic presidents, Bill Clinton and Barack Obama, were both popular, successful politicians who enjoyed reputations as particularly skilled orators. Yet neither leader presented himself or his policies as the representative or product of an ideological movement. Clinton, a self-proclaimed "New Democrat" who intentionally distinguished himself from a tradition of Democratic liberalism that he viewed as politically disadvantageous and substantively out-of-date, openly broke with the left wing of his party on a number of specific issues—including middle-class tax cuts, the death penalty, and welfare reform—while frequently sounding centrist or even conservative rhetorical themes such as fiscal discipline, market competition, and personal responsibility. Clinton's careful respect for the gap between the symbolic conservatism and operational liberalism of the American electorate sometimes led him into bouts of logical incoherence. For example, he famously proclaimed in his 1996 State of the Union address that "the era of big government is over," earning an enthusiastic ovation from the assembled Republican-led Congress, before proceeding to call on the legislative branch to act immediately to raise the federal minimum wage, expand health care access and portability, maintain stringent environmental regulations, subsidize education and retraining programs for American workers, expand Pell grants and work-study programs for college students, provide funding for Internet access in public schools, and enact campaign finance reform, among other government-expanding proposals.

Unlike Clinton, Obama's rhetoric seldom echoed that of his partisan opponents, and he declined to mimic his Democratic predecessor's "triangulation" strategy of separating himself from the positions of his own party's liberal wing as well as from the views of the Republican leadership. Yet Obama, too, pledged to overcome ideological divisions, rather than claiming the mantle of liberalism in an ongoing philosophical battle against the right. Obama's signature oratorical theme, first articulated in his well-received keynote address at the 2004 Democratic National Convention while he was still an Illinois state legislator running for the U.S. Senate, characterized contemporary ideological conflict as an artificial construct of "spin masters," "negative ad peddlers," and "pundits [who] like to slice and dice our country into red states and blue states." "I say to them tonight," declared Obama, "there's not a liberal America and a conservative America; there's the *United* States of America."[11] His presidential campaigns adopted pithy but vague slogans like "Hope," "Change," and "Yes We Can" that allowed liberal Democrats to read an idealistic purpose into his candidacies without risking an overt commitment to liberalism that might alienate swing voters.

Obama's promises to transcend political gridlock and discord undoubtedly appealed to Americans who had tired of the relentless partisan conflict in Washington, as well as fellow Democrats who nurtured optimism that his inclusive manner could persuade Republicans to moderate their opposition. But he risked committing himself to an objective that was impossible for any president—and especially one who took solidly left-of-center positions on most specific issues—to realize in an era of systematic polarization. In his final State of the Union address, delivered in January 2016, Obama himself acknowledged that he had failed to fulfill this goal, remarking that "one of the few regrets of my presidency [is] that the rancor and suspicion between the parties has gotten worse instead of better."[12]

As he prepared to leave office, Obama could claim a number of concrete achievements, including the management of a national recovery after the severe economic crisis of 2008, the enactment of universal health care, the stricter regulation of financial institutions, the rescue of the American auto industry, fair-pay legislation for female workers, a significant advancement in the federal recognition of gay rights, and the negotiation of international agreements on trade, climate change, and nuclear weapons. But he and his party had not defined these specific accomplishments as stemming from a greater cause for which they stood that rose above the interests of specific social groups or the mere exercise of prudent judgment and scientific reasoning. Some liberals ultimately expressed disappointment that the Obama-led Democratic Party had failed to invest its governing record with a wider sense of purpose that could stand in contrast to the Republican opposition's relentless rhetorical advocacy of conservative principles and values. Russell Muirhead argued that Obama, by tending to characterize his political positions and priorities as simply reflecting common sense and the protection of middle-class interests, ultimately failed to uphold his responsibility as a partisan to invoke a more meaningful set of ideals:

> Both liberalism and conservatism, in Obama's view, had lost their relevance to our political circumstance. Obama was more comfortable contrasting himself with liberals than taking the label as his own (even if his opponents viewed him as the liberal of their egalitarian nightmares). Obama denied that politics is essentially contestatory, engaging a recurring contest that engages new particulars in each new iteration even as it is animated by a steady spirit. . . . Obama could not seem to fully own *his* liberalism . . . [and] could not recognize the partisan character of his own convictions. . . . Hidden in this pretense is an arrogant insistence that everyone should agree with us, without the bother of explaining why.[13]

But Obama was hardly the only Democratic president to resist explicitly identifying his, or his party's, policy agenda with a larger commitment to liberal values; the same tendency could be seen in most other prominent Democrats who have assumed leading roles over the course of the party's history. (Even 1988 presidential nominee Michael Dukakis, commonly attacked by Republicans as, and remembered in retrospect as, an archetypical "Massachusetts liberal," declared in his acceptance speech at the Democratic National Convention that the election "isn't about ideology, it's about competence. [And] it's not about meaningless labels.")[14] Like other Democratic leaders past and present, Obama presumably concluded that waving the banner of liberalism would do little to rally public support, even among many members of his own party, while fatally alienating the larger electorate. Paradoxically, he could best serve his ambitious goal of moving public policy to the left on a range of issues by declining to acknowledge that he was seeking to do so.

As Muirhead suggests, however, this strategy may carry a cost. Obama, like Clinton before him, was a personally charismatic leader who nonetheless faced difficulty in transferring his own popularity to other

Democratic candidates or the party's larger organizational apparatus. Lacking a left-of-center counterpart to the conservative media universe that acts as a faithful transmitter of Republicans' views, Democratic politicians often struggle to communicate with their supporters and keep them engaged in the political process during the periods between presidential campaigns. Frequent reliance on the invocation of group-based self-interest may also tend to alienate voters who do not identify with the cited group or groups, or who find such appeals uninspiring or unseemly in comparison to the broader and more symbolic cast of Republican rhetoric. While the Democratic Party continues to convince many Americans of the suitability of its positions on a variety of specific policy issues, it has found much less success in uniting and mobilizing its membership behind an enduring common purpose.

TOWARD A MORE BALANCED TWO-PARTY SYSTEM

The resurgent strength of partisanship in government and the steady growth of elite-level polarization have introduced a number of challenges to the American political system over the past several decades. Today's vigorous and evenly matched parties sit uncomfortably within a constitutional structure designed over two centuries ago by founders who expressed hostility to parties and who sought to divide power among multiple independent actors serving staggered terms of office and representing distinct electoral constituencies. While critics of our contemporary politics occasionally express excessive nostalgia for previous periods of American history—complaints about frequent conflict and gridlock were commonplace even during the weak-party era of the mid-20th century, now often regarded in retrospect as a golden age of national consensus—the governing problems caused by these ceaseless partisan battles are apparent to even the most casual observer of current events.

Yet solutions do not come easily to hand. Some would-be reformers argue that polarization could be reduced, and partisan warfare abated, by tinkering with the mechanics of the political system. They prescribe limits on gerrymandering in order to reduce the number of safe party districts, on the assumption that more competitive seats will produce more moderate or cooperative legislators. Stricter limits on the use of political money, they contend, would reduce the influence of ideologically purist donors and interest groups over elected representatives. Reforms to the party nomination process, such as the use of "top-two" or "jungle" primaries that allow voters to cross party lines to support favored candidates, have been implemented in California and Washington as antipolarization measures. More fundamentally, changes to electoral rules could potentially encourage the formation of new centrist parties that could hold the balance of power in government.

Yet little evidence substantiates the hope that polarization can be easily reformed away. The great partisan divide in American politics is not simply the result of how districts are drawn, campaigns funded, or candidates nominated. Its roots lie deeper, in the activist populations of the two parties, and it is sustained by party politicians' acquiescence to the policy views of two increasingly distinct sets of electoral, geographic, and interest group constituencies.

But the ferocity of today's political battles does not merely reflect the growing ideological gap between the parties. The mutual antagonism between Democrats and Republicans, in the country at large as well as on the presidential campaign trail or floor of Congress, runs deeper than mere policy disagreement. Even citizens who do not subscribe to ideological conceptions of politics or exhibit strong views on specific issues have become more secure in their preferences for one party over the other during the past several decades. Moreover, Democrats and Republicans not only attack each other for subscribing to misguided beliefs about optimal public policy but also regularly question each other's motives, intelligence, and judgment; suggest that their opponents are not making good-faith arguments; and accuse each other of merely doing the bidding of special interests or pandering to popular prejudices.

A significant share of this reciprocal animosity gains its force from a lack of widespread recognition of the fundamental asymmetry between the parties, with partisans on each side misunderstanding the nature of the opposite party and the basis of its mass support. Because the Republican Party is organized as the agent of an ideological movement, Republicans often assume that the Democratic Party is similarly dedicated to the advancement of "leftist" or "socialist" ideas, or to the expansion of government as a good in itself rather than as a means toward more practical ends. Similarly, the emphasis that the conservative movement places on American military strength, its veneration of the Constitution and the nation's founders, and its defense of traditional cultural values often leads Republicans to conclude that Democrats intentionally seek to weaken the United States and to hasten its moral decline. These long-standing misapprehensions served as the basis for several incorrect—and, in some cases, downright ugly—claims that circulated among Republican supporters during the Obama presidency: that Obama subscribed to Marxist beliefs; that he harbored a hatred and rage toward America that motivated his behavior in office; that he had embarked on an international "apology tour" criticizing the nation before foreign audiences; and, most remarkably, that he had not been born in the United States and was constitutionally inel-igible to serve as president. (This last conspiracy theory was sufficiently resilient to prompt Obama to release his birth certificate to the public in April 2011.) Republicans also tend to be overly dismissive of sincere Democratic deference to academic, scientific, and journalistic expertise, characterizing it as mere window-dressing for the advancement of left-wing ideology.

But party asymmetry also leads Democrats astray when appraising their Republican opponents. Because their own party claims to speak for the interests of historically disadvantaged social groups, Democrats too often assume that the conservative ideology espoused by Republicans is little more than a publicly acceptable justification for the otherwise in-defensible maintenance of other groups' existing power and privilege. Democrats regularly accuse Republicans of taking political positions for the sole purpose of currying favor with corporate interests or wealthy supporters, and they are often liable to regard conservative critiques of Democratic policies as merely motivated by racism and other forms of bigotry. Because Democrats view their party as self-evidently defending the interests of "the people," they are quick to dismiss Republican elec-toral or legislative victories as a failure of the democratic system—leading them to systematically overestimate the extent to which process reforms such as stricter campaign finance regulation, restrictions on lobbying, or the loosening of voter registration requirements would produce a deci-sive leftward shift in American politics. Democrats often cite the opera-tional liberalism of the national electorate as evidence of their superior representation of the public's views but frequently dismiss or ignore the equally strong prevalence of symbolic conservatism—in particular, a long-standing and deep-seated suspicion of government—among the same population of citizens. Just as Republicans can be overly mistrustful of Democrats' sincerity in using the levers of government power to ad-dress legitimate social problems, Democrats can be too hasty in conclud-ing that Republican skepticism about the effectiveness and desirability of government action amounts to a denial of, or indifference toward, the ex-istence of the problems themselves.

Improving the mutual understanding of each party's essential nature would not eliminate, or even sharply reduce, the growing divide between the issue positions held by Democrats and Republicans. But it could still have positive effects on American politics. Political rhetoric and debate might be more respectful, substantive, and illuminating. Political leaders might be less likely to cast aspersions on the motives of the other party. A renewed respect on both sides for the views and objectives of the oppo-sition might uncover previously obscured opportunities for cooperation and compromise, even if the parties continued to maintain distinct ideal positions on most policy issues.

A fuller recognition of the distinctive characters of both parties might also work to reduce the growing antipathy expressed by partisan voters toward the opposition. Alan I. Abramowitz and Steven Webster have recently demonstrated that rising party loyalty in the American electorate over the past several decades has primarily reflected increasingly negative feelings held by partisans about the opposing party rather than more positive evaluations of voters' own party.[15] If Democrats and Republicans alike gained greater appreciation of the views and motives of their political rivals, perhaps their partisan attachments would be less dependent upon the maintenance of hostile feelings toward the other side. Trust, and even pride, in the American parties and the political process as a whole might improve from its current worrisome state.

The durable presence of partisan asymmetry over many years of American political history also reflects an enduring mismatch between the operational and symbolic predispositions of the nation's citizenry. The parties have responded rationally to—and further reinforced—this pattern, adapting their strategy, rhetoric, and policymaking efforts to the American public's insistent, if inconsistent, demands for a smaller government that addresses a greater number of problems. Neither party can claim a record of courage in confronting the long-standing incoherence of the national electorate; instead, leaders merely seek to shift the terms of debate to the level of specificity that systematically favors their party's own position.

Our political system would benefit greatly from a more honest reckoning on both sides of the aisle of the necessary connection between broad principles and policy details. For too long, Republicans have promised to shrink the size of government without fully acknowledging that fulfilling this objective would entail sacrificing popular programs and benefits. For too long, Democrats have promised to address the various needs and concerns of a large assortment of social groups without admitting that the realization of their ambitions would require a significant expansion of government's collective authority and cost. Such pledges often succeed in achieving short-term electoral goals, but the persistent gaps between the campaign rhetoric and governing record of each party ultimately provoke popular frustration, anger, cynicism, apathy, and revolt.

While parties and politicians do not always behave admirably, responsibility for their persistently mismatched behavior also lies with the voters themselves. The messages that Americans send to their elected officials are sufficiently contradictory to allow partisan differences to become further entrenched, while the electorate, like its representatives, seeks to avoid grappling with the full implications of its various political preferences. A more realistic and coherent citizenry could bring balance to the enduring asymmetry between the Democratic and Republican parties, forcing both to acknowledge that they only represent a partial expression of the public will. If voters continue to side with Democrats on specific policies while agreeing with Republicans on the broader role of government in society, it can be no surprise that the parties will continue to adopt dissimilar approaches to political competition while each claiming sole authority to speak on behalf of the American people. Building a stronger democracy requires acknowledging—or, even better, resolving—the contradictions in our own collective political mind.

NOTES

CHAPTER 1

1. "Getting Started | Hillary Clinton," YouTube video, 2:18, posted by Hillary Clinton, April 12, 2015, https://www.youtube.com/watch?v=0uY7gLZDmn4.

2. John Dickerson, "Hillary Clinton's Opening Pitch," *Slate*, April 12, 2015, http://www.slate.com/articles/news_and_politics/politics/2015/04/hillary_clinton_campaign_video_announcing_her_presidential_run_she_wants.html.

3. Susan Page, "Second Chance for a First Impression," *USA Today*, April 13, 2015, p. 1A.

4. Megan Carpentier, "In Hillary Clinton's America, There's Room for Equality, Diversity and Pick-Up Trucks," *The Guardian*, April 13, 2015, http://www.theguardian.com/commentisfree/2015/apr/13/hillary-clinton-america-equality-diversity-pick-up-trucks.

5. Robert Kuttner, "Hillary Clinton: From Symbolism to Specifics," *American Prospect*, April 13, 2015, http://prospect.org/article/hillary-clinton-symbolism-specifics.

6. Ruth Marcus, "Hillary Clinton's Insultingly Vapid Video," *Washington Post*, April 13, 2015, http://www.washingtonpost.com/blogs/post-partisan/wp/2015/04/13/hillary-clintons-insultingly-vapid-video/.

7. Maureen Dowd, "Granny Get Your Gun," *New York Times*, April 18, 2015, http://www.nytimes.com/2015/04/19/opinion/sunday/maureen-dowd-granny-get-your-gun.html.

8. Polsby and Mayer (1999, p. 219).

9. Acheson (1955, pp. 23–25, 30–32).

10. Richard L. Lyons, "Vetoes Frustrate Democrats," *Washington Post*, June 17, 1975, p. 12.

11. Mayhew (1966, pp. 151, 153, 155).

12. Plotke (1996).

13. Nie et al. (1976, pp. 200, 209, 196, 202).

14. Polsby (1983, p. 85).

15. Rae (1989, p. 201).

16. Freeman (1986, p. 352).

17. Rohde (1991); Polsby (2004).

18. Ronald Brownstein, "Coalition of New, Old, Equates to Obama Win," *National Journal*, November 7, 2012, http://www.nationaljournal.com/thenextamerica/politics/coalition-of-new-old-equates-to-obama-win-20121107.

19. McCarty, Poole, and Rosenthal (2006).

20. See Fiorina (2005); Abramowitz and Saunders (2008).

21. Levendusky (2009); Bartels (2000).

22. McCarty, Poole, and Rosenthal (2006).

23. Thomas Mann and Norman Ornstein, "Let's Just Say It: The Republicans Are the Problem," *Washington Post*, April 27, 2012, http://www.washingtonpost.com/opinions/lets-just-say-it-the-republicans-are-the-problem/2012/04/27/gIQAxCVUlT_story.html.

24. Horwitz (2013) offers a useful review.
25. Kabaservice (2012, p. xvi).
26. Ezra Klein, "This Is What Makes Republicans and Democrats So Different," *Vox*, January 13, 2016, http://www.vox.com/2016/1/13/10759874/republicans-democrats-different.
27. Downs (1957); Aldrich (1995); for a review, see Hacker and Pierson (2014).
28. Our view of the Democratic Party, described more fully in the following chapter, better matches theories of political parties that emphasize the dominance of "intense policy demanders." See Bawn et al. (2012).

CHAPTER 2

1. "Revolution of 1994," *Frontline*, PBS, aired November 9, 1994, http://www.pbs.org/wgbh/pages/frontline/shows/clinton/etc/11091994.html.
2. *Congressional Record* 141, no. 10, January 18, 1995, p. H308.
3. "Distrust, Discontent, Anger and Partisan Rancor: Section 1: Trust in Government 1958–2010," Pew Research Center, April 10, 2008, http://www.people-press.org/2010/04/18/section-1-trust-in-government-1958-2010/.
4. "Government," Gallup, n.d., http://www.gallup.com/poll/27286/government.aspx.
5. "As GOP Takes Control, Nation Seeks New Course," *USA Today*, January 4, 1995, p. 10A; Dan Balz and Richard Morin, "Public Agrees with Goals of the GOP," *Washington Post*, January 6, 1995, p. A8; David Lauter, "*Times* Poll: Clinton's Image Hurts Him More Than His Ideas," *Los Angeles Times*, January 28, 1995, http://articles.latimes.com/1995-01-28/news/mn-25268_1_times-poll/2.
6. Bill Clinton, State of the Union Address, January 25, 1995, http://millercenter.org/president/speeches/speech-3440.
7. "Text of Clinton Government Shutdown Address," CNN, November 14, 1995, http://www.cnn.com/US/9511/debt_limit/11-14/transcripts/clinton.html.
8. Adam Clymer, "Americans Reject Big Medicare Cuts, a New Poll Finds," *New York Times*, October 26, 1995, http://www.nytimes.com/1995/10/26/us/americans-reject-big-medicare-cuts-a-new-poll-finds.html.
9. Bob Cusack and Kevin Bogardus, "1997 GOP Coup Is Talk of 2012 Primary," *The Hill*, January 31, 2012, http://thehill.com/homenews/campaign/207565-1997-coup-is-talk-of-2012-primary-race.
10. Free and Cantril (1967).
11. Converse (1964).
12. Fiorina (2005); Abramowitz (2010).
13. Broockman and Ahler (2014).
14. Ellis and Stimson (2012, p. 8).
15. Ellis and Stimson (2012, p. 43).
16. Ellis and Stimson (2012, p. 74).
17. Despite the large gap, macro-ideology and macropartisanship are correlated at .53; party identification and ideology track different phenomena but generally rise and fall in tandem.
18. Ellis and Stimson (2012).
19. Abramowitz and Webster (2015) have found that, among partisans, negative feelings toward out-groups are rising faster than positive feelings toward in-groups. For our measure, this is only apparent since 2004. The long-term trends are clear across all indicators: Republicans have slowly felt more warmly about conservatives and less warmly about liberals, and Democrats have felt the reverse.
20. Abramowitz and Saunders (2006); Levendusky (2009).
21. Abramowitz and Saunders (2006).
22. Abramowitz and Saunders (2006).

23. Converse (1964, p. 215).
24. Converse (1964, pp. 215–216).
25. The coding scheme has been reapplied regularly, with high inter-coder reliability. For further information, see Hagner, Pierce, and Knight (1989) and Lewis-Beck et al. (2008).
26. We allowed respondents to define "liberalism" and "conservatism" rather than impose a single definition for each. Most ideological comments made by Republicans referred to a belief in smaller government and more individual responsibility. Ideological responses by liberals, which were less frequent, referred primarily to the need for government or equality. Using long interviews, Robert Lane argued that all citizens' ideological beliefs could be fit together with enough time and coaxing (see Lane 1962). We seek only to show that Republicans reason ideologically more than Democrats—a tendency that has diverse individual-level mechanisms.
27. On the 2000 ANES levels of conceptualization scale, fewer than 10 percent of self-identified liberals were categorized as ideologues, while more than 20 percent were categorized as group benefits voters.
28. The party identification scale is a substantively and statistically significant predictor of the number of group mentions and the number of ideological mentions, even with controls for all of these demographic factors. Other factors showed no large and consistent effects.
29. References to humanism (ANES Code 807), equality or egalitarianism (Code 829), generosity or compassion (Code 831), or democratic values (Code 845) were all made sparingly and were included in the count of ideological mentions. The full coding scheme is available at http://www.electionstudies.org/studypages/2004prepost/nes04app.pdf.
30. Previous studies noticed the disproportionate tendency of Republicans to score higher on the levels of conceptualization scale but focused on the lack of consistent evidence that the hierarchical scale could be used reliably across elections. We do not wish to resuscitate the scale but note the different partisan tendencies captured by the top two levels. See Hagner and Pierce (1982).
31. Brewer (2009, p. 11). The only exception to the Democratic advantage was 1968.
32. Brewer (2009, p. 18).
33. Brewer (2009, p. 46).
34. Lelkes and Sniderman (2015).
35. Although Republicans do not tend to consciously think of themselves as members of discrete groups, they may still be motivated by self-interest. Republicans tend to subsume (or rationalize) that interest within the adoption of a broader ideology, perceiving a who-gets-what style of politics openly based on group identity as a distinctively Democratic phenomenon.
36. Romney's remarks at this private fundraiser were released by *Mother Jones* magazine. Romney incorrectly assumed that the Democratic coalition only comprised people who paid no taxes and received government benefits, but his characterization of the Democratic base as more concerned with direct actions from government than with broad ideological reasoning was more apt. Mother Jones News Teams, "Full Transcript of the Mitt Romney Secret Video," *Mother Jones*, September 19, 2012, http://www.motherjones.com/politics/2012/09/full-transcript-mitt-romney-secret-video.
37. This difference has been consistent in every election since 1972, although partisans have become more knowledgeable about the ideological reputations of the parties. See Lelkes and Sniderman (2015).
38. Abramowitz and Saunders (2006); Lelkes and Sniderman (2015).

39. Green, Palmquist, and Schickler (2002, p. 8).
40. Abramowitz and Saunders (2006, p. 186).
41. Lelkes and Sniderman (2015).
42. Haidt (2012).
43. Jost et al. (2003); Haidt (2012).
44. Liberman et al. (2007).
45. Green, Palmquist, and Schickler (2002).
46. Abramowitz and Saunders (2006).
47. Abramowitz and Saunders (2006).
48. Ellis and Stimson (2012).
49. Valentino and Sears (2005); Hutchings and Valentino (2004). But see Carmines, Sniderman, and Easter (2011) for a contrary view.
50. Hutchings and Valentino (2004).
51. Kinder and Kam (2010).
52. Kinder and Kam (2010, p. 59).
53. Kinder and Kam (2010).
54. Kinder and Kam (2012).
55. Tesler (2012).
56. Hutchings and Valentino (2004).
57. Barreto and Pedraza (2009).
58. Classen, Tucker, and Smith (2015).
59. Baldassarri and Goldberg (2014).
60. Abramowitz and Saunders (2006); Valentino and Sears (2005); Carmines and Stimson (1989).
61. Hutchings and Valentino (2004) provide an overview; Valentino and Sears (2005) respond to some critiques; Carmines, Sniderman, and Easter (2011) contend that the evidence is weak.
62. Abramowitz (2013).
63. Key (1961, p. 246).
64. Petrocik, Benoit, and Hansen (2003).
65. Green, Palmquist, and Schickler (2002).
66. Therriault (2015).
67. Egan (2013).
68. Egan (2003, p. 23).
69. "Question: What's More Important in (Survey Country) Society: That Everyone Be Free . . .," Pew Global Attitudes and Trends Question Database, http://www.pewglobal.org/question-search/?qid=1030&cntIDs=&stdIDs=.
70. McCarty, Poole, and Rosenthal (2006).
71. Liberal intellectuals and interest groups also criticized Obama over issues like the lack of a public option in the Affordable Care Act and spying by the National Security Agency—just as they had criticized Bill Clinton over his ideological "triangulation" in the 1990s. These attacks did not resonate within the mass Democratic base to the same extent that conservative demands regularly challenge Republican leaders.
72. Critchlow (2011).
73. Broockman and Skovron (2014).
74. Broockman and Skovron (2014, p. 18).
75. Free and Cantril first noticed the public's "schizoid combination of operational liberalism with ideological conservatism," which Stanley Feldman and John Zaller explored in attitudes toward social welfare policy. We draw upon the more recent work of Ellis and Stimson. See Free and Cantril (1967, p. 37); Feldman and Zaller (1992); Ellis and Stimson (2012).

76. We use the policy mood measure collected by James Stimson and a composite measure we created from the same dataset of public opinion polls. Both are available at policya-gendas.org.
77. Wlezien (1995).
78. This usage follows Ellis and Stimson (2012), who adapted Free and Cantril's (1967) formulation of "operational liberalism" and "ideological conservatism."
79. Ellis and Stimson (2012).
80. Classen, Tucker, and Smith (2015).
81. Baldassarri and Goldberg (2014).
82. Ellis and Stimson (2012).
83. Ellis and Stimson (2012, p. 101).
84. Ellis and Stimson (2012, p. 172).
85. Ellis and Stimson (2012, p. 183).
86. Ellis and Stimson (2012, p. 173).
87. Jacoby (2000).
88. Ellis and Stimson (2012, p. 159).
89. Schneider and Jacoby (2005).
90. Ellis and Stimson (2012, p. 180).
91. "Presidential Approval Ratings—George W. Bush," Gallup, n.d., http://www.gallup.com/poll/116500/presidential-approval-ratings-george-bush.aspx.
92. Presidential debate transcript, October 15, 2008, http://elections.nytimes.com/2008/president/debates/transcripts/third-presidential-debate.html
93. Henry J. Kaiser Family Foundation, "Whom Does the Public Trust More on Health Care and Medicare?," Kaiser Public Opinion, October 2012, https://kaiserfamily-foundation.files.wordpress.com/2013/01/8371.pdf.
94. "Inside Obama's Sweeping Victory," Pew Research Center, November 5, 2008, http://www.pewresearch.org/2008/11/05/inside-obamas-sweeping-victory/.
95. "Support for Health Care Overhaul, but It's Not 1993," Pew Research Center, March 19, 2009, http://www.people-press.org/2009/03/19/support-for-health-care-overhaul-but-its-not-1993/.
96. Mike Pence, "Press Conference with House Minority Leader John Boehner, Vermont Governor Jim Douglas, House Minority Whip Eric Cantor, South Dakota Governor Mike Rounds, Rep. Mary Fallin, Rep. Mike Pence," Vote Smart, June 24, 2009, http://votesmart.org/public-statement/436578/press-conference-with-house-minority-leader-john-boehner-vermont-governor-jim-douglas-house-minority-whip-eric-cantor-south-dakota-governor-mike-rounds-rep-mary-fallin-rep-mike-pence#.VZbvlouQ3Jo.
97. Jeffrey Young, "Kyl: Health Bill a 'Stunning Assault on Liberty,'" *The Hill*, September 22, 2009, http://thehill.com/blogs/blog-briefing-room/news/59761-kyl-health-bill-a-stunning-assault-on-liberty-.
98. Dave Cook, "GOP Chairman Steele's Assault on Obama Health Plan," *Christian Science Monitor*, July 20, 2009, http://www.csmonitor.com/USA/Politics/2009/0720/gop-chairman-steeles-assault-on-obama-health-plan.
99. "Poll Chart: Obama Health Care Law: Favor/Oppose," *HuffPost Pollster*, n.d., http://elections.huffingtonpost.com/pollster/us-health-bill.
100. Alex Isenstadt, "Town Halls Gone Wild," *Politico*, July 31, 2009, http://www.politico.com/news/stories/0709/25646.html.
101. "Tough Questions, Frustrations Continue in Town Halls," CNN, August 13, 2009, http://www.cnn.com/2009/POLITICS/08/13/town.hall.wrap/index.html?_s=PM:POLITICS.

102. "President Obama Holds a Tele-Townhall Meeting on Health Care with AARP Members," *Washington Post*, July 28, 2009, transcript http://www.washingtonpost.com/wp-dyn/content/article/2009/07/28/AR2009072801444.html.
103. Philip Rucker, "S.C. Senator Is a Voice of Reform Opposition," *Washington Post*, July 28, 2009, p. A01.
104. Nyhan et al. (2012).
105. Kaiser Family Foundation, "Kaiser Health Tracking Poll: March 2013," http://kff.org/health-reform/poll-finding/march-2013-tracking-poll/; Pew Research Center, "Views of the Affordable Care Act and Its Future," May 5, 2014, http://www.people-press.org/2014/05/05/views-of-the-affordable-care-act-and-its-future/.

CHAPTER 3

1. Mitt Romney, Remarks to the Conservative Political Action Conference, February 10, 2012, http://www.presidency.ucsb.edu/ws/?pid=99343.
2. *Washington Post*. 2012. "Republican Primary Debate: January 23, 2012," *Washington Post*, n.d., http://www.washingtonpost.com/wp-srv/politics/2012-presidential-debates/republican-primary-debate-january-23-2012/.
3. Aldrich (1995, p. 17).
4. Desmarais, La Raja, and Kowal (2014); Koger, Masket, and Noel (2009); Masket (2009); Herrnson (2009).
5. Bawn et al. (2012).
6. Karol (2009, pp. 7–9).
7. Bawn et al. (2012, p. 590).
8. For a review, see Galvin (2010).
9. Hacker and Pierson (2014).
10. Nexon (1971, p. 717).
11. Polsby (2008, p. 20).
12. Freeman (1986).
13. Galvin (2010).
14. Galvin (2010, p. 8).
15. Mayer (1996).
16. Skocpol and Williamson (2012, pp. 81–82).
17. Parker and Barreto (2013, p. 3).
18. For a comparison based on the two approaches, see Hood, Kidd, and Morris (2015).
19. McCarty, Poole, and Rosenthal (2006).
20. Noel (2013).
21. Noel (2013, p. 37).
22. Noel (2013, p. 37).
23. Critchlow (2011); Nash (2006).
24. Nash (2006).
25. Conservative activists took over all Republican-affiliated organizations during the early 1960s to slowly build delegate and grassroots support for Goldwater (Brennan 1995).
26. Gross, Medvetz, and Russell (2011).
27. Nash (2006, p. 275).
28. Nash (2006, p. 556).
29. Nash (2006, p. 577).
30. Noel (2013, p. 37).
31. Noel (2013, pp. 42, 96).
32. Cox Richardson (2014); Perlstein (2001); Phillips-Fein (2009); Dochuk (2012); Kazin (2011).

33. Cox Richardson (2014); Perlstein (2001, 2008, 2014); Phillips-Fein (2009); Dochuk (2012); Nash (2006); Rosen (2014); Fones-Wolf (1994); Kruse (2005, 2015); Andrew (1997); Critchlow (2011).
34. Zelizer (2010); Gross, Medvetz, and Russell (2011).
35. Cox Richardson (2014, p. 182).
36. Gerring (1998).
37. Cox Richardson (2014, p. 204).
38. Rosen (2014); Cox Richardson (2014).
39. Dwight D. Eisenhower, Letter to Edgar Newton Eisenhower, November 8, 1954, http://teachingamericanhistory.org/library/document/letter-to-edgar-newton-eisenhower/.
40. Rocco (2015); Perlstein (2001); Kruse (2015).
41. Nash (2006).
42. Perlstein (2001, p. 13).
43. Nash (2006), 198.
44. Zaretsky (2007, p. 232).
45. From the beginning, rightist organizations sought to both sell conservatism to the public and take over Republican Party institutions (see Andrew 1997).
46. Kruse (2015).
47. Dochuk (2012, p. 186).
48. Fones-Wolf (1994, p. 5).
49. Fones-Wolf (1994).
50. Fones-Wolf (1994, pp. 35–36).
51. Burns (2009).
52. Nash (2006, p. 504).
53. Critchlow (2011).
54. Perlstein (2001); Dochuk (2012).
55. Dochuk (2012, p. 143).
56. Cox Richardson (2014, p. 226).
57. Perlstein (2001).
58. Nash (2006, p. 276).
59. Nash (2006, p. 407).
60. Horwitz (2013).
61. Gross, Medvetz, and Russell (2011).
62. Nash (2006). The expansion was made possible by rising conservative foundations like the Scaife Fund, the Olin Foundation, and the Bradley Foundation (see Critchlow 2011).
63. Replacing "liberal" with "progressive" primarily yields references to the Progressive movement of the early 20th century and does not change the main trends. We also conducted searches with different capitalizations and in plural form, finding similar results. The one exception is that "Liberal Democrats" is a term used mostly to identify the British party, even in American books.
64. Perlstein (2001); Dochuk (2012).
65. Perlstein (2001, p. 221).
66. Kabaservice (2013).
67. Brennan (1995); Schoenwald (2001); Andrew (1997).
68. Nash (2006). The campaign also featured a series of new books designed to spread conservative ideology to the electorate (see Critchlow 2011).
69. Perlstein (2001).
70. This means that 1 out of 54 of his voters was out working for the campaign. See Schoenwald (2001).

71. Schoenwald (2001, p. 10); Andrew (1997).
72. Phillips-Fein (2009); Dochuk (2012).
73. Dochuk (2012).
74. Zelizer (2010, p. 94).
75. See Randall Balmer, "The Real Origins of the Religious Right," *Politico Magazine*, May 27, 2014, http://politi.co/1Mk2XE0.
76. Berry (1999).
77. Berry (1999).
78. Dochuk (2012).
79. John King, "Religious Right May Broaden Agenda Beyond Gay Rights," Associated Press, September 8, 1993, http://bit.ly/1Na2JQy.
80. Berry (1999, p. 101). Horwitz (2013) also reviews this history.
81. See Horwitz (2013) for a review.
82. Kabaservice (2004, p. 12).
83. Nash (2006, p. 226).
84. Kabaservice (2004, p. 209).
85. Perlstein (2008, p. 431).
86. Lipset (1960).
87. Kabaservice (2004, p. 341).
88. Katznelson (1989, p. 198).
89. Schoenwald (2001); Critchlow (2011).
90. Weisbrot and Mackenzie (2008, p. 95).
91. Katznelson (1989); Baumgartner and Jones (2015); Weisbrot and Mackenzie (2008).
92. Teles (2008, pp. 52–53); see also Grossmann (2014).
93. Weisbrot and Mackenzie (2008, p. 97).
94. Teles (2008).
95. Teles (2008, pp. 265, 279).
96. Teles (2008).
97. Kazin (2011, p. 7).
98. Burner (1968, p. xiii).
99. Brinkley (1989, p. 94).
100. Brinkley (1989, p. 104).
101. These authors are included in the edited volume by Fraser and Gerstle (1989); the summary of their joint point of view is provided in the introduction (p. xix).
102. Lichtenstein (1989, p. 123).
103. Kazin (2011, p. 157).
104. Katznelson (1989, pp. 186–192).
105. Brinkley (1989, pp. 109–112).
106. Brinkley (1995, p. 10).
107. Plotke (1996, p. 170).
108. Mollenkopf (1983, p. 43).
109. Broder (1971, pp. 69–71).
110. Goodwin (1991, p. 154).
111. Perlstein (2001).
112. Akst (2012). http://wilsonquarterly.com/quarterly/spring-2012-the-age-of-connection/port-huron-statement-manifesto-at-50/.
113. Akst (2012). http://wilsonquarterly.com/quarterly/spring-2012-the-age-of-connection/port-huron-statement-manifesto-at-50/.
114. Isserman and Kazin (1989, p. 213).
115. Kazin (2011, pp. 250–251).
116. Davis (1986, p. 127).

117. Cowie (2011, p. 95).
118. Miroff (2007, p. 130).
119. Miroff (2007, pp. 3, 201).
120. Fraser and Gerstle (1989, p. xxi).
121. Cowie (2011, p. 239).
122. Cowie (2011).
123. Katznelson (1989, p. 204).
124. Cowie (2011).
125. Berry (1999, p. 26).
126. Teles (2008).
127. Berry (1999, p. 29).
128. Teles (2008, pp. 7–8).
129. Davies (2007).
130. Mayer (1996, p. 127).
131. Berry (1999, p. 1).
132. Berry (1999, p. 60).
133. Gross, Medvetz, and Russell (2011).
134. Kazin (2011, p. xv).
135. Kazin (2011, p. 215).
136. Isserman and Kazin (1989); Braungart and Braungart (1990). YAF alums who became influential conservative activists included Richard Viguerie, Howard Phillips, and Paul Weyrich.
137. Kazin (2011).
138. Isserman and Kazin (1989, p. 235).
139. See Byrne (2012).
140. Harold Meyerson, "The Long March of Bernie's Army," *American Prospect*, Spring 2016, http://prospect.org/article/long-march-bernie's-army.
141. This group is not included in Table 3-1 because it was extinct by the beginning of the time period analyzed.
142. DiSalvo (2012, p. 52).
143. DiSalvo (2012, p. 56).
144. DiSalvo (2012).
145. DiSalvo (2012, p. 44).
146. Andrew (1997, p. 178).
147. Klinker (1994).
148. Klinkner (1994, p. 97).
149. Cowie (2010, p. 88).
150. Klinkner (1994, p. 183).
151. Klinkner (1994, p. 167).
152. Klinkner (1994, p. 207).
153. Klinkner (1994, p. 134).
154. Klinkner (1994, p. 77).
155. Klinkner (1994, p. 113).
156. For a full data description, see Volkens et al. (2013).
157. For a full data description, see Kitschelt and Freeze (2010).
158. The party's average across these dimensions is the highest and its standard deviation is low compared to all other parties.
159. Kitschelt (2000).
160. Kitschelt (2000).
161. Cohen et al. (2008).
162. We use data reported in Grossmann and Dominguez (2009).

163. Cohen et al. (2008).
164. Heaney et al. (2012).
165. Rapoport, McGlennon, and Abramowitz (1986).
166. See Shufeldt (2014).
167. Shufeldt (2014).
168. Koger, Masket, and Noel (2009).
169. Koger, Masket, and Noel (2010).
170. Skinner, Masket, and Dulio (2012).
171. This dataset is summarized in Broockman et al. (2014).
172. Broockman et al. (2014).
173. Cooperman and Crowder-Meyer (2015).
174. Noel (2013).
175. These policy positions are listed in Noel (2013). The columns were not coded for their references to social groups or party constituencies.
176. We use a smoothed line (a weighted average with 25 percent based on the previous platform and 25 percent based on the next platform) to compensate for erratic short-term shifts.
177. The Comparative Manifestos Project only differentiates some topic mentions based on social groups, some based on issue areas, and some based on a combination of the two. Gerring (1998, p. 200) finds that the Democrats began regularly discussing minority issues in their platform in the 1940s and spent up to 20 percent of their platform on the subject by the 1990s (although he could not locate his original codes).
178. Manza (2000).
179. Dochuk (2012); Rieder (1985).
180. See Wald (2015) for Jewish voting over time and in international perspective.
181. Kazin (2011).
182. Ferguson (1989).
183. Cox Richardson (2014).
184. Perlstein (2001); Phillips-Fein (2009).
185. Phillips-Fein (2009).
186. Phillips-Fein (2009, p. 44).
187. Teles (2008).
188. Witko (2014).
189. Hacker and Pierson (2005).
190. Grossmann (2012).
191. Grossmann (2012); Berry (1999).
192. See Grossmann and Dominguez (2009).
193. Noel (2013, 87).
194. Kruse (2005).
195. Klinkner (1994, p. 55).
196. Dochuk (2012).
197. Formisano (2004, p. 10).
198. Formsiano (2004, p. 3).
199. Formisano (2004).
200. Rieder (1985, p. 6).
201. Kruse (2005).
202. Kruse (2005, p. 210).
203. Polsby (2004).
204. Polsby (2004, pp. 97–99).
205. Kruse (2005, p. 6).
206. Kruse (2005, p. 245).

207. Johnston and Shafer (2006).
208. Johnston and Shafer (2006).
209. Johnston and Shafer (2006).
210. Kinder and Kam (2010).
211. The lack of political diversity in academia influences the questions asked and consensus answers that develop, especially when it comes to beliefs about conservatism. See Duarte et al. (2015).
212. For the former view, see Valentino and Sears (2005); for the latter view, see Johnston and Shafer (2006).
213. See Schoenwald (2001). Conservative movement organization materials from this period rarely mentioned race or racial issues.

CHAPTER 4

1. *Hannity and Colmes*, "Obama Guilty by Association?," Fox News Channel, transcript, February 29, 2008.
2. Howard Kurtz, "The Military-Media Complex" *The Washington Post*, April 21, 2008, http://www.washingtonpost.com/wp-dyn/content/article/2008/04/21/AR2008042100776_4.html.
3. Cats R Flyfishn, "Fact Check: Obama and Ayers," *Organizing for Change*, April 17, 2008, https://pennsylvaniaforchange.wordpress.com/2008/08/21/fact-check-obama-and-ayers/.
4. Kurtz, "Military-Media Complex."
5. Kate Phillips, "Palin: Obama Is 'Palling Around with Terrorists," *The Caucus* (blog), *New York Times*, October 4, 2008, http://thecaucus.blogs.nytimes.com/2008/10/04/palin-obama-is-palling-around-with-terrorists/.
6. Jack Cashill, "Who Wrote *Dreams from My Father?*," *American Thinker*, October 9, 2008, http://www.americanthinker.com/articles/2008/10/who_wrote_dreams_from_my_fathe_1.html. For later analysis of the controversy, see Brian Montopoli, "Bill Ayers Book Comment Sets Blogs Abuzz," CBS News, October 7, 2009, http://www.cbsnews.com/news/bill-ayers-book-comment-sets-blogs-abuzz/.
7. Ann Coulter, "Radical Loon When Obama Was Only 47," *Human Events*, October 22, 2008, http://humanevents.com/2008/10/22/radical-loon-when-obama-was-only-47/.
8. Ladd (2011, p. 6).
9. Ladd (2011, p. 43).
10. Ladd (2011, p. 46).
11. Ross (1991); Kabaservice (2004); Geiger (2014).
12. Ross (1991); Kabaservice (2004); Geiger (2014).
13. Gross (2013).
14. Gross (2013, p. 7).
15. See Duarte et al. (2015), along with 33 commentaries, all available at http://bit.ly/1Og1Hnw.
16. Ladd (2011).
17. Ladd (2011, p. 74).
18. Ladd (2011, p. 78).
19. Dochuk (2012).
20. Lucas (2012).
21. Formisano (1991, p. 157).
22. Domke et al. (1999).
23. Jamieson and Cappella (2008, p. 169).
24. Barker and Knight (2000).

25. For a summary, see Ladd (2011).
26. Levendusky (2013, p. 13).
27. Groeling (2013).
28. Ladd (2011).
29. Stroud (2011).
30. Jamieson and Capella (2008).
31. Ladd (2011, p. 90).
32. "Press Widely Criticized, But Trusted More than Other Information Sources," Pew Research Center, September 22, 2011, http://www.people-press.org/2011/09/22/press-widely-criticized-but-trusted-more-than-other-institutions/.
33. Ladd (2011, p. 103).
34. "Political Polarization in the American Public: Section 1: Growing Ideological Consistency," Pew Research Center, June 12, 2014, http://www.people-press.org/2014/06/12/section-1-growing-ideological-consistency/.
35. Ladd (2011, p. 189).
36. Ladd (2011, p. 124).
37. Viguerie and Franke (2004).
38. "The Powell Memo (Also Known as the Powell Manifesto)," *Reclaim Democracy*, n.d., http://reclaimdemocracy.org/powell_memo_lewis/.
39. See Judis (2001). Mark Schmitt offers a more nuanced view of the memo's influence in "The Legend of the Powell Memo," *American Prospect*, April 27, 2005, http://prospect.org/article/legend-powell-memo.
40. Bobbitt (2010); Gross (2013).
41. Gauchat (2015, p. 1)
42. Moreno (2011, p. 18).
43. "Brown/Warren Debate "I'm Not a Student in Your Classroom," YouTube video, 1:38, posted by IPAddress, October 2, 2012, https://www.youtube.com/watch?v=5CFqROUc6TA.
44. Gross (2013, p. 4).
45. Gauchat (2012).
46. Gauchat (2015, p. 1)
47. Weidenbaum (2009, p. 40), citing Harris surveys.
48. Hird (2005).
49. Bimber (1996, p. 5).
50. Hemmer (2010).
51. Lucas (2012).
52. Hemmer (2010).
53. Fred J. Cook, "Radio Right: Hate Clubs of the Air," *The Nation*, May 25, 1964, pp. 523–526.
54. Lucas (2012).
55. Perlstein (2001).
56. Hemmer (2010, p. 6).
57. Hemmer (2010, p. 124).
58. Perlstein (2001, p. 368).
59. Bobbitt (2010).
60. Lucas (2012); Bobbitt (2010).
61. Levin (1986).
62. Bobbitt (2010), citing data gathered by the Center for American Progress.
63. Hemmer (2010, p. 222).
64. Sherman (2014).
65. Meagher (2012).

66. Sherman (2014).
67. Sherman (2014).
68. Bartlett (2015).
69. This quote from Hemmer's forthcoming book is cited in Calmes (2015).
70. Viguerie and Franke (2004).
71. Nash (2006).
72. Viguerie and Franke (2004).
73. Hemmer (2010).
74. Hendershot (2011).
75. Lucas (2012).
76. Lucas (2012).
77. Pickard (2015).
78. Lucas (2012, p. 135).
79. It was not immediately clear that conservatives would benefit from this outcome; organizations like the Pacifica Foundation led the charge to deregulate, and conservatives like Weyrich and Pat Buchanan feared that ending the Fairness Doctrine would enable liberal media to expand. See Lucas (2012).
80. Hindman (2009).
81. Seideman (1986, p. 127).
82. Mayer (2004, p. 88).
83. Lasar (1999).
84. Lasar (1999).
85. Bobbitt (2010).
86. Bobbitt (2010).
87. Mayer (2004).
88. Mayer (2004, p. 103).
89. Viguerie and Franke (2004, p. 341).
90. Sherman (2014).
91. Mayer (2004, p. 101).
92. Bobbitt (2010).
93. Mayer (2004).
94. See "In Changing News Landscape, Even Television Is Vulnerable: Section 4: Demographics and Political Views of News Audiences," Pew Research Center, September 27, 2012, http://www.people-press.org/2012/09/27/section-4-demographics-and-political-views-of-news-audiences/.
95. Mayer (2004, p. 102).
96. Calmes (2015).
97. Calmes (2015).
98. Fones-Wolf (2006).
99. Fones-Wolf (2006).
100. Ostertag (2006).
101. Ostertag (2006).
102. Ostertag (2006).
103. Borsook (2000).
104. Grossmann (2012).
105. Hindman (2009).
106. Hindman (2009); Ladd (2011).
107. Halleck (2003).
108. Vasi et al. (2015).
109. Prior (2013).
110. Prior (2007).

111. Arceneaux and Johnson (2013).
112. Matt Bai, "Cable Guise," *New York Times Magazine*, December 2, 2009, http://www.nytimes.com/2009/12/06/magazine/06fob-wwln-t.html?_r=0.
113. Arceneaux and Johnson (2013).
114. E.g., Stroud (2011).
115. Bartlett (2015); Sherman (2014).
116. Morris (2005).
117. Jamieson and Capella (2008).
118. Viguerie and Franke (2004).
119. Levendusky (2013, p. 12).
120. Calmes (2015).
121. Stroud's coding information is available at http://commstudies.utexas.edu/sites/commstudies.utexas.edu/files/attachments/NicheNewsStroudTalkRadioCoding.pdf.
122. Bennett (2009).
123. This measure understates the partisan difference because Republicans are nearly uniformly conservative, whereas many Democrats are not liberal; Stroud (2011, p. 51).
124. Iyengar and Hahn (2009).
125. Garrett and Stroud (2014).
126. Morris (2005).
127. Grentzkow and Shapiro (2011).
128. Amy Mitchell, Jeffrey Gottfried, Jocelyn Kiley, and Katerina Eva Matsa, "Political Polarization & Media Habits," Pew Research Center, October 21, 2014, http://www.journalism.org/2014/10/21/political-polarization-media-habits/.
129. Mitchell et al., "Political Polarization and Media Habits."
130. Mitchell et al., "Political Polarization and Media Habits."
131. Bakshy, Messing, and Adamic (2015).
132. Mitchell et al., "Political Polarization and Media Habits."
133. David Weigel, "The Torch Is Being Passed to a New Generation of Right-Wing Media," *Bloomberg Politics*, December 1, 2014, http://www.bloomberg.com/politics/features/2014-12-01/the-torch-is-being-passed-to-a-new-generation-of-rightwing-media.
134. Calmes (2015).
135. Lucas (2012).
136. Julian Sanchez, "Frum, Cocktail Parties, and the Threat of Doubt," *Julian Sanchez*, March 26, 2010, http://www.juliansanchez.com/2010/03/26/frum-cocktail-parties-and-the-threat-of-doubt/.
137. Julian Sanchez, "Epistemic Closure, Technology, and the End of Distance," *Julian Sanchez*, April 7, 2010, http://www.juliansanchez.com/2010/04/07/epistemic-closure-technology-and-the-end-of-distance/.
138. Jamieson and Capella (2008).
139. Jamieson and Capella (2008).
140. Jamieson and Capella (2008).
141. Jamieson and Capella (2008, p. 161).
142. Levendusky (2013).
143. Bartlett (2015).
144. Jamieson and Capella (2008, p. 127).
145. Barker (2002).
146. Levendusky (2013, pp. 31–32).
147. Fetterman, Boyd, and Robinson (2015).
148. Hemmer forthcoming, p. 351, quoted in Calmes (2015).
149. Lucas (2012).
150. Jamieson and Capella (2008, p. xiv).

151. Lucas (2012).
152. Lucas (2012).
153. Jamieson and Capella (2008).
154. Lucas (2012).
155. Lucas (2012).
156. Fareed Zakaria, "A Way Out of Our Dysfunctional Politics," *Washington Post*, July 20, 2011, https://www.washingtonpost.com/opinions/a-way-out-of-our-dysfunctional-politics/2011/07/20/gIQATEQcQI_story.html.
157. Jonathan Martin, "Gingrey Apologizes Over Limbaugh," *Politico*, January 28, 2009, http://www.politico.com/story/2009/01/gingrey-apologizes-over-limbaugh-018067.
158. Mike Allen, "Steele to Rush: I'm Sorry," *Politico*, March 2, 2009, http://www.politico.com/story/2009/03/steele-to-rush-im-sorry-019517.
159. Calmes (2015).
160. Meagher (2012).
161. Bobbitt (2010).
162. Molly Ball, "Can Scott Walker Save Himself?," *Atlantic*, September 8, 2015, http://www.theatlantic.com/politics/archive/2015/09/can-scott-walker-save-himself/404128/.
163. Calmes (2015).
164. Jamieson and Capella (2008).
165. Barker (2002).
166. Bolce, De Maio, and Muzzio (1996).
167. Jamieson and Capella (2008, p. x).
168. Jamieson and Capella (2008, p. 3).
169. Matt Bai, "Working for the Working-Class Vote," *New York Times Magazine*. October 15, 2008, http://www.nytimes.com/2008/10/19/magazine/19obama-t.html?ref=magazine.
170. Jonathan Bernstein, "Understanding Fox News," *The New Republic*, October 27, 2010, https://newrepublic.com/article/78720/understanding-fox-news.
171. Tim Dickinson, "How Roger Ailes Built the Fox News Fear Factory," *Rolling Stone*, May 25, 2011, pp. 54–84.
172. David Schoetz, "David Frum on GOP: Now We Work for Fox," ABC News, March 23, 2010, http://blogs.abcnews.com/nightlinedailyline/2010/03/david-frum-on-gop-now-we-work-for-fox.html.
173. Cox Richardson (2014, p. 319).
174. DellaVigna and Kaplan (2007).
175. Hopkins and Ladd (2012).
176. Martin and Yurukoglu (2014).
177. Morris (2007).
178. Tsfati, Stroud, and Chotiner (2013).
179. Hollander (2014).
180. Jamieson and Capella (2008).
181. Classen, Tucker, and Smith (2015).
182. Levendusky (2013, p. 7).
183. Arceneaux and Johnson (2013, p. 103).
184. Clinton and Enamorado (2014).
185. Arceneaux et al. (2015).
186. Arceneaux et al. (2015).
187. David Frum, "Waterloo," *FrumForum*, n.d., http://www.frumforum.com/waterloo-page/.
188. Calmes (2015).
189. Calmes (2015).

190. Jamieson and Capella (2008).
191. Jamieson and Capella (2008).
192. Meagher (2012).
193. Sherman (2014); Levendusky (2013).
194. Skocpol and Williamson (2012).
195. Stroud (2011).
196. Gabriel Sherman, "How Roger Ailes Picked Trump, and Fox News' Audience, over Megyn Kelly," *New York*, August 11, 2015, http://nymag.com/daily/intelligencer/2015/08/fox-news-picked-trump-over-megyn-kelly.html.
197. Ryan Lizza, "Donald Trump's Hostile Takeover of the G.O.P.," *New Yorker*, January 28, 2016, http://www.newyorker.com/news/daily-comment/donald-trumps-hostile-takeover-of-the-g-o-p.
198. Groseclose and Milyo (2005).
199. See Brendan Nyhan, "The Problems with the Groseclose/Milyo Study of Media Bias," *Brendan Nyhan*, December 22, 2005, http://www.brendan-nyhan.com/blog/2005/12/the_problems_wi.html. Nyhan (2012) follows up with a full analysis.
200. Groseclose and Milyo (2005).
201. Nyhan, "Problems with the Groseclose/Milyo Study"; Nyhan (2012).
202. Meagher (2012, p. 470).
203. Medvetz (2012, p. 53.).
204. Medvetz (2012, p. 90).
205. Weisbrot and Mackenzie (2008).
206. Medvetz (2012, p. 17).
207. Paul M. Weyrich, "The Most Important Legacy of Joe Coors," March 24, 2003, http://www.enterstageright.com/archive/articles/0303/0303coors.htm.
208. Medvetz (2012, p. 115).
209. Weidenbaum (2009, p. 29).
210. Meagher (2012).
211. "Jim DeMint's Speech at CPAC 2013," *Daily Signal*, March 14, 2013, http://dailysignal.com//2013/03/14/jim-demints-speech-at-cpac-2013/.
212. Medvetz (2012, p. 104).
213. Meagher (2012).
214. Meagher (2012, p. 472).
215. Rich (2004, p. 21).
216. Medvetz (2012).
217. Medvetz (2012).
218. Campbell and Pedersen (2014, pp. 47–48).
219. Rich (2004, p. 10).
220. Weidenbaum (2009).
221. Groseclose and Milyo (2005).
222. Ronald Reagan, "Remarks to the American Enterprise Institute for Public Policy Research," December 7, 1988, American Presidency Project, http://www.presidency.ucsb.edu/ws/?pid=35239.
223. Reagan, "Remarks to the American Enterprise Institute."
224. Abelson (2009).
225. Medvetz (2012, p. 5).
226. Medvetz (2012).
227. Medvetz (2012).
228. Stefancic and Delgado (1996).
229. Bartlett (2015).
230. Fischer (1991)

231. Fischer (1991, pp. 340–341).
232. Jacques, Dunlap, and Freeman (2008).
233. Boykoff and Boykoff (2004).
234. McDonald (2014).
235. Grossmann (2012).
236. Stefancic and Delgado (1996).
237. Stefancic and Delgado (1996).
238. Critchlow (1985).
239. Medvetz (2012).
240. Johnson and Van Ostern (2012).
241. Johnson and Van Ostern (2012, pp. 12–13).
242. Meagher (2012, p. 472).
243. Stefancic and Delgado (1996).
244. Medvetz (2012, p. 129).
245. Brint et al. (2008).
246. Turk-Bicakci (2007).
247. Rojas (2007).
248. Arthur (2011).
249. Levine (1996).
250. Medvetz (2012, p. 171).
251. Medvetz (2012).
252. Rich (2004, p. 10).
253. Stefancic and Delgado (1996, pp. 145–146).
254. Rich and Weaver (1998, p. 249).
255. Rich (2004, p. 79).
256. Rich (2004, pp. 190–197).
257. Weidenbaum (2009).
258. Esterling (2004).
259. Campbell and Pedersen (2014).
260. Campbell and Pedersen (2014, p. 46).
261. Mooney (2006); Mooney (2012).
262. Andrew C. Revkin, "Politics Reasserts Itself in the Debate Over Climate Change and Its Hazards," *New York Times*, August 5, 2003, http://www.nytimes.com/2003/08/05/science/politics-reasserts-itself-in-the-debate-over-climate-change-and-its-hazards.html?pagewanted=all.
263. Bimber (1996).
264. Baumgartner and Jones (2015).
265. Lee Drutman and Steven Teles, "A New Agenda for Political Reform," *Washington Monthly*, March/April/May 2015, http://www.washingtonmonthly.com/magazine/marchaprilmay_2015/features/a_new_agenda_for_political_ref054226.php?page=all.
266. Bimber (1996, p. 51).
267. McCright and Dunlap (2010).
268. Mooney (2012), citing Jost et al. (2003).
269. Mooney (2012), citing Nyhan and Reifler (2010).
270. Mooney (2012), citing Tetlock (1983).
271. Blank and Shaw (2015).
272. Nisbet, Cooper, and Garrett (2015).
273. Schuldt, Roh, and Schwarz (2015).
274. Campbell and Kay (2014).
275. Meagher (2012).

276. Lyndsey Layton, "Conservatives Convinced College Board to Rewrite American History," *Washington Post*, July 30, 2015, http://www.washingtonpost.com/local/education/college-board-rewrites-american-history/2015/07/30/cadadd4c-36d1-11e5-b673-1df005a0fb28_story.html?tid=sm_fb.

277. Layton, "Conservatives Convinced College Board."

278. Republican National Committee Counsel's Office, "Resolution Concerning Advanced Placement U.S. History (APUSH)," https://cdn.gop.com/docs/RESOLUTION_CONCERNING_ADVANCED_PLACEMENT_US_HISTORY_APUSH.pdf.

279. Wyatt Massey, "New AP U.S. History Teaching Framework Released After Controversy," CNN, July 31, 2015, http://www.cnn.com/2015/07/31/living/ap-history-united-states-curriculum-change/.

280. Peter Wood, "AP History and Us," National Association of Scholars, August 6, 2015, https://www.nas.org/articles/ap_history_and_us.

281. Wood, "AP History and Us."

CHAPTER 5

1. Benjy Sarlin and Alex Seitz-Wald, "Hello From the Other Side: When 2016 Reporters Swapped Beats," MSNBC, January 12, 2016, http://www.msnbc.com/msnbc/hello-the-other-side-when-2016-reporters-swapped-beats.

2. Maeve Reston, "Romney Attributes Loss to 'Gifts' Obama Gave Minorities," *Los Angeles Times*, November 15, 2012, http://articles.latimes.com/2012/nov/15/nation/la-na-romney-donors-20121115.

3. John Dickerson, "Why Romney Never Saw It Coming," *Slate*, November 9, 2012, http://www.slate.com/articles/news_and_politics/politics/2012/11/why_romney_was_surprised_to_lose_his_campaign_had_the_wrong_numbers_bad.html.

4. Ginger Gibson, "GOP Returns Romney 'Gifts,'" *Politico*, November 15, 2012, http://www.politico.com/news/stories/1112/83938.html.

5. White (1973, p. 299).

6. Mayer (1996, p. 126).

7. Polsby (1983).

8. Rae (1989, p. 91).

9. Rae (1989, p. 131).

10. Rae (1989, p. 131).

11. Rae (1989, p. 114).

12. Gerald R. Ford news conference, May 26, 1976, http://www.presidency.ucsb.edu/ws/?pid=6061

13. Ronald Reagan, "To Restore America, Ronald Reagan's Campaign Address," March 31, 1976, Ronald Reagan Presidential Library and Museum, http://www.reagan.utexas.edu/archives/reference/3.31.76.html.

14. Reagan, "To Restore America."

15. Reagan, "To Restore America."

16. Dallek (1999, p. 55).

17. See Mann (2009).

18. "Transcript: Read the Full Text of the Second Republican Debate," *Time*, September 16, 2015, http://time.com/4037239/second-republican-debate-transcript-cnn/.

19. Nick Gass, "Watch the GOP Contenders Try to Out-Reagan Each Other," *Politico*, September 14, 2015, http://www.politico.com/story/2015/09/ronald-reagan-gop-candidates-2016-legacy-213597.

20. "Transcript: Read Full Text of Gov. John Kasich's Campaign Launch," *Time*, July 21, 2015, http://time.com/3966802/john-kasich-campaign-launch-transcript/.

21. "Guests: Donald Trump, Trump Organization CEO," Fox News Channel, April 14, 2011, http://www.foxnews.com/on-air/hannity/print/transcript/exclusive-donald-trump-talks-2012-calls-obama-worst-president-ever

22. "Transcript: Richard Viguerie (Conservatives Betrayed by Bush, Jul 30 2007)," *Thom Hartmann program*, July 30, 2007, http://www.thomhartmann.com/blog/2007/07/transcript-richard-viguerie-conservatives-betrayed-bush-jul-30-2007.

23. Palmer (1997, p. 22).

24. "1988: 'Thank You, New Hampshire,'" *Union Leader* (Manchester, NH), May 3, 2011, http://www.unionleader.com/apps/pbcs.dll/article?AID=/99999999/NEWS0605/110509961.

25. Edwards (2002).

26. Michael Grunwald, "Grover Norquist Isn't Finished," *Politico*, October 21, 2015, http://www.politico.com/agenda/story/2015/10/grover-norquist-tax-interview-000288.

27. Grunwald, "Grover Norquist Isn't Finished."

28. James Pethokoukis, "Tax Cuts Aren't Everything," *National Review Online*, April 15, 2013, http://www.nationalreview.com/article/345558/tax-cuts-arent-everything-james-pethokoukis.

29. Mariniss and Weisskopf (1996, p. 142).

30. Busch and Ceasar (2001, p. 87).

31. Brian Knowlton, "Republican Says Bush Panders to the 'Agents of Intolerance': McCain Takes Aim at Religious Right," *New York Times*, February 29, 2000, http://www.ny-times.com/2000/02/29/news/29iht-bush.2.t_9.html.

32. "Los Angeles Times Poll, Study #435/Exit Poll, New Hampshire Primary Election," *Los Angeles Times*, February 1, 2000, http://www.latimesinteractive.com/pdfarchive/stat_sheets/la-timespoll435ss.pdf.

33. Andrew E. Smith and Clark Hubbard, "First in the Nation: Lessons Learned from New Hampshire," *Public Perspective*, May/June 2000, pp. 46–49, http://ropercenter.cornell.edu/public-perspective/ppscan/113/113046.pdf.

34. Busch and Ceasar (2001, pp. 87–88).

35. Busch and Ceasar (2001, p. 88).

36. Mark J. Rozell, " . . . Or as Influential as Ever?," *Washington Post*, March 1, 2000, https://www.washingtonpost.com/archive/opinions/2000/03/01/or-influential-as-ever/e0638920-009c-4eb6-ab38-fbdfa37a9a59/.

37. "Transcript of the Fox News Republican Presidential Candidates Debate," *New York Times*, September 5, 2007, http://www.nytimes.com/2007/09/05/us/politics/06text.html?pagewanted=10;oref=slogin&_r=1.

38. James Prichard, "McCain Says He Would Veto Pork Spending," Associated Press, July 24, 2007, http://www.washingtonpost.com/wp-dyn/content/article/2007/07/24/AR2007072401482.html.

39. Tax Policy Center, "The Romney Tax Plan," March 1, 2012, http://taxpolicycenter.org/taxtopics/upload/Romney-Tax-Plan_March-1-2.pdf.

40. Susan Page and Jackie Kucinich, "Perry, Romney and Others Wrangle over Immigration in Debate," *USA Today*, September 23, 2011, http://usatoday30.usatoday.com/news/politics/story/2011-09-22/gop-debate-florida/50518542/1.

41. Amy Bingham, "The 'Moderate' Skeletons in Mitt Romney's Past," ABC News, January 17, 2012, http://abcnews.go.com/Politics/OTUS/moderate-skeletons-mitt-romneys-past/story?id=15373893.

42. "Republican Debate Transcript, Tampa, Florida, January 2012." Council on Foreign Relations, January 23, 2012, http://www.cfr.org/elections/republican-debate-transcript-tampa-florida-january-2012/p27180.

43. Institute of Politics at the Harvard Kennedy School (2013, p. 57).
44. Douthat and Salam (2008).
45. "Against Trump," *National Review*, January 21, 2016, http://www.nationalreview.com/article/430137/donald-trump-conservative-movement-menace.
46. Molly Ball, "Why D.C. Hates Ted Cruz," *The Atlantic*, January 26, 2016, http://www.theatlantic.com/politics/archive/2016/01/why-dc-hates-ted-cruz/426915/.
47. "Transcript: Republican Presidential Debate," *New York Times*, November 11, 2015, http://www.nytimes.com/2015/11/11/us/politics/transcript-republican-presidential-debate.html.
48. Conor Friedersdorf, "The Defining Moments of the GOP Debate," *Atlantic*, August 12, 2011, http://www.theatlantic.com/politics/archive/2011/08/the-defining-moments-of-the-gop-debate/243502/.
49. Lichtenstein (1989, p. 129).
50. Busch (1997, p. 90).
51. Klinkner (1994, p. 106).
52. "Presidential Vote 2 Major Parties 1948–2012," American National Election Studies, http://www.electionstudies.org/nesguide/2ndtable/t9a_1_2.htm.
53. "Kennedy Declares Presidential Bid," YouTube video, 6:26, posted by ABC News, August 26, 2009, https://www.youtube.com/watch?v=9-UYpwtH0pg.
54. Mayer (2003, p. 97).
55. Jeff Greenfield, "Remember 1984," *Slate*, September 7, 2007, http://www.slate.com/articles/news_and_politics/politics/2007/09/remember_1984.html.
56. "Announcement Speech, Old State House, Little Rock, Arkansas," Bill Clinton for President, October 3, 1991, http://www.4president.org/speeches/billclinton1992announcement.htm.
57. George J. Church, "Is Bill Clinton for Real?," *Time*, January 27, 1992, http://www.cnn.com/ALLPOLITICS/1996/analysis/back.time/9601/29/index.shtml.
58. "Brown Presidential Campaign Announcement," C-SPAN, October 21, 1991, http://www.c-span.org/video/?22189-1/brown-presidential-campaign-announcement.
59. Robin Toner, "While Others Shrank from the Race, Clinton Clung to Dream of Presidency," *New York Times*, July 12, 1992, http://www.nytimes.com/1992/07/12/us/1992-campaign-road-nomination-while-others-shrank-race-clinton-clung-dream.html.
60. "Dem. Primary: New Hampshire," archived version of CNN website, https://web.archive.org/web/20000815063528/http://www.cnn.com/ELECTION/2000/primaries/NH/poll.dem.html.
61. "Results, Exit Polls and Delegate Estimate: Election 2000 Primaries/Caucuses," archived version of CNN website, https://web.archive.org/web/20000803200408/http://www.cnn.com/ELECTION/2000/primaries/.
62. "Entrance Polls: Iowa," CNN, January 19, 2004, http://www.cnn.com/ELECTION/2004/primaries/pages/epolls/IA/; "Exit Polls: New Hampshire," CNN, January 27, 2004, http://www.cnn.com/ELECTION/2004/primaries/pages/epolls/NH/.
63. Dan Balz, "Dean's Rivals Question Campaign's Tone in Iowa," *Washington Post*, November 16, 2003, p. A6.
64. "Democratic Debate Transcript, New Hampshire," Council on Foreign Relations, September 26, 2007, http://www.cfr.org/elections/democratic-debate-transcript-new-hampshire/p14313.
65. Celeste Katz, "Sarcasm Reigns as Hillary Clinton Attacks Barack Obama's Campaign," *New York Daily News*, February 25, 2008, http://www.nydailynews.com/news/politics/sarcasm-reigns-hillary-clinton-attacks-barack-obama-campaign-article-1.307892.

66. George Packer, "The Choice," *New Yorker,* January 28, 2008, http://www.newyorker.com/magazine/2008/01/28/the-choice-6.

67. Fisher (2011, p. 502).

68. "Exit Polls: New Hampshire," CNN, January 8, 2008, http://www.cnn.com/ELECTION/2008/primaries/results/epolls/index.html#NHDEM.

69. "Exit Polls: South Carolina," CNN, January 26, 2008, http://www.cnn.com/ELECTION/2008/primaries/results/epolls/index.html#SCDEM.

70. Fisher (2011).

71. Stephen Stromberg, "The Moment When Hillary Clinton Won the First Democratic Debate," *Washington Post,* October 13, 2015, https://www.washingtonpost.com/blogs/post-partisan/wp/2015/10/13/the-moment-when-hillary-clinton-won-the-first-democratic-debate/.

72. "Democratic Candidates Debate in Milwaukee, Wisconsin," February 11, 2016, http://www.presidency.ucsb.edu/ws/index.php?pid=111520

73. Patrick Healy and Amy Chozick, "Minority Voters Push Hillary Clinton to Victories," *New York Times,* March 1, 2016, http://www.nytimes.com/2016/03/02/us/politics/democratic-primary-results.html.

74. John Dickerson, "Why Senate Republicans Hate Ted Cruz," *Slate,* September 27, 2013, http://www.slate.com/articles/news_and_politics/politics/2013/09/ted_cruz_is_despised_by_senate_republicans_a_list_of_the_reasons_gop_senators.html.

75. Harry Enten, "Racial Voting Lines in Hawaii Senate Primary Leave Pollsters Mostly Clueless," *FiveThirtyEight.com,* August 8, 2014, http://fivethirtyeight.com/datalab/racial-voting-lines-in-hawaii-senate-primary-leave-pollsters-mostly-clueless/.

76. Data from Boatright (2013, 2014).

77. Data from Preuhs and Juenke (2011).

78. Azari (2014).

79. See Jarvis (2004).

80. Rhodes and Johnson (2015).

81. See Fowler, Franz, and Ridout (2016).

82. Henderson (2013).

83. Categorizing taxes as a specific problem rather than as a concern with the size of government changes the party averages to reduce the differences between the parties but does not change the relative emphasis of each party.

84. We use data updated from Rhodes and Johnson (2014).

85. "'Real Change' Ad," YouTube video, 0:31, posted by BarackObama.com, September 11, 2008, https://www.youtube.com/watch?v=R3F18zVblJ8.

86. We use data from Druckman, Kifer, and Parkin (2009).

87. Democratic National Committee website, http://www.democrats.org; Republican National Committee website, http://www.gop.org.

88. Rachel Weiner, "Romney, Citing Safety Net, Says He's 'Not Concerned About the Very Poor," *Washington Post,* February 1, 2012, https://www.washingtonpost.com/blogs/the-fix/post/romney-im-not-concerned-with-the-very-poor/2012/02/01/gIQAva-jShQ_blog.html.

89. Mother Jones News Teams, "Full Transcript of the Mitt Romney Secret Video," *Mother Jones,* September 19, 2012, http://www.motherjones.com/politics/2012/09/full-transcript-mitt-romney-secret-video.

90. Aliyah Shahid, "Mitt Romney to Students Who Want to Start Their Own Business: Borrow Money from Your Parents," *New York Daily News,* April 28, 2012, http://www.nydailynews.com/news/election-2012/mitt-romney-students-start-business-borrow-money-parents-article-1.1069096.

91. Transcript of Bill Clinton's Speech to the Democratic National Convention, *New York Times*, September 5, 2012, http://www.nytimes.com/2012/09/05/us/politics/transcript-of-bill-clintons-speech-to-the-democratic-national-convention.html.
92. We use data summarized by Hayes (2005).
93. Hayes (2005).
94. We use data from Egan (2013).
95. Shufeldt (2014).
96. Theodoridis (2015).
97. Shufeldt (2014).
98. Buchler (2015).
99. Henderson (2013).

CHAPTER 6

1. "Speaker Boehner: 'It's Been an Honor to Serve,'" press release, September 25, 2015, http://www.speaker.gov/press-release/speaker-boehner-it-s-been-honor-serve.
2. "How a Prominent Boehner Critic Sees Congress' Future Without Him," National Public Radio, September 25, 2015, http://www.npr.org/2015/09/25/443489238/how-a-prominent-boehner-critic-sees-congress-future-without-him.
3. Full background on the conflict can be found in Ryan Lizza, "A House Divided," *New Yorker*, December 14, 2015, http://www.newyorker.com/magazine/2015/12/14/a-house-divided.
4. An analysis of Ryan's political position based on DW-Nominate first- and second-dimension scores can be found in Harry Enten, "What Paul Ryan Has that Kevin McCarthy and John Boehner Don't," *FiveThirtyEight*, October 22, 2015, http://fivethirtyeight.com/datalab/what-paul-ryan-has-that-kevin-mccarthy-and-john-boehner-dont/.
5. Mayhew (1974); Fenno (1973); but see Mayhew (1966) for an analysis of differences.
6. See Cox and McCubbins (2005); Rohde (1991); and Krehbiel (1998) for these three views, which are often in contention but agree on this point.
7. McCarty, Poole, and Rosenthal (2006).
8. "Toward a More Responsible Two-Party System: A Report of the Committee on Political Parties, American Political Science Association," *American Political Science Review* 44 (supplement), September 1950.
9. Ranney (1951, p. 499).
10. Mann and Ornstein (2008).
11. Sabatier (2007).
12. The advocacy coalition framework is described in Sabatier and Jenkins-Smith (1993); punctuated equilibrium theory is described in Baumgartner and Jones (1993); independent streams theory is outlined in Kingdon (1984). Sabatier (2007) provides summaries. Grossmann and Hopkins (2014) analyze these theories' relationship to theories of party asymmetry.
13. Weisbrot and Mackenzie (2008); Grossmann (2014).
14. Zelizer (2012, p. 285).
15. Hacker and Pierson (2005, p. 2).
16. Mann and Ornstein (2012, p. x).
17. Mann and Ornstein (2012, p. x).
18. Coleman (1999).
19. Erikson, Mackuen, and Stimson (2002).
20. Data are from Grossmann (2014).
21. Mayhew (2005); Erikson, Mackuen, and Stimson (2002).
22. Data are from Grossmann (2014).

23. Pierson (1994, p. 18).
24. Schaller (2015, p. 234).
25. Perlstein (2001, p. 64).
26. DiSalvo (2012, p. 139).
27. Vogel (1998).
28. Eriksson and Strimling (2015).
29. Zelizer (2012, p. 75).
30. Baumgartner and Jones (2015).
31. Volden and Wiseman (2014).
32. Cohen (2012).
33. Mayhew (2011, Table 2.1).
34. Mann and Ornstein (2012).
35. *Congressional Quarterly* kept track of the appearance of the coalition and its victories until the 1990s.
36. Polsby (2004, p. 10).
37. Polsby (2004, p. 13).
38. Mayhew (2011, p. 120).
39. Matthews (1960).
40. Sinclair (1989).
41. Polsby (2004, p. 14).
42. Lowi (1969, p. 70).
43. Feulner (1983, p. 28).
44. Zelizer (2004).
45. Zelizer (2004, p. 264).
46. Grossmann (2014).
47. Ornstein (1975, p. 90).
48. Rohde (1991, p. 19).
49. Rohde (1991).
50. Zelizer (2012, p. 208).
51. Zelizer (2012, p. 209).
52. Zelizer (2012, p. 209).
53. Sinclair (1995, p. 36).
54. Sinclair (1995, pp. 42–43).
55. Feulner (1983, p. 29).
56. Polsby (2004).
57. Rohde (1991).
58. Sinclair (1989).
59. Sinclair (1989).
60. Sinclair (1989).
61. Sinclair (1989, p. 208).
62. Zelizer (2004, p. 204).
63. Smith (1989).
64. Rohde (1991, p. 158).
65. Zelizer (2004, p. 266).
66. Rohde (1991, p. 50).
67. Singh (1998, p. 51).
68. Singh (1998, Table 6.1).
69. Singh (1998, p. 179).
70. Sinclair (1995, p. 119).
71. Hill (1995).
72. Schaller (2015, p. 53).

73. Schaller (2015, p. 93).
74. Lublin and Voss (2003).
75. Frymer (1999, p. 177).
76. Baker and Cook (2005, p. 227).
77. Rocha et al. (2010).
78. Gamble (2007).
79. Minta (2011).
80. Grose (2011).
81. Juenke and Preuhs (2012).
82. Juenke and Preuhs (2012).
83. Griffin (2014).
84. Griffin (2014).
85. Anderson (2007).
86. These data were provided directly by Jennifer Nicoll Victor and categorized by us. They were analyzed in Ringe and Victor (2013).
87. Lynch, Madonna, and Roberts (2012).
88. Hammond (1998, p. 32).
89. Rohde (1991, p. 124).
90. Hammond (1998).
91. Hammond (1998).
92. Hammond (1998, p. 187).
93. Polsby (2004, p. 55).
94. Feulner (1983, p. 25).
95. Feulner (1983, p. 30).
96. Feulner (1983, p. 3).
97. Feulner (1983, p. 49).
98. Feulner (1983, p. 53).
99. Kondracke and Barnes (2015).
100. Ornstein, Peabody, and Rohde (1989).
101. Rohde (1991, p. 121).
102. Zelizer (2012, p. 266).
103. Polsby (2004, p. 115).
104. Peter C. Stuart, "Why Reagan Is Getting Capitol Hill Endorsements," *Christian Science Monitor*, April 25, 1980, http://www.csmonitor.com/1980/0425/042552.html.
105. "The Long March of Newt Gingrich," *Frontline*, PBS, http://www.pbs.org/wgbh/pages/frontline/newt/.
106. Jacobs and Zelizer (2011, pp. 83–85).
107. Mann and Ornstein (2012, p. x).
108. Polsby (2004, p. 126).
109. Zelizer (2004).
110. Zelizer (2004, p. 214).
111. Zelizer (2012, p. 271).
112. Zelizer (2012, p. 271).
113. Theriault (2013).
114. Zelizer (2012, p. 272).
115. Zelizer (2004, p. 204).
116. "House Session," C-SPAN, May 15, 1984, http://www.c-span.org/video/?171083-1/house-session.
117. Rohde (1991, p. 131).
118. Connelly and Pitney (1994, p. 8).
119. "Long March of Newt Gingrich."

120. Critchlow (2004, p. 719).

121. Theriault (2013, p. 27).

122. Zelizer (2012).

123. Zelizer (2012).

124. Tomz and Van Houweling (2012).

125. Polsby (2004, p. 141).

126. Gingrich (1998, p. 37).

127. Howard and Roberts (2015).

128. Howard and Roberts (2015).

129. Theriault (2013, p. 172).

130. Schaller (2015, p. xi).

131. Fenno (1997, p. 42).

132. Crespin, Gold, and Rohde (2006, pp. 153–154).

133. Maraniss and Weisskopf (1996).

134. Schaller (2015, p. 115).

135. Schaller (2015, p. 117).

136. Cox Richardson (2014).

137. Zelizer (2012, p. 284).

138. Critchlow (2011).

139. Draper (2013).

140. Ben Smith, "Health Reform Foes Plan Obama's 'Waterloo,'" *Politico*, July 17, 2009, http://www.politico.com/blogs/ben-smith/2009/07/health-reform-foes-plan-obamas-waterloo-019961.

141. Mann and Ornstein (2012, p. x).

142. Draper (2013).

143. Mann and Ornstein (2012, p. x).

144. Matt Kibbe, "Fighting a Hostile Takeover of Freedom's Party," *Politico*, November 12, 2013, http://politi.co/1pMFUWA.

145. Heritage Action, "Heritage Action Releases Legislative Scorecard," press release, August 25, 2011, http://heritageaction.com/2011/08/heritage-action-releases-legislative- scorecard/.

146. Eliza Newlin Carney, "Keeping Score: The Power of Lawmaker 'Report Cards,'" *CQ Weekly*, January 19, 2013, http://public.cq.com/docs/weeklyreport/weeklyreport-000004207216.html.

147. Jim Vandehei, Mike Allen, and Jake Sherman, "Double Trouble: House GOP Eyes Default, Shutdown," *Politico*, January 13, 2013, http://politi.co/VmHVxp.

148. Molly K. Hooper, "Fearing Primaries, Republican Members Opted to Shun Boehner's 'Plan B,'" *The Hill*, December 22, 2012, <http://thehill.com/homenews/house/274407-fearing-primaries-gop-members-opted-to-shun-boehners-plan-b>.

149. Rohde (1991).

150. John Boehner Delivers Remarks at Election Night Results Watch, *ABC News*, November 2, 2010, http://abcnews.go.com/Politics/house-republican-leader-john-boehner-delivers-remarks-election/story?id=12040162.

151. The content analysis procedures used here match those used in prior chapters.

152. These letters appear online at http://dearcolleague.us/. We scraped them off the website and coded the text.

153. Wood (2009).

154. Druckman and Jacobs (2015, p. 57).

155. Druckman and Jacobs (2015, p. 59).

156. Zelizer (2012, p. 124).

157. Druckman and Jacobs (2015, p. 49).

158. Pierson (1994, p. 69).

159. Pierson (1994).
160. Harris (2005, p. 18).
161. Harris (2005, p. 78).
162. Harris (2005, p. 261).
163. Harris (2005, p. 436).
164. Zelizer (2012, p. 97).
165. Light (1999, p. 36). The estimate was based on 1997 survey data.
166. Light (1999, p. 19).
167. Morgan and Campbell (2011, p. 5).
168. Light (1999, p. 489).
169. Light (1999).
170. Morgan and Campbell (2011).
171. Morgan and Campbell (2011).
172. Morgan and Campbell (2011).
173. Morgan and Campbell (2011, p. 224).
174. Morgan and Campbell (2011).
175. Steven Teles, "Kludgeocracy in America," *National Affairs*, Fall 2013, pp. 97–114, http://www.nationalaffairs.com/publications/detail/kludgeocracy-inamerica.
176. Hacker (2002).
177. Hacker (2002, p. 16).
178. Hacker (2002).
179. Hacker (2002, p. 22).
180. Hacker (2002, p. 222).
181. Howard (1997).

CHAPTER 7

1. Perrett et al. (1999).
2. Draper (2013, p. xviii).
3. Carl Hulse and Adam Nagourney, "Senate G.O.P. Leader Finds Weapon in Unity," *New York Times*, March 17, 2010, p. A13.
4. Major Garrett, "Top GOP Priority: Make Obama a One-Term President," *National Journal*, October 23, 2010.
5. Karen Tumulty, "The Health-Care Talks: Will Obama Get More Involved?," *Time*, May 5, 2009, http://content.time.com/time/politics/article/0,8599,1895706,00.html.
6. Ginger Gibson, "Right Turns on GOP Obamacare Bill," *Politico*, April 23, 2013, http://www.politico.com/story/2013/04/conservatives-turn-on-gop- obamacare-bill- 090531.
7. Sean Trende, "What Cantor's Loss and Graham's Win Mean," *RealClearPolitics*, June 11, 2014, http://www.realclearpolitics.com/articles/2014/06/11/what_cantors_loss_and_grahams_win_mean_122944.html.
8. Brian Beutler, "The Rehabilitationists," *New Republic*, August 30, 2015, https://newrepublic.com/article/122645/rehabilitationists-libertarian-movement-undo-new-deal.
9. Jonah Goldberg, "After Years of False Alarms, the 'Conservative Crackup' Has Arrived," *National Review*, January 27, 2016, http://www.nationalreview.com/article/430324/donald-trump-conservative-crackup-here.
10. Pew Research Center, "Changing Face of America Helps Assure Obama Victory," November 7, 2012, http://www.people-press.org/2012/11/07/changing-face-of-america-helps-assure-obama-victory/.
11. Transcript: Illinois Senate Candidate Barack Obama, *Washington Post*, July 27, 2004, http://www.washingtonpost.com/wp-dyn/articles/A19751-2004Jul27.html.

12. Remarks of President Barack Obama — State of the Union as Delivered," January 13, 2016, https://www.whitehouse.gov/the-press-office/2016/01/12/remarks-president-barack-obama---prepared-delivery-state-union-address.
13. Muirhead (2014, pp. 209–211).
14. E. J. Dionne Jr., "Dukakis Promises Competence and Daring at 'Next Frontier'; Party Ratifies Bentsen Choice," *New York Times*, July 22, 1988, http://www.nytimes.com/1988/07/22/us/democrats-atlanta-dukakis-promises-competence-daring-next-frontier-party.html.
15. Abramowitz and Webster (2015).

REFERENCES

Abelson, Donald E. 2009. *Do Think Tanks Matter? Assessing the Impact of Public Policy Institutes.* Montreal: McGill-Queen's University Press.

Abramowitz, Alan I. 2010. *The Disappearing Center: Engaged Citizens, Polarization, and American Democracy.* New Haven, CT: Yale University Press.

———2013. "From Strom to Barack: Race, Ideology, and the Transformation of the Southern Party System." *American Review of Politics* 34 (3): 207–336.

Abramowitz, Alan I., and Kyle L. Saunders. 2006. "Exploring the Bases of Partisanship in the American Electorate: Social Identity vs. Ideology." *Political Research Quarterly* 59 (2): 175–187.

———2008. "Is Polarization a Myth?" *Journal of Politics* 70 (2): 542–555.

Abramowitz, Alan I., and Steven Webster. 2015. "All Politics Is National: The Rise of Negative Partisanship and the Nationalization of U.S. House and Senate Elections in the 21st Century." Working Paper. http://stevenwwebster.com/research/all_politics_is_national.pdf.

Acheson, Dean. 1955. *A Democrat Looks at His Party.* New York: Harper.

Adler, Scott E., and John D. Wilkerson. 2014. The Congressional Bills Project. www.congressionalbills.org.

Akst, Daniel. 2012. "The Port Huron Statement: A Manifesto at 50." *Wilson Quarterly* Spring. http://wilsonquarterly.com/quarterly/spring-2012-the-age-of-connection/port-huron-statement-manifesto-at-50/.

Aldrich, John. 1995. *Why Parties? The Origin and Transformation of Political Parties in America.* Chicago: University of Chicago Press.

Anderson, Sarah. 2007. "The Green Machine: Environmental Constituents and Congressional Voting." Working Paper. http://fiesta.bren.ucsb.edu/~sanderson/greenmachine.pdf.

Andrew, John A., III. 1997. *The Other Side of the Sixties: Young Americans for Freedom and the Rise of Conservative Politics.* New Brunswick, NJ: Rutgers University Press.

Arceneaux, Kevin, and Martin Johnson. 2013. *Changing Minds or Changing Channels?: Partisan News in an Age of Choice.* Chicago: University of Chicago Press.

Arceneaux, Kevin, Martin Johnson, Rene Lindstadt, and Ryan J. Vander Wielen. 2016. "The Influence of the News Media on Political Elites: Investigating Strategic Responsiveness in Congress. *American Journal of Political Science* 60 (1): 5–29.

Arthur, Mikaila Lemonik. 2011. *Student Activism and Curricular Change in Higher Education.* Burlington, VT: Ashgate Publishing.

Azari, Julia. 2014. *Delivering the People's Message: The Changing Politics of the Presidential Mandate.* Ithaca, NY: Cornell University Press.

Bakshy, Eytan, Solomon Messing, and Lada A. Adamic. 2015. "Exposure to Ideologically Diverse News and Opinion on Facebook." *Science* 328 (6,239): 1130–1132.

Baldassarri, Delia, and Amir Goldberg. 2014. "Neither Ideologues Nor Agnostics: Alternative Voters' Belief System in an Age of Partisan Politics." *American Journal of Sociology* 120 (1): 45–95.

Baker, Andy, and Corey Cook. 2005. "Representing Black Interests and Promoting Black Culture: The Importance of African American Descriptive Representation in the U.S. House." *Du Bois Review* 2 (2): 227–246.

Barker, David C. 2002. *Rushed to Judgment: Talk Radio, Persuasion, and American Political Behavior.* New York: Columbia University Press.

Barker, David, and Kathleen Knight. 2000. "Political Talk Radio and Public Opinion." *Public Opinion Quarterly* 64 (2): 149–170.

Barreto, Matt A., and Francisco I. Pedraza. 2009. "The Renewal and Persistence of Group Identification in American Politics." *Electoral Studies* 28 (4): 595–605.

Bartels, Larry M. 2000. Partisanship and Voting Behavior, 1952–1996. *American Journal of Political Science* 44 (1): 35–50.

Bartlett, Bruce. 2015. "How Fox News Changed American Media and Political Dynamics." Social Science Research Network Working Paper. http://papers.ssrn.com/sol3/papers.cfm?abstract_id=2604679.

Baumgartner, Frank R., and Bryan D. Jones. 1993. *Agendas and Instability in American Politics.* Chicago: University of Chicago Press.

———— 2015. *The Politics of Information: Problem Definition and the Course of Public Policy in America.* Chicago: University of Chicago Press.

Bawn, Kathleen, Martin Cohen, David Karol, Seth Masket, Hans Noel, and John Zaller. 2012. "A Theory of Political Parties: Groups, Policy Demands and Nominations in American Politics." *Perspectives on Politics* 10 (3): 571–597.

Bennett, Stephen Earl. 2009. "Who Listens to Rush Limbaugh's Radio Program and the Relationship Between Listening to Limbaugh and Knowledge of Public Affairs, 1994–2006." *Journal of Radio and Audio Media* 16 (1): 66–82.

Berry, Jeffrey M. 1999. *The New Liberalism: The Rising Power of Citizen Groups.* Washington, D.C.: Brookings Institution Press.

Berry, Jeffrey M., and Sarah Sobieraj. 2014. *The Outrage Industry: Political Opinion Media and the New Incivility.* New York: Oxford University Press.

Bimber, Bruce. 1996. *The Politics of Expertise in Congress: The Rise and Fall of the Office of Technology Assessment.* Albany: State University of New York Press.

Blank, Joshua M., and Daron Shaw. 2015. "Does Partisanship Shape Attitudes Toward Science and Public Policy? The Case for Ideology and Religion." *Annals of the American Academy of Political and Social Science* 658 (1): 18–35.

Boatright, Robert G. 2013. *Getting Primaried: The Changing Politics of Congressional Primary Challengers.* Ann Arbor: University of Michigan Press.

———— 2014. "The 2014 Congressional Primaries in Context." Paper presented at the Brookings Institution, Washington, D.C., September 30.

Bobbitt, Randy. 2010. *Us Against Them: The Political Culture of Talk Radio.* Lanham, MD: Lexington Books.

Bolce, Louis, Gerald DeMaio, and Douglas Muzzio. 1996. "Dial-In Democracy: Talk Radio and the 1994 Election." *Political Science Quarterly* 111 (3): 457–481.

Borsook, Paulina. 2000. *Cyberselfish: A Critical Romp Through the Terribly Libertarian Culture of High Tech.* London: Little, Brown and Company.

Boykoff, Maxwell T., and Jules M. Boykoff. 2004. "Balance as Bias: Global Warming and the US Prestige Press." *Global Environmental Change* 14: 125–136.

Braungart, Margaret M., and Richard G. Braungart. 1990. "The Life-Course Development of Left- and Right-Wing Youth Activist Leaders from the 1960s." *Political Psychology* 11 (2): 243–282.

Brennan, Mary C. 1995. *Turning Right in the Sixties: The Conservative Capture of the GOP.* Chapel Hill: University of North Carolina Press.

Brewer, Mark D. 2009. *Party Images in the American Electorate.* New York: Routledge.

Brinkley, Alan. 1989. "The New Deal and the Idea of the State." In *The Rise and Fall of the New Deal Order, 1930–1980,* ed. Steve Fraser and Gary Gerstle, pp. 85–121. Princeton, NJ: Princeton University Press.

——— 1995. *The End of Reform: New Deal Liberalism in Recession and War.* New York: Alfred A. Knopf.

Brint, Steven G., Lori Turk-Bicacki, Kristopher Proctor, and Scott Patrick Murphy. 2008. "Expanding the Social Frame of Knowledge: Interdisciplinary, Degree-Granting Fields in American Colleges and Universities, 1975–2000." *Review of Higher Education* 32 (2): 155–183.

Broder, David S. 1971. *The Party's Over: The Failure of Politics in America.* New York: Harper & Row.

Broockman, David E., and Douglas J. Ahler. 2014. "Does Polarization Imply Poor Representation? A New Perspective on the 'Disconnect' Between Politicians and Voters." Working Paper, University of California, Berkeley.

Broockman, David E., Nicholas Carnes, Melody Crowder-Meyer, and Christopher Skovron. 2014. "Who's a Good Candidate? How Party Gatekeepers Evaluate Potential Nominees." Working Paper, University of California, Berkeley.

Broockman, David E., and Christopher Skovron. 2014. "What Politicians Believe About Their Constituents: Asymmetric Misperceptions and Prospects for Constituency Control." Working Paper. http://stanford.edu/~dbroock/papers/broockman_skovron_asymmetric_misperceptions.pdf.

Buchler, Justin. 2015. "Asymmetric Polarization and Asymmetric Models: Democratic and Republican Interpretations of Electoral Dynamics." Paper presented at the Midwest Political Science Association Annual Meeting, Chicago, April 16–19.

Burner, David. 1968. *The Politics of Provincialism: The Democratic Party in Transition, 1918–1932.* New York: Alfred A. Knopf.

Burns, Jennifer. 2009. *Goddess of the Market: Ayn Rand and the American Right.* New York: Oxford University Press.

Busch, Andrew E. 1997. *Outsiders and Openness in the Presidential Nomination System.* Pittsburgh, PA: University of Pittsburgh Press.

Busch, Andrew E., and James W. Ceasar. 2001. *The Perfect Tie: The True Story of the 2000 Presidential Elections.* Lanham, MD: Rowman & Littlefield.

Byrne, Janet. 2012. *The Occupy Handbook.* New York: Back Bay Books.

Calmes, Jackie. 2015. "They Don't Give a Damn About Governing: Conservative Media's Influence on the Republican Party." Shorenstein Center Discussion Paper. http://shorensteincenter.org/conservative-media-influence-on-republican-party-jackie-calmes/.

Campbell, Troy H., and Aaron C. Kay. 2014. "Solution Aversion: On the Relation Between Ideology and Motivated Disbelief." *Journal of Personality and Social Psychology* 107 (5): 809–824.

Campbell, John L., and Ove K. Pedersen. 2014. *The National Origins of Policy Ideas: Knowledge Regimes in the United States, France, Germany, and Denmark.* Princeton, NJ: Princeton University Press.

Carmines, Edward G., Paul M. Sniderman, and Beth C. Easter. 2011. "On the Meaning, Measurement, and Implications of Racial Resentment." *Annals of the American Academy of Political and Social Science* 634 (1): 98–116.

Carmines, Edward G., and James A. Stimson. 1989. *Issue Evolution: Race and the Transformation of American Politics.* Princeton, NJ: Princeton University Press.

Classen, Christopher, Patrick Tucker, and Steven S. Smith. 2015. "Ideological Labels in America." *Political Behavior* 37 (2): 253–278.

Clinton, Joshua D., and Ted Enamorado. 2014. "The National News Media's Effect on Congress: How Fox News Affected Elites in Congress." *Journal of Politics* 76 (4): 928–943.

Cohen, Jeffrey E. 2012. *The President's Legislative Policy Agenda, 1789–2002.* New York: Cambridge University Press.

Cohen, Marty, David Karol, Hans Noel, and John Zaller. 2008. *The Party Decides: Nominations Before and After Reform.* Chicago: University of Chicago Press.

Coleman, John J. 1999. "Unified Government, Divided Government, and Party Responsiveness." *American Political Science Review* 93 (4): 821–835.

Connelly, William F., and John J. Pitney. 1994. *Congress' Permanent Minority?: Republicans in the U.S. House.* Lanham, MD: Rowman & Littlefield.

Converse, Philip E. 1964. "The Nature of Belief Systems in Mass Publics." In *Ideology and Discontent*, ed. David E. Apter, pp. 206–261. New York: Free Press.

Cooperman, Rosalyn and Melody Crowder-Meyer. 2015. "Can't Buy Them Love: Gender, Parties, and Political Donors." Paper presented at the Midwest Political Science Association Annual Meeting, Chicago, April 16–19.

Cowie, Jefferson R. 2010. *Stayin' Alive: The 1970s and the Last Days of the Working Class.* New York: New Press.

Cox, Gary W., and Mathew D. McCubbins. 2005. *Setting the Agenda: Responsible Party Government in the U.S. House of Representatives.* New York: Cambridge University Press.

Cox Richardson, Heather. 2014. *To Make Men Free: A History of the Republican Party.* New York: Basic Books.

Crespin, Michael H., Suzanne Gold, and David Rohde. 2006. "Ideology, Electoral Incentives, and Congressional Politics: The Republican House Class of 1994." *American Politics Research* 34 (2): 135–158.

Critchlow, Donald T. 1985. *The Brookings Institution, 1916–1952: Expertise and the Public Interest in a Democratic Society.* DeKalb: Northern Illinois University Press.

——— 2011. *The Conservative Ascendancy: How the Republican Right Rose to Power in Modern America.* Lawrence: University Press of Kansas.

Dallek, Robert. 1999. *Ronald Reagan: The Politics of Symbolism.* Cambridge, MA: Harvard University Press.

Davies, Gareth. 2007. *See Government Grow: Education Politics from Johnson to Reagan.* Lawrence: University Press of Kansas.

Davis, Mike. 1986. *Prisoners of the American Dream: Politics and Economy in the History of the U.S. Working Class.* London: Verso.

DellaVigna, Stefano, and Ethan Kaplan. 2007. "The Fox News Effect: Media Bias and Voting." *Quarterly Journal of Economics* 122 (3): 1187–1234.

Desmarais, Bruce A., Raymond J. La Raja, and Michael S. Kowal. 2014. "The Fates of Challengers in U.S. House Elections: The Role of Extended Party Networks in Supporting Candidates and Shaping Electoral Outcomes." *American Journal of Political Science* 59 (1): 194–211.

DiSalvo, Daniel. 2012. *Engines of Change: Party Factions in American Politics, 1868-2010.* New York: Oxford University Press.

Dochuk, Darren. 2012. *From Bible Belt to Sunbelt: Plain-Folk Religion, Grassroots Politics, and the Rise of Evangelical Conservatism.* New York: W. W. Norton & Company.

Dominguez, Casey B. K. 2011. "Does the Party Matter? Endorsements in Congressional Primaries," *Political Research Quarterly* 64 (3): 534–544.

Domke, David, Mark D. Watts, Dhavan V. Shah, and David P. Fan. 1999. "The Politics of Conservative Elites and the 'Liberal Media' Argument." *Journal of Communication* 49 (4): 35–58.

Douthat, Ross, and Reihan Salam. 2008. *Grand New Party: How Republicans Can Win the Working Class and Save the American Dream.* New York: Doubleday.

Downs, Anthony. 1957. *An Economic Theory of Democracy.* New York: Harper.

Draper, Robert. 2013. *When the Tea Party Came to Town: Inside the U.S. House of Representatives' Most Combative, Dysfunctional, and Infuriating Term in Modern History.* New York: Simon & Schuster.

Druckman, James, Martin Kifer, and Michael Parkin. 2009. "Campaign Communications in U.S. Congressional Elections." *American Political Science Review* 103 (3): 343–366.

Druckman, James, and Lawrence Jacobs. 2015. *Who Governs?: Presidents, Public Opinion, and Manipulation.* Chicago: University of Chicago Press.

Duarte, Jose. L., Jarret T. Crawford, Charlotta Stern, Jonathan Haidt, Lee Jussim, and Philip E. Tetlock. 2015. "Political Diversity Will Improve Social Psychological Science." *Behavioral and Brian Sciences* 38: 1–58.

Edwards, Lee. 2002. *The Conservative Revolution.* New York: Free Press.

Egan, Patrick J. 2013. *Partisan Priorities: How Issue Ownership Drives and Distorts American Politics.* New York: Cambridge University Press.

Ellis, Christopher, and James Stimson, 2012. *Ideology in America.* Cambridge: Cambridge University Press.

Erikson, Robert S., Michael B. Mackuen, and James A. Stimson. 2002. *The Macro Polity.* New York: Cambridge University Press.

Eriksson, Kimmo, and Pontus Strimling. 2015. "Group Differences in Broadness of Values May Drive Dynamics of Public Opinion on Moral Issues." *Mathematical Social Sciences* 77 (3): 1–8.

Esterling, Kevin M. 2004. *The Political Economy of Expertise: Information and Efficiency in American National Politics.* Ann Arbor: University of Michigan Press.

Feldman, Stanley, and John Zaller. 1992. "The Political Culture of Ambivalence: Ideological Responses to the Welfare State." *American Journal of Political Science* 36 (1): 268–307.

Fenno, Richard F. 1973. *Congressmen in Committees.* Boston: Little, Brown.

——— 1997. *Learning to Govern: An Institutional View of the 104th Congress.* Washington, D.C.: Brookings Institution Press.

Ferguson, Thomas. 1989. "Industrial Conflict and the Coming of the New Deal: The Triumph of Multinational Liberalism in America." In *The Rise and Fall of the New Deal Order, 1930–1980,* ed. Steve Fraser and Gary Gerstle, pp. 3–31. Princeton, NJ: Princeton University Press.

Fetterman, Adam K., Ryan L. Boyd, and Michael D. Robinson. 2015. "Power Versus Affiliation in Political Ideology: Robust Linguistic Evidence for Distinct Motivation-Related Signatures." *Personality and Social Psychology Bulletin* 41 (9): 1195–1206.

Feulner, Edwin J. 1983. *Conservatives Stalk the House: The Republican Study Committee, 1970–1982.* Ottawa, IL: Green Hill Publishers.

Fiorina, Morris P. 2005. *Culture War?: The Myth of a Polarized America.* New York: Pearson.

Fischer, Frank. 1991. "American Think Tanks: Policy Elites and the Politicization of Expertise." *Governance: An International Journal of Policy and Administration* 4 (3): 332–353.

Fisher, Patrick. 2011. "The Gapology of the Obama Vote in the 2008 Democratic Presidential Primaries." *Society* 48 (6): 502–509.

Fones-Wolf, Elizabeth A. 1994. *Selling Free Enterprise: The Business Assault on Labor and Liberalism, 1945–60.* Urbana: University of Illinois Press.

————— 2006. *Waves of Opposition: Labor and the Struggle for Democratic Radio.* Urbana: University of Illinois Press.

Formisano, Ronald. 1991. *Boston Against Busing: Race Class and Ethnicity in the 1960s and 1970s.* Chapel Hill: University of North Carolina Press.

Fowler, Erika Franklin, Michael Franz, and Travis Ridout. 2016. *Political Advertising in the United States.* Boulder, CO: Westview Press.

Fowler, James H. 2010. Cosponsorship Network Data. jhfowler.ucsd.edu/cosponsorship. htm.

Francia, Peter L., Paul S. Herrnson, John C. Green, Lynda W. Powell, and Clyde Wilcox. 2003. *The Financiers of Congressional Elections: Investors, Ideologues, and Intimates.* New York: Columbia University Press.

Fraser, Steve, and Gary Gerstle, eds. 1989. *The Rise and Fall of the New Deal Order, 1930– 1980.* Princeton, NJ: Princeton University Press.

Free, Lloyd A., and Hadley Cantril. 1967. *The Political Beliefs of Americans: A Study of Public Opinion.* New Brunswick, NJ: Rutgers University Press.

Freeman, Jo. 1986. "The Political Culture of the Democratic and Republican Parties." *Political Science Quarterly* 101 (3): 327–356.

Frymer, Paul. 1999. *Uneasy Alliances: Race and Party Competition in America.* Princeton, NJ: Princeton University Press.

Galvin, Daniel. 2010. *Presidential Party Building: Dwight D. Eisenhower to George W. Bush.* Princeton, NJ: Princeton University Press.

Gamble, Katrina L. 2007. "Black Political Representation: An Examination of Legislative Activity Within the U.S. House Committees." *Legislative Studies Quarterly* 32 (3): 421–447.

Garrett, R. Kelly, and Natalie Jomini Stroud. 2014. "Partisan Paths to Exposure Diversity: Differences in Pro- and Counterattitudinal News Consumption." *Journal of Communication* 64 (4): 680–701.

Gauchat, Gordon. 2015. "The Political Context of Science in the United States: Public Acceptance of Evidence-Based Policy and Science Funding." *Social Forces* 94 (2):723–746.

————— 2012. "Politicization of Science in the Public Sphere: A Study of Public Trust in the United States, 1974–2010." *American Sociological Review* 77 (2): 167–187.

Geiger, Roger L. 2014. *The History of American Higher Education: Learning and Culture from the Founding to World War II.* Princeton, NJ: Princeton University Press.

Gerring, John. 1998. *Party Ideologies in America, 1828–1996.* Cambridge: Cambridge University Press.

Gingrich, Newt. 1998. *Lessons Learned the Hard Way: A Personal Report.* New York: HarperCollins.

Goodwin, Doris Kearns. 1991. *Lyndon Johnson and the American Dream.* New York: St Martin's Griffin.

Green, Donald, Bradley Palmquist, and Eric Schickler. 2002. *Partisan Hearts and Minds: Political Parties and the Social Identity of Voters.* New Haven, CT: Yale University Press.

Grentzkow, Matthew, and Jesse M. Shapiro. 2011. "Ideological Segregation Online and Offline." *Quarterly Journal of Economics* 126 (4): 1799–1839.

Griffin, John D. 2014. "When and Why Minority Legislators Matter." *Annual Review of Political Science* 17: 327–336.

Groeling, Tim. 2013. "Media Bias by the Numbers: Challenges and Opportunities in the Empirical Study of Partisan News." *Annual Review of Political Science* 16: 129–151.

Grose, Christian R. 2011. *Congress in Black and White: Race and Representation in Washington and at Home.* Cambridge: Cambridge University Press.

Groseclose, Tim, and Jeffrey Milyo. 2005. "A Measure of Media Bias." *Quarterly Journal of Economics* 120 (4): 1191–1237.

Gross, Neil. 2013. *Why Are Professors Liberal and Why Do Conservatives Care?* Cambridge: Harvard University Press.

Gross, Neil, Thomas Medvetz, and Rupert Russell. 2011. "The Contemporary American Conservative Movement." *Annual Review of Sociology* 37: 325–354.

Gross, Neil, and Solon Simmons. 2006. "Americans Views of Political Bias in the Academy and Academic Freedom." American Association of University Professors Working Paper. http://www.aaup.org/NR/rdonlyres/DCF3EBD7-509E-47AB-9AB3-FBCFFF5CA9C3/0/2006Gross.pdf.

Grossmann, Matt. 2009. "Campaigning as an Industry: Consulting Business Models and Intra-Party Competition." *Business and Politics* 11 (1):1–19.

——— 2012. *The Not-So-Special Interests: Interest Groups, Public Representation, and American Governance.* Stanford, CA: Stanford University Press.

——— 2014. *Artists of the Possible: Governing Networks and American Policy Change Since 1945.* New York: Oxford University Press.

Grossmann, Matt, and Casey Dominguez. 2009. "Party Coalitions and Interest Group Networks." *American Politics Research* 37 (5): 767–800.

Grossmann, Matt, and David A. Hopkins. 2014. "Policymaking in Red and Blue." Paper presented at the Annual Meeting of the American Political Science Association, Washington, D.C, August 28–31.

——— 2015. "Ideological Republicans and Group Interest Democrats: The Asymmetry of American Party Politics." *Perspectives on Politics* 13 (1): 119–139.

Hacker, Jacob S. 2002. *The Divided Welfare State: The Battle over Public and Private Social Benefits in the United States.* New York: Cambridge University Press.

Hacker, Jacob S., and Paul Pierson. 2005. *Off Center: The Republican Revolution and the Erosion of American Democracy.* New Haven, CT: Yale University Press.

——— 2014. "After the 'Master Theory': Downs, Schattschneider, and the Rebirth of Policy-Focused Analysis." *Perspectives on Politics* 12 (3): 643–662.

Hagner, Paul R., and John C. Pierce. 1982. "Conceptualization and Party Identification: 1956-1976." *American Journal of Political Science* 26 (2): 377–387.

Hagner, Paul R., John C. Pierce, and Kathleen Knight. 1989. *Content Codings of Levels of Political Conceptualization, 1956–1984.* Ann Arbor, MI: ICPSR.

Haidt, Jonathan. 2012. *The Righteous Mind: Why Good People Are Divided by Politics and Religion.* New York: Pantheon.

Halleck, DeeDee. 2003. "Indymedia: Building an International Activist Internet Network." *Media Development* 50 (4): 11–14.

Hammond, Susan Webb. 1998. *Congressional Caucuses in National Policy Making.* Baltimore: Johns Hopkins University Press.

Harris, John. 2005. *The Survivor: Bill Clinton in the White House.* New York: Random House.

Hayes, Danny. 2005. "Candidate Qualities Through a Partisan Lens: A Theory of Trait Ownership." *American Journal of Political Science* 49 (4): 908–923.

Heaney, Michael T., Seth E. Masket, Joanne M. Miller, and Dara Z. Strolovitch. 2012. "Polarized Networks: The Organizational Affiliations of National Party Convention Delegates." *American Behavioral Scientist* 56 (12): 1654–1676.

Hemmer, Nicole. 2010. "Messengers of the Right: Media and the Modern Conservative Movement." Ph.D. diss., Columbia University.

Hendershot, Heather. 2011. *What's Fair on the Air?: Cold War Right-Wing Broadcasting and the Public Interest.* Chicago: University of Chicago Press.

Henderson, John. 2013. "Downs' Revenge: Elections, Responsibility and the Rise of Congressional Polarization." Ph.D. diss., University of California, Berkeley.

Herrnson, Paul S. 2009. "The Roles of Party Organizations, Party-Connected Committees, and Party Allies in Elections." *Journal of Politics* 71 (4): 1207–1224.

Hill, Kevin A. 1995. "Does the Creation of Majority Black Districts Aid Republicans?: An Analysis of the 1992 Congressional Elections in Eight Southern States." *Journal of Politics* 57 (2): 384–401.

Hindman, Matthew. 2009. *The Myth of Digital Democracy.* Princeton, NJ: Princeton University Press.

Hird, John A. 2005. "Policy Analysis for What? The Effectiveness of Nonpartisan Policy Research Organizations." *Policy Studies Journal* 33 (1): 83–105.

Hollander, Barry A. 2014. "The Surprised Loser: The Role of Electoral Expectations and News Media Exposure in Satisfaction with Democracy." *Journalism and Mass Communication Quarterly* 91 (4): 651–668.

Hopkins, Daniel J., and Jonathon M. Ladd. 2012. "The Consequences of Broader Media Choice: Evidence from the Expansion of Fox News." *Quarterly Journal of Political Science* 9 (1): 115–135.

Horwitz, Robert B. 2013. *America's Right: Anti-Establishment Conservatism from Goldwater to the Tea Party.* Cambridge: Polity.

Hood, M. V., Quentin Kidd, and Irwin L. Morris. 2015. "Tea Leaves and Southern Politics: Explaining Tea Party Support in the Region." *Social Science Quarterly* 96 (4): 923–940.

Howard, Christopher. 1997. *The Hidden Welfare State: Tax Expenditures and Social Policy in the United States.* Princeton, NJ: Princeton University Press.

Howard, Nicholas O., and Jason M. Roberts. 2015. "The Politics of Obstruction: Republican Holds in the U.S. Senate." *Legislative Studies Quarterly* 40 (2): 273–294.

Hutchings, Vincent L., and Nicholas A. Valentino. 2004. "The Centrality of Race in American Politics." *Annual Review of Political Science* 7: 383–408.

Institute of Politics at the Harvard Kennedy School. 2013. *Campaign for President: The Managers Look at 2012.* Lanham, MD: Rowman & Littlefield.

Isserman, Maurice, and Michael Kazin. 1989. "The Failure and Success of the New Radicalism." In *The Rise and Fall of the New Deal Order, 1930–1980,* ed. Steve Fraser and Gary Gerstle, pp. 212–242. Princeton, NJ: Princeton University Press.

Iyengar, Shanto, and Kyu S. Hahn. 2009. "Red Media, Blue Media: Evidence of Ideological Selectivity in Media Use." *Journal of Communication* 59 (1): 19–39.

Jacobs, Meg, and Julian Zelizer. 2011. *Conservatives in Power: The Reagan Years, 1981–1989.* Boston: St. Martin's Press.

Jacoby, William G. 2000. "Issue Framing and Public Opinion on Government Spending." *American Journal of Political Science* 44 (4):750–767.

Jacques, Peter J., Riley E. Dunlap, and Mark Freeman. 2008. "The Organization of Denial: Conservative Think Tanks and Environmental Skepticism." *Environmental Politics* 17 (3): 349–385.

Jamieson, Kathleen Hall, and Joseph N. Capella. 2008. *Echo Chamber: Rush Limbaugh and the Conservative Media Establishment.* New York: Oxford University Press.

Jarvis, Sharon. 2004. "Partisan Patterns in Presidential Campaign Speeches, 1948–2000." *Communication Quarterly* 52 (4): 403–419.

Johnson, Anne, and Tobin Van Ostern. 2012. "Comparing Conservative and Progressive Investment in America's Youth." Center for American Progress Report. https://www.americanprogress.org/wp-content/uploads/2012/12/CampusProgressLeftVsRight-3.pdf.

Johnston, Richard, and Byron E. Shafer. 2006. *The End of Southern Exceptionalism: Class, Race, and Partisan Change in the Postwar South.* Cambridge: Harvard University Press.

Jost, John T., Jack Glaser, Arie Kruglanski, and Frank Sulloway. 2003. "Political Conservatism as Motivated Social Cognition." *Psychological Bulletin* 129 (3): 339–375.

Judis, John. 2001. *The Paradox of American Democracy: Elites, Special Interests, and the Betrayal of the Public Trust*. New York: Routledge.

Juenke, Eric Gonzalez, and Robert R. Preuhs. 2012. "Irreplaceable Legislators? Rethinking Minority Representatives in the New Century." *American Journal of Political Science* 56 (3): 705–715.

Kabaservice, Geoffrey. 2004. *The Guardians: Kingman Brewster, His Circle, and the Rise of the Liberal Establishment*. New York: Henry Holt and Co.

———— 2013. *Rule and Ruin: The Downfall of Moderation and the Destruction of the Republican Party, From Eisenhower to the Tea Party*. New York: Oxford University Press.

Karol, David. 2009. *Party Position Change in American Politics: Coalition Management*. Cambridge: Cambridge University Press.

Katznelson, Ira. 1989. "Was the Great Society a Lost Opportunity?" In *The Rise and Fall of the New Deal Order, 1930–1980*, ed. Steve Fraser and Gary Gerstle, pp. 185–211. Princeton, NJ: Princeton University Press.

Kazin, Michael. 2011. *American Dreamers: How the Left Changed a Nation*. New York: Alfred A. Knopf.

Key, V. O. 1949. *Southern Politics in State and Nation*. New York: Knopf.

———— 1961. *Public Opinion and American Democracy*. New York: Knopf.

Kinder, Donald R., and Cindy D. Kam. 2010. *Us Against Them: Ethnocentric Foundations of American Politics*. Chicago: University of Chicago Press.

———— 2012. "Ethnocentrism as a Short-Term Force in the 2008 Presidential Election." *American Journal of Political Science* 56 (2): 326–340.

Kingdon, John W. 1984. *Agendas, Alternatives, and Public Policies*. Boston: Little, Brown.

Kitschelt, Herbert. 2000. "Linkages Between Citizens and Politicians in Democratic Politics." *Comparative Political Studies* 33 (6/7): 845–879.

Kitschelt, Herbert, and Kent Freeze. 2010. "Developing and Comparing Cross-National and Cross-Party Programmatic Party System Structuration: Measures with a New Global Data Set." Duke University Working Paper.

Klinkner, Philip A. 1994. *The Losing Parties: Out-Party National Committees, 1956–1993*. New Haven, CT: Yale University Press.

Koger, Gregory, Seth Masket, and Hans Noel. 2009. "Partisan Webs: Information Exchange and Party Networks." *British Journal of Political Science* 39 (2): 633–653.

———— 2010. "Cooperative Party Factions in American Politics." *American Politics Research* 38 (1): 33–53.

Kondracke, Morton, and Fred Barnes. 2015. *Jack Kemp: The Bleeding-Heart Conservative Who Changed America*. New York: Sentinel.

Krehbiel, Keith. 1998. *Pivotal Politics: A Theory of U.S. Lawmaking*. Chicago: University of Chicago Press.

Kruse, Kevin. 2005. *White Flight: Atlanta and the Making of Modern Conservatism*. Princeton, NJ: Princeton University Press.

———— 2015. *One Nation Under God: How Corporate America Invented Christian America*. New York: Basic Books.

Ladd, Jonathan M. 2011. *Why Americans Hate the Media and How It Matters*. Princeton, NJ: Princeton University Press.

Lane, Robert E. 1962. *Political Ideology: Why the American Common Man Believes What He Does*. New York: Free Press of Glencoe.

Lasar, Matthew. 1999. *Pacifica Radio: The Rise of an Alternative Network*. Philadelphia: Temple University Press.

Lelkes, Yphtach, and Paul M. Sniderman. 2015. "The Ideological Asymmetry of the American Party System." *British Journal of Political Science*, advance online publication.

Levendusky, Matthew. 2009. *The Partisan Sort: How Liberals Became Democrats and Conservatives Became Republicans*. Chicago: University of Chicago Press.

——— 2013. *How Partisan Media Polarize America*. Chicago: University of Chicago Press.

Levin, Murray. 1986. *Talk Radio and the American Dream*. Lanham, MD: Lexington Books.

Levine, Lawrence W. 1996. *The Opening of the American Mind: Canons, Culture, and History*. Boston: Beacon Press.

Lewis-Beck, Michael S., Helmut Norpoth, William G. Jacoby, and Herbert F. Weisberg. 2008. *The American Voter Revisited*. Ann Arbor: University of Michigan Press.

Liberman, Nira, Yaacov Trope, Sean McCrea, and Steven Sherman. 2007. "The Effect of Level of Construal on the Temporal Distance of Activity Enactment." *Journal of Experimental Social Psychology* 43 (1): 143–149.

Lichtenstein, Nelson. 1989. "From Corporatism to Collective Bargaining: Organized Labor and the Eclipse of Social Democracy in the Postwar Era." In *The Rise and Fall of the New Deal Order, 1930–1980*, ed. Steve Fraser and Gary Gerstle, pp. 122–152. Princeton, NJ: Princeton University Press.

Light, Paul C. 1999. *The True Size of Government*. Washington, D.C.: Brookings Institution Press.

Lipset, Seymour Martin. 1960. *Political Man: The Social Bases of Politics*. Garden City, NY: Doubleday.

Lowi, Theodore J. 1969. *The End of Liberalism*. New York: W. W. Norton.

Lublin, David, and D. Stephen Voss. 2003. "The Missing Middle: Why Median-Voter Theory Can't Save Democrats from Singing the Boll-Weevil Blues." *Journal of Politics* 65 (1): 227–237.

Lucas, Fred. 2012. *The Right Frequency: The Story of the Talk Giants Who Shook Up the Political and Media Establishment*. Palisades, NY: History Publishing Company.

Lynch, Michael S., Anthony J. Madonna, and Jason M. Roberts. 2012. "Positive Agenda Control and the House Majority Party: Policy Bargaining over Structured Rule Choice." Working Paper. http://spia.uga.edu/faculty_pages/ajmadonn/Rules.pdf.

Mann, James. 2009. *The Rebellion of Ronald Reagan: A History of the End of the Cold War*. New York: Viking.

Mann, Thomas and Norman Ornstein. 2008. *The Broken Branch: How Congress Is Failing America and How to Get It Back on Track*. New York: Oxford University Press.

——— 2012. *It's Even Worse Than It Looks: How the American Constitutional System Collided With the New Politics of Extremism*. New York: Basic Books.

Manza, Jeff. 2000. "Political Sociological Models of the U.S. New Deal." *Annual Review of Sociology* 26: 297–322.

Maraniss, David, and Michael Weisskopf. 1996. *"Tell Newt to Shut Up!"* New York: Simon & Schuster.

Martin, Gregory J., and Ali Yurukoglu. 2014. "Bias in Cable News: Real Effects and Polarization." National Bureau of Economic Research Working Paper 20798.

Masket, Seth. 2009. *No Middle Ground: How Informal Party Organizations Control Nominations and Polarize Legislatures*. Ann Arbor: University of Michigan Press.

Matthews, Donald R. 1960. *U.S. Senators and Their World*. Chapel Hill: University of North Carolina Presss.

Mayer, William G. 1996. *The Divided Democrats: Ideological Unity, Party Reform, and Presidential Elections*. Boulder, CO: Westview Press.

——— 2003. *The Making of the Presidential Candidates, 2004*. Lanham, MD: Rowman & Littlefield.

————. 2004. "Why Talk Radio Is Conservative." *Public Interest* 156: 86–104.

Mayhew, David R. 1966. *Party Loyalty Among Congressmen: The Difference Between Democrats and Republicans, 1947–1962.* Cambridge: Harvard University Press.

———— 1974. *Congress: The Electoral Connection.* New Haven, CT: Yale University Press.

———— 2005. *Divided We Govern: Party Control, Lawmaking, and Investigations, 1946–2002.* 2nd ed. New Haven, CT: Yale University Press.

———— 2011. *Partisan Balance: Why Political Parties Don't Kill the U.S. Constitutional System.* Princeton, NJ: Princeton University Press.

McCarty, Nolan, Keith T. Poole, and Howard Rosenthal. 2006. *Polarized America: The Dance of Ideology and Unequal Riches.* Cambridge, MA: MIT Press.

McCright, Aaron M., and Riley E. Dunlap. 2010. "Anti-Reflexivity: The American Conservative Movement's Success in Undermining Climate Science and Policy." *Theory, Culture and Society* 27 (2–3): 100–133.

McDonald, Lauren. 2014. "Think Tanks and the Media: How the Conservative Movement Gained Entry into the Education Policy Arena." *Educational Policy* 28 (6): 845–880.

Meagher, Richard. 2012. "The 'Vast Right-Wing Conspiracy': Media and Conservative Networks." *New Political Science* 34 (4): 469–484.

Medvetz, Thomas. 2012. *Think Tanks in America.* Chicago: University of Chicago Press.

Minta, Michael D. 2011. *Oversight: Representing the Interests of Blacks and Latinos in Congress.* Princeton, NJ: Princeton University Press.

Miroff, Bruce. 2007. *The Liberals' Moment: The McGovern Insurgency and the Identity Crisis of the Democratic Party.* Lawrence: University of Kansas Press.

Mollenkopf, John H. 1983. *The Contested City.* Princeton, NJ: Princeton University Press.

Mooney, Chris. 2006. *The Republican War on Science.* New York: Basic Books

———— 2012. *The Republican Brain: The Science of Why They Deny Science—and Reality.* Hoboken, NJ: John Wiley & Sons.

Moreno, Jonathan D. 2011. "The Body Politic: An Introduction." *Theoretical and Applied Ethics* 1 (2): 13–22.

Morgan, Kimberly J., and Andrea Louise Campbell. 2011. *The Delegated Welfare State: Medicare, Markets, and the Governance of Social Policy.* New York: Oxford University Press.

Morris, Jonathan S. 2005. "The Fox News Factor." *International Journal of Press/Politics* 10 (3): 56–79.

———— 2007. "Slanted Objectivity? Perceived Media Bias, Cable News Exposure, and Political Attitudes." *Social Science Quarterly* 88 (3): 707–728.

Muirhead, Russell. 2014. *The Promise of Party in a Polarized Age.* Cambridge: Harvard University Press.

Nash, George H. 2006. *The Conservative Intellectual Movement in America Since 1945*, 30th anniversary edition. Wilmington, DE: Intercollegiate Studies Institute.

Nexon, David. 1971. "Asymmetry in the Political System: Occasional Activists in the Republican and Democratic Parties, 1956–1964." *American Political Science Review* 65 (3): 716–30.

Nie, Norman H., Sidney Verba, and John R. Petrocik. 1976. *The Changing American Voter.* Cambridge: Harvard University Press.

Nisbet, Erik C., Kathryn E. Cooper, and R. Kelly Garrett. 2015. "The Partisan Brain: How Dissonant Science Messages Lead Conservatives and Liberals to (Dis)Trust Science." *Annals of the American Academy of Political and Social Science* 658 (1): 36–66.

Noel, Hans. 2013. *Political Ideologies and Political Parties in America.* Cambridge: Cambridge University Press.

Nyhan, Brendan. 2012. "Does the US Media Have a Liberal Bias?" *Perspectives on Politics* 10 (3): 767–771.

Nyhan, Brendan, Eric McGhee, John Sides, Seth Masket, and Steven Greene. 2012. "One Vote Out of Step? The Effects of Salient Roll Call Votes in the 2010 Election." *American Politics Research* 40 (5): 844–879.

Nyhan, Brendan, and Jason Reifler. 2010. "When Corrections Fail: The Persistence of Political Misperceptions." *Political Behavior* 32 (2): 303–330.

Ornstein, Norman J. 1975. "Causes and Consequences of Congressional Change: Subcommittee Reforms in the House of Representatives, 1970–73." In *Congress in Change: Evolution and Reform*, ed. Norman J. Ornstein. New York: Praeger Books.

Ornstein, Norman J., Thomas E. Mann, Michael J. Malbin, and Andrew Rugg. 2013. *Vital Statistics on Congress*. Washington, D.C.: Brookings Institution Press.

Ornstein, Norman J., Robert L. Peabody, and David W. Rohde. 1989. "Change in the Senate: Toward the 1990s." In *Congress Reconsidered*, 4th ed., ed. Lawrence C. Dodd and Bruce I. Oppenheimer, pp. 13–37. Washington, D.C.: Congressional Quarterly.

Ostertag, Bob. 2006. *People's Movements, People's Press: The Journalism of Social Justice Movements*. Boston: Beacon Press.

Palmer, Niall A. 1997. *The New Hampshire Primary and the American Electoral Process*. Westport, CT: Praeger.

Parker, Christopher S., and Matt A. Barreto. 2013. *Change They Can't Believe In: The Tea Party and Reactionary Politics in America*. Princeton, NJ: Princeton University Press.

Perlstein, Rick. 2001. *Before the Storm: Barry Goldwater and the Unmaking of the American Consensus*. New York: Hill and Wang.

———2008. *Nixonland: The Rise of a President and the Fracturing of America*. New York: Scribner.

———2014. *The Invisible Bridge: The Fall of Nixon and the Rise of Reagan*. New York: Simon & Schuster.

Perrett, David I., D. Michael Burt, Ian S. Penton-Voak, Kieran J. Lee, Duncan A. Rowland, and Rachel Edwards 1999. "Symmetry and Human Facial Attractiveness." *Evolution and Human Behavior* 20 (5): 295–307.

Petrocik, John R., William L. Benoit, and Glenn J. Hansen. 2003. "Issue Ownership and Presidential Campaigning, 1952–2000." *Political Science Quarterly* 118 (4): 599–626.

Phillips-Fein, Kim. 2009. *Invisible Hands: The Making of the Conservative Movement from the New Deal to Reagan*. New York: W. W. Norton & Company.

Pickard, Victor. 2015. *America's Battle for Media Democracy: The Triumph of Corporate Libertarianism and the Future of Media Reform*. New York: Cambridge University Press.

Pierson, Paul. 1994. *Dismantling the Welfare State? Reagan, Thatcher, and the Politics of Retrenchment*. New York: Cambridge University Press.

Plotke, David. 1996. *Building a Democratic Political Order: Reshaping American Liberalism in the 1930s and 1940s*. New York: Cambridge University Press.

Polsby, Nelson W. 1983. *Consequences of Party Reform*. New York: Oxford University Press.

———2004. *How Congress Evolves: Social Bases of Institutional Change*. New York: Oxford University Press.

———2008. "The Political System." In *Understanding America: The Anatomy of an Exceptional Nation*, ed. Peter H. Schuck and James Q. Wilson, pp. 3–26. New York: Public Affairs.

Polsby, Nelson W., and William G. Mayer. 1999. "Ideological Cohesion in the American Two-Party System." In *On Parties: Essays Honoring Austin Ranney*, ed. Nelson W. Polsby and Raymond E. Wolfinger, pp. 219–254. Berkeley, CA: Institute of Governmental Studies.

Preuhs, Robert R., and Eric Gonzalez Juenke. 2011. "Latino U.S. State Legislators in the 1990s: Majority-Minority Districts, Minority Incorporation, and Institutional Position." *State Politics and Policy Quarterly* 11 (1): 48–75.

Prior, Markus. 2007. *Post-Broadcast Democracy: How Media Choice Increases Inequality in Political Involvement and Polarizes Elections.* New York: Cambridge University Press.

——— 2013. "Media and Political Polarization." *Annual Review of Political Science* 16:101–127.

Rae, Nicol C. 1989. *The Decline and Fall of the Liberal Republicans: From 1952 to the Present.* New York: Oxford University Press.

Ranney, Austin. 1951. "Toward a More Responsible Two-Party System: A Commentary." *American Political Science Review* 45 (2): 488–499.

Rapoport, Ronald, Alan I. McGlennon, and John Abramowitz. 1986. *The Life of the Parties: Activists in Presidential Politics.* Lexington: University Press of Kentucky.

Rhodes, Jesse H., and Kaylee T. Johnson. 2014. "The Politics of Group Targeting in Presidential Advertisements: A Preliminary Investigation." Paper presented at the 2014 Southern Political Science Association Annual Meeting, New Orleans, LA, January 9–11.

——— 2015. "Class Conscious? Economic Inequality, Party Commitments, and Class Rhetoric in American Presidential Campaigns." Working Paper. https://www.re-searchgate.net/profile/Jesse_Rhodes/contributions.

Rich, Andrew. 2004. *Think Tanks, Public Policy, and the Politics of Expertise.* Cambridge: Cambridge University Press.

Rich, Andrew, and R. Kent Weaver. 1998. "Advocates and Analysts: Think Tanks and the Politicization of Expertise." In *Interest Group Politics,* 3rd ed., ed. Allan J. Cigler and Burdett A. Loomis, pp. 235–254. Washington, D.C.: CQ Press.

Rieder, Jonathan. 1985. *Canarsie: The Jews and Italians of Brooklyn Against Liberalism.* Cambridge: Harvard University Press.

Ringe, Nils, and Jennifer Nicoll Victor. 2013. *Bridging the Information Gap: Legislative Member Organizations as Social Networks in the United States and the European Union.* Ann Arbor: University of Michigan Press.

Rocco, Philip Bartholomew. 2015. "Reorganizing the Activist State: Conservatives, Commissions, and the Politics of Federalism, 1947–1996." Ph.D. diss., University of California, Berkeley.

Rocha, Rene R., Caroline J. Tolbert, Daniel C. Bowen, and Christopher J. Clark. 2010. "Race and Turnout: Does Descriptive Representation in State Legislatures Increase Minority Voting?" *Political Research Quarterly* 63 (4): 890–907.

Rohde, David W. 1991. *Parties and Leaders in the Postreform House.* Chicago: University of Chicago Press.

Rojas, Fabio. 2007. *From Black Power to Black Studies: How a Radical Social Movement Became an Academic Discipline.* Baltimore: Johns Hopkins University Press.

Rosen, Elliot A. 2014. *The Republican Party in the Age of Roosevelt: Sources of Anti-Government Conservatism in the United States.* Charlottesville: University of Virginia Press.

Ross, Dorothy. 1991. *The Origins of American Social Science.* New York: Cambridge University Press.

Sabatier, Paul A., ed. 2007. *Theories of the Policy Process,* 2nd ed. Cambridge, MA: Westview Press.

Sabatier, Paul A., and Hank Jenkins-Smith. 1993. *Policy Change and Learning: An Advocacy Coalition Approach.* Boulder, CO: Westview Press.

Schaller, Thomas F. 2015. *The Stronghold: How Republicans Captured Congress but Surrendered the White House.* New Haven, CT: Yale University Press.

Schneider, Saundra K., and William G. Jacoby. 2005. "Elite Discourse and American Public Opinion: The Case of Welfare Spending." *Political Research Quarterly* 58 (3): 367–379.

Schoenwald, Jonathan M. 2001. *A Time for Choosing: The Rise of Modern American Conservatism.* New York: Oxford University Press.

Schuldt, Jonathon P., Sungjong Roh, and Norbert Schwarz. 2015. "Questionnaire Design Effects in Climate Change Surveys: Implications for the Partisan Divide." *Annals of the American Academy of Political and Social Science* 658 (1): 67–85.

Seideman, David. 1986. *The New Republic: A Voice of Modern Liberalism.* New York: Praeger.

Sherman, Gabriel. 2014. *The Loudest Voice in the Room: How the Brilliant, Bombastic Roger Ailes Built Fox News—and Divided a Country.* New York: Random House.

Shufeldt, Gregory. 2014. "Unequal Parties: Partisan Differences in Political Behavior." Ph.D. diss., University of Notre Dame. http://etd.nd.edu/ETD-db/theses/available/etd-07112014-115448/.

Sinclair, Barbara. 1989. *The Transformation of the U.S. Senate.* Baltimore: Johns Hopkins University Press.

——— 1995. *Legislators, Leaders, and Lawmaking: The U.S. House of Representatives in the Postreform Era.* Baltimore: Johns Hopkins University Press.

Singh, Robert. 1998. *The Congressional Black Caucus: Racial Politics in the U.S. Congress.* Thousand Oaks, CA: Sage Publications.

Skinner, Richard M., Seth E. Masket, and David A. Dulio. 2012. "527 Committees and the Political Party Network." *American Politics Research* 40 (1): 60–84.

Skocpol, Theda, and Vanessa Williamson. 2012. *The Tea Party and the Remaking of Republican Conservatism.* New York: Oxford University Press.

Smith, Steven S. 1989. "Taking It to the Floor." *Congress Reconsidered,* 4th ed., ed. Lawrence C. Dodd and Bruce I. Oppenheimer, pp. 330–350. Washington, D.C.: Congressional Quarterly.

Stanley, Timothy. 2010. *Kennedy vs. Carter: The 1980 Battle for the Democratic Party's Soul.* Lawrence: University Press of Kansas.

Stefancic, Jean, and Richard Delgado. 1996. *No Mercy: How Conservative Think Tanks and Foundations Changed America's Social Agenda.* Philadelphia: Temple University Press.

Stroud, Natalie Jomini. 2011. *Niche News: The Politics of News Choice.* New York: Oxford University Press.

Teles, Steven M. 2008. *The Rise of the Conservative Legal Movement: The Battle for Control of the Law.* Princeton, NJ: Princeton University Press.

Tesler, Michael. 2012. "The Return of Old-Fashioned Racism to White Americans' Partisan Preferences in the Early Obama Era." *Journal of Politics* 75 (1): 110–123.

Tetlock, Philip E. 1983. "Cognitive Style and Political Ideology." *Journal of Personality and Social Psychology* 45 (1): 118–126.

Theodoridis, Alex. 2015. "It's My Party: Partisan Intensity Through the Lens of Implicit Identity." University of California, Merced, Working Paper.

Theriault, Sean M. 2013. *The Gingrich Senators: The Roots of Partisan Warfare in Congress.* New York: Oxford University Press.

Therriault, Andrew. 2015. "Whose Issue Is It Anyway? A New Look at the Meaning and Measurement of Issue Ownership." *British Journal of Political Science* 45 (4): 929–938.

Tomz, Michael, and Robert Van Houweling. 2012. "Political Pledges as Credible Commitments." Working Paper. https://dl.dropboxusercontent.com/u/24724021/Pledges.pdf.

Tsfati, Yariv, Natalie Stroud, and Adi Chotiner. 2013. "Exposure to Ideological News and Perceived Opinion Climate: Testing the Media Effects Component of Spiral-Of-Silence in a Fragmented Media Landspace." *International Journal of Press/Politics* 19 (1): 3–23.

Turk-Bicakci, Lori A. 2007. "The Development of Social Movement Programs and Departments in Higher Education: Women's and Ethnic Studies from 1975–2000." Ph.D. diss., University of California, Riverside.

Valentino, Nicholas A., and David O. Sears. 2005. "Old Times There Are Not Forgotten: Race and Partisan Realignment in the Contemporary South." *American Journal of Political Science* 49 (3): 672–688.

Vasi, Ion Bogdan, Edward T. Walker, John S. Johnson, and Hi Fen Tan. 2015. "No Fracking Way! Documentary Film, Discursive Opportunity, and Local Opposition against Hydraulic Fracturing in the United States, 2010 to 2013." *American Sociological Review* 80 (5): 934–959.

Viguerie, Richard A., and David Franke. 2004. *America's Right Turn: How Conservatives Used New and Alternative Media to Take Power.* Chicago: Bonus Books.

Vogel, Steven Kent. 1998. *Freer Markets, More Rules: Regulatory Reform in Advanced Industrial Countries.* Ithaca, NY: Cornell University Press.

Volden, Craig, and Alan Wiseman. 2014. *Legislative Effectiveness in the United States Congress.* Cambridge: Cambridge University Press.

Volkens, Andrea, Pola Lehmann, Nicolas Merz, Sven Regel, and Annika Werner. 2013. *Comparative Manifesto Project.* Berlin: Wissenschaftszentrum Berlin für Sozialforschung (WZB).

Wald, Kenneth D. 2015. "The Choosing People: Interpreting the Puzzling Politics of American Jewry." *Politics and Religion* 8 (1): 4–35.

Wallsten, Kevin. 2007. "Agenda Setting and the Blogosphere: An Analysis of the Relationship between Mainstream Media and Political Blogs." *Review of Policy Research* 24(6): 567–87.

Weidenbaum, Murray. 2009. *The Competition of Ideas: The World of Washington Think Tanks.* New Brunswick, NJ: Transaction Publishers.

Weisbrot, Robert, and C. Calvin Mackenzie. 2008. *The Liberal Hour: Washington and the Politics of Change in the 1960s.* New York: Penguin Books.

White, Theodore H. 1973. *The Making of the President, 1972.* New York: Harper.

Willnat, Lars, and David H. Weaver. 2014. *The American Journalist in the Digital Age: Key Findings.* Bloomington: School of Journalism, Indiana University. http://news.indiana.edu/releases/iu/2014/05/2013-american-journalist-key-findings.pdf.

Wilson, James Q. 1962. *The Amateur Democrat: Club Politics in Three Cities.* Chicago: University of Chicago Press.

Witko, Christopher. 2014. "When Does Money Buy Votes? Campaign Contributions and Policymaking." In *New Directions in Interest Group Politics,* ed. Matt Grossmann, pp. 165–184. New York: Routledge.

Wlezien, Christopher. 1995. "The Public as Thermostat: Dynamics of Preferences for Spending." *American Journal of Political Science* 39 (4): 981–1000.

Wood, B. Dan. 2009. *The Myth of Presidential Representation.* Cambridge: Cambridge University Press.

Zaretsky, Natasha. 2007. *No Direction Home: The American Family and the Fear of National Decline, 1968–1980.* Chapel Hill: University of North Carolina Press.

Zelizer, Julian E. 2004. *On Capitol Hill: The Struggle to Reform Congress and Its Consequences, 1948–2000.* Cambridge: Cambridge University Press.

——— 2010. "What Political Science Can Learn from the New Political History." *Annual Review of Political Science* 13: 25–36.

——— 2012. *Governing America: The Revival of Political History.* Princeton, NJ: Princeton University Press.

INDEX

Note: Page references followed by *f* or *t* denote figures or tables, respectively. Numbers followed by n indicate notes.

RMD
1